New Metaphysical Foundations of Modern Science

Edited by Willis Harman
with Jane Clark

New Metaphysical
Foundations of Modern Science

Edited by Willis Harman
with Jane Clark

INSTITUTE OF
NOETIC
SCIENCES

Production Staff

Research coordinator:
Nola Lewis

Design, layout and print production:
David Johnson

Editorial Assistant
Carol Guion

Proofreading:
Sienna S'Zell, Susan Sulc

Staff assistant:
Rose Welch

Institute of Noetic Sciences
475 Gate Five Road, Suite 300
Sausalito, California 94965

For permissions, contact the Managing Editor at the Institute of Noetic Sciences. Printed by Edwards Brothers, Ann Arbor, Michigan.

Library of Congress Cataloging-in-Publication Data

New Metaphysical Foundations of Modern Science / edited by Willis Harman with Jane Clark.
    p.   cm.
    Includes bibliographical references and index.
    ISBN 0-943951-11-9
    1. Science–Philosophy.   2. Metaphysics.   I. Harman, Willis W.
II. Clark, Jane.
Q175.M54168   1994
501–dc20   94-6253
                                                     CIP

Acknowledgements

This project could not have been accomplished without the vision, encouragement, and financial support of those with the insight to understand its potential significance. From its inception, the Causality Project, from which this book has grown, has received its primary support from the Fetzer Institute, Laurance S. Rockefeller, and the members of the Board of Directors of the Institute of Noetic Sciences.

It was the Board, in fact, who urged the Institute to undertake a fundamental exploration of scientific difficulties in accommodating the ideas of consciousness as a causal factor in the universe, and agreed to put up initial support.

Many other individuals, inspired by the thought that it is about time science and consciousness are reconciled, helped out with their gifts. These included grants from the Three Swallows Foundation, Seven Springs Foundation, the Waletzky Trust, Don Land Memorial Fund, and Marjorie Milbourne.

Finally, we would like to acknowledge the consistent and wholehearted support of the staff of the Institute—everyone here has had a hand, or sometimes a finger, in helping this book come into being. The book would not exist were it not for this base of support, and we thank you all for the innumerable ways, large and small, in which you have contributed to its emergence.

—Willis Harman
President, Institute of Noetic Sciences

Contents

Foreword

by Jane Clark

The fifteen essays which make up this book cover an extraordinarily wide range of disciplines: physics and biology, the cognitive and neurosciences, psychology and philosophy, engineering and anthropology. What draws them together and justifies their appearance, side by side, in such a volume, is a belief on the part of all the authors that science has reached a point in its development where it urgently needs to reassess its values and its aims. And that this reassessment needs to be fundamental, affecting not only the content and subject matter of scientific study, but also the way in which that study is carried out, and even the very mindset of the scientists whose work has gradually, over the last 300 years, become so central to our civilization.

There are, of course, in the current literature, a host of books which tackle this subject, and many critiques of current science from the point of view of spirituality, ecology, feminism, ethics, the perennial wisdom, etc. What distinguishes this volume from most of these is that the essays presented here have all been written by working scientists and philosophers who are deeply committed to science as an enterprise, both personally and professionally. Their critique is that of the "insider", and when they speak of the need for scientists to extend their definition of what is real to more subtle realms, or to come to a different kind of interaction with nature than that of "objective observation", they are speaking of a need they feel for change in the way they themselves work. The raising of such ideas is still a rarity within scientific institutions, and one of the main hopes in bringing out this book is that it will encourage discussion within the professional community, and put some kind of awareness of underlying meanings back on the agenda.

This book is only one aspect of a long-term project, dubbed "The Causality Project", which Willis Harman and the Institute of Noetic Sciences have been working on since 1989. This project is itself only a part of the general work of the Institute, which is, as its name, from the Greek word *nous* meaning "mind" suggests, is to investigate the role of consciousness within science. To this end, it has undertaken and funded, over the last twenty years, a great number of projects, involving both practical research into anomalous phenomena and the investigation of ideas.

Willis Harman became president of the Institute in 1977, and embarked upon the path which eventually led to this book through his gradual disappointment with the research projects which attempted to tackle consciousness directly. He eventually realized that the reason they were not yielding the kinds of results hoped for was that scientific methodology excludes consciousness from the very start—it denies it in its ground rules, so to speak, as *a priori* assumption—and having done so, can never "re-find" it in the outside world. This drew his attention to the need to look more closely at these ground rules, and he subsequently set up the Causality Project, in conjunction with the Fetzer Institute and the Rockefeller Foundation, to investigate what he saw as one of the key concepts of the scientific worldview.

It soon became clear to him, however, that he was going to have to dig down very deep indeed into the roots of science if he was to reintegrate consciousness. This insight was further clarified when, as part of his research, he came across the work of E. A. Burtt and his seminal book *The Metaphysical Foundations of Modern Physical Science,* published in 1924. Burtt pointed out that behind the methodology of science, underpinning all its findings and theories, were a number of assumptions about the nature of the world and the way in which human beings can understand it—ontological and epistemological assumptions—which were neither articulated nor brought into question during the course of normal research. These he called the "metaphysical foundations" (not to be confused with the kind of metaphysics found within the spiritual traditions) because they do not reside within the material world as such, nor can they be proven by empirical experiments, but they form the ground out of which all our conceptual ideas about the physical world arise.

At the same time, Willis was beginning to understand that science was facing deep and apparently insoluble problems in many areas, and was in some senses in a crisis situation. This, he felt, made it a particularly appropriate time to begin asking the kinds of questions which Burtt had initiated. He was aware, of course, that the majority of scientists would not agree with him, and would deny that science is based on any kind of metaphysics, arguing that out of all the systems of knowledge that the world has known, science is unique in providing us with objective, absolute knowledge. Many of these would also deny that there are any problems with the way that science is currently done; that, on the contrary, we are on the brink of some of its greatest triumphs as we penetrate simultaneously into the innermost secrets of the human constitution (through our genetic research) and the origins of the universe (through cosmology). But Willis was able to make contact with a number of scientists who agreed that there are problems, and who had already, by themselves, been exploring alternative views. So it was that the idea of a book through which their thoughts could be aired to a wider public, which would extend the work that Burtt began and be a kind of tribute to him, was born.

The coming into being of the book, however, did not follow the usual pattern, in which the various contributors were asked simply to send in papers. Willis asked the authors to write a first draft of their essays so that they could be circulated, and then invited all those involved to a meeting in seclusion in the beautiful setting of Asilomar on the Monterey Peninsula of California. There, in November 1992, fourteen people spent three intensive days discussing the papers, and exploring generally the nature of the foundations upon which Western science—the science of Newton and Darwin—has been built.

This retreat, which also marked the beginning of my own involvement in the project, constituted an extraordinary opportunity to consider what form science might take if some of our present assumptions were to change; if we took as our starting point, for instance, the idea that the world is not only divided into discrete, particular bits, but is also (paradoxically) an undivided whole. Or if we began to acknowledge that scientists are intrinsically entangled with their experiments as whole human beings, not merely through their intellects, and that what is really happening (but rarely made conscious) as they work with nature is that they are increasing their self-knowledge. These wide-ranging discussions fed back into the papers, many of which were substantially revised in the months that followed.

Mention of the Asilomar retreat highlights one of the most important aspects of the ideas presented in the pages that follow, and that is their exploratory nature. It is clear to most of the writers that many of the changes they discuss are already underway: that this is not a game of "wouldn't it be nice if...", but their work is part of a new pattern of ideas and understandings which are forming not only within science but within Western society as a whole. At the same time, I do not believe that any of them would claim to see completely just what this new pattern—this "new science"—is, or what it will look like as it develops. It is emerging, or "emergent" in every sense of the word, in that what is intimated is a new conceptual framework which is arising out of the old way of looking at things, but which cannot be reduced to it, nor predicated from it. In the language of Thomas Kuhn, whose book *The Structure of Scientific Revolutions* is perhaps the only work quoted by every contributor, we are in the midst of a paradigm shift. But the final form of the new paradigm is far from manifest to us at this moment.

One knows from looking at past paradigm shifts—for instance, that which Kuhn and several contributors to this volume consider in depth, the switch from the Aristotelian sciences of the middle ages to the Newtonian view in the seventeenth and eighteenth centuries—that they are characterized by a complete change of values, in which not only the contents of our thought, but the whole way in which we organize knowledge, categorize its domains and define disciplines, is radically reconstituted. It is for this reason that we have not attempted to present the papers here in any particular order, or put them into sections according to subject or whatever. There is no doubt that they are very diverse, for in searching for alternative metaphysical systems, the authors have drawn on a huge variety of sources from both the past and the present—the indigenous peoples, the ancient Greeks, the medieval Magi, the spiritual traditions of Buddhism and the Vedas, the scientific writings of Goethe and Rudolf Steiner, William James, Alfred North Whitehead, Henri Bergson, Gregory Bateson, W.V.O. Quine, the philosophic works of the original quantum physicists like Niels Bohr and Erwin Shrödinger, as well as those of contemporary thinkers like David Bohm and James Lovelock.

But what has struck me most as I have worked on these papers is not the diversity so much as the common ground. The same themes arise again and again, albeit couched in different terms, and there is an unexpected degree of consensus about at least some of the features which the new science must have. Willis, in his opening and closing chapters, catches hold of some of these, and begins the important task of placing them into a coherent order. But still there are many other, more subtle resonances and harmonies which appear as one reads these essays as a whole collection (bearing in mind that it is one of the central ideas of the emerging science that the whole is always greater than the sum of its parts), and which give a more qualitative taste of what the science of the twenty-first century might be like.

It is because they already have one foot in the other camp, so to speak, because they are putting to use concepts and ideas which are new or untried to most of us, that the essays in this book are so very challenging. Certainly I have found them to be so, and during the process of editing have come to believe that this is not only because many of them are so intellectually stimulating (which they are), but also because at the heart of the "new science" which they presage there is something other than the kind of dualism which has dominated Western thought for centuries, and which has led us to separate mind from matter, the intellect from emotions, qualities from quantities, the abstract from the practical. The science which is envisioned here is concerned with wholes, and it requires us to engage with vitality at that level. Vine Deloria says, describing the kind of scientist which he believes a new methodology will require,

He must be a whole person; he or she must include their emotional responses to the data and must bring to the gathering of knowledge the sense of self and self-discipline that characterize a whole person.

Such an engagement is demanding for all of us; even for those who have not been through the very specialized education which science requires of its practitioners. For, as both Eugene Taylor and Willis point out, the "mechanistic" mindset—and the technology it generates—has now penetrated into every area of modern life, and influences just about everything we do, from the way that we organize our businesses to the upbringing of our children and our response to the arts. We have all, to some degree, imbibed its values and assumptions, and are therefore part of the total situation within which it finds validation.

At the same time, science itself is reflective of, and often explicitly expresses, the ideas and assumptions of the culture in which it thrives. The questioning to which the scientific process is subjected in this book is clearly an aspect of a much larger movement which is challenging the whole basis upon which our society operates, and which aspires to a more holistic and sustainable—less fragmented—way of life. In exposing these new ideas from the very heart of science to a wider, nonspecialist public, it is hoped that *New Metaphysical Foundations of Modern Science* can make a valid contribution to this collective process, through which people all over the world, scientists and nonscientists alike, are exploring new possibilities, new models for understanding and interacting with the world in a more benign manner.

Introduction

by Willis Harman

The illustrious triumphs of science have never been more evident than they are now. It may thus seem incongruous to raise at this point misgivings about the foundation assumptions of modern science.

However, it is not the first time such issues have been raised. Most specifically, they were put forward in a 1924 classic by philosopher of science E. A. Burtt, entitled *The Metaphysical Foundations of Modern Physical Science*. Burtt traced the origins of the ontological and epistemological assumptions that underlie the physical sciences, and argued that they were adapted to and fashioned by a particular cultural outlook and a particular time in history. In our times, when that context has changed, he claimed that there is need for a reassessment of these metaphysical assumptions. The response at the time was hardly overwhelming; in fact for the next quarter of a century scientists appeared to be, if anything, increasingly committed to the positivistic and reductionistic premises that Burtt had targeted for reassessment.

But that did not mean that the issue went away. It continued to raise its head, in particular in the life sciences where many biologists insisted that the premises assumed in the physical sciences are inappropriate to the biological sciences. The philosopher of science Marjorie Grene, for example, has said:

> Living things, from the cell to human beings, *cannot* be understood purely in molecular terms. Life is radically non-interpretable . . . except in terms of matter *and* form, physical-chemical conditions *and* biotic principles. . . . At least a two-level ontology is needed for the interpretation of all living things. . . . The relation, say, between cellular function and the chemical laws which specify necessary conditions for its operation, is *not* a complementarity like wave and particle. It is a hierarchical complementarity, in which . . . the higher level depends for its existence on the lower level,

but the laws of the lower level, though presupposed by, cannot explain the existence of the higher—although they may suffice to explain its failures. (1974, p. 48)

Biologists Richard Levins and Richard Lewontin (1985) have made a related point. They observe that science is as much a product of culture as culture is a product of science:

Nothing evokes as much hostility among intellectuals as the suggestion that social forces influence or even dictate either the scientific method or the facts and theories of science. . . . [Yet] science, in *all* its senses, is a social process that both causes and is caused by social organization. (p. 4)

As a consequence of the social milieu at the time, Levins and Lewontin perceive that early Western science adopted "four ontological commitments [of Cartesian reductionism]":

1) There is a natural set of units or parts of which any whole system is made.

2) These units are homogeneous within themselves, at least insofar as they affect the whole of which they are the parts.

3) The parts are ontologically prior to the whole; that is, the parts exist in isolation and come together to make wholes.

4) Causes are separate from effects, causes being the properties of subjects, and effects the properties of objects. (p. 269)

These assumptions, according to the authors, introduce numerous distortions into our understandings of organisms and societies, and have further objectionable implications with regard to how that knowledge is applied.

Nobel laureate neuroscientist Roger Sperry has long observed (1981, 1987) that a science based on Cartesian reductionism cannot be complete. Such a science assumes only explanations involving what Sperry (after D. T. Campbell, 1974) terms "upward causation"—that is, elemental phenomena "causing" more holistic phenomena (for example, molecular motion causing the phenomena of temperature and heat flow). An adequate science, according to Sperry, must also include "downward causation" according to which "things are controlled not only from below upward but also from above downward by mental, social, political, and other macro properties. [Furthermore,] primacy is given to the higher level controls rather than the lowest." (1987)

Charles Laughlin et al. (1990) observe that

Beginning in the '50s and '60s, a period of radical transformation of science has led us away from a mechanistic, positivistic, hyperrational conception of science, on a path with two principal themes: (1) A shift away from a fragmented, mechanical, nonpurposive conception of the world toward a holistic, organic, and purposive conception; and (2) a shift away from a concern with objectivity toward a concern with subjectivity—that is, with the role of perception and cognition in the process of scientific inquiry.

Finally, in a remarkably lucid history of the Western worldview, Richard Tarnas (1991) describes the path by which the present impasse has been reached:

> The modern scientific mind found itself beleaguered on several fronts at once: by the epistemological critiques, by its own theoretical problems arising in a growing number of fields, by the increasingly urgent necessity of integrating the modern outlook's human-world divide, and above all by its adverse consequences and intimate involvement in the planetary crisis. The close association of scientific research with the political, military, and corporate establishments continued to belie science's traditional self-image of detached purity.... The belief that the scientific mind had unique access to the truth of the world, that it could register nature like a perfect mirror reflecting an extra-historical, universal objective reality, was seen not only as epistemologically naive, but also as serving, either consciously or unconsciously, specific political and economic agenda, often allowing vast resources and intelligence to be commandeered for programs of social and ecological domination. (p. 364)

If these observations are at all accurate, the basic assumptions of science may be in for a more fundamental shift than any since the scientific revolution. Even the dramatic twentieth-century revolutions in physics left the metaphysical foundations more intact than will the present challenge, or so it would appear.

The Timeliness of the Inquiry

We wish to make it most clear that in arguing for a reassessment of the metaphysical foundations of science we are in no way attacking the fundamental spirit of scientific inquiry. The contributors to this volume are practicing scientists or philosophers of science, with a deep appreciation of the advance in human thought represented by modern science. What we are proposing is the timeliness of science taking a major step in its own evolution.

C. P. Snow pointed out three decades ago, in a much-discussed book entitled *Two Cultures and the Scientific Revolution* (1959), that unlike almost any stable society one could name, modern society does *not* have a single worldview on which there is consensus. Broadly speaking, we have two competing worldviews: the one dominant in the humanities and religions, in which values are important and such things as volition and the human spirit are assumed to be "real", and the other, "scientific" one in which they are not. As a result we have a deep underlying confusion about everything; but, because we have largely learned to live with the contradiction, that perplexity is not widely noted. The most serious consequences come from society's confusion about values and meanings.

Tarnas (1991) has described the predicament of the modern world and its science in terms of the "double bind" concept of anthropologist Gregory Bateson. This "double bind of modern alienation" is as follows:

> 1) The human being's relationship to the world is one of vital dependency, thereby making it critical for the human being to assess the nature of that world accurately. 2) The human mind receives contradictory or incompatible information about its situation with respect to the world, whereby its inner psychological and spiritual sense of things is incoherent with the scientific metacommunication. 3) Epistemologically, the human mind cannot achieve direct communication with the world. 4) Existentially, the human being cannot leave the field. . . . The modern condition is an extraordinarily encompassing and fundamental double bind, made less immediately conspicuous simply because it is so universal. We have the post-Copernican dilemma of being a peripheral and insignificant inhabitant of a vast cosmos, and the post-Cartesian dilemma of being a conscious, purposeful, and personal subject confronting an unconscious, purposeless, and impersonal universe, with these compounded by the post-Kantian dilemma of there being no possible means by which the human subject can know the universe in its essence. We are evolved from, embedded in, and defined by a reality that is radically alien to our own, and moreover cannot ever be directly contacted in cognition. (pp. 419-420)

Recognizing the power of this "double bind", wherein we *have* to have confidence in our picture of the world, and yet the influential worldview presented by modern science is inadequate to live by,

> . . . it should not be surprising what kinds of response the modern psyche has made to this situation as it attempts to escape the double bind's inherent contradictions. Either inner or outer realities tend to be distorted: inner feelings are repressed and denied, as in apathy and psychic numbing, or they are inflated in compensation, as in narcissism and egocentrism; or the outer world is slavishly submitted to as the only reality, or it is aggressively objectified and exploited. There is also the strategy of flight, through various forms of escapism: compulsive economic consumption, absorption in the mass media, faddism, cults, ideologies, nationalistic fervor, alcoholism, drug addiction. When avoidance mechanisms cannot be sustained, there is anxiety, paranoia, chronic hostility, a feeling of helpless victimization, a tendency to suspect all meanings, an impulse toward self-negation, a sense of purposelessness and absurdity, a feeling of irresolvable inner contradiction, a fragmenting of consciousness. And at the extreme, there are the full-blown psychopathological reactions of the schizophrenic: self-destructive violence, delusional states, massive amne-

sia, catatonia, automatism, mania, nihilism. The modern world knows each of these reactions in various combinations and compromise formations, and its social and political life is notoriously so determined. . . . The pivot of the modern predicament is epistemological, and it is here that we should look for an opening. (pp. 420-422)

Pressure to do something about this predicament has increased significantly during the past quarter century. The pressure originates partly from growing disenchantment with some of the consequences of technological application unguided by suitable values; partly, also, from the interest that has developed in meditative spiritual practices and explorations of "altered states of consciousness". As theologian Jacob Needleman wrote in his introductory paragraph to *A Sense of the Cosmos* (1975):

Once the hope of mankind, modern science has now become the object of such mistrust and disappointment that it will probably never again speak with its old authority. [The problems contributed to by modern technologies have] eroded what was once a general trust in the *goodness* of science. And the appearance in our society of alien metaphysical systems, of 'new religions' sourced in the East, and of ideas and fragments of teachings emanating from ancient times have all contributed doubt about the *truth* of science. Even among scientists themselves there are signs of a metaphysical rebellion.

Using a different metaphor, Thomas Berry (1988) has written about how we are searching for a "New Story"—a new account of how things came to be as they are, within which we find a sense of life purpose, a guide to education, an understanding of our suffering, and impetus for energized action. It is apparent to more and more people that the Old Story has become fragmented and nonfunctional. At the heart of the New Story will be, clearly, the insight of science and the facts of evolution. But that story, as it is told in our science classrooms, is incomplete, and, in its incompleteness, distorting. It has displaced the old but not matured sufficiently to serve as the new.

This is a time of unusual flux both within science and in the relationship of science to the broader society. Science is the *only* generally recognized cognitive authority in the modern world; it is the principal definer of truth in modern society. It stands at the gates of legitimation, admitting to our schools and businesses—even our homes—only those concepts which pass its tests. Yet its position as ultimate truth-legitimator is challenged by the spreading "heretical" awareness that important realms of human experience appear to be denied or invalidated by conventional science.

Objectives of This Report

In this collection of essays we aim to propel this important issue into the dialogue, both within the scientific community and the public at large. The influence of science in the broader society is so strong that any question about the adequacy of its foundation assumptions is a matter not only for professional but also public concern. The scientific worldview so permeates and shapes our society that any significant change therein will shake the foundations of every institution in society. The implications of the questions being raised are so profound that there is not one of us who can feel completely comfortable when considering them.

The collective credentials of the authors represented in this collection of essays are such that we trust it will not be treated as a trivial contribution. But they do not speak with a single voice. They agree on the importance and timeliness of the inquiry; they believe it is time for science to evolve past the present unsatisfactory state. They do not propose a single, uniquely "best" solution to the dilemma. Rather, you will find in these chapters a number of alternate suggestions as to the most fruitful approach. The dialogue is open; our one strong recommendation is that it be vigorously pursued. The stakes are high, and the time is right.

A Short Walk Through the Chapters

The problem to which the overall inquiry is addressed is defined in the first chapter. It identifies the assumptions of logical empiricism, the metaphysical foundation which at mid-century was generally agreed to be the solid foundation on which rigorous science should be based, and briefly summarizes some of the challenges to that foundation.

Lynn Nelson further elaborates on the relationship between science and metaphysics. Until the 1960s scientists generally held that their empirical research is a fundamentally different enterprise from philosophy, and does not involve metaphysical commitments. This view was effectively challenged by Thomas Kuhn's (1970) *The Structure of Scientific Revolutions,* which held that metaphysical commitments are tacitly understood by practicing scientists, but are typically neither articulated nor subjected to scrutiny. These metaphysical assumptions may change at times of "scientific revolution", but if they do, the "before" and "after" assumptions are irreconcilable.

Nelson counters both of these views by insisting that metaphysical commitments are incorporated in theories, methodologies, research questions, and hypotheses; such commitments are part of the evidence for theories and models; and attention to metaphysical assumptions should be part and parcel of the doing of science. In other words, scientific knowledge is both socially constructed *and* constrained by evidence.

She goes on to analyze how the present metaphysical foundations have been influenced by the male-orientation of Western society, particularly in its emphasis on dominance as a feature of natural relationships, its attraction to linear and hierarchical causal models of such relationships (including biological determinism), and its de-emphasis of process. Nelson's feminist critique urges the adoption of models that focus on whole organisms and on processes, encouraging recognition of the complexity of relationships and processes, still evolving and not complete—a complexity for which neither biological determinism nor simple environmentalism adequately account.

Michael Scriven continues the philosophical critique of our present form of science. Agreeing with Nelson on the importance of examining the metaphysical commitments that underlie all of science, he focuses on the role of the mind in science—on a "psychological epistemology". The legitimate territory of science, he argues, overlaps that of the objective and the subjective. The question is how to deal with the data of subjective experience.

A variety of extreme views have been developed during this century, none of which, Scriven claims, are suitable for science as a practical discipline. One of these extreme views is idealism, which embodies skepticism regarding the reality of the external world's existence. Logical positivism, on the other hand, accepts the reality of the external world but denies that of the world of inner experience. Another position is instrumentalism, which is the view that the tangible world is real enough, but that the rational order of science has no reality in itself; it is merely a way to facilitate prediction and the simplification of description. As Scriven sees it, instrumentalism is not enough, because a truth that survives new methods of looking is more valuable than a truth that does not. But logical positivism is not enough either, because its model of scientific knowledge and understanding is a very primitive oversimplification of a highly sophisticated set of procedures and their results.

Part of the problem arises because of language. The dichotomy of subjective-objective is commonly used both in an evaluative sense (bias vs. lack of bias) and in a descriptive sense (inner vs. outer). Because these two meanings are confused, doubt arises that the subjective (descriptive sense) can satisfy appropriate tests of objectivity (evaluative sense).

Scriven proposes a radical reanalysis of the logic of science, substituting for terms such as explanation, classification and evidence terms that are more psychologically oriented, such as information and understanding. This would result in a science that includes both the objective and the subjective in the descriptive sense, yet it could be objective in the sense of removal of bias. By placing science on a psychological foundation, its tendencies toward intolerance and overclaiming can be both understood and tempered.

Ilja Maso approaches the epistemological question from the standpoint of the "excellent researcher". He notes the shortcomings and dangers of the too-common concept of scientific research approaching some absolute truth, and proposes an epistemology of open inquiry employing "the totality of the researcher". He urges that the researcher rely on the totality of him/herself—on his potential, abilities and experiences—to (re)create a method appropriate to the question being researched.

The philosophy of life underlying the "truth-seeking" view of science is that science is absolute: that some persons through method can approach truth; that these persons are on top of the earthly hierarchy and have the moral right to try to persuade others. To take into account possible negative consequences of the results of scientific inquiry is nothing more than a nuisance inhibiting scientific progress.

Maso replaces the "truth-seeking" view with a goal of understanding, and the experiencing of truth by the researcher. When research is "excellent", it is because of a special combination of question, method, situation and researcher. In qualitative research, the researcher's relationship must be characterized by threefold openness—to the situation, to the research itself and to oneself. Only by having love and respect for self and others are researchers really able to find profound understanding and take responsibility for their deeds.

Nobel laureate **Roger Sperry,** interestingly enough, confirms the importance of the questions which other contributors are raising, but claims that the resolution is already with us. He agrees on the necessity to break the hold of the physicalism which has dominated science for over two centuries, but argues that the essential insight for this change has already been around since the late 1960s in the form of novel principles of cognitive and emergent causation.

Sperry's basic concept is that mental states (as subjectively perceived) are emergent properties of brain processes. They are qualitatively different from the physical world, although emergent from it. He argues that after a certain point in evolution, a new causative force (consciousness), qualitatively different from the reductionist causes of science, becomes operative and must be included in any adequate scientific accounting for phenomena. Thenceforth, causation ceases to be solely of the "bottom-up" form described by reductionistic science, and has to include "top-down" causation from consciousness.

The most important consequence of this new view of causation, Sperry asserts, is that science is now placed in the position of clarifying issues of morals and values, rather than reductionistically dismissing them. However, he warns against opening the door of scientific inquiry so wide as to readmit the otherworldly and the supernatural.

Another Nobel laureate, **George Wald,** counters with a view of a universe in which consciousness—rather than emerging after billions of years of antecedent evolutionary processes—is characteristic of the whole and "was there all the time." Wald has reached this radical conclusion from his many years of research in the biological sciences, toward the end of which he came to focus on two very fundamental questions: 1) How does it happen that the universe is so favorable toward the creation of living organisms? and 2) How did consciousness evolve and where is it located? His startling conclusion is that consciousness has been prior to, and intimately a part of, the evolutionary process. This view is in stark contrast to the accepted picture of unguided material evolution culminating in the human brain capable of conscious awareness. It implies a replacement of the ontological and epistemological assumptions which have been generally accepted as a proper foundation for science.

Richard Dixey, like Roger Sperry, attempts to reconcile the fact that we are familiar with two quite different types of explanation of events: "mechanical causation", the usual scientific type of explanation, and "volitional causation", the kind of explanation involving human values, perceptions, and choices (Sperry's "upward" and "downward" causation). Science has heretofore included only the former. Dixey argues that we need a "science of qualities". He addresses the problem that we ourselves are a part of the external world we set out to describe with science

> . . . and yet it is as if we have tried to find some way of creating a valid picture of it without ourselves as a component. Rather than proposing that all causes are mechanical and that our own volition is an illusion, why not invert the proposition and argue that all causes are volitional and that meaning is a component of reality? The external does not cease to exist, but the ground of being is recognized as primary. . . . Do we discover or create? Perhaps it is both.

Robert Jahn and **Brenda Dunne** caution that any re-examination of metaphysical premises should be based on direct scientific evidence that not only reveals shortfalls in the established paradigm, but points to specific paths for their remediation—they urge, in other words, that science be kept at the core of its own evolution, and that scientific methodology be retained for the task. Their chapter reviews research at Princeton University on certain anomalies, the findings of which point to the inadequacy of conventional assumptions about the relationship of consciousness to the physical environment. It suggests the need to soften the boundary between "I" and "not I", between self and environment.

The authors hypothesize that quantum physics may hold a key to further progress here. The irreducible wave-particle complementarity of quantum physics is not a property of the physical world per se; it arises in the process of consciousness interpenetrating with its environment. They conjecture that it is consistent to attribute to this same consciousness both wavelike and particulate characteristics.

Mae-Wan Ho also argues from new empirical evidence, focusing in her paper on the disjunction between the quality of our experience and the description of reality in science. The mind-object dualism of Western science presupposes that we can know nature without experiencing her. More than that, scientists are taught that their subjective experiences are unreliable, and must be denied at all cost to preserve the objectivity of science. The history of Western culture through the modern era has been that of progressive alienation from nature and hence from our natural being, while nature has become fragmented into atoms and fundamental particles. Unlike the knowledge systems of indigenous peoples where there is no mismatch between knowledge and experience, the severing of form from content in science lies at the root of its inability to make sense of life. Thus the development of science has led to the progressive flattening of experience and a disenchantment of reality.

Recent research has shown that metabolic energy in the body, rather than being dissipated as heat, is stored in the form of collective modes of electrome-chanical and electromagnetic vibrations that extend over macroscopic distances within the organisms. These "coherent" excitations manifest in the faint emission of light; they also appear to be responsible for long-range order in the living system, as well as for efficient energy conversion. (This is offered as an explanation for the extremely high efficiencies—up to 98 percent—of metabolic energy conversion in animal muscles, compared with the far lower efficiencies of mechanical engines that depend on fuel combustion.) This evidence suggests that organisms are coherent space-time structures, and their existence as such accounts for the remarkable spatio-temporal organization in all living systems—a pattern that is maintained in the face of a constant flux of energy and matter. This is also the basis for the distinction between "self" and a "not-self" within organisms, and explains how living organisms appear to violate the second law of thermodynamics—that is, they maintain or increase order, rather than increasing disorder (entropy).

But the real point of Ho's discussion is that these research findings lend support to Whiteheadian notions of the primacy of process, and of organisms which are their own cause as well as the "cause" of other events or organisms in their environment. She observes that these hypotheses lead to a picture of reality resembling that of the indigenous peoples of the world.

Brian Goodwin, too, sees in the concept of the organism a key to the "new biology". An organism, he says, is a dynamic form engaged in process, *becoming other in order to remain itself.* Organisms integrate dynamically with their environment, being affected both by external conditions and effecting change in their surroundings. The transformations that organisms undergo are expressions of their natures, Goodwin insists, *not*, as the neo-Darwinists proclaim, simply impressions of the environment acting via natural selection to generate a historical entity defined in terms of a contingent strategy of survival encoded in its genes as memory store.

Goodwin directly challenges the adequacy of the neo-Darwinist explanation of evolution, based on the three principles:

1) the transmission of hereditary instructions from generation to generation via self-generating DNA;

2) random variations in the instructions by modifications in the DNA; and

3) selection of the fitter variants in the organisms produced by the altered instructions.

He further challenges the faith that morphogenesis and the developmental dynamics of organisms will be satisfactorily explained by some sort of yet-to-be-discovered "program" in the gene structure.

Combining on the one hand general principles that unite the great diversity of organismic forms as transformations of one another, and on the other hand the Darwinian concept of biological forms evolving through time, Goodwin foresees a new "science of qualities" in which qualities are recognized as major ingredients of a world. This is a world in which we can feel at home, because we are engaged with our feelings and our minds in creating an intelligible and a significant unity expressed through unlimited creative diversity.

In his chapter, cultural anthropologist **Charles Laughlin** urges us to recognize science as an artifact of Western culture, bringing with it an understanding of the universe which is radically different from that of ancient, traditional and indigenous societies. Laughlin observes a distinction between a search for meaning and a search for truth, and raises the question of how scientific models of causation fail to enrich people's lives in any deep or integrating way. Our individual world of immediate experience—our *life-world*—is infused with meaning, and the worldviews of all human societies, as anthropologists attest, purport to reveal the hidden forces that seem to produce or relate experienced phenomena. The Euro-American worldview, however, is very strongly influenced by Western science, in which the "search for truth" is a predominant factor; this denies the kind of meaningful life-world arrived at by individuals through life experience, and thus contributes to a sense of anomie and alienation.

Laughlin identifies the source of this problem in the dualism of Cartesian metaphysics, and as counter to it he urges the increasing incorporation of "mature contemplation" into science. This will, he argues, bring about changes in the metaphysical foundations of science, and hence reduce the discrepancy between scientific models of causation and life-world causation.

In **Vine Deloria's** instructive essay, we learn of the essential difference between the knowledge of the Native American and that of the Western scientist:

> The real interest of the old Indians was not to discover the abstract structure of physical reality but rather to find the road along which, during the duration of a person's life, individuals were supposed to walk. This colorful image of the road suggests that the universe is a moral universe; that is to say, there is a proper way to live in the universe. There is a *content* to every action, behavior, and belief.

In this view it is

> . . . naive to believe that anything can be objectified for any purpose whatsoever without severe damage to the unity of life. The process of objectification is simply that of denying the moral dimension of the universe and rejecting the possibility of experiencing different modes of existence.

In the Indian view, we exist in a living universe within which events and actions have moral content—and that makes all the difference.

Understanding "native science" is useful as a commentary to reduce the hubris of modern science. As Deloria warns, we should not try to transpose concepts and ideas from one cultural context to another:

> Each cultural context has a unity of its own which gathers information into a particular set of interpretations. Removing an idea from one context to another cannot be done successfully because the methodologies by which each culture gathers information are different.

Physicist **Arthur Zajonc** proposes that we take seriously a proposal for the reform of science put forth by the German philosopher J. W. von Goethe. Zajonc sees, in physics, chaos theory, and other disciplines, a shift in Western consciousness toward a non-local and "entangled" imagination of our world. This approaches the perspective articulated long ago by Goethe and Rudolf Steiner, which embodies a fundamental conviction that the relation of the human mind to the world is ultimately not dualistic but participatory. All human knowledge of the world is in some sense determined by subjective principles; but instead of considering these principles as belonging ultimately to the separate human subject, and therefore not grounded in the world independent of human cognition, this participatory conception holds that these subjective principles are in fact an expression of the world's own being, and that the human mind is ultimately the organ of the world's own process of self-revelation. In this view, the essential reality of nature is not separate, self-contained, and complete in itself, so that the human mind can examine it "objectively" and register it from without. Rather, nature's unfolding truth emerges only with the active participation of the human mind. Nature's reality is not merely phenomenal, nor is it independent and objective; rather, it is something that comes into being through the very act of human cognition. Nature becomes intelligible to itself through the human mind.

Historian **Eugene Taylor** reminds us that the nineteenth-century philosopher William James grappled with many of the same questions being addressed in this inquiry, and answered them with his concept of "radical empiricism". For Taylor, science is best represented as an attitude or motive; it is a particular state of consciousness based on certain consensually validated assumptions about the world, held by a community of individuals called scientists. Its justification is that it works in representing and controlling the forces of the physical world. Problems arise because the so-called objectively neutral stance of science has been elevated to the major orienting philosophy of life in the modern world.

Taylor focuses on extending science, especially psychology, to include the phenomenal, subjective realm of the perceiver. Here he turns to one of the fundamental tenets of radical empiricism, that we should put experience, rather than sense perceptions, first. Empiricism deals with the entire phenomena of experience, whether generated from within the person or outside. Empiricism becomes radical when it refuses to admit into its constructions any element that is not directly experienced, nor exclude from them any element that is directly experienced. Thus, within the entire range of human experience, all claims are a potential topic of scientific investigation, although not all may be ultimately verified.

Taylor describes the usefulness of radical empiricism as a philosophical position guiding scientific research. Radical empiricism suggests that the underlying assumptions of all scientific disciplines are at base philosophical, and that the radically empirical view can be brought to bear as a way to 1) critique the work of scientific reductionists in light of their own metaphysical criteria, as well as 2) explain phenomena amenable to a kind of scientific scrutiny which is not limited by the metaphysics of physicalism. The crux of his argument is reserved, however, for a few paragraphs at the end where he emphasizes that at the core of his radical empiricism, James resolves the dualism of the mental and the physical by asserting that the one should not be subsumed under the other, but rather that "no external world of objects can exist *except as a function of some consciousness.*" In Taylor's view "what contemporary definitions of objective science do is clearly not to banish subjectivity, but *to hold the discussion of consciousness in abeyance.*"

The crux of the matter is that when one opens one's self to the uncertainty of pure experience, which is the radically empirical point of view, one runs the risk of being changed ultimately.

Finally, in the last chapter, Harman builds upon what has gone before and proposes a restructuring of science in which nothing is lost, but many present puzzles appear to become resolvable. Present science, tremendously effective in its chosen context, is based on a) an ontological assumption of separateness and b) an epistemological assumption of physical sense data as the sole emprical evidence on which the scientific picture of reality is to be based. The prospect of an "extended science" would build upon a′) an *ontological assumption of oneness, wholeness,* interconnectedness of everything, and b′) an *epistemological assumption that there are two available "windows" onto reality,* namely, the objective, through the physical senses and the subjective, through the intuitive and aesthetic faculties.

Such an extended science naturally employs a participatory methodology, and furthermore emphasizes, as do several of the other essays, the self-transformation of the scientist as an integral component of researching and learning.

The overall thrust of this study is, thus, that a reconstitution of science on a different metaphysical foundation is *intellectually supportable,* potentially *fruitful* in terms of researchable questions and effective methodology, *desirable* in terms of the light it could shed on some age-old scientific puzzles, and *timely* in terms of both a receptive climate and need for a different understanding of our relationship to nature.

References

Thomas Berry, *The Dream of the Earth,* Sierra Club Books, 1988.

E. A. Burtt, *The Metaphysical Foundations of Modern Physical Science* (2nd ed.) Routledge and Kegan Paul, 1932.

Donald T. Campbell, "'Downward Causation' in Hierarchically Organized Biological Systems" in *Studies in the Philosophy of Biology,* edited by F. Ayala and T. Dobzhansky, University of California Press, 1974.

Marjorie Grene, *The Understanding of Nature: Essays in the Philosophy of Biology,* D. Reidel, 1974.

Thomas Kuhn, *The Structure of Scientific Revolutions* (2nd ed.), University of Chicago Press, 1970.

Charles D. Laughlin, John McManus, and Eugene d'Aquili, *Brain, Symbol, and Experience: Toward a Neurophenomenology of Human Consciousness,* New Science Library Shambhala, 1990.

Richard Levins and Richard Lewontin, *The Dialectical Biologist,* Harvard University Press, 1985.

Jacob Needleman, *A Sense of the Cosmos,* E. P. Dutton, 1975.

C. P. Snow, *Two Cultures and the Scientific Revolutions,* republished 1969 as *Two Cultures and a Second Look,* Cambridge University Press, 1959.

Roger W. Sperry, "Changing Priorities", *American Review of Neuroscience,* 1981, 4, 1-15.

Roger W. Sperry, "Structure and Significance of the Consciousness Revolution", *The Journal of Mind and Behavior*, 8 no. 1, Winter 1987.

Richard Tarnas, *The Passion of the Western Mind: Understanding the Ideas That Have Shaped Our Worldview*, Harmony Books, 1991.

A Re-examination of the Metaphysical Foundations of Modern Science:

Why Is It Necessary?

by Willis Harman

Scientists typically assume (or behave as though they do) that the philosophical premises underlying science are not at issue—that they are part of the definition of modern science. More than one scientist has quoted, with some tinge of self-satisfaction, the anonymous remark that "philosophy of science is about as useful to scientists as ornithology is to birds"; this is a part of the legacy of the fragmentation of knowledge that is characteristic of modern times. Yet, many debates that appear to be about scientific matters in fact center around implicit ontological issues about the ultimate nature of reality, and epistemological issues about how we might find out.

Most practicing scientists are preoccupied with solving their own focused and practical problems, and are not at all involved with broader philosophical issues. The prevailing view among most scientists seems to be that they are not aware of any fundamental problems in their work that will not be satisfactorily resolved in time through the workings of normal science. For example: "There are no puzzles in morphogenesis, ontogeny, instinctual behaviors of animals, etc. that will not be satisfactorily explained as we learn more about the programs in the DNA", and "Consciousness will be adequately explained on a neurobiological basis."

Philosophers of science, on the other hand, *have* thought a lot about the foundation assumptions of science. However, on this matter of underlying assumptions, there is not only no consensus among them, there is no generally accepted way of achieving consensus.

Most scientists, therefore, do not see any necessity to reexamine the basic definitions of science, and even see a certain hazard in doing so. Throughout the history of science there has been a felt need to guard the gates against the fake and the mystical, which are ever eager to come in under the umbrella of legitimacy that science enjoys. Thus a sober sense of responsibility is appropriate if one presumes to reexamine that which has come to have a time-honored place, and seems to contribute to such an effective scientific enterprise.

But we have become increasingly aware over the past twenty or thirty years, as a culture, that any society's knowledge system is based on some ontological and epistemological assumptions, and this includes modern science. The issue is, how are these established and how is their adequacy evaluated? Students of science, at least in the earlier part of this century, were typically given the impression of a vast structure within which the fund of knowledge is continually increasing in size and quality, and the more fundamental laws are increasingly certain. It comes as a shock, then, to discover that in fact some of the most basic assumptions underlying science are very much in question—perhaps more so than at any time in the past three centuries.

Anomalous Areas

There are now a number of areas which demonstrate major failures of the prevailing scientific worldview to accommodate well substantiated evidence. Amongst them are the following:

1) The fundamental inquiry within physics into *the ultimate nature* of things does not appear to be convergent. The search for more fundamental particles seems to lead to still more fundamental particles; the search for the ultimate reductionist explanation seems to point to a wholeness. It is a fundamental initial assumption of physics, which has influenced every other area of science, that ultimate reality consists of fundamental particles, separate from one another and interacting through mechanisms (especially fields) which can be discovered and specified. But with Bell's theorem of nonlocality, and its experimental confirmation by Alain Aspect in 1982, quantum physics now displays an inherent contradiction: particles originally assumed to be separate turn out, apparently, to be connected (see Heisenberg, 1958, Bohm and Peat, 1987, Kitchener, 1988).

2) There appears to be evidence for a fundamental *self-organizing force* in living systems, from the smallest to the largest conceivable organisms, which remains unexplained by physical principles. Living systems exhibit a tendency toward self-organization (for example, homeostasis; intricate patterns in flowers

and butterfly wings); toward preservation of integrity (as in healing and regeneration; ontogenesis from a single fertilized egg to an adult organism); toward survival of the organism and the species (for example, complex instinctual patterns for protection and reproduction). The manifestations of this self-organizing tendency cause some scientists to question the accuracy of the received dogma that all inheritance is chromosomal (Lewontin, 1992). The evidences of a cumulative effect, over time, of this self-organizing tendency in evolution cast doubt on the adequacy of the neo-Darwinist orthodoxy (see Denton, 1986, Wesson, 1991).

3) Our scientific knowledge about the universe appears to be incomplete in that there is no place in it for the *consciousness of the observer*—nor, in general, for volition ("free will") or any of the other attributes of consciousness. Nobel laureate Roger Sperry (1987) insists that no science can be complete that does not include "downward causation", from the higher level of consciousness to the lower, physicochemical level.

4) One of the most challenging aspects of the consciousness puzzle is the *concept of the self*. The conscious self is ineluctably involved in observation; yet the science constructed from those observations contains no place for the self. Psychologist Gordon Allport wrote in 1955, in a little volume entitled *Becoming*, "For two generations, psychologists have tried every conceivable way of accounting for the integration, organization and striving of the human person without having recourse to the postulate of a self." The battle is still going on.

5) There is a persistent puzzle of "action at a distance" or *non-local causality*. This shows up, as we have already observed, in the far reaches of quantum physics. It also appears in the area which John Beloff (1977) calls "meaningful coincidences", referring to two or more events where there appears to be a meaningful connection although there is no physical connection. Here "meaningful" may refer either to the subjective judgment of the observer, or to a judgment based in historical data (as in the case of astrology or the *I Ching*). The term "meaningful coincidences" includes Carl Jung's "synchronicity" (Peat, 1987) and most of the range of the "paranormal". Examples include apparently "telepathic" communication, seemingly clairvoyant "remote viewing", and the "coincidence" between the act of prayer and the occurrence of the prayed-for, such as healing. Another example is the feeling of having a "guardian angel" when a person feels warned about a danger, or provided with a particularly fortuitous circumstance in life. A host of historical and anecdotal examples fall into the categories of "miracles" and "psi phenomena" (see Jahn and Dunne, 1987, Jung and Pauli, 1955).

6) Yet another area is that of *altered states of consciousness*, including those states traditionally sought out in a spiritual or mystical context.

Because these areas contain anomalous phenomena or reported experiences does not, of course, necessarily mean that the fault for each is the same. Certainly at first glance that seems improbable. However there is reason to think it may be the case nonetheless.

Reviewing the Nature of Scientific Inquiry

To make the argument for that assertion we need to review some basic aspects of scientific inquiry, and the historical context in which science originally became established.

The dominant worldview of sixteenth century Europe assumed a deep unity between nature and gnosis (knowledge which, though hidden, is accessible to imaginative thought and feeling).[1] What emerged in the seventeenth century was a science based on a profound division between mind and the nature it contemplates, so that an "ontological gulf" exists between consciousness and its object, such that the real is truly an object which stands over against the thinking mind, appearing *to* it but not *in* it. This dramatic change in perception emerged from a struggle for legitimacy and power between the members of groups championing radically different programs of development and reform in Europe at the end of the sixteenth and the beginning of the seventeenth centuries.

One of these programs was a movement for radical change and reform centering around the Renaissance nature philosophy of a group of fifteenth and sixteenth century scholars, including a Franciscan friar named Francesco Giorgi, author of an influential treatise "De harmonia mundi". Others in this group were Johannes Reuchlin, John Dee, and Giordano Bruno.

In this nature philosophy, all of reality was a single coordinated domain, every region of which was related to every other region. Thus to know the region called nature entailed knowing the whole sphere of Being within which nature was embedded. Mind and nature were thus undergoing a continuous cooperative transformation. But to achieve this knowledge and insight, the seeker had to make a spiritual commitment so as to experience *gnosis,* which is knowledge that transforms both self and other, in which mind and nature are simultaneously changing to states of greater harmony and unity. In alchemy, this dual transformation was described as a golden illumination of the mind or soul of the practitioner of the art which occurred at the same time that gold was emerging in the crucible. Thus nature was undergoing transmutation simultaneously with the spiritual illumination of the seeker; neither could occur without the other.

The Parisian monk and mathematician Mersenne saw Giorgi's gnostic nature philosophy as a threat to a very different proposal for reform, one that he deeply felt to be the path of intellectual and political rectitude and stability. Mersenne was a key figure in the early development of science, acting as what might in modern parlance be called a "networker" among Descartes, Desargues, Fermat, Pascal, Galileo, and others. Descartes studied mathematics for two years with Mersenne, an experience which presumably had some influence on his philosophy, and, in turn, Mersenne was instrumental in spreading Descartes' concepts of scientific method.

The science which Mersenne helped to shape in the seventeenth century, and which has come down to us as the dominant tradition of Western scientific and philosophical thought, is based upon dualisms that split the unified world of the Renaissance magi into separate domains of power. The threads of these dualisms can be found running through individual sciences as well as through our social and political structures.

Modern scientific thinking is often assumed to have begun with Descartes. In his *Discourse on Method* (originally entitled *Project of a Universal Science Destined to Raise Our Nature to Its Highest Degree of Perfection*) he outlined the new method of inquiry. The basic tenet of Descartes' philosophy was a dualistic position: he saw the universe as comprised of two distinct kinds of substance, namely mind, the essence of which is thought, and matter, the essence of which is extension in three dimensions. This dichotomy created the so-called "mind-body problem", which is the question of how these two such dissimilar substances can interact—how mind can know matter and affect matter.

The method of Bacon, Galileo, Descartes, Newton, and Leibnitz was characterized by "radical impersonalism". Bacon was deeply suspicious of the active, imaginative mind, advocating the superiority of the disciplined mind as the surer way to scientific truth. The focus of these early scientists on rigorous discursive reasoning eventuated in a described universe whose atomic constituents were only extrinsically correlated with one another, obeyed generic laws of interaction that made no provision for their individual characteristics, and was held together by a mysterious yet clearly non-anthropomorphic force: gravity. In contrast, the world-picture of Renaissance nature philosophy had been of a Cosmos composed of intrinsically correlated elements, hierarchically ordered in accordance with anthropomorphic values, and held together by a force called "love".

The scientific revolution was only one of several seventeenth century "revolutions". The economic doctrine of capitalism and the competition of the market began in Amsterdam and spread through Western Europe. The religious fragmentation of the Reformation continued as political fragmentation. First enunciated in the Treaty of Westphalia, the concept of competing autonomous nation-states, free to do anything they wanted and with the power to defend themselves, replaced the unity of the Holy Roman Empire. Meanwhile, the

"Glorious Revolution" in England presaged the liberal-democratic revolutions of the next century.

Underlying all of this, and more fundamental, was a basic shift in the dominant picture of reality. The cosmic vision of wholeness was replaced by a perception of separateness. Activities became rationally organized around impersonal and utilitarian values rather than around ceremonial and traditional ones. There was a shift from action that is prescribed to action by choice. This secularization of values marked the beginning of modern times. It brought a differentiation of institutions, and social division of labor. Change became expected or desired, and was increasingly institutionalized. There was increasing orientation toward the individual, and toward pluralism in values.

As Tarnas (1991) explains,

> With Galileo, Descartes, and Newton, the new science was forged, a new cosmology defined, a new world opened to man within which his powerful intelligence could act with new freedom and effectiveness. Yet simultaneously, that new world was disenchanted of all those personal and spiritual qualities that for millennia had given human beings their sense of cosmic meaning. The new universe was a machine, a self-contained mechanism of force and matter, devoid of goals or purpose, bereft of intelligence or consciousness, its character fundamentally alien to that of man. The pre-modern world had been permeated with spiritual, mythic, theistic, and other humanly meaningful categories, but all these were regarded by the modern perception as anthropomorphic projections. Mind and matter, psyche and world, were separate realities. The scientific liberation from theological dogma and animistic superstition was thus accompanied by a new sense of human alienation from a world that no longer responded to human values, nor offered a redeeming context within which could be understood the larger issues of human existence. Similarly, with science's quantitative analysis of the world, the methodological liberation from subjective distortions was accompanied by the ontological diminution of all those qualities—emotional, aesthetic, ethical, sensory, imaginative, intentional—that seemed most constitutive of human experience. These losses and gains were noted, but the paradox seemed inescapable if man was to be faithful to his own intellectual rigor. (p. 326)

By the middle of the twentieth century there was general agreement as to the purpose of science—to provide explanations of natural phenomena, albeit with a special emphasis on the ability to predict and control, and hence to manipulate, the physical environment (Rubinstein et al., 1984)—and general agreement on the appropriateness of the foundation assumptions of logical empiricism (Salmon, 1989). This near-consensus existed despite the persistent failures of the prevailing scientific worldview to accommodate well substantiated evidence, as detailed above. The explanation for this paradox lay in the strong faith that satisfactory ways would eventually be found to explain those anomalies within the accepted scientific framework.

Such did not prove to be the case, however. By the 1990s—roughly four decades later—the consensus has evaporated and the issue of appropriate metaphysical foundations is far more alive than it was in the 1920s when Burtt published his *Metaphysical Foundations* (Burtt, 1924).

Quine's 'Theoretical Network' Argument

One of the most important figures in this issue of the relationship of metaphysics to science is W.V.O. Quine, who plays a central role in Lynn Nelson's chapter in this volume. He argued (1962; discussed in Churchland, 1986, pp. 260-267) that the scientific explanation for any phenomenon is embedded in a theoretical network which involves multitudinous assumptions, including:

a) assumptions involved in "observations" of the phenomenon

b) hypotheses about the context of the phenomenon

c) underlying theoretical hypotheses

d) "basic laws" of the pertinent area of science

e) the accepted nature of scientific methodology

f) epistemological assumptions underlying scientific inquiry

g) ontological assumptions about the basic nature of reality

When there is an "anomaly", or a failure of observations to conform to scientific expectations, it means that *somewhere* in that network there is a falsity. But there is no standard logic for discerning just where in the theoretical network the falsity lies. Thus in the face of an anomaly we must consider revising all elements of the network. There is ultimately no such thing as a "crucial experiment" to "prove" a scientific hypothesis.

In short, when experience contradicts science, the science must be changed, but there is no infallible logic for determining exactly what to change in one's theory. Karl Popper's insistence that theories are never proved, but only falsified or not, seemed at one point an important insight; however, in today's science to talk of "verification" or "falsification" of theory sounds naive and simplistic. We must, says Quine, give up any idea that we can use experience either to confirm or to falsify particular scientific hypotheses. A consequence of Quine's view is that even our epistemological convictions about how we acquire knowledge, and about the nature of explanation, justification, and confirmation, are subject to revision and correction.

It is precisely to that point that present-day scientific paradoxes seem to have brought us. Most scientists today would assert that science has moved away from the strict determinism, reductionism, positivism, and behaviorism of a half century ago. But it remains to be discerned what we are moving *toward.*

The Metaphysical Foundations of Modern Science

Among the metaphysical assumptions which have been assumed intrinsic to modern science, perhaps the most important are:

Objectivism: the assumption of an objective world which the observer can hold at a distance and study separately from himself;

Positivism*:* the assumption that the real world is what is physically measurable; and

Reductionism: the assumption that we come to really understand a phenomenon through studying the behavior of its elemental parts (for example, fundamental particles).

These are essentially the assumptions of *logical empiricism*, the consensus position that had been reached by the middle of this century. They amount to the premise that the basic stuff of the universe is what physicists study: namely, matter and physical energy—ultimately, "fundamental particles", their associated fields and interrelationships.

To be sure, these underlying assumptions have been modified with the advent of quantum physics, particularly by the indeterminacy principle and the inherent statistical nature of measurement of the very small. What we are suggesting in this volume is the possibility of an even more fundamental change—change at the level of underlying ontological and epistemological assumptions.

Underlying the above (modified) classical assumptions is *an ontological assumption of separateness:* separability of observer from observed, subjective from objective, causes from effects; separateness of organism from environment, man from nature, mind from matter, science from religion; separateness of "fundamental particles" from one another, of things in general unless there is some "mechanism" to connect them ("action at a distance" precluded); separability of the parts of a system or organism to understand how it "really" works; separateness of scientific disciplines, of investigators, competing over who was first discoverer.

The assumption of separateness leads to the hubris that humankind can pursue its own objectives as though the Earth and the other creatures were here for its benefit; to the myth of the "objective observer"; to reductionist explanations; to the ethic of competition. It implies the locality of causes, that is, it precludes "action at a distance", either in space or time, and the epistemological assumption that our sole empirical basis for constructing a science is the data from our physical senses.

The ontological assumption of separateness, together with the positivistic assumption that what science deals with are ultimately quantifiable aspects of physical reality, leads to interest in certain types of questions, such as:

- If things are apparently separate and yet interact, what is the "mechanism" of the interaction? How to explain the interaction between two fundamental particles? Two celestial bodies? Two remotely located human beings? "Action at a distance" is a major puzzle; attempts to deal with it have centered around concepts of fields (gravitational, electromagnetic, morphogenetic) and particle-exchange.

- Extrapolating backwards to the "Big Bang" or other origin of the universe in its present form, what have been the chief mechanisms of evolution of the physical world and the world of living organisms?

- How does the appearance of purpose arise in the world of living organisms and human experience; that is, how can it be explained in terms of such mechanisms as chance and natural selection?

- How can the experience of conscious awareness, selective attention, etc. be explained in terms of brain functioning and other mechanisms?

- What is the physical explanation for such "meaningful coincidences" or "anomalous phenomena" as apparently clairvoyant remote viewing, or seeming psychokinesis?

If we consider changing some of the basic assumptions of science, then we find that at least as defensible as separateness is the ontological assumption that everything is connected to everything–physical universe and consciousness, mind and matter; all is a wholeness, a unity, a oneness. As an epistemological corollary to this assumption, one might assume that in addition to the "outer" way of interacting with the universe, through the physical senses, there is an "inner" way through one's own consciousness and intuition. If science were to be reconstituted on the basis of these assumptions, the questions of interest might appear quite differently–for example:

- What has been the evolution of the whole system (including the evolution of so-called scientific laws, since the constancy and inviolability of these cannot be taken for granted)? What has been the role of consciousness in evolution?

- If all is one, how does the appearance of separateness arise?

- If individual human minds are parts of a oneness, how do we avoid total confusion because of all the potential communication? Does the brain, then, function as a filter or "reducing valve"?

Not only do the metaphysical assumptions have profound influences within the scientific enterprise; they have social consequences as well. Levins and Lewontin (1985) point out some of the social consequences of the ontological assumption of separateness and the corresponding worldview of alienation:

> For example, medical research and practice isolate particular causes of disease [out of a chain of intersecting causes] and treat them. The tubercle bacillus became *the* cause of tuberculosis, as opposed to, say, unregulated industrial capitalism, because the bacillus was made the point of medical attack on the disease. The alternative would not be a 'medical' but a 'political' approach to tuberculosis and so not the business of medicine in an alienated social structure. Having identified the bacillus as the cause, a chemotherapy had to be developed to treat it, rather than, say, a social revolution. (p. 270)

Toward a New Scientific Paradigm

To consider what a science based upon wholeness rather than separateness might look like is not merely an interesting exercise. There is increasingly widespread agreement, both within and without the scientific community, that science must somehow develop the ability to look at things more holistically; that it has been a mistake of modern society to assume that, ultimately, reductionistic "scientific" causes should explain everything. We should not expect reductionistic science to comprise an adequate worldview. The context of reductionistic science is the desire to gain control through manipulation of the physical environment, and within that context its description of "causes" works amazingly well. Our problems arise when we change the context and attempt to elevate that kind of science to the level of a worldview. That is when we generate conflicts like "free will versus determinism" and "science versus religion".

The advent of quantum mechanics has played an important role in this change to a more holistic approach. Western science, as we have noted, started with an ontological assumption of separateness; the observer was assumed separable from the observed; ultimate reality was assumed to be "fundamental particles", separate from one another. Separateness implied objectivism and reductionism. A positivistic bias followed, so that "consciousness" became essentially absent from the scientific worldview.

Over the next several centuries physics developed from these assumptions, finally concluding (through quantum theory) that observer is *not* separate from the observed; fundamental particles are *not* separate from one another (Bell's theorem); and the consciousness of the observer is *essential* not only to the observation, but to the existence of the thing being observed (since only when an observation is made are the probability functions of quantum mechanics "collapsed" into actualities).

This much is rather generally agreed upon by physicists and other scientists. However, most have been reluctant to take the next step—of going back to the origins and reconstituting all of science on the basis of alternative assumptions—such as that of oneness, wholeness, unity—which might resolve some of the fundamental puzzles it is facing. But in this decade of the 1990s, our attitudes toward science appear to have a new fluidity and humbleness, which makes inquiry into such a sacrosanct topic as its metaphysical foundations possible in a way it probably would not have been even a quarter of a century ago. Scientists are no longer concerned with sounding the death knell of the medieval worldview, and consequently some aspects of that worldview, with its hierarchical, essentialistic, teleological, and even supersensible connotations, are not so threatening. In fact, the very admission of such concepts into scientific discourse frees them from their former association with medievalism.

However, the fear of opening science up to "medieval superstition" is not the only source of resistance to the paradigm shift. There is also a subtle power issue. As Lynn Nelson (1990) points out:

> The picture of an autonomous, self-regulating, self-critical, and non-subjective set of practices that produce 'objective' knowledge continues to shape science's self-image, and therefore, the practice of science. For it works to justify the 'cognitive authority' granted to science and claimed by science as its due. . . . Scientists . . . are granted and exercise a cognitive authority to shape the larger community's understanding of nature, including human nature. In exercising this authority, scientists can and do shape social and political policy based on the understandings of nature they 'certify' and communicate. (p. 140)

A challenge to the foundations of science may seem to threaten that preferred position which scientists hold in modern society.

Nevertheless, the problems with "separateness science" have become so visible that the issue is probably irrevocably joined. The question is: What is the new paradigm?

The eventual form of this modification to science, by which it is to be freed from the problems with the "separateness" assumption, is not at all clear. One possibility is that it should take the form of a *complementary* holistic science, in which consciousness and the physical world have a complementary relationship to one another, a solution which physicist Niels Bohr once proposed. Another is that it might take the form of an "extended" science, within which the science based on the separateness paradigm is included within a broader framework of knowledge, as an approach which applies in special cases where a physical system is relatively isolated from the whole, and no volitional causality intervenes. Yet another possibility is that even the concept of "metaphysical assumptions" is found to imply a structure that is too confining.

All of these possibilities will be explored in the following chapters. Our one objective is to portray the question and the alternative action paths with sufficient vigor and clarity that this important issue becomes widely discussed. The scientific community, influenced perhaps by attitudes of the general public, will then make the decisions which will define science for some time to come.

Note

1. This section is partially based upon Goodwin, 1987.

References

John Beloff, "Psi phenomena: Causal versus acausal interpretation", *Jour. Soc. Psychical Research,* 49, no. 773, September 1977.

David Bohm and F. David Peat, *Science, Order, and Creativity,* Bantam Books, 1987.

E. A. Burtt, *The Metaphysical Foundations of Modern Physical Science,* 2nd ed., Routledge and Kegan Paul, 1924.

Patricia Smith Churchland, *Neurophilosophy: Toward a Unified Science of the Mind/Brain,* MIT Press, 1986.

Michael Denton, *Evolution: A Theory in Crisis,* Adler and Adler, 1986.

Brian Goodwin, "A science of qualities" in *Quantum Implications: Festschrift for David Bohm,* B. T. Hilary and F. D. Peat, eds., Routledge and Kegan Paul, 1987.

Werner Heisenberg, *Physics and Philosophy: The Revolution in Modern Science,* Harper and Row, 1958.

Robert Jahn and Brenda Dunne, *Margins of Reality: The Role of Consciousness in the Physical World,* Harcourt Brace Jovanovich, 1987.

C. G. Jung and W. Pauli, *The Interpretation and Nature of the Psyche,* R.F.C. Hull and P. Silz, trans., Pantheon, 1955.

Richard F. Kitchener, ed., *The World View of Contemporary Physics: Does It Need a New Metaphysics?,* State University of New York Press, 1988.

Richard Levins and Richard Lewontin, *The Dialectical Biologist,* Harvard University Press, 1958.

Richard Lewontin, "The dream of the human genome", *New York Review,* May 28, 1992.

Lynn Nelson, *Who Knows?: From Quine to a Feminist Empiricism,* Temple University Press, 1990.

F. David Peat, *Synchronicity: The Bridge Between Matter and Mind,* Bantam, 1987.

W.V.O. Quine, "Two dogmas of empiricism" in *From a Logical Point of View,* 2nd ed., Harvard University Press, 1962.

Robert A. Rubenstein, Charles D. Laughlin, Jr., and John McManus, *Science as Cognitive Process: Toward an Empirical Philosophy of Science,* University of Pennsylvania Press, 1984.

Wesley Salmon, *Four Decades of Scientific Explanation*, University of Minnesota Press, 1987.

Roger W. Sperry, "Structure & significance of the consciousness revolution", *The Journal of Mind & Behavior*, 8, no. 1, Winter 1987.

Richard Tarnas, *The Passion of the Western Mind: Understanding the Ideas That Have Shaped Our World View*, Harmony Books, 1991.

Robert Wesson, *Beyond Natural Selection*, MIT Press, 1991.

On What We Say There Is and Why It Matters:

A Feminist Perspective on Metaphysics and Science

by Lynn Hankinson Nelson

*T**he conviction persists—though history shows it to be a hallucination—that all the questions that the human mind has asked are questions that can be answered in terms of the alternatives that the questions themselves present. But, in fact, intellectual progress usually occurs through sheer abandonment of questions, together with both of the alternatives they assume—an abandonment that results from their decreasing vitality and a change of urgent interest. We do not solve them: we get over them.*

—John Dewey

Getting Over the Metaphysics/Science Dichotomy

Two views of the relationship of metaphysics to science developed in philosophy of science during the 1960s. These have remained influential in the natural and social sciences, and have often been regarded as representing the only possible approaches to that relationship. One is a view associated with the "post-logical" positivist tradition of Carl Hempel and Ernest Nagel, the immediate intellectual heir of logical positivism. A central tenet of this tradition, like that of its predecessor, was that metaphysics and science are fundamentally distinct enterprises or entities; more to the point, that science, both as practice and product (theories, models, ontologies, and so on), is anchored firmly in sensory evidence, and that metaphysics, as either project or product, is "non-empirical".

Although developments in philosophy of science over the last three decades have led many in the field to abandon the view that science is (or could be) without metaphysical commitments (see, for example, Addelson, 1983, Dyke, 1988, *Biology and Philosophy,* 1986-present, Kuhn, 1970, and Lakatos, 1970), the legacy and focuses of the Hempel/Nagel tradition continue to underwrite an emphasis on the justification of (already "complete") scientific theories—an emphasis that effectively precludes attention to metaphysical commitments. And, as science critics note, many practicing scientists remain loath to admit that the theories, models, research, and hypotheses they generate and adopt either presume or advance metaphysical commitments (Addelson, 1983, and Keller, 1985). This is despite widespread commitments to "laws of nature" (or to a more general assumption that nature is orderly); to the existence of a unique, true theory of nature; and/or to physicalism or materialism. These are obviously metaphysical in nature, but neither the early nor later version of positivism, nor many scientists, acknowledge them as such.

The second view of the relationship of metaphysics to science, which has also been influential in philosophy of science and the sciences (particularly the social sciences), is associated with Thomas Kuhn, emerging in (or at least attributed to) *The Structure of Scientific Revolutions,* first published in 1962. In his analysis, Kuhn argued that "quasi-metaphysical commitments" are at work in science, tacitly implied by the paradigms which, on his account, both under-write and shape the practices of normal science (Kuhn, 1970, pp. 39-47). But Kuhn also implied that metaphysical commitments are not—and more impor-tantly, could not be—subjected to evaluation. Along with other "rules" (for example, methodological principles and statements of law and theory), Kuhn maintained that metaphysical commitments are not articulated in normal science, and that among the scientists whose practice they shape, knowledge of such commitments is at best tacit. "One is at liberty," Kuhn maintained, "to suppose that somewhere along the way the scientist has intuitively abstracted rules of the game for himself, but there is little reason to believe it" (ibid., p. 47).

It is only during periods of crisis, Kuhn argued, that metaphysical commitments and other rules come to be an issue with which scientists need to contend. But because Kuhn viewed the paradigms competing in such periods as both "constitutive of nature" and "irreconcilable", he was led to argue that the paradigms at issue, and the metaphysical commitments they incorporate, are unable to be compared by reference to "evidence" or "the world" (ibid., sections IX and XII). Kuhn's views continue to be influential in the social sciences and they are evident in some recent sociology of science and science criticism (Addelson, 1983, Bleier, 1984, and Keller, 1985).

It is a common view that the account of the relationship of metaphysics to science advocated by the Hempel/Nagel tradition and that advocated by Kuhn (or at least implied in his analysis) are contradictory—more to the point, that Kuhn's account revealed the bankruptcy of the positivist position. It is my contention that these accounts are more aptly and usefully viewed as two sides of the same coin, alternatives which, to paraphrase Dewey, "we need to get over". It is a consequence of each position, for instance, that the presence and role of metaphysical commitments are indications that something is wrong. From the positivist position, such commitments represent a "failure" of scientific method (specifically, a failure to filter out "non-empirical" elements). From the Kuhnian position, although metaphysical commitments are common features of science (and perhaps unavoidable features), they are not and could not be subject to empirical constraint. Hence, both positions underwrite the view that metaphysical commitments are irrational. I argue below that these continuities are underwritten by deeper assumptions common to the two traditions: a view that individual theories or paradigms "face" experience in isolation from a larger system of theories and practices, and a (related) view that science is an autonomous entity or enterprise (see, also, Nelson, 1990).

Alternative Views

As I noted at the outset, it is also a common view that the positivist and Kuhnian positions exhaust the possible understandings of the relationship between metaphysics and science. But there is an alternative to both and to the view of metaphysics they serve to underwrite, and it is to that that much of this chapter is devoted. Building from and extending the positions advocated by W.V.O. Quine, the heir apparent of the positivist tradition, I argue that metaphysical commitments are incorporated in theories, methodologies, research questions, and hypotheses—indeed, in everything we say about the world; that such commitments constitute part of the evidence for particular theories, research projects, models, and methods, and are themselves subject to empirical constraint; and that attention to the metaphysical commitments incorporated in models, methods, and theories needs to become part of the doing of science.

Support for these positions comes from two sources: a theory of evidence that is broader than that embraced by the positivist and Kuhnian traditions, and issues raised in and by feminist science criticism. Both indicate that metaphysical commitments constitute part of the evidence for individual theories and claims, and that such commitments can be exposed and evaluated. Moreover, both allow us to see that science can lead to better metaphysics. The view of evidence builds from Quine's arguments for holism, but the consideration of feminist science criticism leads to a broader construal of the theories and experiences that function as evidence than Quine envisioned.

For instance, while Quine maintains that there is a real boundary between science and values (it may, in fact, be the only boundary he recognizes), feminist science criticism indicates that metaphysical commitments are often political, reflecting and reinforcing the social relations and practices—including those involving gender, race, and class—that characterize our larger community. More to the point, feminist criticism indicates that these relationships obtain not just in cases in which the charge of "bad science" is appropriate, but also when the charge is not appropriate. I use these points to further the argument that subjecting metaphysical commitments to scrutiny must become part of what we expect and demand of good science.

The project I undertake involves, then, a general consideration of the relationship between science and metaphysics and a call for self-conscious and extensive scrutiny of metaphysical commitments, rather than a critique or defense of any specific metaphysics. Philosophy, of course, affords no more access to a goddesses' eye view of things than does science, and there are general assumptions and interests underwriting my approach. Some are pragmatic (at least, in a Quinean sense). For instance, I view theories, models, and ontologies as tools to organize, explain, and predict experience, rather than pieces added incrementally to a unique, true theory of nature. But as my discussion of evidence indicates, a pragmatic view of science does not entail that we eschew questions of "truth" or abandon an empiricist account of evidence. Experience is a constraint on all of our theorizing, and our collective experience indicates that not all of the tools we construct are equally warranted: predictions fail, theories wither, and we can and do get things wrong. Moreover, in the absence of "Archimedean" standpoints, there seems no vantage point from which to declare that all of our attempts to organize and explain nature are fictions (see, also, Nelson, 1990, 1992).

Alternatively put, my discussions of evidence and feminist science criticism suggest the view that knowledge is both socially constructed and constrained by evidence, and that the generation of ontologies and general metaphysical commitments (for example, to linear or non-linear models of biological processes, to reductionist or to anti-reductionist approaches) is part of the building of knowledge. Other assumptions at work in the discussion are shaped by categories, questions, and interests that have become possible as a result of feminist participation in and attention to the sciences. I am concerned with the androcentrism that feminist science criticism reveals in methods, ontologies and theories in various sciences, and with the more general assumption that dominance relations are a ubiquitous feature (if not the most fundamental feature) of human and non-human nature. Androcentrism and commitments to dominance relations raise questions concerning empirical adequacy (for example, whether androcentric models lead to partial accounts of social life), as well as questions concerning the political implications of the commitments incorporated in and implied by scientific research and theories. They also raise questions for the epistemology of science: for our accounts of how we go about generating theories, and of the nature and scope of the evidence we have for doing so.

I do not directly defend these assumptions, although some support for each will emerge in the larger discussion. I am aware, however, that they violate some long-standing and fervently-held "either/ors"—the alleged dichotomies of political advocacy and objectivity, of sociology of science and epistemology, of feminism and empiricism, to name some of the more obvious, as well as the alleged dichotomy between metaphysics and science on which I focus. I ask that readers consider whether the approaches I take shed light on the relationship between metaphysics and science, and between each of these and politics, and whether these issues warrant our attention.

I. What We Say There Is

I begin to lay the groundwork for a discussion of Quine's account of the relationship between metaphysics and science by identifying the assumptions common to the Hempel/Nagel and Kuhnian positions. The summary is brief, serving primarily as counterpoint for positions I later advocate.

Hempel/Nagel

As the intellectual heir of logical positivism, the tradition that has come to be called the "Hempel/Nagel" tradition in philosophy of science shared several assumptions with its predecessor. One was the view that a (if not *the*) central task of an epistemology of science is to specify the "logic" of science—the logical structure of theories and the logic of explanation, and the logic of the connection between sensory evidence and theories. It is the work done within the tradition to articulate the connection between evidence and theories that shapes its approach to metaphysics, and, hence, the work on which I focus here. A second assumption common to the early and later versions of positivism was that securing the connection required that science be free of anything that was not grounded (ultimately) in sensory evidence. And like their predecessors in logical positivism, Hempel and Nagel assumed that the latter required, in turn, a sharp boundary between science on the one hand, and metaphysics and values on the other.

Abandoning the positivist insistence that "meaning" could be equated with a method of verification (as Ayer, for example, had insisted. See Ayer, 1950), Hempel specified conditions for determining whether a sentence is "cognitively significant" (Hempel, 1965). Not surprisingly, given the goals and assumptions noted above, the criteria preserve precisely the distinction between "sense" and "nonsense" that the positivists designed in order to banish metaphysics and values from science. On Hempel's criteria, only those sentences which can in principle be tested by empirical evidence (synthetic sentences), or whose truth or falsity is a matter of the "meanings" of their terms (for example, mathematical and logical sentences), are part of the body of knowledge that the tradition regards as constitutive of science (Hempel, 1965, pp. 101-102).

Problems raised by the positivist attempt to show that theories are (ultimately) a construction from sense data led Hempel and Nagel to locate the connection between science and evidence in something other than the ways theories are generated (Hempel, 1966, and Nagel, 1961). Arguing that "there is no logic of discovery", they introduced a distinction between the contexts of discovery (the context in which theories or hypotheses are generated) and that of justification (the context in which such theories are tested and justified), and maintained that the connection between theories and evidence is forged in the second context (Hempel, 1965). Developing a comprehensive account of the logic of confirmation, Hempel argued that confirming hypotheses by observation statements insures that the hypotheses admitted into the "body of scientific knowledge" are appropriately constrained by evidence (Hempel, 1965, pp. 95-96). (The emphasis on the logic of justification also characterizes Karl Popper's philosophy of science. But there are important differences between the two approaches. For one thing, Popper focused on the logic of falsification rather than confirmation; more important, perhaps, many of the problems I note below with Hempel's assumptions are recognized by Popper [see Popper, 1959, and Nelson, 1990].)

Now, Hempel's faith in the objectivity of the knowledge so produced was partly underwritten by the fact that the relationship between theories and evidence that he analyzed and specified is a logical relationship (with "observation sentences" replacing the illusive—if not illusionary—"sense data" that figured in logical positivism). But it was also underwritten by other features of his account, and it is these which effectively banish questions about metaphysical commitments from the epistemology of science. First, Hempel assumed an "ideal" language of science. He defined observation sentences, for example, as sentences about "directly observable attributes of things and events" that are couched in "a well-determined language of science" (Hempel, 1965, p. 22). The definition, together with the alleged distinction between contexts of discovery and justification, effectively limits the epistemology of science to the testing of already "complete" hypotheses and theories, by observation sentences that are themselves (already) couched in a "well-determined" language of science. In short, how we arrive at what Hempel calls "the definite language of science" (statements of theory as well as "observation" sentences), how questions come to be deemed interesting or worthy of attention, and how ontologies and methodologies come to be propounded and adopted to answer these, are relegated to "questions about discovery". Given the alleged distinction between discovery and justification, such questions are deemed irrelevant to the epistemology of science on the grounds that they are (ultimately) irrelevant to the content of science.

Other assumptions and arguments underwrote the view that issues involving metaphysical commitments could be safely ignored. First, Hempel's account of the logic of confirmation assumed that individual sentences (observation sentences, for example) have specifiable empirical content: that is, a list of sensory stimulations that will confirm or disconfirm them in isolation from a larger body of theory and assumptions. The latter is, of course, one of the assumptions that Popper recognized as unwarranted; he describes observation sentences (which he calls "basic sentences") as the product of "judicial decisions" and denies that these (or anything else) provide a "foundation" for science (Popper, 1959, pp. 110-111). Second, while acknowledging that what he called "background assumptions" complicate the logic of using observation sentences to "confirm" individual hypotheses and theories, Hempel's account suggested that individual theories face the evidence (with the latter recorded in observation sentences) in isolation from a larger body of theory. Third, for those in the tradition, the objectivity of science seems insured by the view, as Nagel explicated it, that:

> [while] common-sense knowledge is largely concerned with the impact of events upon matters of special value to men [sic], the statements of science appear to be only tenuously relevant to the familiar events and qualities of daily life. (Nagel, 1961, p. 10)

Together, these assumptions underwrite the view that science is anchored firmly in evidence: a self-regulating activity, it is governed by a logic internal to it and the definitive evidence of nature.

It is worth noting one additional assumption that has functioned as support for the view that issues of discovery, including questions about the generation and propounding of ontologies, can be safely ignored. Hempel and Nagel apparently assume that there is a determinate set of sentences, a determinate theory of nature, that will constitute science at the end of inquiry (Nelson, 1990). Given that assumption, how particular pieces of the unique, true theory come to be discovered can be regarded as unimportant. If, on the other hand, the various assumptions I have identified are unwarranted, then writing off the context of discovery, and writing off questions about the presence and nature of metaphysical commitments in science, are not defensible.

Thomas Kuhn

In approaching science as an activity rather than a body of knowledge, and in terms of its account of that activity, Kuhn's analysis has been viewed as refuting the most basic tenets of the Hempel/Nagel tradition and its predecessor—and there are, of course, some striking differences. First, Kuhn argued that within "normal science" (non-crisis or non-revolutionary science), there is no effort to confirm or falsify theories. Second, he maintained that the outcomes of scientific revolutions are determined by "conversions" rather than empirical evaluations and comparison of competing theories (or paradigms) (Kuhn, 1970). What drives, underlies, and determines normal science and revolutionary science—and thus determines what comes to be certified as scientific knowledge—on Kuhn's analysis, are adherence and allegiance to a paradigm and the sociology of science communities.

I focus here on the view of metaphysical commitments that contributes to these positions, but I note at the outset that Kuhn's work is a matter of some controversy. I am not convinced that the view of the relationship of metaphysics to science that I outline is the only view to be found in Kuhn's work—or that it is the view he himself intended to convey (see, for example, Kuhn, 1972, and his Postscript to 1970, and Lakatos and Musgrave, 1970). My claim is (only) that the view is compatible with things Kuhn has said about metaphysical commitments in his accounts of normal and revolutionary science, and that this has been influential in sociology of knowledge and science. As such, it is part of what contributes to a general skepticism about the rationality of metaphysical commitments.

For our purposes, it will be sufficient to focus on Kuhn's account of crisis and revolutionary science. Unlike his account of normal science in which "quasi-metaphysical" commitments function, so to speak, behind the scenes, Kuhn's account of revolutionary science grants metaphysical commitments a consequential role. Not only do such commitments function to determine "the population of the universe" (Kuhn, 1970, p. 102), but, along with other features of a paradigm, they preclude the possibility that choices between competing paradigms can be made on the basis of comparison between them (a comparison which might indicate, for example, that one paradigm surpasses the other in explanatory range), or between each paradigm and "the world" (ibid., section II). There are several grounds for these claims and they are worth separating.

First, the paradigms at issue in crisis and revolutionary science—the old, now well articulated, and the new, as yet comparatively unarticulated—are described by Kuhn as "disciplinary matrices" (Postscript to Kuhn, 1970). Each incorporates a distinct worldview, for the paradigms at issue are "constitutive of nature" (Kuhn, 1970, p. 149), and "provide all phenomena except anomalies with a theory-determined place in the scientists' field of vision" (ibid., p. 97). Moreover, each paradigm incorporates a definition of science. Paradigms, Kuhn notes, are "the source of the methods, problem-field, and standards of solution accepted by any mature scientific community" (ibid., pp. 102-103).

Second, Kuhn maintains that the paradigms at issue in crisis and revolutionary science are irreconcilable. "The differences between successive paradigms are both necessary and irreconcilable," Kuhn argued. "Competing paradigms tell us different things about the population of the universe and about that population's behavior" (ibid., pp. 102-103). In other words, paradigms are "closed systems". And hence, Kuhn maintains, there is nothing else, no higher tribunal—either in terms of evidence or logic—that can be appealed to.

> . . . the choice [between competing paradigms] is not and cannot be determined by the evaluative procedures of normal science, for these depend in part upon a particular paradigm, and that paradigm is at issue. . . . Like the choice between competing political institutions, that between competing paradigms proves to be a choice between incompatible modes of life. (ibid., pp. 93-94)

Finally, we need to note that Kuhn's scientific communities are themselves closed systems. Describing the education of a prospective member of a science community as an initiation rather than the learning of theory, and defining membership as itself a matter of allegiance to a paradigm, Kuhn's communities are both self-regulating and insulated. He notes that:

> One of the things a scientific community acquires with a paradigm is a criterion for choosing problems that, while the paradigm is taken for granted, can be assumed to have solutions. To a great extent these are the only problems that the community will admit as scientific or encourage its members to undertake. (Kuhn, 1970, p. 37)

Now, if, as Kuhn believes, paradigms are self-contained, "world determining" and determining of what counts as science, if competing paradigms are irreconcilable, and if science communities are themselves closed systems, then the weight of the course of events during crisis can only be carried by the sociology of the community—by techniques of persuasion and professional pressure, rather than anything like rational comparison of paradigms in the light of evidence and/or explanatory power. Epistemological recourse, for the reasons outlined above, is impossible. "As in political revolutions," Kuhn argues, "so in paradigm choice—there is no standard higher than the assent of the relevant community" (ibid., pp. 93-95).

Hence, and ironically, it is on the basis of a cluster of assumptions that he shares with Hempel and Nagel that Kuhn is led to the view that revolutions in science force or incorporate epistemological chasms, and that such crises are (and could only be) resolved by "conversions". These views are a consequence of assuming that only sensory evidence constitutes evidence (the flip side of the view that individual theories, or paradigms, "face" the evidence in isolation from anything else), and of assuming that scientific communities are self-regulating systems governed by a logic internal to them. We turn next to a view that challenges these assumptions and, by so doing, avoids the skepticism with which the Hempel/Nagel and Kuhnian traditions view metaphysical commitments.

W.V.O. Quine

Almost four decades ago, Quine began a discussion of metaphysics and science by asking the question "What is there?", and answering "Everything" (Quine, 1963). There was both an epistemological and metaphysical point to the question and the answer, reflecting the central argument of Quine's discussion, that it is impossible to discuss ontology (what there is) without discussing theory (what we say there is). What there is, Quine's answer suggests, is what our theories say there is; that is, what we posit in the way of objects in the process of organizing and explaining what goes on—in short, what we are willing to talk about. Quine's initial statement of what there is is meant to convince or remind us of the scope of our common-sense "there is" idiom—an idiom, he maintains, that is involved in all of our dealings with the world (Quine, 1969A, p. 105).

In posing and so answering the question, Quine was concerned to undermine several specific views. One is the view that there are degrees or kinds of existence (that there is a distinction, for example, between "theoretical" objects and "real" objects, or "actual" and "potential" objects). The objects which figure in our ways of organizing experience (both those of common sense and science) are, in Quine's view, both theoretical and real (see also Quine, 1966).

Other targets include the views that metaphysical commitments are somehow avoidable (as the emphases of the Hempel/Nagel tradition suggested) or that such commitments are "free-floating" or hidden (as Kuhn's analysis of normal science implied), as well as the view, strongly implied by both traditions, that metaphysical commitments are pernicious. Metaphysical commitments,

Quine maintains, are not lurking in the background or laid down prior to the construction of theories. They are incorporated in theories—indeed, in all of our theories. In building a theory, we accept the ontology it brings with it, pending the evolving of a better theory.

> We commit ourselves to an ontology containing numbers when we say there are prime numbers larger than a million; we commit ourselves to an ontology containing centaurs when we say there are centaurs; and we commit ourselves to an ontology containing Pegasus when we say Pegasus is. (Quine, 1963, p. 8)

In insisting on the interdependence between ontology and theory, and between metaphysics and epistemology, Quine also insists that "absolute" metaphysical questions do not make sense. We cannot separate ontology from ideology, there are no "things in themselves". Ontological questions are always relative to some background theory which, for the time, is taken at face value.

To clarify these points and their implications, I briefly summarize one of Quine's explorations of physical-object ontology. In a discussion whose main thrust (like all of Quine's discussions of ontology) is epistemological, Quine argues against the logical positivist claim that physical-object ontology is a construction from pre-theoretic sense data. Physical-object ontology, Quine maintains, is our "conceptual first". It is highly theoretical (Quine, 1969B), in that our introduction to physical objects is inseparable from our learning of physical object theory. Indeed, it is impossible to "get on to" physical object ontology without simultaneously grasping physical object theory (see also Quine, 1960).

> It is only when a child has got on to the full and proper use of individuative terms like 'apple' that he [sic] can properly be said to have taken to using terms as terms, and speaking of objects. To learn 'apple', it is not sufficient to learn how much of what goes on counts as apple; we must learn how much counts as an apple, and how much another. . . . Only at this stage does it begin to make sense to wonder whether the apple now in one's hand is the apple noticed yesterday. (Quine, 1969C, pp. 7-10)

In this discussion and others, Quine generalizes the argument to all ontologies. All, he maintains, are theoretical and inseparable from the process of constructing theories. We do not first posit molecules, he says in another discussion, and then decide what to say about molecules; the positing of molecules is inseparable from what we say of them and from the theorizing which led us to posit them.

> One tends to imagine that when someone propounds a theory concerning some sort of objects, our understanding of what he is saying will have two

phases: first we must understand what the objects are, and second we must understand what the theory says about them. (Quine, 1960, p. 16)

But, Quine maintains, our understanding of "what the objects are" in fact awaits the second phase: "we do not learn first what to talk about and then what to say about it" (ibid., p.16). Thus, science, in Quine's view, is permeated with metaphysics, and metaphysics, as Kuhn had maintained, is part of science.

But unlike Kuhn, Quine argues that metaphysical commitments are not pernicious. We can always, he points out, expose the ontic commitments we honor by rendering our sentences in first order quantification theory–a language which includes the quantifier (itself the logical equivalent of "there is")–to find out what, in the way of ontology, a theory commits us to. Such commitments are exposed when we look to what the domain of a theory contains (Quine, 1963). Even "the highly theoretical statements of ontology"– those commitments most broadly and deeply embedded in the network of common-sense and scientific theories (the current commitments, for example, to linear relationships, to reductionism, and/or to physicalism)–are statements of what our current theories commit us to. And we can reveal a general metaphysical commitment to how things happen, by looking at our theories, methodologies, and questions, and determining what objects and kinds of natural relationships (for example, linear or nonlinear) these commit us to. As it is being appealed to here, logic does not tell us what there is; it reveals the commitments contained within our current theory of nature.

I have so far noted two ways in which Quine challenges the assumptions that underwrote the positivist and Kuhnian views of the relationship of metaphysics to science. But there is more to be gained from Quine's position. One way of evaluating a theory, he notes, is by analyzing the ontic commitments it carries with it and considering whether these are congenial with our broader theories. He maintains that our broader theory or views do indicate some criteria and that these render some ontic commitments more suspect than others. The particular criteria Quine advocates, which include simplicity and clarity of identity criteria, are by no means uncontroversial. Nor are some of the positions to which they have led him. He rejects, for example, theories which commit us to propositions or mental entities, on the grounds that these alleged entities do not have clear identity criteria, that they make for a more complicated ontology, and that the benefits to countenancing such entities are insufficient to counterbalance these shortcomings (see, also, Nelson, 1990).

I am not concerned here to defend Quine's criteria (indeed, it is not clear that simplicity is an appropriate criterion in evolutionary biology, or that we can or should expect that our most inclusive theory of nature will be a first-order theory). Nor do I wish to defend the specific decisions he uses the criteria to underwrite (for example, the decision to not countenance "mental entities").

But I do want to defend the assumptions underlying such decisions: that ontological decisions can and should be made, and that some will be important (that is, whether we admit into our overall ontology entities like "attributes" or "minds"). Further, that making such decisions is relative to a background theory and set of criteria, and part and parcel of evaluating and selecting theories, not antecedent to, separable from, or inherently compromising, of that endeavor. Hence, Quine would argue that the criteria he suggests have themselves evolved within science. In other words, not only does science incorporate metaphysics, it can lead to better metaphysics.

But recognizing the evaluation of metaphysical commitments as part of doing science requires, as a first step, that we give up the myth that metaphysical commitments cannot be evaluated or subjected to empirical constraint (an implication of both the positivist and Kuhnian positions), as well as the view that we can use a theory to organize experience and be free to reject the metaphysics inherent in it.

II. Evidence

Quine's arguments notwithstanding, the view that special attention to metaphysical commitments is unnecessary can still be maintained if one continues to believe one or both of the following:

1) that science is about the business of discovering the pieces of a unique, true theory of nature

2) that the ontologies and broader metaphysical assumptions that are incorporated in scientific models, research, and theories have no social or political consequences.

I delay discussion of the second assumption until later sections, turning in this section to arguments which indicate that the first assumption is unwarranted, and to an account of evidence that supports Quine's account of the interdependence shared by metaphysics and science.

One True and Unique Theory

If we were to assume, as Hempel and Nagel did (and many practicing scientists still do), that there is one full and unique truth about the world, then it follows that the way in which pieces of that truth come to be discovered and "added to" our larger theory of nature is of no (or negligible) consequence—or at least of little or no consequence for the epistemology of science. Like Popper, for example, we might maintain that such questions are of little intrinsic interest to epistemologists and can safely be left to psychologists (Popper, 1959); or, like many philosophers and sociologists, we might believe that sociology of knowledge and epistemology are distinct enterprises with little to offer one another.

If we also assume—as Harvard physicist Sheldon Glashow recently proposed as part of a "creed" or "article of faith" shared by practicing scientists (Glashow, 1989)—that our sensory organs are sufficiently refined to discriminate such a unique, true theory from alternative candidates, and that science is a process that will lead, at some finite point, to a view that decisively and finally rules out all alternatives, it might also be reasonable to assume that wrong-headed metaphysical commitments would be exposed as such, at least eventually.

If, on the other hand, as I now wish to argue, none of these assumptions are warranted, then those of us who are not tempted by either radical skepticism or judgmental relativism have some work to do. Minimally, and most importantly perhaps, we need to wrestle with the issue of evidence. I begin by locating "us", so to speak, using Glashow's assumptions as a counterpoint. The arguments I develop closely follow those I offered in more detail in Nelson (1990 and 1992).

a) Science is a process that will lead, at some finite point, to a view that decisively and finally rules out all alternatives.

Many of us have come to recognize that this assumption cannot be justified. Consider a piece of current scientific theory, the nature of supernovae, which, in outlining his "article of faith", Glashow offered as an example of an "eternal", "extra-historic", and "universal" truth (Glashow, 1989). However much evidence we have for our current account of supernovae, and however much we ever will have, we are not in a position, and will never be, to know that future experience will not cause us to abandon it, or to organize things in ways that no longer include it. (That is that we do not have to assume we would come to reject our current theory as "false".) There is nothing in our experience to date to rule out the possibility of a future theory commensurate with all of our experience to date but incompatible with our current theory about supernovae, for what we say about supernovae far exceeds the evidence we have and ever will have.

The point, as Quine noted decades ago, holds for all of our theories. All of our theories are under-determined by all the evidence we have or ever will have (Quine, 1960; see also Longino, 1990, and Nelson, 1990). It is commensurate with our collective experience to date (however unlikely it may seem) that we will eventually abandon our common-sense way of organizing things in terms of physical objects and events, for a theory that is commensurate with much of our current experience but incompatible with physical object theory (Quine, 1969B).

b) Our sense organs are sufficiently refined to discriminate a best theory of nature (assuming there is one) from alternative candidates.

It is commensurate with our collective experience that our sense organs are refined to a degree that they are an important part of what has enabled us to survive (so far) through organizing and predicting features of the world and future experience. But there is nothing in that experience, or in what we currently know about our sense organs, to warrant the inference that they are adequate to the task of encompassing *all* that goes on, *all* the rhythms and order (or, perhaps, an inherent disorder) of nature. As a product of natural selection, our sense organs are more likely the product of "jury-rigging" of available parts, and probably only one of the possible results (Gould, 1982).

c) That here is one unique, final theory of everything.

It is commensurate with our collective experience and knowledge, including developments in philosophy of science, that indefinitely many theories would enable us to successfully explain and predict experience. That is, it is commensurate with our experience that no single system would be better than all others and, hence, that there is not "one, unique and full account" to be discovered (Quine, 1960). It is commensurate with that experience, for example, that an alternative "theory of nature" that did not include Boyle's Law—or, in fact, any "law"—might equally well explain and predict what we experience (Nelson, 1990; see also Keller, 1985, and Potter, 1992).

It is important to be clear about what these arguments do and do not establish. They do not suggest that any or all alternatives will do. On the contrary, I would maintain that the notion of a "reasonable" claim or theory makes sense; nor is this relativism a consequence of what I have said by way of criticizing the assumptions above. Each of the points made so far has been made on the basis of our collective experience and other aspects of current knowledge (for example, evolutionary theory, empirical psychology, philosophy of science), and it is not compatible with these that any belief, or any way of organizing things, will do. That there is a world that constrains what it is reasonable to believe is a hypothesis woven through most of our current theories, and with good reason: it makes the most sense of what we experience. At the very least, nature is a point of resistance that constrains what it is reasonable to claim and believe (Keller, 1989). My point has been that we are not warranted in assuming that only one system could organize the world, or that the world is of a determinate nature, specifiable in categories our sense organs will lead us to discover. The arguments reflect, in fact, the consequences of a thorough-going empiricism.

An Alternative View of Evidence

I turn now to an account of evidence that is compatible with the view, to use Quine's phrase, that science is "a bridge of our own making" which is constrained by evidence. In this view (which I want to emphasize is a theory of evidence, and not a theory of truth), the over-arching constraint on theories and beliefs is coherence, which is understood as a dual constraint. Individual theories (as well as claims and beliefs) must be coherent with experience and they must be coherent with a larger system of current theory and practice—which system incorporates, necessarily, metaphysical commitments. To explicate the view, I begin by considering (in broad and general strokes) the evidence for a current piece of knowledge: that which we know about subatomic particles.

The evidence for subatomic particles and their behavior includes a larger body of current theory in physics within which subatomic particles figure directly, as well as theories and practices in other fields (such as mathematics and technology) which underwrite or support these. I am using the terms "underwrite" and "support" in a strong sense, in an evidential sense, suggesting that a body of accepted knowledge and practices is, to use a Quinean metaphor, akin to an arch—each piece sharing supports (sensory supports and, hence, meaning) with the others (Quine, 1960, and Nelson, 1990).

In this view, the evidence for our knowledge about subatomic particles and their behavior obviously includes theories, methodologies, and standards from other areas of physics, chemistry, mathematics, and technology. But it also includes theories and standards of a broader reach, including "common-sense" knowledge and experience of macroscopic objects and events, for it is in terms of these that the evidence for—including the explanatory power of—more esoteric theories becomes apparent. Indeed, it is in terms of these common-sense standards that theories that posit subatomic particles come to have empirical significance (Quine, 1960 and 1966). As Quine has said:

> Lacking [direct sensory experience of unobservable objects], what evidence can the physicist muster for his doctrine of molecules? His answer is that there is a convergence of indirect evidence, drawn from such varied phenomena as expansion, heat conduction. . . . Any defense [of the molecular doctrine] has to do with its indirect bearing on observable reality. (Quine, 1966, p. 238)

Physicist Leon Lederman, explaining to a lay audience what it is like working in high-energy physics, implicitly makes the same argument:

No subatomic object is ever observed directly. Two particles collide and spew debris and new matter inside the accelerator. Physicists infer the existence of new particles from the fact that they collide with other particles which leave electromagnetic tracks in a $65 million detector. Think of a bus that drives by your house everyday. One afternoon while you're at work the bus collides with a Subaru. The bumper flies off the Subaru and hits your mailbox, which is hurled through your window. When you come home, you look at the pattern of shattered glass and say, 'Hmmm, a Subaru'. That's not unlike what high-energy physicists do for a living. (Lederman, 1989, p. 103)

In short, a theory that posits subatomic particles and describes their behavior does not stand alone, but shares an interdependence with common-sense theory, as well as with a current body of scientific theory and accepted practices (including the various theories, methodological principles, and assumptions that underwrite the view that the piece of equipment Lederman speaks of is, in fact, a subatomic particle detector).

Wider Implications

Finally, as the last point indicates, broader metaphysical and methodological commitments incorporated in current scientific practice constitute part of the evidence for our knowledge of and about subatomic particles. These commitments include the assumptions that there are objects and events that are not "directly observable" which explain, more systematically, what happens on the macroscopic level, and that particular macroscopic events (instrument readings, for example, or debris and electromagnetic tracks) are evidence of these. These commitments are incorporated in theories and methodologies, and they are part of the evidence to which a physicist would point when questioned about how and why physicists came to posit subatomic particles, and how they justify their claims about their behavior, as the passage from Lederman indicates. In other words, our knowledge about subatomic particles is not discrete or isolatable from a larger system of theories, practices, and standards of evidence—systems which include other aspects of scientific knowledge and practices (such as physics, mathematics, and technology), common sense, and broader metaphysical commitments and their analogues in accepted methodologies.

Of course, as I mentioned above, internal consistency is not the sole criterion (or an adequate one) for reasonable beliefs and explanations. Part of the evidence for our current knowledge about subatomic particles is experience. Subatomic particles (or, more aptly, theories that posit them) both organize and are compatible with our experiences, and such objects (or, again, more aptly theories that incorporate them) have explanatory power, in that they allow us to explain and to predict some of what happens. I am not suggesting that there are any "immediate experiences" of subatomic particles. The account of evidence I have outlined suggests, in fact, quite the opposite: namely, that the sensory experiences that are currently possible and that we view as relevant to claims about subatomic particles are themselves shaped and mediated by a larger system of public theory and accepted practices (for some public)—a system, as I argued above, that also constitutes part of the evidence for such particles and for our claims about their behavior.

It might be objected that the account of evidence I have outlined is appropriate in terms of highly theoretical or esoteric objects, but not generalizable. But as Quine's arguments about the theoretical nature of physical-object ontology suggest, the account is no less appropriate for our knowledge in any area. Our evidence for rabbits is not different in kind from that for subatomic particles, in that part of the evidence is a larger conceptual scheme or theory that includes physical objects, with rabbits among these, and part of the evidence is that rabbits (or, more aptly, a theory that includes them) help us to organize, explain, and predict some of what happens. As individuals, our abilities to recognize rabbits depend on public theories and practices that organize our sensory experiences into coherent and recoverable accounts (see also Nelson, 1990). Quine points out that an alternative theory of nature might have allowed us to herald rabbit events (or instantiations of "Rabbithood") rather than visits from middle-sized physical objects (Quine, 1969B).

Now, this account of evidence provides a viable alternative to the narrow construal of evidence that characterized the Hempel/Nagel and Kuhnian traditions, broadening, as it does, the scope of what we consider to be relevant evidence supporting individual theories to include theories and practices of a broad reach. It illuminates how metaphysical commitments constitute part of the evidence for our theories and beliefs, and it assumes no "sub-basement", in terms either of pre-social experience or a determinate reality specifiable in only one way (or any best way). At the same time, it does not support wholesale skepticism or relativism, for it proposes that there are two constraints on the theories we construct: sensory experience, and larger bodies of accepted knowledge and practice.

Such a view implies that the evaluation of the metaphysical commitments incorporated in theories and research needs to be recognized as necessary to good science. I turn next to issues in feminist science criticism which support Quine's contention that such scrutiny is possible, and provide additional support for the claim that such scrutiny is necessary.

III. Why What We Say There Is Matters

The discussions of the last two sections indicate, of course, that meta-physical commitments matter. Such commitments are incorporated in all that we say, they contribute to or undermine the empirical adequacy of a theory, and they function as evidence. Issues raised in and by feminist criticism support these points, but they also take this discussion in a new direction—adding additional, but somewhat different support for the claim that the metaphysical commitments incorporated in science must be subjected to scrutiny. They indicate that the commitments incorporated in the theories, methodologies, and research projects of various sciences both reflect and reinforce political relations and practices in our larger community. I outline two specific focuses within feminist criticism: research which indicates that androcentrism is a factor in science; and a current debate concerning linear, hierarchical models in the biological sciences (see also Bleier, 1984, 1988, Harding, 1986, 1991, Keller, 1985, Longino, 1990, and Nelson, 1990, for overviews of issues in feminist criticism).

Androcentrism in Science

Feminist scientists and science critics claim that in a number of sciences the language used to describe phenomena, the questions pursued, the models adopted, the interpretation of data and observations, and the theoretical frameworks developed reflect the fact that science is and has been practiced in societies dominated by men. These critics claim that androcentrism or male bias is evident in many research programs and theoretical frameworks, and that it affects the content of science. Its presence, they argue, leads to faulty method-ologies and models, and, ultimately, to partial or distorted accounts of various aspects of human and nonhuman nature.

Some of the cases of androcentrism cited by feminist critics are straight-forward. A number of research programs and theoretical frameworks have started out to provide (and, in many cases, have claimed to provide) an account of some aspect of human experience, but they have begun (and, in some cases, ended) their research and analyses with the experiences and behavior of men. As feminists point out, the methodology not only reflects a commitment to the view that men can provide the norm for the species, but it also affects the content of theories. One consequence has been that when women are studied and do not fit the models provided by the initial research (for example, in developmental psychology), scientists have concluded that there is something wrong with women (for an overview, see Harding, 1986).

Feminist scholarship indicates that the methodology is widespread in psychology, the social sciences, and history. In addition to its obvious relationship to the "woman questions" which have resurfaced time and again in the history of science, feminist criticism reveals that the methodology has the following results (for overviews, see Bleier, 1984, Harding, 1986 and 1991, Nelson, 1990, and Tuana, 1989): important areas of social life are overlooked or misdescribed when men's activities and behavior serve as the only or primary focus; women's activities are often subsumed under men's, completely ignored, or misdescribed; the differences between women's and men's positions (or, more generally, the role of gender relations in social dynamics) are not incorporated in theories that purport to provide adequate descriptions of social life, psychology, and so on.

The example of androcentrism on which I want to focus is more subtle. I use it because it reveals how metaphysical commitments span sciences and fields, and function as evidence for specific theories and methods. Before outlining the example, I spend a moment clarifying the claim that androcentrism is a factor in science. Elsewhere I have suggested that the perspectives at issue in feminist science criticism are better characterized as "androcentric" rather than "male biased" (Nelson, 1990), and I adopt the former term and the perspective in what follows. Describing the perspectives at issue as "biased" suggests that scientists could and should be disengaged observers, and while such disengagement has been long associated with objectivity, feminist criticism suggests that self-conscious attention to our locations within specific social, historical, and cultural relations, and to the role such locations play in shaping our understandings, may be both a more realistic and a more rigorous ideal of objectivity (see, especially, Harding, 1991). The term "bias" also suggests the conscious manipulation of data and theories, and such manipulation, if and when it occurs, is uninteresting from the perspective of the epistemology of science.

I have also argued that characterizing the perspectives at issue as "male" should be viewed with suspicion, on the grounds that the description suggests both a universality and a connection with biology that is belied by cross-cultural and historical differences in how gender is perceived and organized, and by the fact that various biological processes (including the extensiveness of postnatal neurobiological development) make a connection between "ways of knowing" and biological sex highly suspect (Bleier, 1984, 1988, Longino, 1990, and Nelson, 1990). More to the point, the perspectives at issue in feminist science criticism are straightforwardly connected to contemporary Western practices, views, and assumptions to do with gender. Hence, my discussion focuses on "male-centered" methodologies, categories, organizing principles, and theories in various sciences, and I understand "male-centered" as both historically and culturally specific.

'Man the Hunter' Theories

The example on which I focus involves an organizing principle that feminist research has exposed as shaping methods, observations and theories in primatology, anthropology, animal sociology, and evolutionary theory, as well as other fields. This is the principle that males are socially oriented; that is, that their activities are skilled and determining of social organization and, in the case of humans, of culture as well; and that females are biologically oriented; that is, that their activities are largely reproductive (assumed, in turn, to be "natural" and unskilled), and without consequence for the most important (and, in the case of humans, the "distinctly human") features of social dynamics. In models and theories incorporating this organizing principle, feminist scientists and critics note, females are satellites to male actors who dominate and determine social dynamics (Bleier, 1984, Haraway, 1988, 1990, Longino and Doell, 1983, and Tanner and Zihlman, 1976). The "Man the hunter" account of human evolution constitutes a particularly useful example of the organizing principle in action, because those who developed and advocate the theory synthesized and appealed to theories and observations in other fields (geology, population genetics, primatology, anthropology, among these). Hence, the theory illuminates two factors identified in the last section: that metaphysical commitments span sciences and fields, and that they function as evidence.

As its feminist critics note, the "Man the hunter" account of human evolution credits the evolution of Homo sapiens to what its advocates assumed were activities and behaviors engaged in and exhibited by our male ancestors. The theory attributes the evolution of bipedalist and "speaking man" to the invention of tools and the development of social organization, and they explain both as necessary to the hunting of larger animals by men (Fox, 1967, Washburn and Lancaster, 1976, and Wilson, 1978). The activities of our female ancestors (when they are mentioned at all) appear to have been exhausted by childbearing, lactating, and childrearing—with none of these viewed as contributing to the evolution of bipedalist and "speaking man".

But feminists argue that, without the androcentric organizing principle, there is no reason to assume that our female ancestors were completely occupied with procreation and childrearing activities, or that male dominance hierarchies characterized early hominid and human groups (Hubbard, 1982). So stated, however, the criticism is misleading for it implies that the "Man the hunter" account emerged in a vacuum. While it is true that some of the theory's advocates simply declared that only males hunted, that males were dominant over females and children, and that hunting was the most important source of food, many others used accounts provided by anthropologists of contemporary hunter/gatherer societies to reconstruct early hominid and human social dynamics. And some of the theory's advocates, including sociobiologists, use observations and theories in primatology as evidence for early human behavior and social organization (for example Barash, 1977, and Wilson, 1978. Longino and Doell, 1983, explore the various theories and assumptions drawn on by advocates of "Man the hunter" theory which, as I note above, extend beyond the biobehavioral sciences and anthropology to population genetics, evolutionary biology, geology, paleontology, etc.). And, indeed, feminists in anthropology, primatology, and animal sociology have shown that a similar organizing principle has shaped observations and accounts of social dynamics and behavior in primate groups and in contemporary hunter/gatherer societies (Bleier, 1984, Haraway, 1988, Harding, 1986, and Slocum, 1975). In addition, feminist critics frequently note the convergence between "Man the hunter"'s reconstruction of early hominid and human life, and contemporary (Western) gender stereotypes and social relations.

In other words, feminist criticism reveals that the organizing principle at the heart of the "Man the hunter" account, far from being unwarranted, was supported by a vast feedback system across disciplines and fields, as well as "common-sense" gender stereotypes and assumptions. If we construe evidence broadly, as my arguments of the last section suggest is appropriate, we would expect to find that other current theories and models constitute part of the evidence for the "Man the hunter" account. Indeed, such synthesizing of results is generally recognized as a mark of good science.

What feminist criticism reveals which we did not expect to find is that our experiences of gender and of gender relations are also factors in the theorizing and observing we do in science communities, and that they are reflected in the metaphysical commitments that function as evidence for particular theories and models.

Consequences

The androcentric organizing principle has two general consequences that warrant attention. One involves issues of empirical adequacy; the other, the political implications of theories and models incorporating the principle. I begin with the first issue, using anthropology as an example.

In studying contemporary hunter/gatherer societies, anthropologists long focused on the hunting of animals by men in these societies, in effect writing off women's gathering activities as unskilled, of little intrinsic interest, and without much consequence (Bleier, 1984, Harding, 1986, and Reiter, 1975). Their accounts of the social dynamics within such groups suggested that women are primarily concerned with procreative and reproductive activities, and that these activities limit women's contribution to "productive" activities—keeping them close to home, for example, while males hunt (Bleier, 1984). An assumption that procreative and reproductive activities are "natural" (a result, at least in part, of not studying them or engaging in cross-cultural comparisons) also effectively precluded any analysis that would have challenged the assumption: of variations across such groups or historical periods, of the relation of such activities to specific physical and social environments, or of the role such activities have in determining other social arrangements (see, for more extensive discussion, Bleier, 1984, Reiter, 1975, Slocum, 1975, and Tanner and Zihlman, 1976).

Evidence that such accounts are empirically inadequate comes from research that does not make use of an androcentric organizing principle, but which suggests a very different picture of the social dynamics of hunter/gatherer societies. For example, it has been found that women's gathering in such societies is actually highly skilled, requiring knowledge of hundreds of plants and other ecological factors, and that it is a fundamentally social, rather than individual and unskilled, activity. In addition, gathering provides as much as 80 percent of the sustenance for hunter/gatherer groups, and in some hunter/gatherer groups, women are as much away from home as their male counterparts, with childcare shared among male and female members. And while most hunter/gatherer societies incorporate a division of labor by gender (divisions which typically result in only males hunting), these divisions are flexible and respond to changes in environmental conditions. They are affected, for instance, by proximity to other groups, by adopting a settled as opposed to nomadic life, and by the influence of missionaries (Bleier, 1984). Finally, women's productive activities frequently determine the spacing of children and childcare arrangements, rather than, as anthropologists and others long assumed and many sociobiologists currently argue, vice versa (Bleier, 1984 and 1988, and Reiter, 1975).

It is only because we now have extensive research that does not incorporate the androcentric organizing principle that we are in a position to see that its underlying and related assumptions have been consequential in shaping methodologies, observations, and theories. And it is because of such research that we are therefore able to argue that such assumptions have precluded an adequate analysis of the role that female activities would have played in human evolution. Without androcentric assumptions, very different accounts of the social dynamics of various cultures and animal groups emerge, as do the criteria we bring to a reconstruction of human evolution (Harding, 1986, Longino, 1990, Slocum, 1975, and Tanner and Zihlman, 1976). Hence, it is not surprising that we currently find alternative accounts of both social dynamics and evolution in which females have at least as central a role as their male counterparts (see, for example, Slocum, 1975, and Tanner and Zihlman, 1976).

What do cases of androcentrism suggest about the rationality of metaphysical commitments, and about the objectivity of views shaped by social and political experience and assumptions? If we were concerned to maintain the view that politics and science are (or should be) separate domains, we would need to write off the "Man the hunter" theory, as well as a good deal of work in the bio-behavioral sciences and anthropology, as examples of bad science. But the conclusion is not warranted. There was evidence for the "Man the hunter" account of evolution; its advocates drew on anthropology, primatology, and the biobehavioral sciences, and the evidence was no less relevant or appropriate than that provided by current theories and models in geology, paleontology, and population genetics.

Moreover, feminist criticism of "Man the hunter" theory (and of research and models on which its advocates relied), and the alternatives that feminist scientists are currently constructing, are by no means apolitical or free of metaphysical commitments. To try to separate feminist criticism of androcentrism, or the alternatives feminists propose, from feminist politics would be as ludicrous as attempting to separate the androcentrism feminists have uncovered in psychology, sociology, history, philosophy, primatology, anthropology, and evolutionary theory from the androcentrism and sexism of the societies in which scientists live. Some scientists who find feminist claims warranted are also tempted by the view that feminist scientists and science critics are not doing "anything special" (Gould, 1984). But this view requires a highly improbable coincidence between those who are feminists and those who recognize androcentrism and sexism to be factors in science. It also leads, of course, to the following question: if the problems with methods and theories in, say, development psychology that were identified by Carol Gilligan's analysis were "so obvious" (as a scientist claimed recently at a symposium on politics and science), so, too, the problems in anthropology that Slocum and Tanner identified, and so too the problems Hubbard identified in evolutionary theory, and so on . . . then, why, prior to feminist criticism and the current women's movement, didn't anyone see them?

I can see two, and only two, alternatives to recognizing a connection between feminist politics and feminist criticism: one is that feminists (for some reason other than their politics) just happen to be better scientists (more careful observers, more creative theoreticians, more logically adept, etc.); the other is that scientists (pre-feminism) deliberately distorted their accounts of humans and other species to construct androcentric theories. I know of few scientists who would opt for either of these alternatives.

So while we must recognize that androcentrism is present in science, and that it leads to what are, at best, partial accounts of behavior and social dynamics in human and nonhuman groups, we cannot conclude that experiences stemming from gender and other political relations, or metaphysical commitments, are inherently distorting. We need, instead, a more sophisticated view of the relationship between politics and science, one which recognizes that our broader metaphysical commitments constitute part of the evidence for our theories, and that the scope of the interdependence—the scope of the commitments that so function—includes, as Quine puts it, the commitments incorporated in "everything we say about the world".

Master Molecule Theories

Recently feminists have extended their criticism of models in which dominance relations are central to include models in molecular biology, and, in particular, to what biophysicist Evelyn Fox Keller calls "master molecule" theories (Keller, 1985). Keller, biologists Ruth Bleier and Ruth Hubbard, and other feminists have questioned the appropriateness of linear and hierarchical causal models in the characterization of biological processes (Bleier, 1984, Hubbard, 1982, and Keller, 1985). Feminist critics are not alone, of course, in criticizing such models; a substantial body of criticism directed at linear and hierarchical models of biological and evolutionary processes is currently being offered by biologists and philosophers of science (see, for example, Dyke, 1988, Lewontin, 1976, 1981, and *Biology and Philosophy*, 1986-present).

Feminist scientists and science critics are also criticizing what they view as a broader metaphysical commitment to the universality of dominance relationships, a commitment that Keller argues is reflected in the positing of "laws of nature" (Keller, 1985), and that she and other feminists relate to the view that the goal of science is "to dominate nature" (Bleier, 1984, and Merchant, 1980). In considering the criticism of linear and hierarchical models of natural relationships, I limit my discussion to two lines of argument: that such models are an inappropriate approach to cellular protein synthesis, and that the prevalence of such models in our approaches to human and nonhuman nature reflects and serves to justify Western political experience. While it is not possible to predict either the directions or the outcome of the debates on which I touch, the issues involved on both sides of the debate support various claims I have made in the discussion so far.

I note first that feminists and other critics of the "master molecule" theory of cellular protein synthesis have had little difficulty in explicating the metaphysical commitments incorporated within the model. The "executive DNA" model, these critics claim, incorporates a commitment to what Ruth Hubbard and other biologists call "genetic reductionism"—a phrase used to refer to what are, in fact, a cluster of metaphysical assumptions: that genes are irreducible and separate things that determine events; that complex traits are discrete; and that such traits are genetically determined (Bleier, 1984, Dyke, 1988, Gould, 1981, Hubbard, 1982, and Rose, 1982).

The second thing to note is that feminists and other critics of the executive DNA model have had little difficulty in evaluating these commitments. They have argued that the dominant role assigned to genes in the model obscures and distorts what are in fact more complex relationships involved in cellular protein synthesis. Hubbard argues, for example, that the model of gene action fails to encompass the actions of other molecules, and the effects of the biological environments and processes within which genes act. In cellular protein synthesis, she claims, although genes specify the sequence of elements within particular protein molecules, protein molecules have to "fold up" into three-dimensional configurations and the particular configuration affects their function. These patterns of folding are not themselves genetically determined; they are a consequence of the larger biological environment of the organism and the organism's environment (Hubbard, 1982, p. 85). In short, according to Hubbard and Bleier, the model dichotomizes, and then arranges in hierarchical causal sequences, the discrete gene and its alleged discrete effects from the environment of the larger organism—an environment, they maintain, of complex processes.

As we found in our consideration of "Man the hunter" theory, there are two lines of criticism discernible in the feminist literature addressing linear and hierarchical models in the biological sciences. One issue involves the empirical adequacy of such models; the other, their political implications. In terms of the first issue, feminists and other critics argue that the assumption that natural relationships are linear and hierarchical distorts the actual relationships in biological processes. In terms of the second issue, critics argue that linear, hierarchical models (of biological processes, social dynamics, and nature more broadly) both reflect and reinforce our political experiences, including those of dominance (Bleier, 1984, Hubbard, 1982, Rose, 1982). "Master molecule" theories, they argue, render biological determinist theories more plausible than they are in fact, and such models reflect and reinforce Western political experience. Questions concerning both empirical adequacy and political implications are discernible in Bleier's appraisal:

> Underlying the methodological problems in biological determinist theories of human behavior, the fundamental scientific issue is the role of genes and biology in determining characteristics and behavior. It is a controversy that serves to obscure social and political origins of inequality and to undermine change. (Bleier, 1984, p. 40)

> Hierarchies, relations of domination, subordination, power, and control are not necessarily inherent in nature but are an integral part of the conceptual framework of persons bred in a civilization constructed on principles of stratification, domination, subordination, power, and control, all made to appear natural.... It is important to know causes for events

and phenomena, for without that 'knowledge' one cannot know how to intervene effectively in order to remain or be in control. (Bleier, 1984, pp. 200-202)

As I noted earlier, the debate concerning linear, hierarchical models of gene action is part of a larger debate that has been surfacing for more than a decade—and metaphysical commitments are also at the core of that larger debate. There has been a re-emergence of related questions concerning the status of biology as an autonomous science, critiques of various forms of reductionism, and questions about whether physics (at least classical physics) can serve as a model for biology and other sciences (Ayala and Dobzhansky, 1974, Dyke, 1988, Keller, 1985, Mayr, 1988, and *Biology and Philosophy*,1986-present). Part of the debate concerns the general metaphysical commitment to linear and hierarchical relationships in human and non-human nature. Keller maintains, for example, that not only does the commitment limit our approaches to nature, it also underwrites our views of mature science. And both, she maintains, have had substantial consequences for biology.

> Our understanding of what constitutes a law (in nature as in society) is of course subject to change, and not all laws necessarily imply coercion. Certainly not all scientific laws are either causal or deterministic; they may, for example, be statistical, phenomenological, or, more simply, just the 'rules of the game'. . . . But in many, perhaps most, scientific disciplines, the finality of a theory continues to be measured by its resemblance to the classical laws of physics, which are both causal and deterministic. (Keller, 1985, pp. 131-33)

Alternatives to linear, hierarchical models, alternative metaphysical commitments, are also important elements of the criticisms I have outlined. Keller, for example, suggests an alternative view of the scientific project. Rather than viewing it as a search for the laws of nature (or law-like behavior in nature), she suggests an approach based on a metaphysical commitment to order, in which biology, rather than physics, would hold central place.

Order, Keller notes, can include linear and hierarchical causal relationships, but it can also encompass other kinds of relationship, including the nonhierarchical and nonlinear relationships that feminist and other scientists claim actually obtain within biological processes, and within other aspects of human and nonhuman nature.

> Order is a category comprising patterns of organization that can be spontaneous, self-generated, or externally imposed; it is a larger category than law precisely to the extent that law implies external constraint. Conversely, the kinds of order generated or generable by law comprise only a subset of a larger category of observable or apprehensible regularities, rhythms, and patterns. (Keller, 1985, p. 132)

In terms of the second line of criticism directed at linear, hierarchical models, their relationship to political experience and relations, feminist critics are also clearly articulating alternative commitments. As we saw earlier, Bleier argues that models in which dominance is a central feature, including linear and hierarchical models of gene action, not only reflect Western political experience but serve to reinforce it. Genetic reductionism, she and other critics note, underwrites biological determinist theories, and the latter are frequently used to justify divisions in power. Thus, Bleier and the other feminist critics I have cited explicitly relate the models and theories they criticize, and the alternatives they propose, to political experiences and interests. As Bleier describes one of the goals underlying her critique of genetic reductionism,

> My hope and intent is the discarding of the genes/environment contro-
> versy and the dichotomy between nature and nurture or biology and
> learning, because the dichotomy is impossible, unresolvable, and scientifi-
> cally meaningless. It is a controversy that serves to obscure social and
> political origins of inequality and to undermine change. (Bleier, 1984, pp.
> 40-41)

By contrast, the adoption of alternative models that focus on whole organisms and on processes, on all social dynamics rather than just (or most centrally) dominance hierarchies and relationships, would allow for the recognition of the complexity of relationships and processes, still evolving and not complete, which the assumption of linear, hierarchical relationships does not permit (see also Bleier, 1984, and Gould, 1981).

Thus, the debate over "master molecule" theories involves large metaphysical and methodological issues, including the appropriateness of linear and hierarchical causal models in the biological sciences, the universality of such relationships throughout the natural and social world, and the related issue of biological determinism. It also involves more specific issues: the status of genes as dominant entities that determine discrete effects, and the appropriateness of assuming there are "masters" or single causes of complex processes and relationships.

The Nature of Science

There is one additional approach to the issues I have considered that is relevant to the larger themes of this chapter. I want to use the current example to further the point (a point already made in the discussion of "Man the hunter" theory) that metaphysical and methodological commitments are neither random nor arbitrary, nor the result of personal quirks or idiosyncrasies. While there seem to be clear relationships between the positing of "masters" and "executives" of biological process and Western political experience, between our political experience and our positing of laws to govern all that happens, the relationship is, once again, broader than that between such experience and specific models or theories. As was the case with "Man the hunter" theory, so, too, it is the current state of science—other current research and theories—that shapes and underwrites the commitment in the biological sciences to linear, hierarchical models.

As Keller and other critics of "master molecule" theories note, the metaphysical assumptions that came to dominate genetics in the period between the 1930s and the 1950s were shaped by the success of physics and a conscious effort to make biology more like it. Both underwrote the adoption of linear and hierarchical models as well as great successes in molecular biology (Keller, 1985). The assumption that physics should serve as a model for a serious biology, and specifically as a model for genetics, came in one of its most influential forms from Max Delbruck, a theoretical physicist who came to the United States in 1937 and invited biologists to view the gene as a "molecular object" (ibid.). As a physicist, Keller notes, Delbruck came from a tradition that "revered simplicity rather than complexity", and the search for simplicity came to dominate genetics under his influence and that of others who shared an interest in making biology "more serious"—that is, more like physics (Keller, 1985, pp. 159-61). Among the various factors at work in the revolution, Keller argues, there was the fact "above all, [that] the principal characters [of the revolution] came from disciplines far removed from classical genetics, ... from biochemistry, microbiology, X-ray crystallography, and perhaps especially, from physics" (Keller, 1985, p. 159), all of which are traditions committed to simplicity and to isolating discrete objects and events.

Hence, part of the evidence supporting the adoption of linear and hierarchical models of gene action was a substantial body of theory and practice (and, in particular, classical physics), and a view—based at least in part on the success of physics, but also one assumes on the view that how things worked on the most basic level was likely to be how they worked on more complex levels— that a "serious science" should incorporate linear models, discrete entities, and simple explanations. This is not to deny a relationship between political experiences and metaphysical commitments. It is to maintain that we need to cast our net wider, to incorporate a substantial body of theory that incorporates science as well as "common sense", as part of the evidence that underwrites our broader metaphysical commitment, including those to linear, and hierarchical relationships.

IV. Conclusion

This chapter began with a call for the abandonment of the metaphysics/science dichotomy. I supported the call with arguments to several ends: that the views which long underwrote the dichotomy included a too narrow construal of evidence and a view of science as an autonomous enterprise. Quine's arguments, and my extrapolations from these to an account of evidence, provided an alternative to both. They also provided support for the claim that science is permeated with metaphysics. Further support for the latter, and for the claim that metaphysical commitments can be articulated and evaluated, was found in issues raised in and by feminist participation in and criticism of science.

If we grant that metaphysical commitments constitute part of the evidence for our theories and claims, it becomes clear, I argued, that we need to subject such commitments to evaluation. The various relationships between science and politics that are revealed in and by feminist science criticism further the case, for we cannot interpret the lesson of feminist science criticism as meaning that we need stricter methodological controls to filter out all of our experiences of politics and gender. The relationships between political context and experiences of gender, and our approaches to human and nonhuman nature, are neither overcome nor absent in feminist criticism or in the alternatives feminists are developing.

There is a continuity between my arguments which appeal to the evidentiary role played by metaphysical commitments and the need for empirical adequacy, and the arguments which appeal to the political implications of our metaphysical commitments, and it is this: scientists, feminists and nonfeminists, work within a body of theory they inherit and, in their small ways, alter—alterations which are made on the basis of their experiences, and bodies of accepted and evolving theories and practices. And they can do nothing else.

What we are not free to do, as scientists or laypersons, as feminists or nonfeminists, is to accept a theory and reject the metaphysics inherent in it. What we say there is matters, and must be accorded our most self-conscious, collective, and reflective attention.

References

K. P. Addelson, "The man of professional wisdom" in *Discovering Reality*, edited by S. Harding and M. Hintikka, D. Reidel, 1983.

F. J. Ayala and T. Dobzhansky, editors, *Studies in the Philosophy of Biology: Reductionism and Related Problems,* University of California Press, 1974.

A. J. Ayer, *Language, Truth, and Logic,* Dover, 1950.

D. Barash, *Sociobiology and Behavior,* Elsevier, 1977.

Biology and Philosophy, D. Reidel, 1986-present.

R. Bleier, *Science and Gender: A Critique of Biology and Its Theories on Women*, Pergamon Press, 1984.

R. Bleier, editor, *Feminist Approaches to Science*, Pergamon Press, 1988.

C. Dyke, *The Evolutionary Dynamics of Complex Systems*, Oxford University Press, 1988.

R. Fox, *Kinship and Marriage*, Pergamon Press, 1967.

S. Glashow, "Positivism lives", *New York Times,* Oct. 22, 1989.

S. J. Gould, *The Mismeasure of Man*, W.W. Norton, 1981.

S. J. Gould, *The Panda's Thumb*, W.W. Norton, 1982.

S. J. Gould, "A feeling for the organism", *New York Review of Books,* March 26, 1984.

D. Haraway, "Primatology is politics by other means" in *Feminist Approaches to Science*, edited by R. Bleier, Pergamon Press, 1988.

D. Haraway, *Primate Visions: Gender, Race, and Nature in the World of Modern Science,* Routledge, 1990 .

S. Harding, *The Science Question in Feminism*, Cornell University Press, 1986.

S. Harding, "Whose science? Whose knowledge?" in *Thinking from Women's Lives,* Cornell University Press, 1991.

C. Hempel, *Aspects of Scientific Explanation and Other Essays in the Philosophy of Science,* Free Press, 1965.

C. Hempel, *Philosophy of Natural Science,* Prentice-Hall, 1966.

R. Hubbard, "Have only men evolved?" in *Biological Woman–The Convenient Myth,* edited by R. Hubbard et al., Schenkman, 1982.

E. F. Keller, *Reflections on Gender and Science,* Yale University Press, 1985.

E. F. Keller, "The gender/science system" in *Feminism and Science,* edited by Nancy Tuana, Indiana University Press, 1989.

T. S. Kuhn, *The Structure of Scientific Revolutions,* 2nd ed., University of Chicago Press, 1970.

T. S. Kuhn, "Second thoughts on paradigms" in *The Structure of Scientific Theories,* edited by F. Suppe, University of Illinois Press, 1972.

I. Lakatos, "Falsification and the methodology of scientific research programs" in *Criticism and the Growth of Knowledge,* edited by I. Lakatos and A. Musgrave, Cambridge University Press, 1970.

I. Lakatos and A. Musgrave, *Criticism and the Growth of Knowledge,* Cambridge University Press, 1970.

L. Lederman, "An interview with Leon Lederman", *Omni,* October, 1989.

R. C. Lewontin, "Sociobiology–A caricature of Darwinism", *Journal of Philosophy of Science* 2, 1976.

R. C. Lewontin, "Sleight of hand", *The Sciences,* July/August, 1981.

H. Longino, *Science as Social Knowledge: Values and Objectivity in Scientific Inquiry,* Princeton University Press, 1990.

H. Longino and R. Doell, "Body, bias, and behavior: A comparative analysis of reasoning in two areas of biological science", *Signs: Journal of Women in Culture and Society* 9, 1983.

E. Mayr, *Toward a New Philosophy of Biology,* Belknap Press of Harvard University Press, 1988.

C. Merchant, *The Death of Nature: Women, Ecology and the Scientific Revolution,* Belknap Press of Harvard University Press, 1980.

T. Nagel, *The Structure of Science: Problems in the Logic of Scientific Explanation,* Harcourt, Brace and World, 1961.

L. H. Nelson, *Who Knows: From Quine to a Feminist Empiricism*, Temple University Press, 1990.

L. H. Nelson, "Epistemological communities" in *Feminist Epistemologies*, edited by L. Alcoff and E. Potter, Routledge, 1992.

K. Popper, *The Logic of Scientific Discovery*, Harper and Row, 1959.

E. Potter, "Epistemic negotiations" in *Feminist Epistemologies,* edited by L. Alcoff and E. Potter, Routledge, 1992.

W.V.O. Quine, *Word and Object,* MIT Press, 1960.

W.V.O. Quine, *On What There Is. From a Logical Point of View, revised ed.,* Harper and Row, 1963; First printing, 1953.

W.V.O. Quine, *Posits and Reality, The Ways of Paradox and other Essays,* Random House, 1966.

W.V.O. Quine, "Existence and quantification" in *Ontological Relativity and Other Essays*, Columbia University Press, 1969A.

W.V.O. Quine, "Epistemology naturalized", ibid., 1969B.

W.V.O. Quine, "Speaking of objects", ibid., 1969C.

R. R. Reiter, editor, *Toward an Anthropology of Women,* Monthly Review Press, 1975.

S. Rose, editor, *Against Biological Determinism,* Allison & Busby, 1982.

S. Slocum, "Woman the gatherer" in *Toward an Anthropology of Women*, edited by R. R. Reiter, Monthly Review Press, 1975.

N. Tanner and A. Zihlman, "Women in evolution", *Signs: Journal of Women in Culture and Society* 1, 1976.

N. Tuana, editor, *Feminism and Science*, Indiana University Press, 1989.

S. Washburn and C. S. Lancaster, "The evolution of hunting" in *Kalahari Hunter-Gatherers,* edited by R. B. Lee and I. DeVore, Harvard University Press, 1976.

E. O. Wilson, *On Human Nature,* Harvard University Press, 1978.

The Psycho-Logical
Foundations of Modern Science

by Michael Scriven

Introduction

1) The intent of this chapter is to sketch a restructuring of the foundations of science and indicate how it can lead to solutions of some well-known problems about the nature of science—and to some specific changes of direction in certain areas of scientific and metascientific research. The general features of the account given are more in line with what practicing scientists think of as "the common-sense view" than those proposed by philosophers of science like Comte, Carnap, and Popper—or Habermas and Foucault today. The specific results are not so obvious (and not established in detail here): they include implications for the analysis of the concepts of probability, taxonomy, information, evaluation, randomness, causation, measurement, and many others, all of these results having significant (but not shocking) effects on the practice of scientific research and the teaching of science.

The song that is sung in these pages has two melodies that were alien music to the neo-positivists: an emphasis on the *subjective* element in science, meaning the internal cognitive element, and an emphasis on the *context* of epistemic activities rather than the content of epistemic claims. While this song is not the war-cry of their traditional opponents, it is hoped that a new harmony emerges which may appeal to those on both sides looking for new music.

2) The metaphysical foundations of science—and hence science itself—are in some crucial but elusive way involved with the nature and limitations of the mind. Toward the end of his famous analytic study, *The Metaphysical Foundations of Modern Physical Science*, E. A. Burtt says:

The whole vast realm which science reveals finds its rational order and meaning in the knowing activity of the human mind.[1]

The key question is whether—or to what extent—the order that science "reveals" is imposed by the mind on the world or by the world on the mind.

3) In the classical form of the view referred to by philosophers as idealism, even the existence of the outside world is rejected; hence all of its apparent order comes from the mind which creates it. This view has recently had a revival of popularity in association with critical theory, and various versions of constructivism such as social constructionism, deconstructionism, post-modernism. Another radical possibility is instrumentalism—the view that the tangible world may exist, but that the invisible entities and laws of science which provide it with its "rational order" are merely mnemonic devices invented to facilitate prediction and the simplification of description, with no claim to reality. A stronger version of this treats the hypothesis of the existence of the external world as itself a device for improving predictions. Burtt himself favored the view that most of the order is in the mind,[2] but allowed that there is some kind of external world. However, he thought that the mind was a mysterious entity that "must find its total explanation beyond the material world".[3]

4) The view put forward here differs from each of these positions.

i) It proposes a radical reanalysis of the logic of science—that is, of the framework concepts for the whole body of science, concepts such as explanation, classification, evidence, probability—in terms of two quasi-psychological (specifically, cognitive) concepts. The concepts are those of knowledge and understanding—and their "communication counterparts" information and explanation.

ii) The method of analysis itself is novel, and is based on the same approach, which lays much more emphasis on the importance of context and communication than does classical logic.

iii) The position taken is that the requisite sense of these concepts—and hence of all science—is on the one hand subjective, in a sense that justifies some but not most of what the anti-objectivists have claimed. However, it is objective in a sense that supports most, but not all, of what is claimed by those proclaiming the traditional objectivity of scientific claims. (In the usual technical language, it is close to realism but with some concessions to instrumentalism; constructionist but with little concession to relativism.)

iv) One perspective on these conclusions is to say that understanding the role of the mind in science, properly conceived, clarifies much about the nature of science; in particular about its essentially evaluative functions, including its real standards of evidence and theoretical adequacy, by contrast with its too-frequent intolerance; and its real power, by contrast with its occasional forays into megalomania and paranoia.

Psychological Epistemology: Preliminaries

5) The view here should be referred to by a label that reflects its roots in the fusion of the psychic with the logical, the subjective with the objective, the internal world with the external world. The language of the title of this chapter might therefore be read with the hyphen explicit, as "The Psycho–Logical Foundations of Modern Science". Correspondingly, the tool discipline to which we are referring might be thought of as psychologic—where we can without ambiguity drop the hyphen—and the underlying philosophy as psycho-logical epistemology. An alternative terminology might try to reflect the fusion here of a new approach to information theory with logic, but the term "info-logic" has been used in another context with another meaning, so we will use the first alternative. This choice has another advantage: the similar term "psychologism" was regarded as derogatory by the logical positivists, for invalid reasons, and we need to confront their rejection with reinstatement of the psychological element in the logic of science.[4]

A third reason for the suggested term is the belief that psychology itself needs to stabilize after the swings from introspection to behaviorism to constructionism, and in the face of the current tension between phenomeno-logical and clinical psychology, on the one hand, and cognitive and experimen-tal psychology on the other. The term "psycho-logical" points the way toward a greater respect for the role of reasoning in the study of psychology, a counterpart to the movement that has recently emerged in sociology with the emergence of the "rational-action paradigm".[5]

6) Although only a sketch of a new approach is presented here, it represents a move toward a more balanced approach in which we render considerable domains both to the material world of Caesar and to the spiritual or mentalistic realm of "the inner life". There is nothing new about attempting some kind of reconciliation; the trick here, as in human affairs, is to get the relationship right. It is not enough that the two domains recognize the legitimacy of each other—although one should bear in mind that sometimes even this is going too far, as in the way some theologians divide the turf of life between science and religion—for science has more to say about mental phenomena than merely to acknowledge their reality. It is, however, too strong to talk of complementarity, for there are parts of either territory which have no complement in the other (the stab of pain itself, on one side; the psi function, on the other).

It is also too strong to propose unity under one government or the other (epiphenomenalism or idealism), and too much to argue for a single citizenship (an identity theory). We must insist that the territory of science overlaps much—but not all—of those of the other two jurisdictions, because it is defined in a different way, as the territory of the Kurds overlaps the countries of Iraq and Turkey. Thus the appropriate treatment of the external world and the internal world is not achieved by trying to destroy the Skin Curtain that separates them, nor by denying the reality of what is on one or the other side of it, but rather by recognizing that the legitimate territory of science is defined on an overlay, on a second level. The solution must be sought in the foundations of that meta-territory, in the discipline which links and analyzes all of science's specific subject-matters—in the "grammar of science", which, in this account, is referred to as psycho-logical.

7) Thus, the psycho-logical approach follows the common-sense and scientific position in rejecting skepticism about the external world's existence and order (hence it is, in the philosopher's sense, a form of realism).[6] It equally rejects skepticism about the internal world's reality, which is the behaviorist's position. It rejects the conventionalistic aspect of instrumentalism without jumping into the opposite camp of supposing the order to be entirely "out there". While it is perfectly consistent with the first quote from Burtt, it differs from his interpretation of the situation in several ways. For example, it differs from his further conclusion about the mind, in that it takes the mind to have a total explanation within the material world, while conceding that there are aspects of the mental life—its flavor, so to speak—that cannot be reduced to the language of (the rest of) science although they can be extensively related to it.

The mind-body problem is no more a legitimate philosophical problem than it is an impediment to normal discussions of how one's feelings are affected by one's circumstances or by medication. The more extreme versions of physicalism and reductionism are not supported here, that is the versions that deny the reality of these other aspects of the mental life or insist they are "nothing more than" the physical reduction of them.

8) The order in the world of which Burtt spoke is, however, one of the matters that can be clarified by reference to the physical explanation of the mind's operation. In these terms, it presupposes (depends on, recognizes) a reality that is indeed ordered in the sense of being far from chaos, but a reality in which much of the order is a byproduct of the evolutionary attempt of our limited brains to cope with—to describe and explain—the complexity of the universe.

9) This sounds like "evolutionary epistemology", but the approach here is crucially at variance with that of those associated with that label, notably Popper and Campbell,[7] who incorrectly (and unnecessarily) denied the exist-

ence of a legitimate form of inductive inference in favor of the "random trial and selective retention" account. One might say that they insisted on a first-level analogy with the way evolutionary adaptation takes place, when they should have seen the necessity for an extension to the second level, where new abilities and senses evolve that cut through the laborious process of trial and error.

10) So the position taken here is that there is an external world, and that it is more or less as we normally and scientifically describe it—these two types of description being complementary, contrary to the Eddington et al. incompatibilism thesis ("The scientist has shown that what appears to be a solid table is really mostly empty space" etc.). But this assertion involves no acceptance of the kind of infallibilism that is so often ascribed to science (by its enemies), or to the logical positivist interpretation of science, by its critics.[8] We can be sure that many details, some important facts, and some major perspectives that we have accepted in a certain period in the history of science will turn out to be wrong. But these errors are, at any historical moment, quite minor compared with the constancy of the overall picture comprising the findings of all sciences (and other inquiry disciplines). It is in fact because the changes are incremental that they can be recognized at all, and for the same reason the idea of wholesale skepticism is essentially self-contradictory. Those who say that everything is uncertain have not realized that their claim refutes itself. If they do sense this, they naively suppose that this in some way supports their position, not realizing that they have rejected all positions, not all positions besides their own. They want to eat their cake and have it too; to be right in their conclusion, although reaching it by denying the legitimacy of all conclusions.[9] If you kill enough civilians in a war you haven't liberated the country from a tyrant, you've become one. The fact that many legal cases are appealed does not support the view that law is arbitrary.

11) While this is not the place to deal with the whole problem of epistemological skepticism about the external world, it may be useful to indicate a secondary reason for rejecting the leading versions of it, because it provides a preliminary example of one kind of analysis—"bootstrapping"—that is part of the repertoire for the reanalysis of all the concepts in the logic of science.

The highly skeptical view about the external world that philosophers refer to as idealism—because of its emphasis on the reality of "ideas" rather than an external reality—essentially involves a confusion between the nature of experience and the nature of what we infer from experience. While our knowledge of many sensory and other experiences is, with respect to a particular claim, more reliable than most conclusions we form about the external world, there is nothing logically improper about hypothesizing the existence—and properties—of that world, and confirming that hypothesis in the usual ways. Eventually, the level of confirmation by many people and long experience may make public claims about the external world more reliable than the claims of any one person about their experiences, and in some cases more credible than the shared beliefs of large numbers of people about their experiences. The primacy of sensory information in the normal process of inference should not be confused with its ultimacy.

The mistake made by the idealists in claiming that only ideas are real is like that of supposing that only the detective's clues are real whereas the crime is imaginary. The crime is just as real as the clues, although we will never see it directly as we do the clues. But there are no grounds for supposing that the real is restricted to what we can see on demand.

Of course, the deeper insight is that we cannot even learn the language for describing the world of experience without reference to the external world, or indeed without reference to things which exist although we cannot see them— either now or, in some cases, even when we wish to. The idea that the existence of the outside world is more problematic than that of the world of experience is, of course, exactly the same mistake which seduces the skeptic about induction into thinking that the present is certain but the existence of the future is problematical. The manner of the crime or the matter of the future are indeed inferred rather than directly observed but in due course, as the evidence accumulates, they not only become reliable beliefs but more reliable than most of the individual evidences from the senses on which we build their existence.

12) Even if one continues to believe in the reality of that part of the external world which could in principle have been observed (or could be observed in the future), another radical suggestion has been widely canvassed— the instrumentalist claim that abstract or theoretical-scientific concepts are mere mnemonics, convenient inventions to facilitate thought, but lacking any ontological status. That view was proved simplistic as instruments improved to the point where we came to see the molecules and then the genes which were supposedly only *façons de parler*. While in principle the instrumentalist position might still be true of other entities besides the ones where it was proved wrong, it has failed as a logical point: theoretical constructs are, in general, entries in the reality stakes and often successful ones. Thus, independently of the historical refutation of specific instrumentalist claims, exactly the same argument against instrumentalism can be used as was applied above to the other skeptical positions. The argument is simply reinforced by the historical examples.

13) Finally, the approach here leaves the door open for some—but not all— of the new forms of knowing or knowledge that have recently been advocated by critics of the narrow-mindedness of traditional science, which is better described as the simplistic interpretation of scientific method by many scientists. Several of the other essays in this collection are devoted to explorations of

this latter possibility, but no attempt to review them is provided in this essay, which might be described as primarily concerned with establishing the limits and legitimacy of the general domain of the subjective in science, and of the objective in the realm of the mind. Its target is thus nearer to the original one aimed at by Burtt, but more directly aimed than his paper at reconstructing the logic of science than the epistemology of science.

Going Beyond Logical Positivism

14) It may be helpful to see the present approach to the logical analysis of science as a natural extension of efforts from two opposing directions. In the first place—the perspective addressed in this section—it is a "natural" extension of the reductionist program of the logical positivists (logical empiricists, operationalists, etc.), but an extension which for them was completely taboo. The extension from the other end was an extension of the reductionist effort made from the very different starting point of the phenomenologists, constructionists, and others. Whereas the logical positivists wanted to reduce the concepts of science to observational data, the other approach wanted to reduce even the observations to something more mentalistic—sense data, phenomena, mental constructs. Both efforts have proved unsuccessful—in principle and not just in practice—although not refutable in quite such a straightforward way as instrumentalism. We need to understand the reason for the failure, and how it suggests a natural extension of the effort.

15) The reductions attempted by the logical positivists in the early days of the Vienna Circle—that is, their attempts at definition of, for example, theoretical entities in terms of observational ones and historical events in terms of present ones—was restricted to the use of syntactic (purely grammatical) procedures of explicit definition, and, later, recursive definition and implicit definition via sets of axioms. With this restriction it eventually became clear that the project was impossible—theoretical entities could not be defined away in terms of observational predicates.[10]

In the effort to increase the plausibility of the reductionist thesis, the later logical positivists, notably Carnap and Tarski, then extended the allowable analytic techniques to semantic analysis, where meaning rules involving linkages to the external world—not just from one linguistic entity to another—were allowed. (Ostensive definition was the paradigm.) This yielded negligible further success, although for some time it was a cult approach that extended to general philosophy (for example Sellars). The natural third step would have been to draw on the third and last division of semiotic—pragmatics—for analytic tools. In this approach, some reference would have been allowed to parameters referring to the specific contexts of use. But the logical positivists drew the line at this, which they felt went beyond the spirit of logic as they conceived it, and the spirit of logical positivism as they defined it.[11]

16) The most distasteful aspect of this step, for them, was the inevitability of having to include reference to the knowledge-states of the people using the terms—for example, in the case of "explanation", they would have had to include reference to what the audience knew. This is what they called "psychologism". They felt that this kind of reference was part of the "context of discovery"—a matter of historical or biographical interest but not relevant to logic, which involved the "context of justification". Definitions—the real meaning of terms—had to be appropriate for the latter context, and hence independent of considerations which dominate the former.

17) In this essay it will be argued that the extra step, the inclusion of "pragmatic" (a.k.a. contextual, a.k.a. psychologistic, a.k.a. cognitive state) considerations, if done in a certain way, does in fact lead us to an improved analysis of the concepts and understanding of the nature of science. This view involves a sense in which scientific objectivity is, in a way, eventually subjective, while showing that the sense in which this is true is one in which the subjectivity is no threat to validity. Thus the logical positivists' critics—today, for example, the constructionists—were right in supposing that the logical positivists' separation of the agent, the scientist, from the world was unsound, but wrong in supposing that the objectivity of science was illusory. It is merely an elusive ideal, like justice. It is right to point out that we quite often miss it, even when the whole scientific establishment thinks it has been attained; but it is a blunder to suppose that we usually miss it, or may have entirely missed it. The routine process of the law, as of science, attracts little publicity mainly because there is little news value in just punishment for conceded or irrefutably demonstrated offenses, as there is little scientific excitement about the accurate measurement of samples of conventional substances. It does not follow that justice or accurate measurement is an illusion; it is no more an illusion than the external world or the future—or the present. But sometimes we are wrong about it.

Falling Short of Phenomenology

18) Extending logical positivism beyond the point at which it ceases to accept the extensions does not salvage it as logical positivism, but it does establish some continuity with the proposals made there, and it can show how the movement stopped on the brink of breakthrough to a workable analysis. In the same way, restraining the claims of phenomenology—and of its allies in the cause of subjectifying science—will also make the position unacceptable to the originators, perhaps in part because we take away the cachet of the iconoclast. However, it does create a viable position rather than a self-contradictory one,

and it does locate it in a context which shows it shares a border with the opposition. To perform this task, however, we need to clarify the key notions of objectivity and subjectivity. As we will see, a great deal of the confusion involves switching from one to the other of two quite different interpretations of these terms.

The Two Faces of Subjectivity

19) The key to the trouble is that "subjectivity" has both an evaluative sense and a descriptive sense. (A parallel situation applies to "objectivity".) These senses are best understood in terms of their contrasting concepts as well as their connotations. In the evaluative sense, subjectivity (or "subjective") connotes unreliability, a mere matter of opinion, unreality, or fallibility; it contrasts with factuality and validity. In the descriptive sense, it connotes something private, idiosyncratic, personal, or specific to a particular subject, and it contrasts with what is intersubjectively observable or determinable. The antonym, objectivity (and "objective" in one of its many senses), refers directly to the contrasting concepts, that is, in the evaluative sense it refers to lack of bias, to truth or validity, and in the descriptive sense it refers to what is public or "external to the mind". [12]

Behaviorists often argued for the move from introspectionism in psychology to behaviorism by incorrectly identifying the two senses of objectivity, that is, by rejecting all purely personal experiences as lacking in the kind of objectivity that can be of value to science. But the sense in which personal experience is (necessarily) subjective does not support the conclusion that it is necessarily unreliable; otherwise, general practitioners, psychotherapists, optometrists, and space medicine specialists would be hard put to do competent work. A less partisan view of the situation would have been that an *excessive* focus on introspection as *the* method of psychology had led to undervaluing what could be done in terms of intersubjectively testable claims. The use of the latter type of claim was of course so successful in the physical and biological sciences of the time that it was inevitable a movement would begin in psychology to jump on that bandwagon.

However, to do so—that is, to restrict validity-objectivity to intersubjectively verifiable experience—is simply a mistake. Introspection, about some matters, when practiced by some observers, in some conditions, can pass the tests to establish objectivity in the sense in which it connotes an unbiased account; that is, in the sense that establishes the phenomena experienced as deserving the status of (putative) facts. Perhaps the most important example of this arises in research on drug effects where the reports of the subjects on their experiences are a crucial part of the data, and are of a type that investigators often have no basis for inferring from prior data or their own experience. The kind of tests such data must pass of course overlap with the ones appropriate for external events, to a degree that ensures they both refer to the same quality of reality. Hence they include tests of internal consistency; test-retest consistency; the use of analogies with publicly accessible experiences; information content which can be partly verified in other ways; truth-telling tests or track record (especially where the incentive to deliberate deception can be minimized); the identification of brain, electrogalvanic, or sensorimotor correlates; overt behavior cues; and reports from other subjects of their own private experiences. Only some of these are relevant in most cases, but the accumulation of those available makes it unreasonable to deny the data status of the reports—as reports of inner experience, not just of shared verbal behavior (cf. religious revelations which claim to provide knowledge about the external world).

20) In the more recent rush to jump off the behaviorist bandwagon, many people have continued to treat the two senses of subjective/objective as one and have simply reinstated the fallen angel of subjectivity (in the personal-experience sense) as the leading divinity in the pantheon of knowledge. This gives it an epistemological role it cannot support, and ensures contemporary opposition and a return swing of the pendulum in the future. Even in the misleading epistemological picture, according to which we infer from inner experiences conclusions about outer reality, it is clear that there is a distinction between the truth—that we only access the external world via our perceptions or sensations (etc.)—and the related error of supposing the world to be no more than a construction out of sensations (etc.). On that distinction hangs the difference between fact and fantasy, the difference between the crime and the clues. We will not make progress by merely reversing the earlier mistake.

21) The behaviorists were precipitate; they oversimplified the situation and ran into absurdity, at its most absurd in the position of the "radical behaviorists" led by Skinner who argued for the mind as merely a fiction for explaining overt behavior. This was no more and no less foolish than arguing for the world as a fiction for explaining mental events. But the behaviorists were not wrong to suppose that: i) there are great difficulties in verifying claims about personal experience; ii) there is no way to define all the concepts of science in terms of such claims; iii) a great deal of scientific research in psychology (and other social sciences) could be done without depending in the slightest on assumptions about the nature and content of the mind; and iv) one cannot even define many of the crucial mental states, such as knowledge, without conceding that some of the necessary conditions for its applicability are external, and that some sets of external conditions are sufficient for its application.

Nor, on the other hand, were the idealists of whatever stripe wrong in stressing the reality of the mental world, the privileged access to it of one individual, and the impossibility of constructing the external world by some simple process of defining its entities in terms of mental events. We have now moved to a better understanding of the complex truth about the relation of language about mental events, states, and processes, to language about behavior, through the work of Wittgenstein, Ryle, Austin, and others following them, but spelling the story out in detail is not essential for the purposes of the present exercise.[13]

22) The solutions to the ontological problem about the status of the mind, and to the epistemological problem about the nature of scientific knowledge, do not lie in a straightforward proof that the construction which one of them thought impossible is in fact feasible. Given the construction tools they knew about and accepted, both constructions were impossible. The solution lies in improving the tools, thereby reconceptualizing the problem. Using the improved tools, the realist turns out to be right, but given the old tools, used in the traditional way, the idealists were equally well entitled to their conclusion. However, the way we save the realist requires an immediate rejection of the logical positivist position. It is not done by embracing idealism but by insisting on what the positivists rejected as "psychologism".

The Program for Psycho—Logic

23) Thus both parties, the idealists and the realists (in the first decades of this century the two parties were mainly represented by the metaphysicians and the logical positivists) labored under three handicaps. Their definition of subjectivity was confused; their definition of definition was excessively restrictive; and their conception of legitimate inference was also too narrow. We have already suggested some refinements in the first of these, and have indicated how the second and third caused trouble. The aim of the rest of this essay is to follow through the strand of subjective (mentalistic, psychologistic, etc.) involvement in the conceptual apparatus of science, in order to understand the underlying fusion of the subjective and objective. The three concepts just referred to are only three of the many to which we will refer. The key set includes and does not go far beyond the following twenty groups with sixty elements, although we'll only provide comments on a representative subset:

- concepts
- observation and observable entities
- data, facts, information, propositions, and discoveries
- description
- estimation and judgment

- evaluation
- classification
- ideal types and natural kinds
- generalizations and laws
- prediction and correlation
- explanation and reduction
- causation, experimentation, and determinism
- meaning and definition; criteria and indicators; necessary and contingent connections
- measurement
- approximation
- truth, probability, and possibility
- confirmation, corroboration, justification, verification, and falsification
- scientific evidence and inference (including deduction, induction, abduction, and probative inference); significance; and proof (demonstration)
- parsimony and simplicity
- models, analogies, theories, paradigms; theoretical (abstract) entities
- subjectivity and objectivity

It will be clear from the sections above that it is also being suggested that the reconceptualization of these concepts provides a basis for reconstruing some of the important issues in the philosophy of science. In fact, it seems plausible to suggest that such a reconceptualization affects most of the important methodological, epistemological, and ontological issues involved in understanding science, although determinism is the only position included in the above list.

24) So the main contention here is simple enough to describe, although not so simple to establish. It is maintained that more elaborate and imaginative notions of logical construction, definition, and inference (in particular) make it possible to retain the appropriate degree of objectivity for scientific concepts while allowing the degree of mental involvement that is essential if we are to provide a reasonably plausible analysis of the grammar of science and the functions of thought in science. The recipe involves getting the analysis of scientific concepts extended beyond syntactics and semantics into the

"psychologistic" domain of pragmatics. Unless we do this, the analyses are wrong; if we do this, a lasting marriage of the subjective and the objective can be accomplished. The secondary contention, which is independent of the other, is that the notions of knowledge and understanding (or information and explanation) are the only epistemological primitives in the set required for the logic of science; that is, the rest are reducible to these.

The Concepts of 'Basic Meaning' and 'Standard Context'

25) Each of the terms we will deal with has a basic meaning which includes contextual, "psychologistic", state of mind, or "subjective" factors.[14] It is in terms of this basic sense that we come to understand the concepts, and we often have to turn back to this basic sense in order to resolve puzzles involving the concepts. But each of the terms also has one or more standard contexts where the psychological element "falls away" because it is so well understood that the reference to it becomes implicit, a hidden assumption. In those contexts, we can often employ the standard dictionary kind of definition, which is usually a syntactical translation rule, sometimes a semantic rule; and where that fails, we can often turn to the definition implicit in a set of axioms or laws—or even just true statements—which involve the term. The most common standard contexts for scientific contexts are those of the science classroom and the scientific research community. The existence and familiarity of these standard contexts misled logicians into thinking that the real meaning of the concept was encapsulated in the syntactical definitions. But even the scientific meaning was not encapsulated in the syntactical definition used by the scientific community, as we quickly saw when problem cases arose, and a switch to another definition was made (thermodynamics): not a paradigm shift, just a parachute switch; that is, the use of a built-in escape mechanism.

Discovery

26) We start with an example of historical interest because it is the one to which the logical positivists appealed in their distinction between real logic—the appropriate tool in the "context of justification"—and history/biography, which is the "context of discovery". The concept of a scientific discovery, or any other kind of discovery, clearly refers to the knowledge-context of the time when the discovery is supposed to have been made. A discovery is an increment in what is known. Here the logical positivists illustrated psycho–logic admirably, with an example which does not form a significant element in the logical vocabulary of science, so they could afford to concede the involvement of the psychological

or cognitive element. There is an interesting although simple problematic application of the concept of discovery which forces us to be clear about that element. Even though this case does not come from the philosophy of science, it illustrates the kind of problem which we will find there in connection with other concepts.

The problem concerns a comment that used to be in every history text, to the effect that "Columbus discovered America". Of course, this refers to the personal knowledge context of Columbus in particular, readily generalized to the standard context of European knowledge of the time. Today, most of us understand why it is offensive to Native Americans to find this in school history texts, since it disregards their many cultures–for whose knowledge context "America" was not a discovery but a foreign name for their homeland.

27) This simple example leads us on to a more profound problem with the separation of the context of discovery from that of the context of justification, and the attempt to discard the former for purposes of "real logic". This problem arises because the way we learn every concept is in the context of discovery, and, with nearly all concepts that involve reference to "states of the mind", this means that the logical criteria for the concept initially include both intersubjectively observable phenomena and the "inner states". One can hardly argue that these terms change their meaning after we learn them, since in that case it would not be these concepts that one had learnt. So it is always inappropriate to treat them as divorced from the inner states–as behaviorism does–just as it is always inappropriate to treat them as divorced from the external criteria–as the idealist, phenomenologist, or constructionist does (or has difficulty not doing).

Note that this is different from the way in which we learn about invisible causes. These are defined from the beginning in terms of a definite description, as "the hidden cause of these things you can see". While this is marginally defensible as a way to introduce, for instance, the language of phenomenal pain through pointing at pain behavior in others, it is not the way in which we introduce notions such as knowledge and understanding. They must always meet external tests as well as internal ones, since we are often wrong about our beliefs concerning the extent of our knowledge and understanding. (If not, we could replace marking examinations by taking a lie-detector test.) And it is those concepts which form the basis for the whole structure of science.

Knowledge and Information

28) Knowledge and understanding–so it is suggested here–are the building blocks for all other concepts in the repertoire of the logic of science. As commonly and correctly used, whether in science or outside it, the basic sense

of each involves a crucial reference to the psychological—specifically, the cognitive—state of some individual, audience, or recipient (not necessarily human) and to some externally observable criteria. The concept of knowledge is in most respects the simpler of the two; although its content overlaps with the notion of understanding (a.k.a. comprehension, or, sometimes, insight), context will always distinguish them.

Closely related to the concept of knowledge is the concept of information, just as the concept of understanding is closely related to the concept of explanation. In each of these conjugate pairs, the second notion involves the communication or acquisition of the first. Information is knowledge that is conveyed, or set up to be read or conveyed, or acquired by a knower from a process of observation or reflection. By a slight extension of meaning, perhaps not even metaphorically, we speak of the information in DNA being read by RNA because the RNA has the ability to "read" the structure of DNA; note the way that transmittal comes in. In the same way we speak of Watson and Crick as those who broke the code, meaning only that they worked out (the general principles of) how to interpret—acquire particular information from—the structure of genes. Analogously, explanations are the vehicles of understanding, devices whose criteria of merit include their comprehensibility to another agent as well as their truth.

29) The "communication-conjugate" in each pair of concepts is developmentally prior to it. That is, the way in which we learn the concept of knowledge is via the passage of information (about, in particular, the use of the term "knowledge"); the concept of understanding is only understood because it is explained to us. This developmental primacy is another reason, besides the external criteria consideration, for being very careful that in throwing out the context of discovery one does not also throw out the essence of the context of justification.

30) In general terms, then, information is knowledge transmitted or received via a communication process (or encoded for transmittal in such a process)—or acquired from a process of observation or inference—whereas the knowledge itself may be just an "inner state".[15] Information is thus a configuration which conveys or can convey some truth about some thing or state. While information is often configured by an agent using a conventionalized code, it may be incorporated in any configuration whose significance becomes understood. For example, the meteorologist gleans information from configurations of atmospheric conditions, the physician is informed by examination of the patient's condition. Analogously, explanations are understanding-transporters and must themselves be phrased or cast in terms of some communication procedure.

31) Information is a narrower concept than knowledge since the latter clearly includes "knowing-how" (Ryle) (or tacit knowledge [Polanyi])—our "procedural" knowledge of how to do things that involve skills which must be acquired by demonstration, practice, and mentoring, and cannot be acquired by following a stateable procedure.[16] The cognitive, rather than the manual-dexterity sub-species of this kind of knowledge, is important in science, although one might argue that manual skills with instruments, including computers, has more importance than has commonly been acknowledged. Knowledge also includes experiential knowledge, our knowledge of the taste of things, the flavors that only experience can bring; the respect for participant observation field experiences in anthropology is an important example of recognition of the importance of this in science.

There can be external studies of these two kinds of knowledge (its causes and effects, etc.), and the results of those studies can be communicated, but that communication and the information it contains does not contain the knowledge to which it refers. Acquisition of a skill and of experience, while they are cases of learning, of knowledge acquisition, are not naturally described as acquiring information, although a determinist might argue that in such cases one's brain, even if not one's mind, has acquired information. It is commonly supposed—but not obviously true—that such knowledge is less important to science than communicable and inferrable information, especially propositional knowledge. Yet even there we have underestimated the range of the processes of communication, explanation, and education in science, which include not just the written or spoken word, but demonstration, training, portrayal, and acting (role-playing). Still, science is mainly a public activity whose history is not biography nor poetry nor art, where the other kinds of knowledge are of paramount importance.

32) The basic sense of information—the sense with which we must begin—is far more general and psychologistic than the Turing/Shannon notion, as developed in conventional "information theory".[17] Theirs was a convenient and fruitful surrogate, immensely powerful in highly stylized contexts, but far from the core meaning. It deals well with situations where the range of possibilities can be clearly delineated in advance, and information is incorporated in some message by selecting a particular combination from among the possibilities. Of course, it can do little with those parts of scientific knowledge that involve knowing-how or experiential knowledge, but it is also of little use in many important cases of propositional scientific knowledge, which is the kind of information we commonly convey in science education and research. The simplest version of the theory has some difficulty with defining the information content of a message without reference to the linguistic repertoire of the recipient. Is the information conveyed by a message in French the same as that

of the translation of that message into English? The natural answer is to say that it depends on what languages the recipient understands. Of course, that is a psychologistic answer, referring to the "context of discovery" not the context of justification; but it is the right answer for understanding the basic sense of the term "information". There are other types of context-dependent information; besides those which depend on the cognitive context, that is, involve "pragmatics" or "psychologistic" considerations, there are also "semantic" examples which also involve explicit reference to features of the physical context, local or more general, for example the information conveyed by "You were accused by the man on your left", when uttered in an appropriate context. (There are also borderline cases, like "He's not a very tall man, by our standards".) This kind of information can only be expressed in terms of the technical definition if we start the process of building information about the environment into the information content of a proposition, not a process for which it is easy to give rules.

There are many other problems. The "technical definition" of information (as we'll call the Turing-Shannon definition) can do little with the subtleties of metaphor, and since most theories are or embody metaphors, it can do little with the information contained in many theoretical claims and hypotheses. Now the process of explaining the meaning of important terms in science involves, to a crucial extent, subtle nuances that cannot be—certainly never have been—expressed in any finite set of propositions, and hence cannot be reduced to bits of information.

The technical concept can do even less with the information created by modes of presentation or by techniques of analysis. The format of information may create further information, and reformatting may alter the amount of information "in" a dataset.[18] Thus, in the Turing-Shannon sense, a table of figures may represent facts, hence constitute data, which is information; but the information it contains may only be of an item-by-item type. When graphed or represented in some other pictorial way, such as by using pseudo-coloring, that dataset may reveal a trend or a feature which represents further information.[19] Appropriate statistical analysis can similarly create information; it is not a mere transformation of the same amount of information into a different publishing format. Supercomputers similarly may create information when they do data-crunching exercises that were previously impossible. Their role is then closely analogous to that of the electron microscope and not just to that of the calculator; both make the invisible visible, and thus, sometimes, they convert theoretical concepts into observable ones. Relatedly, maps of terrain, models of molecules, diagrams of instruments and machines, may be informative where no verbal description of the same phenomena is informative, although it may "contain the same information".

The subtleties of graphical representations, where the configuration conveys information but at a level we have not yet succeeded in atomizing, is a crucial matter in clinical diagnosis, for example, where it has been shown that graphical representation of the results of tests conveys more than tabular representations—the work on the Minnesota Multiphasic Personality Inventory has perhaps been the most intensive.

The technical concept of information cannot even cope with the difference between informative and trivial tautologies—that is, between "Triangles have three angles", a definition incorporating only linguistic knowledge, and Pythagoras' Theorem, a great discovery even though it demonstrably contains no more Turing-Shannon information than the definitions from which it can be deduced. Since a number of key physical and economic laws are expressed in terms that make them definitionally true, defining information in that way rules out the expression of a great deal of knowledge. The positivists of course rejected all tautologies, including all mathematical theorems, as lacking in "empirical content". But it is simply implausible to say that Pythagoras' Theorem tells us nothing about the length of the sides of physical triangles; surveyors use it all the time exactly because it does just that. The positivists were right to stress that geometry is not like simple empirical generalizations, but they failed to realize that it is very like virtually every actual physical law or theory, since these are nearly always expressed in terms of abstractions or idealizations.

However, the fundamental point they missed was the fact that geometry is a conversion device, just like a computer or graphics, and these devices create information about whatever it is applied to, because information is in the mind of the audience. They insisted that the information had to be in the propositions themselves, regardless of how they were massaged, combined, or portrayed—and that is just not the nature of information. It led them to an absurd position on this as on many other issues. Tautologies, such as interesting theorems and theories, are discoveries which enable us to create information—not about linguistic rules or abstract entities, but about whatever we apply them to. They are intellectual microscopes, making visible what was invisible, making new and important information out of what was unenlightening data.[20]

Thus the basic, that is, the psycho-logical, sense of information takes it as the knowledge passed on by some message or inferred from something perceived, and the extent as well as the value of that information will depend on the interpretive skills and the prior knowledge of the recipient or inferrer. There is, it should be clear, no way in which all this is subject to quantitative assessment, indeed the attempt produces a serious loss—along with some benefits, the saving grace of the technical definition. It should be equally clear that the technical definition is hopelessly inadequate to cover even the range of scientific knowledge and information. But we do not need to throw away its conceptual contributions: the relation of entropy to thermodynamics, of noise to randomness, are still insights in terms of the psychological sense. But we must expand the technical notion in order to handle its problems, and be cautious about how we interpret its results.

33) What Turing and Shannon did was entirely justifiable, if not taken too literally. It follows the long tradition of definition by simplification—especially definition by reduction to a roughly related but clearly quantifiable concept—that has generated great bodies of useful theory and practice, from the kinetic energy definition of temperature to the relative frequency approach to probability. But one must understand that such "definitions" are merely convenient equivalences, limited in their applicability and utility, often to be abandoned as we see beyond them to a larger vision, and always subject to modifications based on our increasingly richer understanding of the concepts. Taking them literally, as sound conceptual analyses, is like taking radical behaviorism or inductive skepticism literally. Considering them seriously is a sensible intellectual exercise, but acting on them is absurd in any practical terms. In this essay, that kind of absurdity is taken seriously as a reason for abandonment of the approach, contrary to the view of many philosophers, who think that a little geocentric complexity is no problem for an ontological theory.

34) Even for practical application, these approaches had serious problems. The relative frequency theory turned out to have great difficulties with a notion that it needed to be able to count on, the notion of the limit of the ratio of two types of event in an actual sequence of events. It turned out to be simply inapplicable to the probability of the single case—most importantly, the probability of a new hypothesis or theory. The psycho-logical sense of probability is the fundamental one, and in that sense it refers to the most reasonable betting level. (We discuss this concept a little more below.)

In the case of information, systems with definite discriminable states turn out to be less common than was supposed, outside the special worlds of fundamental particles, thermodynamics, circuits, and computers, and in particular, little of the brain's functioning meets that requirement. We now find that the "co-localization of neurotransmitters and growth factors in neurons . . . [results in the use of] entirely different combinations of signals at different times, dictated by the environment."[21] This can be construed as a nudge from the neurons toward developing contextual (pragmatic) definitions rather than content-only (syntactic) ones.

For the psycho-logical sense of information used here, these difficulties are avoided. There are no reductionist definitions, the meaning of the terms is contextual and flexible, never fully expressed in quantitative terms, but not arbitrary or subjective in the pejorative sense.

Understanding and Explanation

35) Understanding or comprehension of a phenomenon, as of a communication, might be called "second-order knowledge". It is the capacity to answer a range of questions about the explanand (whatever it is that is said to be explained or understood). The relation of knowledge to understanding is like the relation between knowing the meaning of the words on a menu in Italy and being able to discuss the chef's approach with the waiter in Italian. Thus understanding is a process of coming to master, or having mastered, the keys to a cognitive network—one in which the phenomenon or communication is embedded, and which meets certain standards of relevance and quality, enabling those who have mastered it to accommodate new questions or occurrences. Sometimes the range of relevance may be very limited ("I understand why he did it" is very close to "I know why he did it", that is, his motive), but in general the range is quite wide (for example understanding the phenomenon of diffraction). Understanding modifies the understander's set toward further information, and often renders the new information redundant. Understanding, like information, may be created by reformatting or reanalyzing data; one may "understand what's happening" only when one runs a correlation matrix, or a pseudo-color timeslicing animation of the data. Understanding is therefore a property of sets made up of related items of information, information-generating propositions like laws and classifications, and information formats.

36) Understanding is communicated via explanations, although not all understanding can be thus communicated, for some of the same reasons that ensure not all knowledge can be converted into information. The criteria of merit for an explanation are therefore its truth and the extent to which its recipient can pass the tests for understanding. Explanations are thus judged like teaching, and of course much teaching consists in giving explanations, a considerable skill which goes well beyond mere understanding. The extent of the gap is clear when one finds people with advanced credentials in an esoteric discipline who are very poor at explaining it—they can even be found on the faculty of universities.

37) The logical positivists and the neo-positivists naturally rejected the notion of understanding as psychologistic, part of the context of discovery, and nothing to do with scientific explanation. The best they could do was to equate "explaining X" with "proving X to be true (or probable)", which is a completely different enterprise. People who are puzzled by X already accept (presuppose) that X is true; it is not enlightening for them to have this proved, let alone shown that it is likely. Nor were the logical positivists entirely consistent in their approach. They had to deny that explaining the meaning of something was a case of scientific explanation, because of course the inquirer in such a case is

clearly not asking the explainer to prove that the puzzling passage (for example) is true; yet it did not occur to them that the same applies to the inquirer about a scientific phenomenon. The difference between the two is simply one of subject matter. To explain a physical phenomenon one needs (normally, that is in standard contexts) to explain it in terms of other physical phenomena. Exactly which phenomena should be appealed to naturally depends on what the inquirer already understands, individually or as assumed in some standard context.[22]

Concepts and Laws

38) Understanding is best seen as the most complex in a series of cognitive survival mechanisms which the brain develops to handle the influx of sensory and internally generated information. Some of that information is the knowledge stored in memory which provides the wherewithal to find food stores, game trails, and recognize allies. The problem for the brain is surfeit and sorting this knowledge. If it cannot be organized, it cannot be stored in the finite space available, and, more importantly, it cannot be quickly retrieved in the limited time when it can save its possessor. So there first develops the concept—and, if language is available, its linguistic representation, the word—followed by the explicit version of a concept, the classification and then the generalization, the law, the model or metaphor and eventually the theory. Constancies in the sensory (etc.) field are the referent of, and presupposed by, concepts, and explicitly formulated in classifications and generalizations.[23]

Probability

39) The first cushion which allows knowledge claims to be both mnemonic and comprehensive is the slippage in the loose definition of concepts we have already discussed—definitions in terms of criteria, examples and contrasts rather than necessary and sufficient conditions, as in geometry. This was something the positivists saw as weakness, but which was in fact a success in terms of the task of survival with a finite mind in an untidy world.

The next two buffers were probability and approximation. In the case of probability something very significant occurred, because we find the neopositivists, notably Carnap in his later stages, conceding a minor legitimacy to the psychologistic element by allowing that there was one sense of probability which referred to degree of belief. However, he made the almost inevitable mistake of thinking that in this sense a probability claim was incorrigible. That is, they took "belief" to be entirely subjective, not logically evaluable in the way that a scientific statement would be. This was a blunder. The simple fact is that we have a large experience with the evaluation of beliefs as reasonable or unreasonable, and if they had not been so anxious to depart the realm of the "subjective" for the context of justification, it might have occurred to them to define probability in terms of degree of reasonable belief, that is, support without guarantees. As Toulmin rightly and devastatingly pointed out, we know very well how to criticize someone's probability estimate, although it correctly reports their own degree of belief.[24] Thus the "subjective" area of degree of belief is entirely corrigible by considerations from the objective domain of public evidence.

The neo-positivists, however, quickly moved on the more congenial "logical sense" of probability—the implicit definition of probability in the axioms of probability theory—and the "empirical sense"—the relative frequency notion. The logical sense requires saying that obviously corrigible claims about the probability of an event, or theory, are analytically true, which is an absurd conclusion. (Of course, they may be analytically true relative to one's assumptions but the positivists had long since rejected that kind of defense for astrology; truth claims bring one's assumptions and not just one's deductions into question.) Since it was clear and not disputed by anyone that the relative frequency sense cannot handle the probability that a new hypothesis is true— and some other important cases—the neo-positivists were left without a plausible account of probability, just because they were unwilling to accept the double-aspect feature of epistemic concepts such as knowledge, understanding, and now probability.

They were forced to the multiple-meaning approach simply because they had such a narrow conception of meaning. There is not the slightest reason to suppose there is more than one sense of "probability"—one which reflects itself a) in the "subjective sense" because we try to believe what's true, b) in the logical sense because we try to make our axioms reflect the truth about the concept being axiomatized, and c) in the relative frequency sense because that is a useful standard context. Of course, probability is a function of the state of our knowledge at a particular time; in the basic meaning, it is the knowledge of an individual, and, in standard contexts, it is the pooled knowledge of the scientific community at a particular time, as when we talk about the plausibility of a new scientific theory.

Approximation

40) It was significant that the logical positivists never discussed approximation, and came pretty late to probability. Their paradigm of scientific truth was the exceptionless generalization, and they thought that natural laws were

normally of that kind, whereas, in fact, there are almost no such laws. The importance of laws is that they are simple and usefully near the truth for a useful part of the range of their variables; in fact, almost all of them are simply approximations, and inaccurate by several hundred percent for large slices of their range.[25] We are lucky to get that much; it makes survival possible. And also wholesale self-destruction.

Approximation is simply one more survival device. Our brains are not capable of memorizing anything like the true graph showing the behavior of the simplest gas of all (hydrogen), let alone the differences between that and other gases. We settle for the General Gas Law. If we need exact figures, we determine them experimentally, but we rarely have that need. What we constantly need is a general sense of how gases behave, and the approximation gives us that; it gives us an understanding more precious by far than specific factual knowledge, because it is so much more far-reaching. It gives us the link to the kinetic theory of gases, the explanation of how internal combustion engines work, and a million other insights. A little inaccuracy is a small price to pay for all that—if you approach these matters pragmatically, not in terms of mathematics as an ideal and with demands for stand-alone syntactic translation rules for your definitions.

Idealization

41) Ideal types and natural kinds are further elements in the pragmatics of the mind/brain struggle for survival. They emerge implicitly in concept formation, and come to the front as an explicit element in the definition of taxons in developing classifications. And we have just seen the thin end of the wedge that gets them into the formulation of laws; by defining the ideal gas as one that obeys the General Gas Law, the perfectly elastic body as one that obeys Hooke's Law, and so on, we are able to formulate the laws as correct instead of incorrect (albeit approximately true) generalizations. In fact, they become tautologies, but properly understood remain as enlightening as ever, contrary to the positivist view that they must then cease to be informative about the external world.

Idealizations are not accidentally given names like "ideal gas", "perfectly elastic body", names that have evaluative connotations, as does the term "idealization" itself. Such substances are ideal for the purposes of science and of understanding. And those are the purposes with which the scientist is concerned. This terminology is a clue to the true function of the logic of science, namely to discover the way in which concepts and laws are formed, found, and framed, so as to resolve the tension between the mental limitations and the physical complexity which have to be co-ordinated in order to develop a satisfactory science.

Causation

42) Analysis of the concept of cause provides a particularly illuminating example of Psycho-logic. One still encounters the simplistic suggestion that cause means necessary condition,[26] despite the obvious counter-examples, for example those provided by overdetermination. There are still lingering beliefs that causation cannot operate at a distance, whereas the simplest thought-experiment about a new power that operates instantaneously and without the benefit of a propagating field shows we would not hesitate to use causal language about its—what can we call them except—effects. The best account that can be given in syntactic terms (that a cause is "a non-redundant member of a set of conditions which are jointly sufficient") was established long ago and it still leaves counter-examples.[27] The crucial further step is to bring in contextual criteria, which is most easily done by introducing the notion of a "contrast class".[28] Thus, to someone in a room watching someone else closing all the windows, the last of which breaks, the answer to the question "Why did that window break?" must be in terms of differentiating of that closing-event from the other closing-events, that it was slammed harder, or already had a crack. But for someone who walks into that room after the window breaks and asks exactly the same question (that is, uses the same language), a more appropriate answer will be to point to the person who was closing the window and say that s/he broke it when closing it. The contrast class for the first inquirer is the windows that did not break under conditions that seemed to be the same; for the second inquirer, the contrast class is with the broken window's unbroken state a few minutes earlier. Causes are mini-explanations, and hence must relate to the gaps or tensions in the understanding of those who call for or seek them. There is no syntactic solution to analyzing causes any more than explanations, but, on the other hand, there is nothing invalid, unreliable, or idiosyncratic about the answers provided. We see here the general message: the concepts in the logic of science are designed to work in—and hence they involve implicit reference to—a cognitive (psychological) context because, to put it bluntly, that is what science itself is created to do.

43) And that is the context of what has been called "volitional causation" or the "rational-action paradigm" referred to earlier. The entire misguided attack on "reasons-explanations", spearheaded by Weber's attack on the value of suicide notes, was just another example of the overreaction to anything which had an element of reference to internal states: a kind of paranoia that confused something that was descriptively subjective with something that was evaluatively

subjective, that is, unreliable and not meeting the standards of science.[29] It led, unfortunately but inexorably, to the denial of the legitimacy of free will in the strong sense in which that holds, again because of the insistence that the inner story must be superficial and the true (reductionist) story correct. There is indeed a sound idea behind reductionism, which can be expressed simply by saying that explanatory reduction is a legitimate ideal. But ontic reduction is not only counter-intuitive; there are no sound or even plausible arguments for it now.

One of the great stumbling blocks in the way of understanding the mind has been the implicit acceptance of the idea of explanation as proof, even by those in the anti-positivist camp. Thus, it is thought to be an objection to reasons-explanations that they may be given of two different actions, between which an agent is trying to decide. But why not? That is the logic of causation, something which has served us admirably throughout the history of science and before that throughout the history of technology. Explanations are usually just proximate causes, not sufficient conditions. That is a limitation, indeed, but only in the sense in which having a net worth of between a million and a billion dollars is a limitation in buying a house. Certainly, there is something fancier than a causal explanation, but what it provides is enough to change the universe. Moreover, it is attainable by mere mortals.

Evaluation

44) If there was one concession the logical positivists were less likely to make than adding psychological factors to the logical analysis of scientific concepts, it was that of adding evaluation to the list of legitimate scientific activities. Indeed, they tarred it with the same brush, in that they thought evaluation was just one more example of bringing in psychological factors, since they made the same kind of mistake they made with the careless dismissal of belief in working on the analysis of probability. That is, they smelled the odor of subjectivity (in the descriptive sense of internal access), and concluded that this meant objectivity (in the evaluative sense of validity) had been banished. They thought that evaluation was just the expression of opinion, taste, or preference, an entirely subjective matter—and of course, that meant subjective in the bad sense as well as the descriptive sense. They were far off the mark on both points; evaluation is neither the mere expression of taste, nor is it necessarily, or even typically, non-objective.

This would have become obvious to them if they had been more serious in their examination of the process of science, since that process essentially involves, and is impossible without, evaluation—the evaluation of experimental designs, of the quality of research papers, of data, of arguments, of instrumentation, and so on. Their model of an evaluative statement was a straw man: for a budding researcher to say that she or he likes to work in cryogenics is an expression of personal, subjective, value. To say that cryogenics is a good area for a beginner to work in, or that someone has just done some very good work in cryogenics, on the other hand, is to go much further—and also less far. It requires support of an entirely different kind, and has entirely different consequences.

The nature of evaluation and its place in science have recently been elaborated at great length by the present author, so the temptation to go into it any further here will be resisted,[30] except for one short comment. Properly done, evaluation serves, amongst other purposes, the data-synthesis task served by measures in descriptive statistics. The letter grade awarded to a student, by the same social scientist who proclaims that evaluation is just an expression of preference, is an extremely efficient, concise and objective measure of their work for certain crucial purposes (when appropriate care and skill is exercised). Thus evaluation serves as one more weapon in the armory of the brain in dealing with the complex world; we remember which brand to buy, which restaurant to visit, although we have long forgotten the details of the proof of its merit.

45) The logical positivists here overestimated the psychological element in a concept, whereas in other cases they underestimated it. The result in either case was to seriously handicap, not just the philosophy of science, but science itself. It seems likely that we lost most of the contribution the social sciences could have made to human affairs in the twentieth century mainly because the doctrine of value-free science dominated their practice.

It is somewhat ironic that the attacks on the value-free doctrine from the "left wing"—critical theory, neo-constructionists, et al.—are essentially irrelevant since they misunderstood the doctrine itself just as badly as the logical positivists misunderstood evaluation. Supporters of the value-free doctrine never argued that scientists do not have values that influence their choice of areas to work in, and which sometimes inappropriately affect their conclusions; nor did they deny that science can be put to use in the cause of many values, often immoral ones. To produce those truisms as the death knell for the doctrine of value-free science is to announce that you have just killed a straw man. The doctrine of value-free science is much more sophisticated, and supported by interesting arguments from Hume, Moore, and others; for example about the impossibility of drawing evaluative conclusions from factual premises. It is the doctrine that within science one cannot infer values from facts, and hence that value conclusions have no place within science. Nevertheless, the doctrine fails miserably, for reasons which are so straightforward that the failure to see them suggests there were some other factors at work besides simple errors of reasoning. One possibility is the fear of evaluation which haunts us all since we know very well how vulnerable we are to its strictures; another is the wish not to confront the power elite, which was certainly Weber's motivation when he introduced the doctrine to sociology.

Inference and Proof

46) If evaluation was the last candidate the logical positivists would ever accept, deductive proof was the last they would give up—or perhaps next to last, after observation. Proof was derivation by use of logical principles of inference, and it was an "effective" notion in the technical sense of being checkable for validity in a routine way without special skill. Thus it was the epitome of objectivity in the sense of intersubjectivity, and with the connotation of desirability. However, the notion of proof is far from routine. Wittgenstein's most literate student, John Wisdom, once put the psychologistic view of proof in these terms:

> Logic is proof, proof persuasion, and philosophy logic played with especially elastic equations.

The logical positivists would have said that persuasion is the task of rhetoric, not logic, and the trouble with philosophy was simply the tendency to get into the areas where questions were not decidable, because not expressed in terms of observables. Proof was safe haven: Whether or not someone was persuaded by a proof was their business—subjective business—but a proof was a proof, objectively so.

This view became increasingly untenable, first with the constraints of the Gödel theorems, then as the full significance of the non-Euclidean geometries and intuitionistic mathematics sank in, and finally with the use by Reichenbach and others of bridge laws, ostensive, and other semantic definitions, which made the validity of proofs about physical world entities dependent on the consistency of bridge laws and their application, a chancy business at best. Today there is the extra problem of whether computer-created proofs are really proofs. The objectivity of proofs, as the logical positivists conceived that objectivity, has evaporated. Of course, while this meant the end of the Erlanger program along with various other dreams of the Vienna Circle, it did not mean the end of rigorous proof, because rigor is something a little less than machine-effective, and that little less salvages all the objectivity we need. It doesn't mean there are never any errors, or even that machines can do the work for us; but we can have almost no errors and machines can do a great deal of the routine work for us. In the end however, we have to look at our hole card—the ultimate assumptions of the proof—and we have to settle the pragmatic question about which assumptions are most appropriate for the particular kind of proof we are interested in.

Thus, there was no need to panic at the sight of a subjective element in the sense of a reference to the present cognitive states, and even the foundational assumptions of the participants. We can manage those and we cannot eliminate them. They are no more threatening to sound science than the Supreme Court is to sound justice.

47) When it came to the other half of scientific inference—inductive or abductive inference—the logical positivist stance was bivalent. The Carnap team went for statistical inference as a legitimate option, although validation was always a worry (hence Hempel's introduction of the "requirement of total evidence"). The Popper group (and the evolutionary epistemologists) rejected the very idea, settling instead for guessing, checked out by confirmation and rejection. Both were in trouble because both took too narrow a view of evidence, inference, and hence proof. They made the mistake of thinking it had to be governed by stateable rules, following on their commitment to the idea that definition had to be in terms of stateable rules, even if expanded to include semantic or implicit ones. They could hardly maintain the effectiveness of proof and allow sloppy definitions, since deduction is, in a sense, just derivation by means of the rules that define the meaning of the terms involved.

The absurdity of the idea that scientists should be considered to be reduced to guessing at every non-deductive conclusion they espouse never bothered the US wing of the neo-positivists and was the UK (Popperian) *piece de resistance*. They were, they said, not concerned with analyzing matters to suit current usage, only with correct analysis. However, it was their analysis which was at fault. Once we have seen the extent to which the intuition of highly trained mathematicians still enters into deductive proof, and is normally highly reliable, it should hardly be unbearable to concede that the same is true in science.

What are the hallmarks of a type of sound non-deductive inference that is not just guessing (that turns out to be right)? It must be notably more successful than mere guessing, and it must be learnable, teachable, and on most occasions testable. Now we all know that it is possible to teach science students, for example, medical students, how to infer conclusions from evidence, and that their level of reliability in doing so can become very high in relatively stable evidential environments. How should we describe this achievement? Of course, the correct description is that this is teaching and learning inductive scientific inference in the medical field. This process is assisted by "rules of thumb" of various kinds, sometimes even by generalizations of an exceptionless kind. But it is not reducible to deduction from any set of such rules. Considerable judgment is involved in the application of the rules, and in training students to make appropriate responses in cases where no rules come near to supplying the answer.

It is here that evolution exercises its powers to select those who have or can learn a "feeling" for the natural order. The evolutionary epistemologists only needed to carry their line of reasoning one step further, so that evolution's role would not just be weeding out false conclusions but the reasoning processes that generate them. They were too fascinated by the chance of improving the analogy with evolution by letting random variation correspond to something, and finished up making it correspond to guessing.

All that can legitimately be meant by "guessing" in Popper's sense is that the step to the conclusion is not deductive. Nobody thought it was, except perhaps the other wing of the logical positivists who kept coming up with ways to reduce induction to rule-governed inference and then faced the problem of how they would know that the rules were correct. Inductive inference is often highly reliable, highly learnable and teachable, and checkable; only someone on a philosophical binge could suggest that it should be called guessing.

So inference of either type involves a psychological element, even a judgmental element, as well as heavy contextual elements. This is the element of truth in all attacks on the logical positivist program; but it does not justify to even the slightest extent the skeptical or relativist conclusions.

Conclusion

48) We could pursue these matters considerably further, for example by looking at measurement, at the paradigmatic psycho-logical concept of randomness, and in more detail at the way in which the concept of law serves as an information compression device that helps us to deal with the future information input flood, and not just the past, despite our limited memory space and calculating power. But perhaps enough has been said to help us see the scientist's struggle to discover the truth about the world and its inhabitants as a struggle to meet needs for knowledge and understanding, both of which have survival value. Of course such studies also have intrinsic interest, as we evolve more esoteric value systems; but their pragmatic context should be seen as their main driving force.

So instrumentalism is not enough, because truth that survives new methods of looking is more valuable than truth which does not. Logical positivism is not enough, because its model of scientific knowledge and understanding was a very primitive oversimplification of a very sophisticated set of procedures and their results. The phenomenological and constructivist alternatives are too much to be workable and too relativistic to be sensible. Yet they were entirely right to fight back against the superficial arguments for the dismissal of the mental. The internal world is as legitimate a world for study as the external, although it needs somewhat different tools and contains significantly different phenomena. The legitimation of that world need not, however, be at the expense of the legitimacy of the study of the other. And neither study should be pursued without careful investigation of the links between the two worlds.

In this paper we have tried to explicate an approach that provides some of those links, at the methodological level. It has tried to extend what we now know, in ways that still make sense, toward a synthesis of the inner and outer worlds, a synthesis that offers a step forward in the logic of science—and a foundation for steps forward in science itself.

Acknowledgments

Many thanks to the other contributors to this volume who were at Asilomar for their comments and especially to Willis Harman for valuable suggestions about the second draft, several of them incorporated here.

Notes

1. P. 322 of the Humanities Press edition (1952) of the 1932 (revised) version.

2. "The natural world after all is more the home and theater of mind than its unseen tyrant . . ." (loc. cit., p. 324)

3. Loc. cit., p. 324

4. The term "psychologism" as used here is defined below. It was used in another sense by Popper and those who followed him in time as well as spirit, and has recently acquired a slightly different sense again.

5. One symptom is the founding of the journal *Rationality and Society*, under James Coleman's editorship. Another is the new effort by sociologists to avoid the excesses of the New Sociology: a valuable and scholarly contribution to this effort is Jeff Coulter's *Mind in Action* (Polity/Blackwell, 1989).

6. Unsurprisingly, philosophers are not unanimous in their definition of realism. Thus Arthur Fine opens his contribution to the anthology *Scientific Realism* (University of California, 1984) with the words "Realism is dead", but goes on to give Bohr as an example of a non-realist or anti-realist (he calls him "the archenemy of realism"). It seems simpler to say that Bohr's position is that the entities inhabiting the sub-atomic level do not have the same properties as those at the macro level. Fine goes on to support a position himself which many would take to be realism; its key component is accepting the literal truth of scientific claims. This is not much better than Piaget's definition of realism as the view that one's own conclusions are always objective, a straw man that he knocks down even more quickly than Fine knocks down his version.

7. Together with their antecedents—Poincaré, and others—well identified in Campbell's essay in his recent anthology, and their successors such as Hallden in *The Strategy of Ignorance: From Decision Logic to Evolutionary Epistemology* (Theoria Press, 1986).

8. The rejection of positivism in this paper is so thoroughgoing that perhaps it will not be dismissed as defensive to say that criticism of the kind referred to here is one of many ways in which the increasingly "politically correct" anti-scientist/anti-positivist line makes a straw man out of the opposition. It is well to remember that logical positivism was a considerable advance on the miasmic metaphysics it replaced. We stand on the shoulders of giants, in the metasciences as in the sciences that metascience studies.

It should also be remembered that what Burtt defined as positivism we are more inclined today to call empiricism, since the current discussion tends to ignore the crucial distinctions between positivism and logical positivism. The definition of positivism provided by the term's originator (Comte) involved, for example, the denial of the legitimacy of the search for causes and theories involving abstract entities, something which Russell, who called himself a logical empiricist, also endorsed, but the later logical positivists completely rejected. (While this is not intended to be a scholarly review of the literature of positivism, the interpretations it involves are based on many years of interaction with Feigl, Carnap and Tarski.)

9. Another way to approach this fundamental flaw in relativism/skepticism is via the impossibility of defining "error" within such a system of thought. (Bunge stresses this flaw among others in an excellent essay which also deals with counter movements in science: "A Critical Examination of the New Sociology of Science", especially Part 2, which is in *Philosophy of the Social Sciences*, March 1992.)

10. Apart from the trivial case of Craig's Theorem which showed the reduction was possible in the useless hypothetical case where one could employ an infinite number of axioms, and under the always false assumption that one could sharply demarcate the observation predicates from the theoretical ones.

11. Specifically, Carnap defined the logic of science as a subject which involves "*abstraction from* the psychological and sociological side of the language". By "abstraction from" he meant the elimination of reference to "beliefs, images, etc., *and the behavior influenced by them*" (emphasis added in both quotes, which are from the opening section of "Logical Foundations of the Unity of Science", in the *International Encyclopedia of Unified Science*, Volume I, Chicago, 1938).

12. The quote is from the *Random House Dictionary*, Unabridged Second Edition. A much longer discussion of this crucial case of linguistic schizophrenia can be found in "Objectivity and Subjectivity in Educational Research", in the *Seventy-first Yearbook of the National Society for Study of Education* (1972), published by The National Society for the Study of Education.

13. It is well described from a point of view that does the best that can now be done for the behaviorist position ("linguistic behaviorism" perhaps) in Jeff Coulter's book referenced earlier.

14. In the language of semiotic, that means the definition has to go beyond syntactic and semantic considerations into the realm of pragmatics.

15. The quotation marks are intended to remind the reader that while cognitive states are convention-ally referred to as inner states, the reason for this is simply to stress that they are the possession of an individual who normally has access to them and who normally has the knowledge that they have that knowledge. These are the criteria for non-evaluative subjectivity, not for the pejorative sense of subjectivity. However, this way of describing cognitive states oversimplifies their status. They also have external criteria that (logically) must be satisfied. For example, since knowledge is only knowledge if it is true, the external world will have to match the knowledge claim in order for it to represent knowledge. And understanding is only understanding if the person said to have it is in fact able to deal with problems related to the matter said to be understood. That is, cognitive states are not like pain, which is conventionally thought to be (this is still an oversimplification, but a less gross one) uniquely accessible to those who have it.

16. Experiential and procedural knowledge are not entirely distinct, since an act of recognition is often expressed in both ways ("I know how to identify *agaricus campestris* by sight" and "I know what *a. campestris* looks like").

17. Any monotonic increasing function of the number of possibilities is acceptable, usually the logarithm to the base 2.

18. It is thus better to say "the information associated with (or implicit in)" a dataset rather than "contained in" or "represented by" the dataset.

19. One of the most important examples today is to be found in computer-assisted EDA (exploratory data analysis) where a three-dimensional representation of a dataset is made to rotate steadily while changing with time to exhibit the dependence on a fourth variable. This approach often reveals patterns and aberrations in a way that no finite approach through conventional statistical analysis has any real chance of uncovering. This is indeed the context of discovery, but it is now being treated as something really important instead of being caricatured as "guessing" in the neo-positivist and evolutionary epistemologist approaches. There is no "context of justification" until there is a discovery, and the process of discovery is one where the yield from exploration can be vastly improved by systematic procedures, without jumping into the absurdity of supposing that there can be an algorithmic procedure for making all discoveries. Further excursions toward multi-media will do more still; the use of sound, motion, and true 3D, via virtual imaging, will eventually be followed by true tactile and, no doubt, olfactory representations. These will tell us more, show us more, teach us more—although perhaps not enough more to make all of the increments worth their considerable cost.

20. A better analysis goes one step further, to deny the claim that the propositions of mathematics and logic are tautologies at all, and reconcile Mill with Wittgenstein.

21. *Information in the Brain* by Ira B. Black (MIT, 1991), p. xiii. It is ironic that this book contains no definition, explicit or implicit, of the concept of information. This can be taken as indirect evidence of the need for a more general concept than that provided by information theory.

22. The decline and fall of the neo-positivist attempt to keep cognitive states out of the logic of science began in the early 1950s, when William Dray began his attack on the covering law analysis of historical explanation, and I began a series of critical analyses of the corresponding analysis of scientific explanation, which I named "The deductive model of explanation". Hempel's extension of the model to probabilistic inference I christened "the inductive model"—together termed "the inferential model". Details of the attack are in 1956 in my Oxford D.Phil. thesis "Explanations" (reproduced by the University of Illinois library in 1962); some later installments were in "Definitions, explanations and theories" in *Minnesota Studies in the Philosophy of Science*, Vol. I, 1958, pp. 99–195, and in "Explanations, predictions and laws", in *Minnesota Studies in the Philosophy of Science*, Vol. II, 1962, pp. 170–230.

23. A considerably more detailed analysis of processes discussed in this section is to be found in "The concept of comprehension: from semantics to software", in *Language Comprehension and the Acquisition of Knowledge,* edited by R. O. Freedle and J. B. Carroll (V. H. Winston & Sons, Washington, DC, 1972). In that paper a "Comprehension Theorem" is proposed, which argues that exactly those information structures required for survival-oriented information-storage purposes provide the condition referred to as comprehension.

24. For example, we may decide that a doctor did in fact believe that a certain medicine was very unlikely to hurt a certain patient (a probability claim) but—far from accepting this as proof that in Carnap's sense of probability as degree of belief, the claim is incorrigible—we may be able to prove that this belief in the low probability of harm was incorrect, and even culpable. And we would do this, not by switching to one of the other definitions, but in terms of the standards of reasonable belief about likelihood.

25. The aversion to discussions of the concept of approximation persists, as we can see by the absence of the term from the index, let alone the glossary, of the recent 800-page anthology of key work in the philosophy of science referenced earlier. The extent of the resistance to the notion was brought home to me when I introduced the discussion of it in "The Key Property of Physical Laws—Inaccuracy" (in *Current Issues in the Philosophy of Science,* edited by Feigl and Maxwell [Holt, 1961], pp. 91–101). Herbert Feigl, one of the editors of this volume, implored me to change the title of my paper since he thought I couldn't *really mean what it implied.*

26. As is mentioned in the glossary for the 800-page anthology *The Philosophy of Science,* edited by Boyd, Gasper, and Trout (MIT Press, 1991).

27. See, for example, "Causes, Connections, and Conditions in History", in *Philosophical Analysis and History,* edited by William Dray (Harper and Row, 1966), pp. 238–264; reprinted in whole or part in various anthologies in the US and Italy; e.g. *Causation,* edited by Ernest Sosa and Michael Tooley (Oxford University Press, 1993), pp. 56-60. John Mackie's analysis was essentially similar.

28. Originally done in the citation of the last footnote, and now widely accepted.

29. An extension of the same point leads naturally to the compatibility of conventional accounts of free will and determinism.

30. "Introduction: The Nature of Evaluation" in *Evaluation Thesaurus* (4th edition, Sage, 1991), pp. 1–43.

The Excellent Researcher

by Ilja Maso

Already during his education at the Royal Jesuit College of La Fleche, Descartes discovered that "there was no body of knowledge in the world of such worth as . . . [he] had previously been led to expect" (Descartes, 1958, p. 96), that is, knowledge that would enable him to distinguish the true from the false (ibid., p. 99). Thus he discovered that in philosophy "there is not a single thing of which it treats which is not still in dispute, and nothing, therefore, which is free from doubt", and he considered "how many diverse opinions regarding one and the same matter are upheld by learned men, and that only one of all these opinions can be true". As regards the other sciences, inasmuch as they borrow their principles from philosophy, he judged that "nothing solid can have been built on foundations so unstable" (ibid., p. 98).

It was due to these disappointments that Descartes decided to study everyday life to see whether the distinction between true and false could be found there. To this end he visited a broad variety of people and places. However, there he found "almost as much diversity. . . [as he] had previously found in the opinions of the philosophers" (ibid., p. 99). This experience taught him "not to be too confident in any belief to which . . . [he] had been persuaded merely by example or custom" (ibid., p. 100).

One day, after still not having found truth in science and everyday life, Descartes resolved to withdraw as far as possible from his country and his books to be able to take himself as the subject of study, and to employ all the powers of his mind in choosing the path that would lead him to true knowledge (ibid., pp. 99-100). According to his own account, he succeeded thus in developing a method which enabled him to slowly but surely make progress with the search for truth without having the pretension that everyone should follow this method "for the right conduct of his reason"[1] (ibid., p. 95). This method embodies four rules he firmly resolved always to observe:

> The first was to accept nothing as true which I did not evidently know to be such, that is to say, scrupulously to avoid precipitance and prejudice, and in the judgments I passed to include nothing additional to what had presented itself to my mind so clearly and so distinctly that I could have no occasion for doubting it.
>
> The second, to divide each of the difficulties I examined into as many parts as may be required for its adequate solution.
>
> The third, to arrange my thoughts in order, beginning with things the simplest and easiest to know, so that I may then ascend little by little, as it were step by step, to the knowledge of the more complex, and, in doing so, to assign an order of thought even to those objects which are not of themselves in any such order of precedence.
>
> And the last, in all cases to make enumerations so complete, and reviews so general, that I should be assured of omitting nothing. (ibid., pp. 106-107)

By applying these rules, this method, to the problems of algebra, Descartes discovered that it afforded him the assurance to employ his reason in all matters as well as it was in his power to do.[2] Besides, he discovered that it enabled him to apprehend the objects of his research more and more precisely and distinctly (ibid., p. 109).

He also realized that, at twenty-three, he still was too young to apply his method to the philosophical foundation of sciences other than algebra. To prepare himself for this task, Descartes understood that he had to spend considerable time eradicating from his mind all the mistaken opinions he had hitherto been holding, to lay up a store of experiences to serve as matter for his reasonings, and to practice constantly his self-prescribed method so as to strengthen himself even more in the effective use of it (ibid., pp. 109-110).

Hoping to be in a better position to do this through intercourse with his fellow-men, Descartes left his stove-heated room (with the winter still not yet over), and roamed the world for nine years. When this period was over, he set himself to the task of meditating on the philosophical foundations of the sciences. To succeed, he thought he had to distance himself from all the places where he might meet acquaintances. So in 1628 he retreated to Holland.

The first meditation he made concerned the application of the first rule of his method, the "Cartesian doubt", to opinions, to the senses, to reasoning and to thoughts. He concluded that

> while . . . [he] was thus disposed to think that all was false, it was absolutely necessary that [the] 'I' who thus thought should be somewhat; and noting that this truth 'I think, therefore I am' was so steadfast and so assured that

the suppositions of the skeptics, . . . could not avail to shake it . . . [he] concluded that . . . [he] might accept it as the first principle of . . . philosophy. (ibid., pp. 118-119)

Next, on examining what this "I" was, he concluded that it was

a substance whose whole essence or nature consists entirely in thinking, and which, for its existence, has no need of place, and is not dependent on any material thing; so that this 'I'—that is to say, the soul by which I am what I am—is entirely distinct from the body, and is indeed more easy to know than the body, and would not itself cease to be all that it is, even should the body cease to exist. (ibid., p. 119)

He then proceeded to consider what is requisite to the truth and certainty of a proposition. Considering his "I think, therefore I am" which he knew to be true and certain, he noted that in this proposition nothing assured him of its truth save only that he saw very clearly that in order to think it is necessary to be. Therefore he judged that he could take as being a general rule

that the things we apprehend very clearly and distinctly are true—bearing in mind, however, that there is some difficulty in rightly determining which are those we apprehend distinctly. (ibid., pp. 119-120)

Reflecting in accordance with this rule on the fact that he doubted, and that consequently his being was not entirely perfect (seeing clearly that it is a greater perfection to know than to doubt), he inquired whence he had learned to think of something more perfect than he himself was; and he saw clearly that it must proceed from some nature that was indeed more perfect, that is, God (ibid., p. 120).

René Descartes is usually seen as the founder of modern philosophy. This is especially due to his method[3] and some of the conclusions, outlined in the foregoing summary of the first four of the six parts of *The Discourse on Method* (1637), which he reached through it: that is his "I think, therefore I am", his distinction between mind and body, and his certainty that things which are apprehended clearly and distinctly are true. Many of these conclusions are nowadays abandoned or viewed as highly doubtful. In this article it will be shown that this does not mean that the tale he tells of the way he discovered these principles has to meet the same fate, for it encloses insights which go beyond what is normally seen as typically Cartesian. That is why some important parts of it are reproduced here, as much as possible in Descartes' own words. In this way, it can and will be demonstrated that this tale can teach us things about method and truth that are relevant to present scientific practice.

The Application of Method

One of the first things Descartes discovered about his method was that it afforded him the assurance to employ his reason in all matters as well as it was in his power to do. Besides, he discovered that this enabled him to apprehend the objects of his research more and more precisely and distinctly (ibid., p. 109).

This passage is interesting, because Descartes is not saying that he uses his reason exactly as prescribed by the rules of his method.[4] No, he is suggesting that his method is a device to use his reason. This suggestion is strengthened when he states that he has to put his method frequently into practice to be able to make effective use of it.

With these remarks Descartes is referring to something every researcher knows: that the rules of a method can never be simply applied to answer every question in every situation, but that rules, questions and situations have to be interpreted, time and time again, to discover just how they have to be applied in a particular situation in order to answer a specific question.[5] In many cases this interpretation is not limited to a simple "translation" of method, question and situation. These often have to be supplemented or changed, totally or partly ignored, or replaced by other approaches, questions or situations. Moreover, this process does not (and should not) happen exclusively by reason. Doubting, understanding, imagining, confirming, wanting, presuming, feeling, intuiting, trying, etc. will often be just as important.

So, all in all, method appears as a more or less general idea about the way particular kinds of research have to be done, an idea that in the practice of research has to be again and again elaborated, supplemented, changed, partly ignored, and sometimes replaced.

To see the relevance of this statement, we have to realize that when we are speaking about a scientific method, we are usually referring to a number of prescriptions that tell us how to do research. But a method is more than that. It is also perhaps the most powerful rhetorical tool we know in science. By pointing to the scientific method that is used, findings are not only made acceptable but also, more often than not, accorded the status of truth.

The rhetorical power of a method is strengthened by the suggestion that it is the method and nothing but the method that has led to the findings concerned. From this point of view, researchers are seen as necessary nuisances who, unfortunately, are needed to put a method into practice. Even researchers collaborate in this mystification by disclaiming any responsibility for the results of that practice, and presenting them as inevitable consequences of the method that was used.[6]

The insight that a method is little more than a guideline which time and again must be adjusted or replaced in the concrete practice of research undermines the rhetorical power of method and restores the responsibility of the researcher. It reveals that researchers who refer merely to a general method as the one that was actually applied in their work, are really engaged in the task of trying to persuade others of the scientific (that is, truthful character) of their research. It also makes it evident that researchers who clarify how they had to extend, change, supplement, neglect or replace method in order to answer the research question in that situation—that is, who are taking responsibility for every aspect of their research—are the ones who are really scientific for the sole reason that their method, their decisions, accidents, coincidences, etc., can be truly inspected and assessed.

If we accept this insight, then the sacred character of method will be profaned, and this will inevitably result in a loss of its rhetorical power and thus, possibly, in a loss of power of the scientific enterprise as a whole. I say "possibly", because we do not have to assume that the standing of method cannot be supplanted by the standing of the researcher. In fact, it is part of the notion of "the excellent researcher" that we could come to understand that it is precisely the adjustment or replacement of method (and the rest), that gives researchers the opportunity to find and to show their excellence, and thus demonstrate the excellence of (or at least, a part of) the scientific enterprise.

The (Re)Creation of Method

Wanting to know how to distinguish true from false, Descartes discovered that an answer to his question could not be found in philosophy, in science or in everyday life. He only found things in dispute, knowledge erected on unstable foundations, and a diversity of opinions. That was why he decided to withdraw as far as possible from his country and his books—to be able to take himself as a subject of study, and to employ all the powers of his mind in choosing the path that would lead him to true knowledge, realizing that it was much more likely that the discovery of such a path would be made by one man than by all and sundry. In doing so, he succeeded in developing a method that enabled him to distinguish truth from falsehood.

Descartes is a good example of researchers who, because of the question they want to answer, and because of the inadequacy of the answers that have been given and the inadequacy of the ways by which those answers have been generated, rely on the totality of themselves—on their own potential, abilities and experiences—to (re)create a method which they can use to reach the desired answers. This relation to the totality of himself is, perhaps, the reason why Descartes could develop a method that, in its application, did not have to be restricted to some particular realm of human reality, excluding others. The rules of his method were such that they enabled him, for instance,

- to find metaphysical and empirical "truths", i.e. "truths" about "the existence of God and of the human soul" and–to be found in the fifth part of his *Discourse*–about "the heart's motion and of certain other difficulties pertaining to medicine" (ibid., p. 92)

- to discover the relationship between aspects of himself (and his situation) and some of these "truths"; for instance, between his "I think, therefore I am", the distinction of the soul from the body, his idea of truth, and the existence of God.

By contrast, the most important present-day methods do not seem to be founded on the totality of human being; in fact, they have been specially designed to exclude important parts of human reality from scientific research, and to accentuate other parts.

So, in his first book *The Logic of Scientific Discovery*, one of the founding fathers of modern thought on method, Sir Karl Popper, asks the question: "What constitutes scientific knowledge?" He asked this question when it was widely accepted that universal statements (that is, scientific knowledge) could be inferred from singular ones. For Popper "any conclusion drawn in this way may always turn out to be false: no matter how many instances of white swans we may have observed, this does not justify the conclusion that *all* swans are white" (Popper, 1968, p. 27). Popper adds to this criticism of the "inductive method" by arguing that it also

> does not provide a suitable 'criterion of demarcation'. . . between the empirical sciences on the one hand, and mathematics and logic as well as 'metaphysical' systems on the other. (ibid., p. 34)

Because if, as the inductivists maintain, elementary statements of experience are the criterion for determining whether a concept or a statement is scientific[al], the natural sciences are not scientific "for sciential laws . . . cannot be logically reduced to elementary statements of experience" (ibid., p. 36).

Against this Popper advocates a deductive method of testing: "the view that a hypothesis can only be empirically tested–and only after it has been advanced" (ibid., p. 30). How hypotheses or, more generally, theories have been conceived is, in his view, irrelevant (ibid., pp. 31-32); what is relevant is to test theories, and select them according to the results of tests. The latter means, among other things, to deduce predictions from the theory–especially those which are easily testable or applicable, which are not derivable from current theory, or, better, which the theory contradicts–and to compare them with the results of practical applications and experiments. The result can be verification (and that means that for the time being the theory has passed the test), or falsification, which means that the theory has been falsified indeed (ibid., p. 33).

Because verification of a prediction does not mean verification of the theory from which that prediction is deduced, theories are never empirically verifiable (ibid., p. 40). That is why, according to Popper, it is not the possibility of verification, but only that of falsification, which can serve as a demarcation criterion, that is, "it must be possible for an empirical scientific system to be refuted by experience" (ibid., p. 41).

Nowadays, more and more criticism is directed against methods which:

- exclude the more metaphysical from the empirical part of human reality

- accentuate only the part of empirical reality that can be used and/or researched (which, consequently, reflects on the way society is organized)

- fail to express the interrelatedness of the (situation of the) researcher, his or her observations, and the situation of that which has been observed.

Two important examples of this kind of criticism are those of Hans-Georg Gadamer and Paul Feyerabend.

Gadamer's objection to (his idea of) the present-day scientific method is that not only does it fail to answer many religious, philosophical and existential questions but it also marks those questions as meaningless.[7] This is the case, says Gadamer, because in science only those phenomena which fit in with its method of discovering and verifying of truth have meaning (Gadamer, 1986, p. 45). In this way, "it is only what is typical and regular that is taken account of" (Gadamer, 1988, p. 322). According to Gadamer, it is also the case that, because of the scientific demand that a statement can only be said to be true after it has been verified (by comparing it to objective reality), truth has been replaced by certainty. This limitation of knowledge to that which can be verified finds, he says, its fulfillment in reproduction, that is, imitation. That is why Gadamer considers science, and method in particular, to be the cause of the development of planning and technology, and thus of the problems of our civilization (Gadamer, 1986, p. 48).

This view on method has led Gadamer to investigate its foundation: understanding. Following Heidegger, Gadamer sees understanding not as a methodological concept but "as the original character of the being of human life itself" (Gadamer, 1988, p. 230). This means that understanding and what is understood are not essentially the same, "but draws its significance from the particular nature of the mode of being that is common to both of them . . . the mode of being of historicalness" (ibid., p. 232). This is why understanding

neither involves 'neutrality' in the matter of the object nor the extinction of one's self, but the conscious assimilation of one's own foremeanings and prejudices. The important thing is to be aware of one's own bias, so that the . . . [object] may present itself in all its newness and thus be able to assert its own truth against one's own fore-meanings. (ibid., p. 238)

And it is because "history does not belong to us, but we belong to it" that self-awareness of our own bias and prejudices, far more than that of our judgments, constitutes awareness of the historical reality of our being (ibid., p. 245). It is within this historical consciousness that, for instance, religious, philosophical and existential phenomena can assert their own truth.

Feyerabend's objections to the scientific method are, generally speaking, identical to those of Gadamer. Like Gadamer, he emphasizes the dominant role of science, in particular method, in the organization of society (Feyerabend, 1976, p. 384), and the limited applicability and poor results of the scientific method. More particularly, Feyerabend compares the poorness of scientific results with the richness of reality. Speaking about history, Feyerabend for instance rhetorically asks:

> Are we really to believe that the naive and simple-minded rules which methodologists take as their guide are capable of accounting for such a 'maze of interactions'? (Feyerabend, 1978, pp. 17-18)

And two pages further down:

> Who can guarantee that they [that is, epistemological prescriptions] are the best way to discover, not just a few isolated 'facts', but also some deep-lying secrets of nature? (ibid., p. 20)

These observations have led Feyerabend to the view that:

> To those who look at the rich material provided by history, and who are not intent on impoverishing it in order to please their lower instincts, their craving for intellectual security in the form of clarity, precision, 'objectivity', 'truth', it will become clear that there is only one principle that can be defended under **all** circumstances and in all stages of human development. It is the principle: anything goes. (ibid., pp. 27-28)

According to Feyerabend, "anything goes" means the development of theories or facts that deviate more or less from existing, accepted and corroborated theories and facts, and, with the help of other ideas, the attempt to improve them so that they can compete with accepted ones (ibid., pp. 29-30). "Knowledge so conceived," says Feyerabend,

> is not a series of self-consistent theories that converges towards an ideal view, it is not a gradual approach to the truth. It is rather an ever increasing ocean of mutually incompatible (and perhaps even incommensurable) alternatives, each single theory, each fairy tale, each myth, that is part of the collection forcing the others into greater articulation and all of them

contributing, via the process of competition, to the development of consciousness. Nothing is ever settled, no view can ever be omitted from a comprehensive account. (ibid., p. 30)

Gadamer and Feyerabend's criticism of modern, scientific method can be seen as a criticism of the restrictions this method imposes upon the possibility of researchers finding and showing their excellence by (re)creating method.

In all the—necessarily very incomplete—examples given above, the different philosophers (Descartes, Popper, Gadamer and Feyerabend) act as excellent researchers. They have formulated a question, they criticize the established answers (or the lack of them) and the established approaches that have generated these answers (or have failed to generate them). This process of question and criticism results in the construction of a new approach that has the pretension not to entail the perceived problems and to be able to answer the question concerned. In all cases, question and criticism are such that they present a completely different perspective on the established answers or approaches, and the new approach which is consequently created is highly original, able to yield new phenomena, or shed a new light on familiar phenomena.

But it must also be said that, although acting as an excellent researcher, in one of these examples the philosopher concerned is using his question, criticism and new approach to limit the possibilities of scientific research. Popper's demarcation criterion (and that of the logical positivists he is criticizing) and the resulting method aim at making it impossible for science to generate or to test theories that are not refutable by empirical reality.

The consequences for researchers who, in learning and using this method, are trying to do excellent research are devastating. Gadamer suggests that researchers who implement Popper's approach are not doing anything better than blindly following the rules of method to give the impression of having done scientific work (Gadamer, 1986, p. 50), while Feyerabend informs us further what "blindly following the rules" actually means. According to him, it implies a present-day scientific education that is simplifying its students by separating the research domain from the rest of history and giving it a "logic" of its own. The training in such a "logic" then "conditions those working in the domain; it makes their actions more uniform and it freezes large parts of the historical process as well" (Feyerabend, 1978, p. 19). This education entails the inhibiting of the student's intuitions, religion or metaphysics, sense of humor, imagination and language. "This is," adds Feyerabend, "reflected in the nature of the scientific 'facts' which are experienced as being independent of opinion, belief, and cultural background" (ibid., p. 19).

In the remaining three examples—those of Descartes, Gadamer and Feyerabend—important parts of human reality are not excluded. This means that researchers using (and thus recreating) these kinds of approach are not

frustrated but are, on the contrary, stimulated in relying on their own—
potential—abilities and experiences through which they have the real possibility
of finding and showing their excellence.

Inherent to this view of research is its methodical perspectivism. Different
methods are seen as answering different questions and, in so doing, yielding
different phenomena or perspectives on phenomena; and no method is, in this
respect, seen as better than any other.[8]

This does not alter the fact that methods have fallen into disrepute and
have been embraced because of the questions asked, the approaches taken, and
the answers given. And behind and beyond the evaluation of these characteristics there has always been an evaluation of the idea of truth that the methodical
approach concerned is employing. The examples of the criticism of Popper
against the logical positivists, and of that of Gadamer and Feyerabend against
the modern scientific method give some inkling of those evaluations.

Because of the connection between method and truth, the idea of truth
is, as will be seen, also an important aspect of excellent research.

Truth

According to the first rule of Descartes' method, we must not accept
anything as true if we are not absolutely sure that it is so. And we only know it
is true when we have scrupulously avoided precipitation and prejudice and have
not added anything to what has so clearly and distinctly been presented to us
that we could not doubt it. It is obvious that Descartes is convinced that there
is something like the truth, and that this truth, under certain conditions, can be
known. From his writings, it is also obvious that there is only one truth about
anything, and that through method(s), it is the task of philosophy and science
to discover that truth.[9]

Nowadays there are still many philosophers and scientists who endorse
Descartes' opinions about truth. The ideas of such an influential thinker as
Popper are an example. Like Descartes, he assumes that there is only one truth
and that it is the task of science to search for it.[10] According to him "it is only
with respect to this aim, that we can say that though we are fallible, we hope to
learn from our mistakes" (Popper, 1989, p. 229).

But although Popper, like Descartes, thinks that it will be possible to
discover the truth, he maintains, contrary to Descartes, that we never can be sure
that we have discovered it (Popper, 1979, p. 30). This opinion is a consequence
of his falsification principle, and of the fact that Popper sees truth as a statement
or an assertion that corresponds to the facts (Popper, 1989, p. 224) and not "as
a special kind of mental state, or as a disposition, or as a special kind of belief"
(ibid., p. 225). "What we should do," Popper suggests,

is to give up the idea of ultimate sources of knowledge, and admit that all knowledge is human; that it is mixed with our errors, our prejudices, our dreams, and our hopes; that all we can do is to grope for truth even though it be beyond our reach. . . . [If we admit this], we can retain that truth is beyond human authority. And we must retain it. For without this idea there can be no objective standards of inquiry; no criticism of our conjectures; no groping for the unknown; no quest for knowledge. (ibid., p. 30)

This means that for Popper there cannot be a method to establish whether we have discovered the truth. The only thing we can do is "to search for . . . [the truth of an assertion] by persistently searching for our errors; by indefatigable rational criticism, and self-criticism" (ibid., p. 16). In this way method can only help us to approach nearer and nearer to the truth (Popper, 1979, pp. 47-60).

The observations presented in the previous two sections of this paper result in a different idea of truth than that advocated by Descartes and Popper. We have seen that to answer a question in a certain situation by using a specific method, we have to alter or to adjust, one to the other, the question, the method and the situation, to the best of our abilities and experiences. The inevitable contingency of this practice makes it impossible to assume that the result of research can be something like "The Truth". This does not mean that the result cannot be excellent. Of course it can. That is the argument of this paper. But if it is excellent, it is excellent due to the special combination of question, method, situation and researcher.

But does this mean that we have to abandon the idea of truth altogether? In telling his tale, Descartes shows the long way he had to go to develop a method which, after a nine-year practice of eradicating from his mind all the mistaken opinions he had hitherto been holding, of laying up a store of experiences to serve as matter for his reasonings, and of practicing this method to strengthen himself in using it effectively, would enable him to find the truth. Only after having obtained such a background could Descartes convince himself and others that the application of his method was yielding nothing but truths.

This story teaches us, first and foremost, to be aware of our own shortcomings and abilities, to work hard to overcome these shortcomings as far as possible, to extend our abilities, and to take our time. Second, it teaches us that researchers must not try to bite off more than they can chew. So the researcher's shortcomings and abilities have also to be part of the adjustment of question, approach and research question to one another. In this way researchers really do have the possibility to be excellent. Third, it teaches us that if, in their work, researchers are aware of their relationship with the subject of their research,[11] and if they are certain, to the best of their knowledge, ability and experience, that they have properly collected and reviewed all the relevant information, there will come a time when they—in an attempt to organize their knowledge, insights, intuitions etc. into a meaningful unity—are convinced that they have found the truth. This is a sign of excellence. But simultaneously they must—on a more cognitive level—realize that this truth is analogic to their perspective. In this respect, Popper is right in stressing that all knowledge is human. Descartes' mistake was that he did not realize this.

Contrary to both Descartes and Popper, the aforementioned means that the idea of "The Truth" is abandoned and replaced by the experience of truth by the researcher. This has important consequences.

According to philosophers such as Popper, the idea of "The Truth" offers a criterion that is elevated beyond all kinds of individual, associational and communal interests, making it possible to objectively criticize scientific activities and results. In this respect, truth is something that exists beyond ourselves, and which applies to all times and situations.

It has to be understood that behind this idea of truth is hidden a philosophy of life in which the absoluteness of God, the super-being, has been replaced by—or overlaps with—the absoluteness of truth. In this philosophy some men can—under certain conditions, that is, by method—gain access to that absoluteness or can approach it. Those men are on top of the earthly hierarchy, and the place of the rest of the world is determined by the degree with which they resemble those men.[12] This philosophy implies that there are no limits set in the search for truth. Seekers of the truth see this earthly existence as nothing more than a subjective, ever changing shadow of that truth, as a necessary starting point on the way to truth. To take into account the possible negative consequences of (the results of) this quest is, in this philosophy, considered to be nothing more than a nuisance inhibiting scientific progress.

In this way, the philosophy of absolute truth is one of the causes of the problems induced, directly or indirectly, by science.

Bringing truth (and responsibility) back to the experience of the individual researcher prevents such consequences and provides a better point of departure in creating a better world.

Conclusion

Methods fall into disrepute and others, for the time being, are embraced. Each new method opens up new phenomena and new perspectives on familiar ones—on humans, on society, on existence, on being, etc.—and thus new possibilities for action in science as well as in society. But new phenomena and perspectives necessarily entail one-sidedness and excessiveness. So after a time of exuberance about the new possibilities, there will inevitably come a time of doubt, resistance, accusations and boredom with what has become standard in a certain period.

Nowadays we are living in such a time. The use of the current scientific standard did not result in the world becoming a better place in every way. It has solved some problems, it has created others, but it has not been able to touch the growing severity of most of them.

This is part of the reason for Gadamer's attack on the present-day scientific method as not being able to answer many religious, philosophical and existential questions; as replacing truth by certainty; and as leading to planning and technology and thus to the problems of our civilization. It also partly explains Feyerabend's ridiculing of scientific method as not being able to discover more than just a few isolated "facts" that do not in the least represent the richness of reality.

The idea of the excellent researcher endorses the criticism of Gadamer and Feyerabend. It endorses also some aspects of the new approaches they have each been formulating: their emphasis on an approach that appeals to the totality of the researcher and, consequently, to the totality of human reality, and their abandoning of the philosophy of absolute truth. Where the idea of the excellent researcher differs from those of Gadamer and Feyerabend is that it does not imply a preference for any particular approach. Different methods are seen as answering different questions, and consequently yielding different phenomena or perspectives on phenomena. In this respect, no method is seen as being better than any other. This realization makes it possible to try to answer the important questions of today by developing, if necessary, new methodologies which tackle them.

Also different from Gadamer and Feyerabend is the emphasis on the responsibility of researchers: first, for the conducting of their research, that is, for the adjustment or replacement of question, method and situation, and for the dealing with their shortcomings and abilities; and second, for the results of their research, for the genuineness of their conviction of having found the truth (for only this gives them the moral right to try to be as persuasive as possible in order to convince others of the truth they have found), for the acceptance of these findings by others (by their rhetorical power), and thus for both the negative and positive consequences of the reality they have been instigating. In this respect, researchers have to realize the interconnectedness of everybody and everything. They have to realize that every move, every thought, every feeling has consequences for the animate and inanimate,[13] and that in this respect research is a powerful means to influence others. Only by having love and respect for themselves and others are they really able to take responsibility for their own deeds.

Notes

1. Reason, or good sense is, according to Descartes, "the power of judging well and of distinguishing between the true and the false" (Descartes, 1958, p. 93).

2. I am deviating here from the English translation of Descartes' text. "But what pleased me most in this method I had discovered was that it afforded me assurance that in all matters I should be employing my reason" is in my opinion an incorrect translation of "Mais ce qui me contenait le plus de cette methode etait que, par elle, j'etais assure d'user en tout de ma raison" (Descartes, 1966, p. 49).

3. And, not discussed here, to his use of expressing "proportions" by numbers or letters (Descartes, 1958, p. 108), that is, his use of mathematics.

4. a) See also his assertion that he was taking care, in a general manner, to be all the time conducting his thoughts in conformity with the rules of his method (Descartes, 1958, p. 116).

b) How much Descartes' application of the rules of his method in concrete situations is in agreement with his "firm and unswerving resolve never in a single instance to fail in observing them" (ibid., p. 106), is anybody's guess.

5. See, for instance, Lynch, Livingston and Garfinkel (1983, pp. 207-208).

6. That does not alter the fact that researchers are seen as responsible for the way they present their results, for the display of their rhetorical power.

7. Note that this observation cannot be an attack on Popper's demarcation criterion. This criterion does not imply that all kinds of metaphysical theories (and questions) are seen as meaningless. According to Popper, falsifiability separates the empirical from the non-empirical and not the meaningful from the meaningless (Popper, 1968, p. 40, note 3). But Gadamer's attack could be rightly directed to the purpose of that demarcation criterion: to place important metaphysical questions outside empirical science.

8. This, of course, does not exclude the possibility that one method is better than another in answering the same question.

9. Note, for instance, his remark that "on each particular issue there is but one true solution, and that whoever finds it knows all that can be known regarding it" (Descartes, 1958, p. 109).

10. This opinion was only formulated by Popper after he discovered Tarski's idea of "truth as correspondence with the facts" (Popper, 1968, p. 274, note 1).

11. In qualitative research, for example, the researchers' relationship with what they are researching is expressed by what I have called "trifurcate openness". This means that a researcher has to be open to three sides: to the research situation, to the research, and to oneself. Openness to the research situation means awareness of the way in which this situation reveals and conceals itself to the behavior and appearance of the researcher, and the way this situation invites and discourages him or her. Openness to the research means awareness of the obligations of that research: one must, for instance, observe and/ or record specific aspects of the research setting, ask certain questions, and to a certain extent control the situation. Openness to oneself means that researchers are aware of themselves in the research situation, and their presuppositions, prejudices, feelings etc. about that situation; and of the changes in their behavior, appearance, presuppositions, prejudices etc., because of what they are experiencing during and in that situation (Maso, 1992).

12. This philosophy is directly connected to the unholy thinking in higher and lower, in truth and false, in eternal and temporal, and in science and society.

13. See, for instance, Whitehead (1934) stating: "Any local agitation shakes the whole universe. The distant effects are minute, but they are there. . . . There is no possibility of a detached, self-contained existence" (ibid., p. 181).

References

R. Descartes, "Discourse on method: Of rightly conducting the reason and of seeking for truth in the sciences" (1637), in *Descartes: Philosophical Writings,* The Modern Library, 1958, pp. 91-144.

R. Descartes, "Discours de la methode: Pour bien conduire sa raison et chercher la verite dans les sciences" (1637) in R. Descartes, *Discours de la Methode,* Garnier-Flammarion, 1966, pp. 31-95.

P. Feyerabend, *Against Method: Outline of an Anarchistic Theory of Knowledge* (1975), Verso, 1978.

P. Feyerabend, "Logic, literacy, and professor Gellner", *The British Journal for the Philosophy of Science* 27, 1976, pp. 381–391.

H. G. Gadamer, "Was ist Wahrheit?" (1957) in H. -G. Gadamer, *Hermeneutik II. Wahrheit und Methode. Gesammelte Werke,* 2, J.C.B. Mohr, 1986.

H. G. Gadamer, *Truth and Method* (1960), Sheed and Ward, 1988.

M. E. Lynch, E. Livingston and H. Garfinkel, "Temporal order in laboratory work" in *Science Observed: Perspectives on the Social Study of Science,* edited by K. D. Knorr-Cetina and M. Mulkay, Sage, 1983.

I. Maso, "The phenomenological chameleon", *Proceedings of the Science and Vision Conference,* 1992.

K. R. Popper, *The Logic of Scientific Discovery* (1959), Harper & Row, 1968.

K. R. Popper, *Conjectures and Refutations: The Growth of Scientific Knowledge* (1963), Routledge, 1989.

K. R. Popper, *Objective Knowledge: An Evolutionary Approach* (1972), Clarendon Press, 1979.

A. N. Whitehead, *Nature and Life,* Cambridge, 1934.

Holding Course Amid Shifting Paradigms

by Roger W. Sperry

Ionce suggested that the 1980s might well be called "the decade of emerging new paradigms". This semi-serious assessment refers to the explosive outburst during this period of new worldviews, new "visions of reality", "new sciences" (of mind, of life, of qualities, wholeness ...), new epistemologies, ontologies and what not. Beyond a growing sense that we are in a period of fundamental ideologic change, we yet lack any consensus regarding the exact nature of what this change is, or its cause, meaning, or where it may be leading. It is in the context of this unprecedented upsurge in novel world outlooks and the associated flux in shifting and emerging paradigms that I try to support a case for holding firm to a scientific view of reality that we already have—specifically, the view spawned some 20 years ago in the widely documented, so-called cognitive, consciousness or mentalist revolution of the 1970s (Baars, 1986, Dember, 1974, Gardner, 1985, Matson, 1971, Palermo, 1971, Sperry, 1987).

Following an era of some two centuries or more of "scientific materialism", the recent turnabout in the conception and treatment of the conscious mind has vastly transformed previous scientific descriptions of ourselves and the world. A changed way of thinking, explaining, and understanding is instilled. New principles of cognitive and emergent causation supersede the older atomism, mechanism and value-empty determinism of prior physicalist views, and affirm human values to be today the most strategically powerful driving force governing the course of world events—the key to our global predicament and its solution.

Described as "a virtual Copernican Revolution" (Manicas and Secord, 1983) and a "reenchantment of science" (Griffin, 1988), among other things, the new outlook most assuredly calls now for a global mind change, a thoroughgoing shift to a new value-belief system, new transcendent guidelines, life goals,

97

and new ways of thinking and living. Upholding a changed scientific interpretation of the creative forces that made and move the universe, it yields a changed set of answers to some of humanity's deepest questions. Intrinsic evolutionary directives provide an ultimate moral-spiritual basis for environmentalism and wilderness values, population balance, protecting the rights and welfare of future generations, and for other measures which would serve to help insure a high-quality, sustainable world with an ever-evolving future. Implemented worldwide (through the United Nations, for example), the resulting type of global mind change would go far to rectify today's self-destructive trends and to preserve and enhance the evolving quality of the biosphere.

Even so, examination of the underlying conceptual developments behind this sweeping paradigm turnaround does not, I believe, encourage hope for a continuing further shift in wished-for directions that might, for example, provide some sort of supernatural transcendence or afterlife for the conscious self. In other words, I think today's new trends toward "wholeness", "subjectivity", "qualities", and so on, do not presage a further degree of general loosening or change in the conceptual foundations of mainstream science—nor imply either that science ought hereon to be viewed as "enculturated" after some two centuries of common-sense understanding that if there is any enterprise in the human venture that stands out as being relatively free of cultural or other conceptual bias, it is science.

At least that is the position I try to support and recently expressed as follows:

> . . . our new acceptance in science of consciousness and subjectivity, the mental and cognitive, or spiritual does not—as frequently inferred—open the doors of science to the supernatural, the mystical, the paranormal, the occult, the otherworldly—nor, in short, to any form of unembodied mind or spirit. The strength and promise of the new macromental outlook is in just the opposite, that is, in taking our ultimate guideline beliefs, and resultant social values out of the realm of the supernatural and otherworldly uncertainties and grounding them in a more realistic realm of knowledge and truth, consistent with science and empiric verification. (Sperry, 1991a, p. 255)

This being an area, however, where final answers still lie far beyond us, my aim in what follows is simply to explain a possible analytic interpretation of the recent outburst of new approaches in science and its conceptual foundations along with some supporting considerations—not with the idea that these lead to any final conclusion, but merely in hope that these factors and the related arguments may be better recognized and taken into account in further appraisals of the many pros and cons.

Introductory Resumé

In brief overview, the principal reason I think the current wave of paradigm shifts and new thinking in science is not apt to continue into a further stage of a more extreme brand of metaphysical reality is that most of these recent trends can be traced to, and appear to be best viewed as outcomes of the consciousness revolution that immediately preceded them. If this is so, they are then dependent upon an interactionist model of the mind-brain relation which would logically rule out the existence or transmission of conscious experience in a disembodied state. More specifically, our new treatment of the contents of subjective experience established by the 1970s' cognitive revolution is based upon the idea that conscious mental states are emergent properties of brain processes. As such, any separate existence apart from the living functioning brain, of which they are dynamic properties, would seem to be a logical impossibility—as would also their manifestation, expression, or transmission in phenomena such as telepathy, reincarnation, channeling, clairvoyance, psychokinesis, and such like.

In this view, science, during the past two and a half decades, has already undergone a major corrective transformation in its conceptual foundations. The result, as I see it, places basic science and its conceptual approach in a more complete, coherent and stable state today than was the case with its preceding reductive physicalism or materialism, which itself has been a paradigm of unquestioned spectacular success in many ways, and appeared to be irrefutable for more than two centuries.

Dependence Upon Special Interpretation

My case for holding to, and working with, the newly defined scientific paradigm that we already have is based on a particular analysis and interpretation of both the cognitive revolution and also the current boom in emerging new paradigms. It is an interpretation that is definitely open to correction, with some half dozen or so competing alternative accounts currently being proposed for these same worldview developments. What follows, therefore, becomes in large part an attempt to support and justify this special interpretation in the light of various contested alternatives. In order to judge its relative credibility, it is essential that we start from an accurate understanding, which in the past has not always been easy. The following account, spelled out in greater detail than elsewhere and expressed largely in nonspecialist terminology, may well appear to some readers to be overly simple and often redundant. The key concepts, however, though quite straightforward and obvious once they have been grasped, nevertheless do not fit into the traditional philosophic dichotomies with which we are familiar and, for this and related reasons, already have a long history of misinterpretation (see Natsoulas, 1987, Ripley, 1984, Sperry, 1991b, 1992).

In a time when it has become common to observe that there are almost as many theories of consciousness as people writing on the subject, it is important to note, first, that the interpretation defended here is not just another individual opinion. Rather it represents the mainstream working conceptual framework, over the past twenty years, for a whole discipline of science, that which specializes in mind and behavior. We thus deal not so much with philosophic opinion as with the factual recorded history of a paradigm shift. The leading question is not whether mentalism or materialism may ultimately be correct, or reductionism or holism and so on, though these and related concerns are directly involved. Primarily, however, the question is one of factual historical record, "What happened in psychology to cause the 1970s' shift from behaviorism to mentalism or cognitivism?"

The answer I arrive at will attribute the shift toward cognitivism—and also, therefore, the present-day trends toward "wholeness", irreducibility and subjectivity—to conceptual developments in the mind-brain, behavioral and cognitive sciences. It is an answer that largely by-passes the "new physics", Bell's theorem and "nonlocality" (see Klotz, 1988), and also ecologic interconnectedness, Whiteheadian "process" philosophy, and various other things to which these same trends have also been ascribed. This includes general systems theory, information theory, philosophic realism, structuralism, computer science, and nonlinear dynamics, to mention just some of the other alleged sources. Many of these alternatives undoubtedly helped contribute to today's outlook in various secondary, supportive, reinforcing, and/or sociologic roles. In my analysis, however, the critical key factor was the overthrow of the determinist logic of traditional reductive physicalism with its centuries-old reasoning that formerly had been taken to rule out any real functional or causal role for the mind or consciousness.

I assume throughout that it is now an agreed fact of history that behavioral science in the 1970s underwent a major paradigm shift in which long-dominant behaviorist doctrine denouncing mentalistic explanations gave way to a new cognitivism, and that this involved a diametric turnabout in the explanatory status of conscious mental constructs. Conscious awareness and all contents of subjective experience had previously been banned from the explanations of science on the grounds that, in addition to formidable methodologic difficulties, the materialist paradigm already provided a complete, closed, and coherent system. In theory and in principle, materialist doctrine left no place for conscious or mental forces, and it had absolutely no need or use for them. Their inclusion, furthermore, would seemingly have to violate the conservation of energy and other established laws. "Mental states cannot interact with physical states", or "Mind does not move matter" was the long-accepted verdict, and "No physical action waits on anything but another physical action." Nevertheless, in the early 1970s after a half century of strict behaviorist renunciation, conscious subjective states quite suddenly, "almost explosively" (Pylyshyn, 1973), gained acceptance in mainstream behavioral science as causally interactive agents, legitimate for scientific explanation of conscious behavior and its evolution (Baars, 1986, Dember, 1974, Gardner, 1985, Matson, 1971, Palermo, 1971, Sperry, 1987). In my interpretation the achievement of this long-delayed breakthrough was finally effected only through recourse to a different form of causal determinism. In other words, it was achieved only by making a change in the basic ground rules of scientific explanation.

A Modified Form of Causal Determinism

In the traditional atomistic or "microdeterministic" view of science, everything is determined from below upward following the course of evolution. In this view, brain states determine mental states, but not vice versa. In the new view, however, things are determined reciprocally, not only from lower levels upward, but also from above downward. In the reciprocal "two-way" or bidirectional model, a molecule, for example, rather than being governed solely by its atomic make-up, becomes also the "master of its inner atoms" and electrons. In chemical interactions the space-time course of its atomic components is determined by the overall configurational properties of the molecule as a whole, as well as the other way around (Sperry, 1964). This is illustrated, for example, in the often very different chemical properties of mirror image forms of the same molecule. In reference to brain function

> the simpler electric, atomic, molecular, and cellular forces and laws, though still present and operating, have been superseded by the configurational forces of higher-level mechanisms. . . . these include the powers of perception, cognition, reason, judgment, and the like, the operational, causal effects and forces of which are equally or more potent in brain dynamics than are the outclassed inner chemical forces. (Sperry, 1964, p. 20)

Thus the traditional one-way "bottom-up" view, based in a heretofore supposedly closed, complete scheme for describing the entire natural order including brains, was perceived in the new outlook to have a flaw or inadequacy in its one-way logic that omitted the downward control. A shortcoming was perceived that left an opening by which conscious subjective experience might be included in a causal interactive role (Popper, 1972, Sperry, 1965).

By combining the old "bottom-up" atomistic determinism with an added concept of "top-down emergent determinism", a way was found at long last by which subjective causality might be included within the classic objective account of science. Moreover, the new bidirectional approach made this possible without any loss in the many proven benefits of the conventional one-way approach (except, of course, for former assumptions that materialist determinism had been a logically airtight and complete system). In the reformed scheme, the microdeterminist chains of causation already covered in the brain-behavioral and other sciences need not be disrupted, intervened or disposed of. Mostly they are maintained in their existing form and simply surrounded, enveloped, or "supervened" by higher-level cerebral systems. The resultant downward causal effects are evidenced not in a reordering of events within the local details of the brain process, but in the way the lower-level components are ordered relative to things outside the given cerebral process.

The bidirectional emergent interaction model places emergent properties in a stronger role. Their irreducibility is demonstrated, as is their downward control over lower-level components. Their evolution as novel causal entities is held to introduce into the cosmos (and to science) new control phenomena and forces in their own form and in their own right. Inclusion of both the bottom-up plus the top-down type of inter-level determinism is claimed to be necessary in order to obtain a complete picture of (causal) reality. This double-way, reciprocal form of causal determinism applies not only within the brain, but throughout nature to emergent properties in general. It follows accordingly that traditional "scientific materialism" as applied throughout the sciences has been in error all along. For, in its exclusive atomistic, reductive physicalist approach, it has logically excluded not only mental but also, in principle, all autonomous macro emergent or holistic causation. Instead, it has made these all reducible to the elemental forces of physics and eventually, in principle, to an even more elemental "theory of everything".

For neuroscience, acceptance of mental causation in the above form does not imply any alterations within the already described chains of neuronal causation—as did, for example, trying to insert conscious influences through "quantum jump" effects at synaptic junctions between brain cells, attempted unsuccessfully in the past by Arthur Compton, John Eccles (1953, 1992), and many others. Instead, consciousness is inserted within higher (cognitive) domains of brain processing, which are as yet neither described nor understood (Sperry, 1965). Mental states, as they successively emerge, for example in a train of thought, are conceived to interact functionally, as emergent wholes, at their own cognitive level in a progression governed by its own special mental dynamics. These higher-level yet-to-be-discovered dynamics of mental progression are presumed to be determined by emergent network properties interacting as irreducible entities, and as subjectively experienced. The dynamics and laws for causal progression at the mental or cognitive level are thus quite different from those in the lower-level neurophysiology.

Such a sequence of higher-level cognitive dynamics exerts concomitant downward control over its neurocellular, molecular, atomic, subatomic and other embedded and enveloped constituents by programming their schedule and course of activation—again, as seen from outside the system and thus without disrupting the laws of microchain causation within these embedded lower-level components. At the same time, as traditionally assumed, the higher-level mental dynamics are also reciprocally determined by, and dependent upon, their lower-level neurocellular, biophysical, chemical, and other components. We are not yet at this date in a position to visualize in detailed or concrete form just how the emergent cognitive patterns might operate as functional wholes in neural network dynamics. That they nevertheless do, however, is strongly indicated in several lines of evidence, such as that from gestalt psychology. What we subjectively perceive, feel or remember, as demonstrated in early gestalt studies, can be shown to depend on the gestalt, pattern or configuration of the neurocellular elements involved, as much as and, in some contexts, more than it depends on which particular neural elements carry the pattern. Subjective meaning is thought to be acquired on the so-called "functionalist" principles of modern computational philosophy (Fodor, 1981, Gardner, 1985), involving interaction of these brain-process gestalts with one another as wholes, and also with the ongoing contextual matrix of network dynamics (Sperry, 1952)—just as a word may acquire different meanings in different sentences and contexts.

Our current "macromental" model of causal determinism is actually a micro plus macro plus mental model, in which emphasis is given to the new macro and mental features. The mental is a special instance of the macro—but sufficiently special to warrant separate mention. In this "double-way" bi-directional model, neither of the reciprocal upward and downward systems of "causal" control are of the common single-level, sequential type of causation ordinarily thought of as a cause-effect sequence. Both the upward and downward control systems are exerted continuously and concomitantly over time during a given sequence of cognitive processing. It is important to note further that these inter-level upward and downward forms of determinism are not symmetric, but quite different in kind. Thus the two counter-flow control systems do not collide, conflict, or in any way counteract each other.

As indicated above, a relativity factor also is involved. The programming influence of the mental on the lower-level constituents is not evident from within the given cognitive brain process itself, where the known laws of neuroscience still apply. Relative to the rest of the organism and the outside world, however, the programming of the constituent neurocellular activation is determined also, and more prominently, by the surround of higher-level cognitive dynamics, with the higher-level process carrying the lower-level elements. This idea has been simply demonstrated in what has been called "the rolling wheel analogy", in which it can been seen that a wheel rolling downhill carries along its embedded molecules and atoms "regardless of whether the individual molecules and atoms happen to like it or not" (Sperry, 1969). Each individual molecule is governed in the usual physiochemical manner relative to neighboring events within the wheel. Relative to the rest of the world, however, the behavior of the molecule is determined more prominently by the macro properties of the wheel as a whole. More than a mere shift in frame of reference (Vandervert, 1991), the inclusion of both frames of reference for describing causation takes us from the former incomplete reductionist paradigm to the more complete emergent interactionist, neomental, or "macromental" position.

The new model involves an added emphasis on the space-time or pattern factors in causation as opposed to the material, physical factors. The space-time patterning of component entities, in and of itself, is endowed with causal efficacy. The collective spatiotemporal arrangement of physical masses, particles, forces, fields, and so on becomes in itself causal, with effects not accountable for in terms of the lower-level laws. In any but perhaps the most ultra simple cases, these space-time interrelations are far too complex (over and above those of the three-body problem) to be explainable by, or reducible to, existing laws for lower-level interaction. These critical space-time factors are thus lost in attempts to reduce lawful explanations at a given level into laws that apply to the lower-level components. In contradiction to continuing contentions that the causal paradigm of classical Newtonian physics allows no room for consciousness (for example, Stapp, 1991, Popper, 1972) the above described solution for inserting the causal influence of mental states in brain function is achieved within the general Newtonian framework.

The Turning Point: Relevant Chronology

To more precisely distinguish the interpretation supported here, it will help, first, to further extend the historical background beyond the disciplinary level of mainstream doctrine to include that of individual personal precursor views that appeared in the decade prior to the 1970s' turnaround in mainstream psychology. Second, we need also to recognize that the closely involved reductionist-holist debate has an extremely long history, traced by some philosophers back to Aristotle and Democritus. This debate is still going strong today. The issues therefore are by no means simple, or easily settled. For the historical background, there is thus good reason to focus first of all not on any particular individual arguments but on the prevailing majority view and its fluctuations in recent decades.

Following a prolonged period in which scientific reductionism and "logical positivism" had been in favor, the majority view in the 1920s underwent a strong swing toward recognition of emergence and holism, particularly in writings on emergent evolution (such as Morgan, 1923, Ritter, 1919, Smuts, 1926). By the 1940s and '50s, however, emergent-holist theory again was gradually losing ground to reductionism and by the early 1960s had sunk to an extreme low, overwhelmed by a strong pervasive upsurge of reductionism, occasioned in part by continued successes in physics but generated especially by dramatic new advances in molecular biology. Thus, by the early 1960s, reductionism again reigned—not only in physics (Feynman, 1963), but also in biochemistry (Platt, 1959), molecular biology (Crick, 1966), psychology (Skinner, 1964), information theory (Simon, 1962), philosophy, (Armstrong, 1968, Dennett, 1969, Hook, 1960, Klee, 1984, Putnam, 1960, Smart, 1963), and nearly everywhere—including even in gestalt psychology, the early prime stronghold of configurational theory (Khler, 1960). General Systems Theory also at this time was accepting reductionist logic as a basic structural principle (Bertalanffy, 1956, Sperry, 1991b).

This strong upswell of reductive physicalist thinking, described by philosopher Thomas Nagel (1971) as a "wave of reductionist euphoria", was soon again, however, to give way to an opposing wave of holism, emergence and "irreducibility" (for example, Bertalanffy, 1968, Koestler and Smythies, 1969, Laszlo, 1972, Pattee, 1973, Polanyi, 1968, Popper, 1972). This most recent holist movement has since continued to burgeon into an extreme new high that still today is gaining further ground both within and outside science, extending even into cosmology (Harris, 1991), and a "postmodern" theology (Griffin, 1988). This latest mainstream swing from one extreme to the other, rather abrupt in terms of historical precedents, poses a key question: "What happened that served to break the 1960s' wave of reductionism and turned it around into a general new all-time high for wholism, a development so marked that today it prompts proposals for a new 'science of wholeness'?" (Harman, 1992). What was it that turned the "reductionist euphoria" of the 1960s into the current boom in holistic "new sciences"? Also, in this same period, what prompted the rise of "The New Philosophy of Science" (Manicas and Secord, 1983)? The logical answer, I believe, is found in the same conceptual developments that enabled the revolutionary turnabout in our understanding of consciousness.

The five-year period starting from about the mid 1960s thus becomes, in this analysis, a crucial turning point in the history of both the reductionist debate and also that of the mind-body relation. Secondarily, it also will be seen that this same period becomes a turning point as well for the fact-value or science-values dichotomy (Edel, 1980), and also for the ancient paradox of freewill and determinism (Deci, 1980). Further, it is these collective changes that, in our present view, are inferred to have set the stage for the subsequent rush of epistemic outbursts of the 1970s and '80s. In this interpretation, the current swing from reductionism to wholism has much in common with the concomitant swing from behaviorism to mentalism. Both shifts can be seen to be interlinked and inseparable. Both are dependent upon the new model of causality which includes "top-down" emergent determinism. The same modified concept that placed mental states in a causal role also refuted the adequacy of traditional "bottom-up" physicalism and gave emergent macro qualities in general (including the mental) a new irreducible causal status. This "flow of history" analysis, as I tend to think of it, accounts as well for the broad array of new epistemic trends of the past two decades, all of which appear to share in common the rejection of traditional materialism. Four major transformative developments visible in the recent literature are taken to be involved, all related, and all traceable, to origins in the same critical five-year period. These include

1) the diametric turnabout in the causal status of consciousness

2) the shift from extreme reductionism to extreme holism

3) a new recognition and wide acceptance of "top-down" emergent determinism

4) a sudden, still-continuing upsurge in radical new outlooks and paradigms in science and philosophy.

All four can be understood and accounted for in terms of the basic concepts required for the turnabout on consciousness.

This brings us to another critical point in my argument, namely, its dependence upon an assumption that the 1970s' changeover in mainstream psychology from behaviorism to cognitivism and my own similar shift to mentalism were both effected on the same theoretical basis, that is, on the same shift to the same new mentalist paradigm. Support for this is twofold: first, it hardly seems plausible that the powerful, seemingly incontestable physicalist paradigm of science with its rigorous exclusion of mentalistic explanation—along with its behaviorist counterpart in psychology—could suddenly, after having successfully fended off all challenges for centuries, have been toppled twice within a few years by two different mentalist theories. The ruling dictum of the materialist era that mind does not interact with matter, and its time-tested reasoning, supposed to be logically cohesive, complete, and irrefutable, is hardly something in which one would expect to suddenly find two separate errors. This alone appears to justify the assumption that in both instances the rational basis behind the new mentalist/cognitive thinking has to be, in essence, one and the same.

Second, the assumption gains added support from the historical record and chronologic correlations evident in the following brief outline of the early expressions of the new "mentalism".

- **1964** An initial brief statement of downward causation in application to evolution, molecular and organismal behavior, including nonreductive downward control of the mental over the neuronal in brain function (Sperry, 1964, pp. 2, 20). This posed a direct challenge to the then-prevailing reductionist outlook and came at a time well before the onset of any awareness of a coming paradigm shift (for example Eccles, 1966, Feigl, 1967, Nagel, 1971, Rogers, 1964, Skinner, 1964).

- **1965** First full presentations (Popper, 1972, Sperry, 1965). The new outlook was described by Karl Popper as "a solution to . . . the classical Cartesian body-mind problem", explaining "interaction of mental and physical states" and bringing "a different view of the world". I presented it as "An Alternative Mentalist Position" that "restores the mind to the brain of objective science", and "a long sought unifying view" that "would eliminate the old dualistic confusions, dichotomies, and paradoxes"; also as a scheme that gives "plenty of free will, provided we think of free will as self-determination", and finally as an "objective explanatory model of brain function that neither contradicts nor degrades but affirms age-old humanistic values". The mentalist/cognitive paradigm is still viewed today in very much these same terms.

- **1966** Wide exposure in a reprinting in *The Bulletin of the Atomic Scientists* (Sperry, 1965) instigated by biochemist-futurist John Platt. This bulletin, with its famous "doomsday clock" and subtitle *Journal of Science and Public Affairs*, gave very broad exposure in those years, not just among physicists.

- **1969** More specialized presentations: 1) in *Proceedings of the National Academy of Sciences* (Sperry, 1969a), later published in full; 2)in *Psychological Review* (Sperry, 1969b); 3) in philosopher Marjorie Grene's international "Concepts of Mind" Workshop (Grene, 1974); and 4) in the 1969 *Proceedings of the Association for Research of Nervous and Mental Diseases, a Program on Perception and its Disorders* (Sperry, 1970a).

- **1970** *Critique in Psychological Review* by Dalbra Bindra (1970), and my response to Bindra (Sperry, 1970b) also in *Psychological Review* (perhaps these two combined were most influential in tipping the scales). By the following year publications in psychology were beginning to express growing awareness of a general paradigm shift (Palermo, 1971).

A competing concept, the "computer program analogy" of mental function, also could be said to qualify in respect to chronology, and is frequently cited as having had a strong influence in bringing about the consciousness revolution. Presented at length in a 1960 book by Miller, Galanter, and Pribram (1960) and more pointedly in a later text by Ulrich Neisser (1967), the computer analogy was surely influential in opening the way to a new appreciation of cognitive factors in a control role in brain function. The computer-program relation, however, can equally well be viewed, like most other physical phenomena, in traditional analytic reductive physicalist terms, and generally was so taken prior to the introduction of downward causation in the mid 1960s. In itself, the computer-program analogy does not demand a shift to mentalism, nor to a causal or emergent view of conscious experience, and it clearly had not done so by 1963-64 when the ongoing debates in psychology between behaviorists and phenomenologists (for example Koch, 1964, Rogers, 1964, Skinner, 1964, Wann, 1964) continued in the same vein as before, essentially unaffected by any new mentalism. Further, the impact of the volume by Miller et al., plus the influence of related work of this period with computers, information theory and Artificial Intelligence, had failed collectively to alter the basic "in-principle" reductionist position and thinking of leaders in the field (Simon, 1962).

The factors responsible for psychology's sudden swing to use of mentalistic explanation (Pylyshyn, 1973), following a half century of rigorous renunciation, were not clear at the time and still today remain subject to ongoing controversy. Mainstream psychologists tend to overlook emergent interaction and the above cluster of related developments in favor of various others more directly affiliated with research programs and theory within psychology itself. As yet, however, there is no consensus. The various subfield groups still vie with one another in ascribing the origins to their own specialty (examples: Amsel, 1989, Baars, 1986, Bolles, 1990, Dember, 1974, Gardner, 1985, Matson, 1971, Palermo, 1971). In my estimation, the majority of these alternative views either fail to stand up in historical examination or they deal with subordinate theories of the behaviorist period which are not critical to behaviorism *per se* as an overarching paradigm making psychology consistent with neuroscience and the other natural sciences (Reese and Overton, 1972, Skinner, 1964).

Behaviorist doctrine, for example, was heavily invested, in its early stages, in conditioned reflex learning (Koch, 1964). This included reliance on pre-natal conditioning to an extent that the very concept of instinct as posited in European ethology (Lehrman, 1953, Lorenz, 1937) had become a term of derision. Behaviorism's denunciation of any inheritance of behavior traits was supported by abundant, seemingly unequivocal experimental evidence that the growth and formation of nerve connections is, by its very nature, entirely diffuse and nonselective (Hamburger, 1990, Weiss and Taylor, 1941). The case against instincts, however, was totally turned around in the early 1940s by new experiments showing that intricate inherited nerve networks can indeed be grown into the brain directly, unaided by learning, and organized with great precision through an elaborate scheme of genetically controlled chemical coding of individual cells (Sperry, 1951).

Soon after this, another serious flaw in behaviorist theory was pointed out by Karl Lashley (1951) in his critique of chained associations as a basis for serial order in behavior. Lashley used language as a main example, and this was reinforced by linguist Chomsky (1959) with an added suggestion that the deep structure of language is not learned, but inherited. Such inheritance, previously unthinkable, by the mid-1950s had become theoretically plausible as a result of the growing evidence of the high precision and complexity of inherent chemoaffinity factors in fetal brain organization (Sperry, 1956). Other theoretical thrusts of the behaviorist era, including the extreme peripheralism, the environmental or "empty organism" emphasis, and Hull's Stimulus-Response scheme for a comprehensive theory covering all behavior, also came into decline and helped contribute to a growing loss of confidence in the so-called behaviorist answers.

For present purposes, the main point to note here is that none of these kinds of theoretical setbacks, individually or collectively, served to overthrow behaviorism *per se* as a conceptual framework, a philosophy of science, or overriding metatheory that rejects introspective mentalistic explanations and restricts behavioral science, like the other natural sciences, to what is objectively observable and measurable. Remaining "behaviorists" today defend their position with claims that the exclusion of mental constructs had been only a methodological principle. Actually at the time, and in harmony with brain research, physics, and the rest of science, it was much more than this. Behaviorist thinking, through the 1950s as in the rest of science, excluded any interactive influence of conscious subjective qualities on the course of physical brain function. Conscious states, that is, were held to be epiphenomenal, not causes of behavior (Skinner, 1964, Wann, 1964, p. 135).

Mind Merged with Matter: Is It Materialism? Dualism? Mentalism? . . . Or?

The new conception of mental states in a causal interactive role was classified by Popper (1972), and by many others since, as a "dualistic" solution. This was in accord with past terminology in which "mentalism" had traditionally been equated with dualism. In contrast, however, I have described this new form of mentalism from the start (Sperry, 1965) as a quite different intermediate position which is monistic, not dualistic. In my view, mental phenomena as dynamic emergent properties of physical brain states become inextricably interfused with, and thus inseparable from, their physiologic substrates. At the same time, they are taken to be distinguishable from the brain substrate in the way that an emergent property is distinguished from its infrastructure, even though it is critically dependent upon the dynamic spacing and timing of the component events. Though mental states, at present, are not observable or measurable, they are presumed, in principle, to be something accessible to eventual scientific description "like the interior of the Earth" (Sperry, 1969), with further advances in technology. It thus becomes a moot question as to whether this modified concept of a mental state as a dynamic emergent retaining its subjective quality or "raw feel" should now be called a "material" or a "mental" process.

Either way, the overall outcome is a coherent hierarchic view of nature with increasingly complex physical systems having diverse emergent properties which include the mental emergents of the brain-mind system, all part of a monistic natural order. The traditional difference between the physical and the mental (as subjectively perceived) is deliberately retained, but with these previously separate, dual realms now inextricably merged. Questions and opinions are continually raised as to whether this type of mind-brain solution ought to be called materialistic or mentalistic. It is only natural that persons with previous investments in one or the other should want to call it a modified form of their former position. Confirmed dualists Popper and Eccles (1977), for example, espoused it as dualistic "psychophysical interaction", whereas I preferred to call it a nondualistic "new", "neo-" or "alternative" mentalism (Sperry, 1965). The latter better serves to distinguish the new features. It emphasizes the reductive physicalist errors of the past, and also the revolutionary, radically revised world-outlook and story the new solution brings to science. I have outlined elsewhere other reasons (as in Sperry, 1965, 1980, 1987, 1991b) why "mentalism" seems to me, overall, to be preferable to "materialism", at least from the standpoint of behavioral science.

About ten years after Popper and I had separately described this new solution to the mind-brain problem (Popper, 1972, Sperry, 1965), and some four years after its adoption by mainstream psychology in its new mentalist paradigm (Dember, 1974, Matson, 1971, Palermo, 1971), the same solution was rediscovered by philosopher Mario Bunge (1977, 1980), but renamed as a new "emergentist materialism"—with myself conveniently misclassified as a dualist, and psychology's shift to cognitivism not mentioned. This ongoing controversy over terminology has caused puzzlement and confusion from the start (Bindra, 1970, Sperry, 1970b). Psychologist Thomas Natsoulas (1987), specializing in the history of consciousness, correctly points out that the new answer blends together features from previously opposed solutions, and then, in reaction to its misclassification as "dualism", calls it a type of "physical monism". Certainly Bunge's "materialism" and Natsoulas' "physicalism" find more ready acceptance in modern science and philosophy than does "mentalism". In retrospect, it might accordingly have been wiser had I used an emergent materialist/physicalist label from the beginning. However, it still seems to me a mistake overall to abandon the age-old common-sense distinction between mind and matter, the mental and the physical. This basic common distinction long preceded the varied philosophic jargon and scientific terminology. The highly distinctive specialness of conscious states with their subjective qualities does not go away just because they are taken to be emergent properties of physical brain processes.

Background Assumptions

The views here outlined reflect a background mainly of experimental research in the brain-behavioral sciences, but undertaken initially with the riddle of consciousness as the ultimate guiding attraction, and accordingly with some heed to associated mind-brain philosophy (Trevarthen, 1991). In these days when it seems to be open season on theories of consciousness, it is still worth remembering that the brain-behavior sciences provide a rich and special source of direct, pertinent evidence regarding the nature of consciousness and its correlates and requisites. This includes many kinds of variations in the comings, goings and quality shifts of consciousness in correlation with different forms of electrical, chemical and surgical intervention, changing brain states, different brain structures, innate anomalies, and so on and on. Any proposed theory should be, at the least, consistent with this accumulated mass of data.

The issue remains unproven as to whether everything is endowed from the start with an inner psychic or nouminous dimension (Berry, 1988) or whether, as is more commonly inferred, psychic experience is instead a relatively late achievement of evolution and confined to brain networks. Like most neuroscientists, I believe a wide collection of observations strongly favors the latter, such as the fact that consciousness is found not in the heart or the liver, but in the brain, where, in turn, it is associated not with all but with only certain cerebral systems. Further, these special cerebral systems, in turn, exhibit awareness selectively, in some states only and not others (such as dreamless sleep, coma, or epileptic seizures). Overall, the evidence of this kind has long been taken in neuroscience to rule out the central tenet of Whiteheadian and of recent "process" philosophy that attributes to most physical entities an inner mental or psychic dimension. The recent upsurge in the acceptance of consciousness, nevertheless, has had a reinvigorating effect in process philosophy where the change tends to be interpreted as vindication by modern science of the tenets of Whitehead (Berry, 1988, Birch and Cobb, 1981, Griffin, 1981). These panpsychic concepts of Whitehead and process philosophy, however, were around for decades earlier and actually played little or no part in the cognitive/consciousness revolution.

The secret of the mind-matter mystery thus appears in mind-brain science to narrow not only to the brain, but to certain select structures and processes within the brain which vary consistently in the evolutionary ladder. Color perception apparently exists in the tiny hummingbird brain, presumably with something similar to the same conscious color sensation we ourselves experience—probably also true for the pinhead brain of the honeybee and many insect species, at least in prototype. All in all there is growing reason to suspect that the secret trick for generating consciousness could turn out to be some relatively simple form of network processing or programming, something that computer-cognitive science may already be close to discovering. A remaining key question at present, however, is whether the infrastructural network components for the emergent subjective quality must be living. Or can subjective emergents be formed from a non-living infrastructure? In either case, one of the most profoundly important implications of the final answer regarding the generation of consciousness, once it is in, is bound to be its bearing on the other central question with which we deal here, namely, "Is consciousness (however it is generated) causally interactive, or is it an acausal epiphenomenon? Is it consequential or inconsequential?"

The views expressed above come also from a background that is not particularly conducive to reliance on "deep intuitive inner knowing" as an alternative to the scientific mode. One learns, for example, of forms of insanity in which inner "voices", a radio, TV, or computer, or some other such fantasized inner delusion is defended with elaborate and quite rational inner logic. This and many other examples demonstrate the general principle that the mind's inner knowing and reasoning, left to itself, may arrive at all kinds of weird and wonderful convictions. The logical "computational" sequence of cerebral reasoning seems a relatively simple feature of information processing that may be much the same whether used to defend a scientific or an insane conclusion. The critical difference lies in how the inner mental conclusion checks out when tested by interaction in the outside "real" world.

The scientific method has been characterized and defined in a variety of ways. To me its real essence lies not in special cognitive features, types of conceptual organization, technological approaches, and such like, so much as in the insistence that any "truth" arrived at, via whatever inner cognitive processing, is not to be trusted until checked and double checked, by experiment or otherwise, for its consistency with outside reality. This checking process which occurs naturally in the course of ordinary behavior is assumed to be an important natural aspect of the evolution of mind. Science, however, formalizes and maximizes the principle in contrast to other avenues to "truth" such as inner revelation, authoritarian dogma, philosophy, or faith. Historically, this is how science got its start and has since proven itself whenever directly challenged by other modes of knowing. It is a view that puts science beyond the culturally dependent status claimed for it in the recent conjecturing of postmodern (sic), anti-foundationalist philosophy (Rorty, 1982). It lifts scientific reasoning out of the realm of conceptual contingencies of culture, tradition, metaphysics, and so on, to ground it directly in the interactions of reality itself.

A related assumption that the mind-brain system evolved within, and in close integration with, the outside real world, means also that subjective "common-sense" impressions acquire a fundamental reality status not easily undermined by philosophic conjecture or by scientific theorizing, including, for example, the weirdness of non-locality, Bell's theorem, wholesale instantaneous interconnectedness, an "observer-dependent reality", or other counterintuitive figments of the "new physics"–that Einstein himself and other physicists could not accept (see Klotz, 1988). Like most biologists exposed to the study of evolution, I take a realist position that assumes a world exists out there regardless of whether I or anyone else happens to perceive it. The laborious excavation of a giant ammonite or a large dinosaur femur from its cretaceous matrix leaves little patience with a philosophy that these and their world did not exist until our observation.

An Already Powerful Paradigm Made Stronger

Science, over some three hundred years, has proven itself against all rivals to be our most successful and effective means for explaining, understanding and for working in and with the world in which we live. More than any other approach–philosophic, religious, mystic or occult, or that of secular humanism, or of just plain common-sense–science has succeeded in being able to "clear the mystery and show the way" in the realm of the natural world. All this success, however, is counterbalanced in that this same science has insisted, as its basic premise, that the entire universe, including the human psyche, is driven throughout solely by mindless physical forces of the most elemental kind. These elemental forces are inferred to rule a cosmos that is utterly indifferent, purposeless and fatalistic, devoid of any higher meaning, values, freedom of choice, or moral priority. The stark descriptions of science add up, from a human standpoint, to an overall life-view of "cosmic meaninglessness" (Provine, 1988). This bleak outlook, plus today's growing uneasiness about the kind of world into which an "age of science" seems to be leading, along with recent indications of emerging changes in our worldview presuppositions (Harman,

1980), collectively give good reason for intensive reexamination of the metaphysical (and also of the supposed physical) foundations of science.

Such reexamination in my own case has served mainly to freshen and further strengthen a general earlier impression that modern science, fortified with its recently modified concepts of consciousness and causation, is today stronger than ever, and that it provides the best route available to an understanding of the true nature and meaning of existence. I continue to see the key to long term, high quality survival to be in a shift worldwide to faith in the type of truth upheld by science (Sperry, 1972, 1991a). It cannot be overemphasized that in this conviction I do not refer to the traditional materialist science of the past two centuries, but rather to the new science spawned by the cognitive (consciousness) revolution of the 1970s with its revised principles of subjective and emergent causation, and top-down determinism. I am presuming further that these new principles, since their establishment in psychology, have gained sufficient ground in other disciplines that they now can be judged to represent the dominant majority view. In other words, what started as a revolution within a single discipline has become a revolution for all science.

Throughout the different sciences, previous inadequacies inherent in traditional materialism are increasingly being recognized and variously resolved within subdisciplinary specialties. Within the behavioral sciences, for example, the new treatment of mental states, applicable to the animal as well as human mind, promptly brought a more cognitive, mentalist approach in comparative psychology and ethology (Griffin, 1988)–not to mention strengthened "animal rights" concerns. It provided also a long-sought sound determinist basis for the cognitive, humanistic, and therapy-centered schools of psychology, plus other approaches involving introspection such as research on personality, values, motivation, and the like, proponents of which during the reign of behaviorism had been obliged to put up with second-class rating because they were "not scientific". The way was cleared as well for a return movement to so-called common-sense or "folk" psychology (impossible under behaviorism) and for the ascendance of a largely new cognitive science encompassing computer science, artificial intelligence (AI) and information theory in conjunction with cognitive psychology and cognitive neuroscience. Many participants with backgrounds in physics have sensed the makings of an emerging "new science" that stands in striking contrast to conventional reductive physicalism.

The bidirectional model of causal determinism, applicable to causal understanding in general, has found ready welcome also beyond psychology in biology, systems theory, evolutionary theory, and other disciplines including philosophy and theology. Systems theory, for example, since the mid 1960s has become a different entity, infused now with emergent interaction, irreducibility of the emergent whole (in principle as well as in practice), and down-level causal determinism, all implanted by the conceptual developments requisite for shifting conscious experience from a noncausal into a causally interactive role (Sperry, 1991b).

Of most interest, in respect to possible metaphysical or cultural bias in science, are those impacts that affect the overall scientific worldview as a whole, bringing changes that help, for example, to bridge the former "two cultures" gulf between the humanities and the sciences—changes of a kind that now enable, for the first time, a logical derivation of moral directives from the type of physical reality upheld by science. Especially critical is the changed treatment of human values, and also the changes in the age-old freewill-determinism paradox. Both of these are central and basic to concepts of the self, personal agency, intentionality, ethics and morality.

The long-established antithetic relation of science and values, known as the science-values or fact-value dichotomy (Bixenstine, 1976) and recognized to be one of the outstanding shortcomings of traditional physicalism, is today diametrically turned around. Subjective values, no longer treated as being merely parallel or epiphenomenal to brain function, become instead causally interactive in the new treatment and thus qualify as legitimate causal constructs. Science no longer spurns values, nor is its cosmology value-free. According to the new mentalism, we are ruled not merely by the fundamental forces of physics, but also, and more critically, by human values. Human values, as indicated at the outset, become the most strategically powerful force shaping modern civilization, the key to our global predicament and its cure.

Today's turnaround in the traditional science-values dichotomy is effected, further, in that the new descriptions of non-human as well as human nature no longer eradicate the rich emergent macro phenomena and qualities we customarily value in our world by reducing them to the elemental forces of physics. All the higher emergent macro, mental, vital and social forces are now given their due as causal realities. In an additional corrective thrust, current views of the brain's methods for cognitive processing recognize a sequence of steps by which subjective moral values can be logically derived on the basis of scientific facts; that is, the old "naturalistic fallacy" is avoided (Rottschaefer, 1987, Sperry, 1985, 1988). Since the mid-1970s, it has become increasingly evident overall that we are in an entirely new era with respect to values (Edel, 1980). From an ethical or humanistic standpoint, the consciousness revolution might equally well be called also a "values revolution".

Another legendary problem with the physicalist paradigm has been its bothersome principle of complete causal determinism (or quantum "probabalism") in that such determinism directly contradicts our universal common-sense impression that we possess freedom of will. The free will-determinism paradox is probably the most notoriously baffling riddle posed by scientific materialism and, from the humanistic standpoint, the most damaging, in that scientific determinism logically destroys any real purpose, intention or moral responsibility. Up through 1964 this age-old enigma was still being looked upon as a deep unfathomable paradox of nature, something we just have to learn to live with (Rogers, 1964). Today's mentalist doctrine provides a resolution of this old dilemma in an answer that preserves both determinism and free will, but each in a modified form (Deci, 1980, Sperry, 1965, 1980).

Free will is maintained, but not in a manner that makes us or our volitions completely free of all causation. This would make our decisions and behavior meaningless, reflecting mere random caprice, unaccountable and insignificant with no predictive reliability. This is not what we want, nor is it what we subjectively experience. What we experience, rather, is the capacity to do what we personally, voluntarily choose, wish, intend, or decide to do. This kind of subjective power to determine what we say and do is exactly what is provided in our new mentalist view. A person's behavior is still determined, but not, as science previously asserted, by the brain's unalterable physico-chemical processes, nor by external environmental factors. Rather, what we cognitively will to do is determined by the higher-level complex cognitive properties of the conscious mind or self. The key determinants take the form of non-reductive emergent and subjective properties of the high-order brain processes of volition and intentionality. The "inexorable" laws of brain physics and chemistry are still important determinants, but, as a result of evolution, these lower-level forces are now controlled and programmed by the higher-level mental agents. Our behavior accordingly is mentally determined and moral responsibility is preserved.

Conclusion

Science today is very different from the science we knew 30 years ago. The change is not in the approach, methodology, or everyday practice of science, which are little affected. The change, rather, is in the type of truths and physical reality science upholds, and the projected picture of ourselves and the world. The natural order as posited by science is no longer, on the new terms, incompatible with human values or the most precious and sacred things in life (Byers, 1989). The new cosmology, embracing emergent causation, makes possible the derivation of transcendent moral guidelines from the worldview of mainstream science. The current outlook on existence supports a more biocentric, less anthropocentric "man is the measure of all things" morality. Context-dependent principles replace the moral absolutes of 2000 years ago, and social priorities emerge that are more realistic, sustainable, and more adequate for the type of world we face today. The result, in effect, is a new moral compass based in the credibility and universality of science. Being neutral and nonexclusive, it has exceptional potential for global acceptance by diverse ethnic, national and cultural constituents and can, if implemented soon enough, offer a humane, non-catastrophic way out of our current global crisis.

The one remaining outstanding negative feature of science, still not rectified in the new outlook, is the continued scientific renunciation of the existence of conscious experience in unembodied forms, thus denying the possibility of a conscious afterlife. The question of whether this is indeed a negative rather than positive feature (when all the pros and cons are rationally balanced out) remains open to debate. In an earlier, brief discussion of this and related problems (Sperry, 1992), I was convinced that an improved, more wise and sophisticated interpretation of existence and its meaning, in terms of the new paradigm, might conceivably succeed in dispelling, through a higher level of understanding, the natural inherent human desire to continue in a conscious future, even after life.

This issue, however, and all others raised in these re-examinations of science, may not matter in the light of a very real and rapidly growing possibility that the enormous built-in momentum in today's global population explosion and the irreversibility in related ecologic degradation could now carry us and the ecosphere past "the point of no return". This mounting threat of total cosmic oblivion overrides today all other concerns, and overturns many ethico-moral imperatives that prevailed without question in the past. Traditional, national, ethnic, religious and cultural loyalties become subsidiary to survival. New higher moral perspectives of survival must now overrule even long-esteemed humanitarian traits which evolved in human nature itself, but without regard to the projected effects in today's kind of world. In the context of today's worsening global situation and our imperiled future, perhaps the most important feature of the described new outlook of science is its provision of a prescription for long term, high quality survival and a way out of our current global predicament.

Without going through the intervening logic, recently reviewed elsewhere (Sperry, 1991a), the type of global mind change and moral priorities that emerge may be inferred from a few of the more salient features, sketched in brief as follows: the implicit supreme plan for existence by which moral right and wrong are determined (Fletcher, 1987), traditionally imputed to divine intellect, is reconceived in terms of the overall design and upward thrust of evolving nature, with special focus on our own biosphere. Humanity's creator thus becomes the vast interwoven fabric of all evolving nature. The creative forces and creation itself become inextricably interfused, making it immoral, even sacrilegious, to degrade earthly existence or to treat it merely as a way station. The evolutionary process, no longer governed merely from below by chance gene mutations, becomes a gradual emergence of increased direction, purpose, and meaning among the forces that move and govern living things. An unpredictable, ever-evolving open-ended future becomes a *sine qua non* for higher meaning. The "highest good"–no longer reduced to subatomic physics or set apart in another, dualistic existence–works out to be an open-ended, ever-evolving quality of life and all existence, and includes protecting the "rights of the unborn" billions of the many generations hopefully to come.

In short, the working paradigm of science, that has proven itself to be tremendously successful for over two hundred years, has now been further rectified and improved in a manner that retains former strengths and corrects some serious humanistic weaknesses. Nothing is lost and we gain a whole new and better way of perceiving and understanding ourselves and the world.

Acknowledgements

The work was supported by a fund of the California Institute of Technology donated for research on the mind-brain problem. I thank Norma Deupree for helpful editorial suggestions and Patricia Anderson and Mary Jeffries for assistance in compiling the references and processing the manuscript.

References

A. Amsel, *Behaviorism, Neobehaviorism, and Cognitivism in Learning Theory: Historical and Contemporary Perspectives,* Erlbaum, 1989.

D. M. Armstrong, *A Materialist Theory of Mind,* Routledge and Kegan Paul, 1968.

R. J. Baars, *The Cognitive Revolution in Psychology,* Guilford, 1986.

T. Berry, *The Dream of the Earth,* Sierra Club Nature and Natural Philosophy Library, 1988.

L. von Bertalanffy, "General systems theory" in *General Systems,* Vol. 1, edited by L. von Bertalanffy and A. Rapoport, Society for General Systems Research, 1956, pp. 1-10.

L. von Bertalanffy, *General Systems Theory,* Braziller, 1968.

D. Bindra, "The problem of subjective experience: Puzzlement on reading R. W. Sperry's 'A modified concept of consciousness'", *Psychological Review* 77, 1970, pp. 581-584.

L. C. Birch and J. B. Cobb, *Liberation of Life: From the Cell to the Community,* Cambridge University Press, 1981.

E. Bixenstine, "The value-fact antithesis in behavioral science", *Journal of Humanistic Psychology* 16 (2), 1976, pp. 35-57.

R. C. Bolles, "Where did everybody go?" *Psychological Science* 1 (107), 1990, pp. 112-113.

M. Bunge, "Emergence and the mind", *Neuroscience* 2, 1977, pp. 501-509.

M. Bunge, *The Mind-Body Problem,* Pergamon Press, 1980 .

D. M. Byers, editor, *Religion, Science and the Search for Wisdom,* US Catholic Conference, Inc., 1987.

N. Chomsky, Book review of *Verbal Behavior* by B. F. Skinner, *Language* 35, 1959, pp. 26-58.

F. Crick, *Of Molecules and Men,* University of Washington Press, 1966.

E. L. Deci, *The Psychology of Self-Determination,* D. C. Heath, 1980.

W. N. Dember, "Motivation and the cognitive revolution", *American Psychologist* 29, 1974, pp. 161-168.

D. C. Dennett, *Content and Consciousness,* Routledge and Kegan Paul, 1969.

J. C. Eccles, *The Neurophysiological Basis of Mind: The Principles of Neurophysiology,* Clarendon Press, 1953.

J. C. Eccles, editor, *Brain and Conscious Experience,* Springer, 1966.

J. C. Eccles, "Evolution of consciousness", *Proc. Natl. Acad. Sci. USA* 89, 1992, pp. 7320-7324.

A. Edel, *Exploring Fact and Value,* Vol. 2, Transaction Books, 1980.

H. Feigl, *The "Mental" and the "Physical"* (with "Postscript after ten years"), University of Minneapolis Press, 1967.

R. Feynman, *The Feynman Lectures on Physics,* Vol. 1, Addison-Wesley, 1963.

J. Fletcher, "Humanism and theism in biomedical ethics", *Perspectives in Biology and Medicine* 31 (1), 1987, pp. 106-116 .

J. A. Fodor, "The mind-body problem", *Scientific American* 244 (1), 1981, pp. 114-123.

H. Gardner, *The Mind's New Science: A History of the Cognitive Revolution,* Basic Books, 1985.

M. Grene, "Workshop on 'Concepts of Mind'", in M. Grene, *The Understanding of Nature,* Reidel, 1974, pp. xiv-xv.

Donald R. Griffin, *The Question of Animal Awareness,* Rockefeller University Press, 1981.

David R. Griffin, *The Reenchantment of Science,* SUNY, 1988.

V. Hamburger, "Historical landmarks in neurogenesis", *Trends in Neuroscience* 4, 1981, pp. 151-155.

V. Hamburger, "The S. Kuffler Lecture: The rise of experimental neuroembryology: A personal reassessment", *International Journal of Developmental Neuroscience,* 8, 1990, pp. 121-131 .

W. W. Harman, "Where is our positive image of the future?", *Institute of Noetic Sciences Newsletter, Winter* 1980 .

E. E. Harris, *Cosmos and Anthropos,* Humanities Press International, 1991.

S. Hook, editor, *Dimensions of Mind,* Collier Books, 1960.

R. L. Klee, "Micro-determinism and concepts of emergence", *Philosophy of Science* 51, 1984, pp. 44-63.

A. H. Klotz, "On the nature of quantum mechanics", *Synthese* 77, 1988, pp. 139-193 .

S. Koch, "Psychology and emergent conceptions of knowledge as unitary" in T. Wann, editor, *Behaviorism and Phenomenology,* University of Chicago Press, 1964, pp. 1-45.

A. Koestler and J. R. Smythies, editors, *Beyond Reductionism: New Perspectives in the Life Sciences,* The Alpbach Symposium 1968, Hutchinson, 1969.

W. Köhler, "The mind-body problem" in S. Hook, editor, *Dimensions of Mind,* Collier Books, 1960.

K. S. Lashley, "The problem of serial order in behavior" in L. A. Jeffress, editor, *Cerebral Mechanisms in Behavior,* John Wiley and Sons, 1951, pp. 112-146.

E. Laszlo, *The Systems View of the World: The Natural Philosophy of the New Developments in the Sciences,* Braziller, 1972.

D. Lehrman, "A critique of Konrad Lorenz's theory of instinctive behavior", *Quarterly Review of Biology* 28, 1953, pp. 337-363.

K. Lorenz, "The establishment of the instinct concept" in K. Lorenz, *Studies in Animal and Human Behavior,* Vol. 1, Harvard University Press, 1937, pp. 259-315.

P. T. Manicas and P. F. Secord, "Implications for psychology of the new philosophy of science", *American Psychologist* 38, 1983, pp. 399-413.

F. W. Matson, "Humanistic theory: The third revolution in psychology", *The Humanist* 31 (2), 1971, pp. 7-11.

G. A. Miller, E. H. Galanter, and K. H. Pribram, *Plans and the Structure of Behavior,* Holt, Rinehart and Winston, 1960.

C. L. Morgan, *Emergent Evolution* (The Gifford Lectures, delivered 1922), Holt, 1923.

T. Nagel, "Brain bisection and the unity of consciousness", *Synthese* 22, 1971, pp. 396-413.

T. Natsoulas, "Roger Sperry's monist interactionism", *The Journal of Mind and Behavior* 8, 1987, pp. 1-21.

U. Neisser, *Cognitive Psychology,* Appleton-Century-Crofts, 1967.

D. S. Palermo, "Is a scientific revolution taking place in psychology?", *Science Studies* 1, 1971, pp. 135-155.

H. H. Pattee, editor, *Hierarchy Theory: The Challenge of Complex Systems,* George Braziller, 1973.

J. R. Platt, "Book review of W. M. Elsasser 'The physical foundation of biology' (1958). (Pergamon Press)", *Perspectives in Biology and Medicine* 2, 1959, pp. 243-245.

M. Polanyi, "Life's irreducible structure", *Science* 160, 1968, pp. 1308-1312 .

K. R. Popper, "Of clouds and clocks. (Second Arthur Holly Compton Memorial Lecture, presented April 1965)", in K. Popper, editor, *Objective Knowledge,* Clarendon Press, 1972, pp. 206-255.

K. R. Popper and J. C. Eccles, *The Self and Its Brain,* Springer, 1977.

W. Provine, "Evolution and the foundation of ethics", *MBL Science* 3, 1988, pp. 5-29 .

H. Putnam, "Minds and machines", in S. Hook, editor, *Dimensions of Mind,* Collier, 1960, pp. 138-164.

Z. W. Pylyshyn, "What the mind's eye tells the mind's brain: A critique of mental imagery", *Psychological Bulletin* 80, 1973, pp. 1-24.

H. W. Reese and W. F. Overton, "On paradigm shifts", *American Psychologist* 27, 1972, pp. 1197-1199.

C. Ripley, "Sperry's concept of consciousness", *Inquiry* 27, 1984, pp. 399-423.

W. E. Ritter, *The Unity of the Organism,* The Gorham Press, 1919.

C. R. Rogers, "Freedom and commitment", *The Humanist* 29 (2), 1964, pp. 37, 40.

R. Rorty, *The Consequences of Pragmatism: Essays, 1972-1980,* University of Minnesota Press, 1982.

W. A. Rottschaefer, "Roger Sperry's science of values", *The Journal of Mind and Behavior* 8, 1987, pp. 23-35.

H. Simon, "The architecture of complexity", *Proceedings of the American Philosophical Society* 106, 1962, pp. 467-482.

B. F. Skinner, "Behaviorism at 50" in T. Wann, editor, *Behaviorism and Phenomenology,* University of Chicago Press, 1964, pp. 79-108.

J. J. C. Smart, *Philosophy and Scientific Realism,* Routledge and Kegan Paul, 1963.

J. C. Smuts, *Holism and Evolution,* Macmillan, 1926.

R. W. Sperry, "Mechanisms of neural maturation", in S. Stevens, editor, *Handbook of Experimental Psychology,* Wiley, 1951, pp. 236-280.

R. W. Sperry, "Neurology and the mind-brain problem", *American Scientist* 40, 1952, pp. 291-312.

R. W. Sperry, "The eye and the brain", *Scientific American* 194 (5), 1956, pp. 48-52.

R. W. Sperry, *Problems Outstanding in the Evolution of Brain Function,* James Arthur Lecture Series, American Museum of Natural History, 1964.

R. W. Sperry, "Mind, brain and humanist values" in J. R. Platt, editor, *New Views of the Nature of Man,* University of Chicago Press, 1965, pp. 71-92; abridged reprinting, *Bulletin of the Atomic Scientists* 22 (7), 1966, pp. 2-6.

R. W. Sperry, "Toward a theory of mind. [Abstr.]", *Proceedings of the National Academy of Sciences* 63, 1969a, pp. 230-231.

R. W. Sperry, "A modified concept of consciousness", *Psychological Review* 76, 1969b, pp. 532-536.

R. W. Sperry, "Perception in the absence of the neocortical commissures", *Perception and Its Disorders, Proceedings of the Association for Research in Nervous and Mental Diseases* 48, 1970a, pp. 123-138.

R. W. Sperry, "An objective approach to subjective experience: Further explanation of a hypothesis", *Psychological Review* 77, 1970b, pp. 585-590.

R. W. Sperry, "Science and the problem of values", *Perspectives in Biology and Medicine,* 16, 1972, pp. 115-130; reprinted in *Zygon, Journal of Religion and Science* 9, 1974, pp. 7-21.

R. W. Sperry, "Mind-brain interaction: Mentalism, yes; dualism, no", *Neuroscience* 5, 1980, pp. 195-206; reprinted in A. D. Smith, R. Llinas, and P. G. Kostyuk, editors, *Commentaries in the Neurosciences,* Pergamon Press, 1980, pp. 651-662.

R. W. Sperry, "Changing priorities", *Annual Review of Neuroscience* 4, 1981, pp. 1-15; reprinted *Science and Moral Priority,* Greenwood/Praeger, 1985.

R. W. Sperry, "Structure and significance of the consciousness revolution", *The Journal of Mind and Behavior* 8, 1987, pp. 37-65.

R. W. Sperry, "Search for beliefs to live by consistent with science", *Zygon, Journal of Religion and Science* 26, 1991a, pp. 237-258.

R. W. Sperry, "In defense of mentalism and emergent interaction", *The Journal of Mind and Behavior* 12, 1991b, pp. 221-245.

R. W. Sperry, "Paradigms of belief, theory and metatheory", *Zygon, Journal of Religion and Science* 27, 1992, pp. 245-259.

H. P. Stapp, "Quantum propensities and the brain-mind connection", invited contribution to the *Volume of Foundations of Physics* honoring Sir Karl Popper, 1991.

C. B. Trevarthen, *Brain Circuits and Functions of the Mind,* Cambridge University Press, 1991.

L. Vandervert, "On the modeling of emergent interaction: Which will it be, the laws of thermodynamics or Sperry's 'wheel' in the subcircuitry?", *The Journal of Mind and Behavior* 12, 1991, pp. 535-540.

T. Wann, editor, *Behaviorism and Phenomenology,* University of Chicago Press, 1964.

P. A. Weiss and A. C. Taylor, "Further experimental evidence against neurotropism in nerve regeneration", *Journal of Experimental Zoology* 95, 1944, pp. 233-257.

The Cosmology of Life and Mind

by George Wald

The great thing about science is that the questions are so much more important than the answers. Almost any scientist can find an answer if he/she can only find a good question. I think that theology tends to make the mistake of straining for answers, even answers that claim to be final. Science lives with the questions. All its answers are tentative, and breed further questions. The really great questions—those a bright child might ask—are never finished answering.

I come toward the end of my life as a scientist facing two great problems. Both are rooted in science, and I approach both as only a scientist would. Yet I believe that both are irrevocably—forever—unassimilable as science. And that is hardly strange, since one involves cosmology, and the other, consciousness. I will begin with the cosmology.

I. A Universe That Breeds Life

We know now that we live in a historical universe, one in which not only living organisms but stars and galaxies are born, mature, grow old and die. There is good reason to believe it to be a universe permeated with life, in which life arises, given enough time, wherever the conditions exist that make it possible.

How many such places are there? Arthur Eddington, the great British physicist, gave us the formula: one hundred billion stars make a galaxy; one hundred billion galaxies make a universe. Our own galaxy, the Milky Way, contains about one hundred billion stars. It is a vast thing. And yet the Milky Way is just a tiny spot in the universe we know. The smallest estimate we would consider of the fraction of stars in the Milky Way that should have a planet that could support life is one percent. That means a billion such places in our own home galaxy, and with a billion such galaxies within reach of our telescopes, the already observed universe should contain *at least* a billion billion—10^{18}—places that can support life.

And now for my main thesis. If any one of a considerable number of the physical properties of our universe were other than they are—some of those properties fundamental, others seeming trivial, even accidental—then life, that now appears to be so prevalent, would be impossible, here or anywhere.

We have too short a time to do more than sample that story here. To give this account a little structure, however, I shall meanwhile climb the scale of states of organization of matter from small to great.

Elementary Particles

I want to say something of two fundamental properties of the elementary particles themselves, involving their masses and their electric charges.

Mass

Every atom has a nucleus composed of protons and neutrons except the smallest atom, hydrogen, which has only one proton as nucleus. About the nucleus electrons are weaving at distances relatively greater than separate our sun and planets. But a proton or neutron in the nucleus has almost 2,000 times the mass of an electron—1,842 times the mass when I last looked. Hence the entire mass of an atom is in its nucleus, and this maintains its position regardless of how the electrons are moving about it.

That is the only reason why anything in this universe stays put, the only reason that our universe has solid structures, and that the small and large molecules that constitute living organisms maintain definite shapes and fit together as they do. The great disparity in mass between the nucleons (protons and neutrons) and the electron is one of the necessary conditions for life.

Electric Charge

How is it that particles so altogether different as a proton and an electron have electric charges that are exactly equal numerically—that the proton is exactly as plus-charged as the electron is minus-charged? It will help to accept this as a legitimate scientific question to know that in 1959 two of our most distinguished astrophysicists, Lyttleton and Bondi, published a paper in the *Proceedings of the Royal Society of London* proposing that in fact the proton and electron differ in charge by the almost infinitesimal amount $2 \times 10^{-18}e$, in which **e** is the already tiny charge on a proton or an electron: so two billion billionths of **e**. The reason they made that proposal is that, given that nearly infinitesimal difference in charge, all the matter in the universe would be charged, and in the same sense, plus or minus. Since like charges repel one another, all the matter in the universe would repel all the other matter, and so the universe would expand, just as it is believed to do.

The trouble with that idea is that yes, the universe would expand, but—short of extraordinary special dispensations—it would not do anything else. For even that almost infinitesimal difference in electric charge would be enough to completely overwhelm the forces of gravity that bring matter together. Hence we should have no galaxies, no stars or planets, and—worst of all—no physicists.

No need to worry, however, for John King, at the Massachusetts Institute of Technology, has since checked this possibility and found that the charges on the proton and electron are numerically exactly equal. That is an extraordinary fact, and not made easier to understand by the present belief that though the electron is a single, apparently indivisible particle, the proton is made up of three quarks, two of them with charges of plus $2/3e$, and one with charge minus $1/3e$.

The Elements

And now, to leave the elementary particles and go to atoms, to elements. There are 92 natural elements, but 99 percent of living matter is made of just four: hydrogen (H), carbon (C), nitrogen (N) and oxygen (O). I have long been convinced that that must be true whenever life exists in the universe, for those four elements possess wholly unique properties, exactly the properties upon which life depends.

These four elements also provide an example of the astonishing togetherness of our universe. While H, O, N and C make up the "organic" molecules that constitute living organisms on a planet, the nuclei of these same elements interact to generate the light of its star. Then the organisms on the planet come to depend wholly on that starlight, as they must if life is to persist. So it is that all life on the Earth runs on sunlight.

The Molecules

And now, to molecules. By far the most important molecule to living organisms is water. No water, no life, anywhere in the universe. I think that water is also the strangest molecule in the whole world of chemistry, and its strangest property is that *ice floats*. If ice did not float I doubt that life would exist in the universe.

Ordinarily, upon cooling, everything contracts. So does water, down to four degrees centigrade. Then, from four degrees centigrade to zero, where it freezes, water expands, so rapidly that the ice when it forms is lighter that water and floats.

Nothing else does that. If water behaved like everything else, it would become increasingly dense as it cooled. The denser water would constantly be sinking to the bottom; freezing would begin at the bottom instead of the top as now, and would end by freezing the water solidly. A really large mass of ice takes very long to melt even when warmed. As it is, under the relatively thin skin of ice at the surface, all forms of life, animal and plant, survive the winter, and when the weather warms, the ice quickly melts. If ice did not float, it is hard to see how any life could survive a cold spell. On any planet in the universe, if a freeze occurred even once in millions of years, that would probably be enough to block the rise of life, and to kill any life that had arisen . . .

Cosmic Principle

Finally we have a cosmic principle. This universe is motivated by two great forces: the force of dispersion or expansion, powered by the Big Bang, and the force of aggregation, powered by gravity. If the force of expansion had dominated, all its matter would have gone on flying apart. There would be no large solid bodies, hence no *place* for life. If, on the other hand, gravity had dominated, the initial expansion produced by the Big Bang would have slowed up and come to an end, followed by a universal collapse—what some astrophysicists call the Big Crunch—perhaps in preparation for the next Big Bang. Then there would have been no *time* for life.

One can suppose that these forces might have taken any values whatever. Actually, they prove to be in exact balance, so that though the universe as a whole is expanding, locally it is held together by gravitation.

It is just this exact balance between the steady expansion of the universe as a whole and its stability locally that affords both enormous reaches of time and countless sites for the development of life.

A Living Universe

The burden of this story is that we find ourselves in a universe that breeds life and possesses the very particular properties that make that possible. The more deeply one penetrates, the more remarkable and subtle the fitness of this universe for life appears. Endless barriers lie in the way, yet each is surmounted somehow. It is as though, starting from the Big Bang, the universe pursued an intention to breed life, such is the subtlety with which difficulties in the way are got around, such are the singular choices in the values of key properties that could potentially have taken any value.

It is not surprising that this realm is being explored much more vigorously by physicists than by biologists, for it is concerned mainly not with life itself but with the physical preconditions for life. Some physicists have recently introduced the term "Anthropic Principle" to characterize a dominant theme of such discussions. It recognizes that "We could only be present in a universe that happens to supply our needs"[1], and that "What we can expect to observe must be restricted by the conditions necessary for our presence as observers"[2].

In this connection, I heard long ago a witticism that runs: "Why is the world five billion years old?"—and the answer is: "Because it took that long to find that out!" That interchange is of the essence of the Anthropic Principle, for no meaning can be attached to such a statement as that the Earth is 4.8 billion years old that does not imply the readiness of this universe to breed life, and the entire evolution on this planet of such creatures as physicists. And if one adds, "Yes, but the Earth really *is* 4.8 billion years old!"– what could that possibly mean out of its current human context? The reality is that such a statement says more of the nature of man than it does of the Earth.

One can draw a parallel Anthropic Principle in the realm of religion. Do gods create humans, or the other way around? I have imagined sometimes that Genesis I contains a mis-translation, that it should have read, "For man created God in his own image, in his own image created he Him, and gave Him dominion over the land and the sea and all manner of living things"—for that is what I think really happened. I was deeply moved to read lately in the Gnostic Gospel of Philip the passage: "That is the way it is in the world—men make gods and worship their creation. It would be fitting for the gods to worship men!"[3]. Men know of the gods only what they have said of them. An Anthropic Principle applied in this realm would recognize that all theologies say more about the nature of the men who made them than about the gods.

Just to choose a few points from the already sparse argument presented above. If the atomic nuclei were not so much more massive than the electrons weaving about them: if the electric charge on the proton did not exactly equal that on the electron: if ice did not float: if the forces of dispersion and aggregation in the universe were not in exact balance—then there might still be a universe, but lifeless. From our self-centered point of view, this is the best way to make a universe. But what I want to know is—how did the universe find that out? That leads me to my other great problem, that of consciousness.

II. The Problem of Consciousness

For me that problem was hardly avoidable, for I have spent most of my life in science studying mechanisms of vision. I learned my business on the eyes of frogs. The retina of a frog is very much like a human retina. Both contain two kinds of light receptors, rods for vision in dim light, cones for bright light. Both contain visual pigments based on vitamin A, that are very similar chemically and in their reactions to light. Both retinas are composed of the same three nerve layers and have parallel connections to the brain.

But I know that I see. Does a frog see? It reacts to light; so does a photoelectrically activated garage door. Does the frog know that it is reacting to light, is it self-aware? Now the dilemma: there is nothing whatever that I can do as a scientist to answer that kind of question.

I have of course preconceptions. A primary fact is my own consciousness. I have all kinds of evidence that other persons are conscious; our mutual communication through speech and writing helps greatly. I think that probably all mammals are conscious; and birds—why else would they sing at dawn and sunset? With frogs I begin to worry; with fish even more. I have worked on the eyes of many invertebrates—scallops, for example, that have eighty beautiful blue eyes in the mantles that line the borders of their shells, perhaps the most complex eyes anatomically in the animal kingdom—yet I have never seen any evidence that scallops use their eyes. And there is a class of marine worms found only in warm seas (Alciopids) that have great bulging eyes with everything one could hope for in an eye. The eyes yielded fine electrical responses to light, but I could never get the worms themselves to respond to light. There is no way whatever to shore up scientifically one's prejudices about animal consciousness.

One is in the same trouble with nonliving devices. Does that garage door resent having to open when the headlights of my car shine on it? I think not. Does a computer that has just beaten a human player at chess feel elated? I think not. But there is nothing one can do about those situations either.

The simple fact is that consciousness gives us no physical signals. What I have said of vision is equally true of any other sensory modality. We have no way of identifying either the presence or absence of consciousness, let alone its content.

That raises the problem of the location of consciousness. I had the joy of knowing Wilder Penfield, the great Canadian brain surgeon. In the course of his therapeutic work he had unprecedented opportunities to explore the brains of perfectly conscious unanesthetized patients. The point is, as he told me, that once the surface of the brain is exposed, it can be touched and probed without discomfort. For some years Penfield had hoped to find a center of consciousness in the brain. I once asked him, why did he think it was in the brain, why not in the whole nervous system, the whole body. He laughed and said, "Well, I'll keep on trying." When we met about two years later he said, "I'll tell you one thing: it's not in the cerebral cortex!"

I had already for some time taken it as a foregone conclusion that the mind—consciousness—could not be located. It is essentially absurd to think of locating a phenomenon that yields no physical signals, the presence or absence of which, outside of humans and their like, cannot be identified.

But further than that, mind is not only not locatable, it *has no location*. It is not a *thing* in space and time, not measurable; hence, as I said at the beginning of this chapter, not assimilable as science. And yet it is not to be dismissed as an epiphenomenon: it is the foundation, the condition that makes science possible. The entire point of science is to bring ever deeper and subtler aspects of reality to recognition in our consciousness. That recognition is itself virtually an act of creation. What would it mean to assert that something exists for which we have no "evidence"? We encounter here deep ambiguity between being and being known. Our consciousness is not only the precondition for science, but for reality: what exists is what has become manifest to our consciousness.

The problem of consciousness tends to embarrass biologists. Taking it to be an aspect of living things, they feel they should know about it and be able to tell physicists about it, whereas they have nothing relevant to say. But physicists live with the problem of consciousness day in and day out. The very crux of twentieth-century physics is the recognition that the observer cannot be excluded from his observations; he is an intrinsic participant in them.

Let me give a simple example. All of you surely have heard that radiation—like light—and all the elementary particles have simultaneously the properties of particles and of waves, though those properties are altogether different, indeed, mutually exclusive. That recognition was the basis for Niels Bohr's principle of complementarity, which notes that numbers of phenomena, in and out of physics, exhibit such mutually exclusive sets of properties; one just has to live with them.

Consider a physicist setting up an experiment on radiation. Enter his consciousness. He chooses beforehand which set of properties he will encounter. If he does a wave experiment, he finds wave properties; if he does a particle experiment, he finds particle properties. To this degree all physical observation is subjective.

III. Mind and Matter

I have propounded two riddles: 1) the very peculiar character of a universe such as ours, that breeds life; and 2) the problem of consciousness, mind, which is a phenomenon that lies outside the parameters of space and time, that has no location.

A few years ago it occurred to me that these seemingly very disparate problems might be brought together. And this could happen through the hypothesis that mind, rather than being a very late development in the evolution of living things, restricted to organisms with the most complex nervous systems—all of which I had believed to be true—has been there always. And that this universe is life-breeding because the pervasive presence of mind had guided it to be so.

That thought, though elating as a game is elating, so offended my scientific sensibilities as to embarrass me. It took only a few weeks, however, for me to realize that I was in excellent company. That kind of thought is not only deeply embedded in millennia-old Eastern philosophies, but it has been expressed plainly by a number of great and very recent physicists.

So Arthur Eddington said (1928):

> The stuff of the world is mind-stuff.... The mind-stuff is not spread in space and time.... Recognizing that the physical world is entirely abstract and without 'actuality' apart from its linkage to consciousness, we restore consciousness to the fundamental position.[4]

And Erwin Schrödinger said:

> Mind has erected the objective outside world of the natural philosopher out of its own stuff. Mind could not cope with the gigantic task otherwise than by the simplifying device of excluding itself... withdrawing from its conceptual.[5]

I like most of all Wolfgang Pauli's formulation:

> To us ... the only acceptable point of view appears to be the one that recognizes both sides of reality—the quantitative and the qualitative, the physical and the psychical—as compatible with each other, and can embrace them simultaneously.... It would be most satisfactory of all if physics and psyche (i.e. matter and mind) could be seen as complementary aspects of the same reality.[6]

What this comes down to is that one has no more reason to deny an aspect of mind to all matter than to deny the properties of waves to all elementary particles. Pauli here is calling again upon Bohr's principle of complementarity. Mind and matter are the complementary aspects of all reality.

Let me say that it is not only easier to say these things to physicists than to my fellow biologists, but easier to say them in India than in the West. For when I speak of mind pervading the universe, of mind as a creative principle perhaps primary to matter, any Hindu will acquiesce, will think, yes, of course, he is speaking of *Brahman*. The Judeo-Christian-Islamic God *constructed* a universe and just once. Brahman *thinks* a universe and does so in cycles, time without end. As the Upanishads tell us, each of us has a share in *Brahman*, the *Atman*, the essential Self, ageless, imperishable. "Tat tvam asi"—Thou art That! That is the stuff of the universe, mind-stuff; and yes, each of us shares in it.

This article is adapted from Synthesis of Science and Religion: Critical Essays and Dialogues *published by the Bhaktivedanta Institute, 1988.*

References

1. R. H. Dicke, *Nature,* 192, 1961, p. 440.

2. B. Carter, in *Confrontation of Cosmological Theories with Observation,* edited by M. S. Longair, Dordrecht, 1974.

3. *Nag Hammadi Library,* Harper and Row, 1981, p.143—written probably in Syria in the late 3rd century CE.

4. *Nature of the Physical World* by Arthur Eddington, Cambridge University Press, 1928, pp. 276-277.

5. *Mind and Matter* by Erwin Schrödinger, Cambridge University Press, 1958.

6. *Interpretation of Nature and the Psyche* by C. G. Jung and W. Pauli (each writing separately), Bollingen, 1955, pp. 208-210.

Man, Matter and Metaphysics:
Can We Create a Total Science?

by Richard Dixey

Causes are the stuff of science; when a scientist appears, people look to him to be able to say "because"—to give reasons and explanations for occurrences, and to link them by causal connections proved by experimental reason, safe and secure.

At least that is the reason why I became fascinated by science. I can remember the day: I was 13, lonely at a new school where again I was boarding a long way from home. I found a book in the library, a book of biology which began with the water cycle and the food chain; there were diagrams showing where all animals belonged, and how they related one to another. It was ordered yet universal, precise yet everything had its place. There was symmetrical interrelationship, balances and energy flows, the seeming multiplicity of life revealed as an expression of an underlying order. I was hooked.

Yet even as I was becoming entranced with this wonder, there were loud rumblings at its foundations. For behind the rhythmic spaces of the textbook diagrams—that belong with baroque music and classical architecture in that love of reasoned harmony which I know now to be a taproot of Western culture—there were voices questioning its validity and relevance, questioning whether science could be held to be universally true, questioning its historical role as a reliable source of knowledge, opportunity and progress.

This was the time of the astronauts and the Apollo program, and looking back, it seems ironic that those who experienced almost the apogee of scientifically generated experience, those brave men who flew into the skies in devices that displayed quite astonishing feats of technical achievement, should have come back to Earth talking not of Dan Dare and the next horizon, but of meaning, and humanity, and of the greater purposes of life.

These concerns echoed my own early experiences, as I began to perceive that at the heart of the scientific endeavor there was a problem that refused to go away. For science was utterly silent on those great issues that seemed to be its very fruit, and silent not by choice but seemingly by definition. Man the observer was an onlooker for real, pawn rather than player, his perceptions and the meanings he ascribed to them irrelevant to the world of harmonies and order, reason and law—that very same world that had seemed, at one time, so attractive.

It dawned on me slowly but surely. I hung on grimly to a notion of truth as a kind of transcendent actuality—like the dark stone in Kubrick's "2001"—but even that seeming certainty, that I was learning something definite about the world, came under attack and eventually buckled utterly.

This is not the place to rehearse the arguments that have led to the collapse of the confident assertions of the special nature of scientific truth. For me, it started with Gödel, who brought me to the realization that no truly objective statement was possible. But of course a rounded approach to this problem would also entail Popper's denial of the possibility of verification, substituting in its place the idea that what makes science special is the fact that it deals in statements that are intrinsically falsifiable, and, further, the collapse of *that* notion with the final acceptance that no statements of fact can be made without other theoretical reference. A comprehensive discussion of these matters can be found in the excellent *Criticism and the Growth of Knowledge* edited by Lakatos and Musgrove.[1]

Of course none of these arguments made a blind bit of difference to how science was carried out or indeed taught. Like many others, I experimented with giving it up altogether as a complete waste of time, and going off to explore the esoteric and Eastern views of the world. But then I returned, and for a specific reason. I came back because it seemed to me that for all its faults, science tries to operate by a truth criterion, and although it was the corrigibility of that criterion that had been coming in for so much attack, I began to see that it was of considerable value. Without such a criterion, who can distinguish between truth and falsity? Too often such a decision is based on political or personal power.

So why concentrate on causation? The upshot of all the critical arguments seems to be the inevitability of viewing science as a language: a view, among other ways, of viewing and describing the world. But it is a language with a truth claim attached. It endeavors to be both descriptive and yet explanatory—that is, it tries to find reasons for what is observed. That those reasons are themselves subject to further analysis is the basis for the downfall of absolute verifiability—or indeed total falsifiability—but the structure still stands, even though, as Popper so aptly put it, it is standing on piles driven into the mud!

What interests me now is the way in which strategies of explanation, which are in themselves the expression of systems of causation—ways of fielding the word "because"—influence and limit the applicability of the scientific language. It is the problem of demarcation as Popper so astutely pointed out,[2] but now, true to the spirit of the post modern age, the issue is not how we can narrow the net of scientific respectability so as to keep other ways of seeing the world out, but rather how we can widen it so as to make science more inclusive and universal.

People and Things

This issue comes into sharpest focus in dealing with the personal realm. The question can be put simply: are people things? Can people be assimilated within a single worldview, a single interlocking system of causation, or are people different in some way? In turn this leads to another question, as to whether scientific knowledge can be truly universal, or whether there are large areas of experience about which science must always remain silent.

And this relates directly to causation, for if there are people and then there are things, it follows that there are two types of cause: volitional cause and mechanical cause. The problem is that in a person the two are mixed; so I might say that "I went to the grocery store because I was hungry" and feel that I had explained my action. But mechanistically, my behavior could be restated as the effect of falling blood sugar triggering the firing of cells in the hypothalamus which in turn stimulated the commencement of a learned behavior pattern. So did I really decide anything at all? It goes without saying that if people are really things, then the first explanation must be a subset of the second; that is, that only one type of cause is truly operating.

But if people are not things, how can the first type of cause, the causal action particular to people, be explained? It can only be explained in terms of the reasons, backgrounds, experiences of people themselves. The person is then seen as a cause rather than as the result of causes, and mechanical causation is reversed.

Representing and Intervening[3]

Before getting onto causation as such, however, I would like to make some observations about how scientific knowledge is generated. These arise from the metaphor of science as a special kind of language—"organized common sense" as it was put in the Victorian era. This notion leads naturally to the idea that scientific knowledge is a special type of perception, often instrumentally aided, and that through the operation of the instruments that are used, whether they are microscopes or space ships, science gives us a wider and deeper view of physical reality.

Were that the case, then the truth claim that attaches to scientific knowledge would be far less problematical, and the process of scientific analysis would be neutral with respect to what was seen or discovered, like a good lens on a camera. But the truth is that the process is active rather than passive; it is a system of representation rather than perception, and much of the knowledge is generated through intervention rather than by passive observation.

In these two respects modern science is quite different from that of the ancient Greeks, for whom true knowledge could only be generated through the classification of naturally occurring objects. Any other form of information—say that generated by experiment—was specifically excluded as unnatural and thus of no value. As a result, Greek science represented itself as a search for Truth in some absolute sense. The problem is that this idea of the search for Absolute Truth is still applied to the modern scientific enterprise, even though the Greek principle of non-intervention was overturned during the Renaissance in a process that reached its peak in the writings of Bacon and Galileo in the sixteenth century.

I have described the historical development of the scientific worldview in other publications,[4] and will not, therefore, rehearse the long story here. The decisive move from observation to intervention can be found in the writings of Francis Bacon, most notably in the *Organum*, where he is explicit in arguing for the validity of knowledge "wrest from Nature" rather than that passively gathered. This alone leads to the problem of the validity of such knowledge and the famous problems inherent in inductive generalization that came to dominate the philosophical concerns of the period that followed.

But were this the only development that occurred in the sixteenth century, the radical changes that transformed the generation of scientific knowledge would not have come about. Just gathering more and more information, even if it is from unusual and strange places, is not enough to start the "engine of discovery" in the way that Bacon described; any reading of the early annals of the Royal Society reveals how that very same engine was initially swamped by a mountain of extraneous and irrelevant information generated by the unregulated experimental program that Bacon recommended.

For what is not so often said, although it perhaps leads to a more fruitful insight into the nature of scientific knowledge, is that it fell to Galileo to make the other crucial transition—the transition from perception to representation—in this fundamental reformulation of the acquisition of knowledge.

Working from an Ideal World

The process to which I am referring is the introduction by Galileo of suppositional logic in his analysis of mechanics.[5] This logical form had been developed over the preceding one hundred years in the proving of herbal remedies, and it is interesting to note that Galileo worked at the medical university of Padua when he carried out his most fruitful work.[6] The process he introduced was a form of argument, a system of logic, that led to a complete reversal of the way to find true causes, and lay behind much of the controversy that surrounded him. Supposition is to use the form "if we suppose this, then that will happen . . ." in the analysis of physical processes. In particular, Galileo used the supposition of the motion of objects on ideal planes, perfectly flat and without resistance, to develop the mathematics that he then applied, with added constants and other factors, in a description of the perceived motion of objects in the actual world. Such devices were necessary to allow the application of mathematics to motion, just as they had been effective in enabling the use of ratios in the proving of herbal mixtures.

But what was different about Galileo's approach was that he applied this process in a most general way. Not content with merely using it in mechanics, he sought to justify its use through a total reformulation of the conception of the external world. In his hands this was no mere tool, but evidence that the physical world was very different from what we see and feel it to be. Galileo argued most persuasively that all that actually exists is a collection of simple entities described by shape, motion and weight, and that all the other characteristics of the perceivable world are hallucinations generated by the process of perception and which stand in the way of genuine insight. Indeed with regard to the latter point, nowadays it is recognized that even common perceptions are really representations, and that common sense is a form of construct just as much as more obviously theoretical statements.[7]

This profound event justifies extensive scrutiny. Scientific analysis uses a technique that has been firmly embedded from the time of Galileo: a technique that creates an idealized model of whatever is to be explained, and then curve fits it to what is actually observed. Such curve fitting, with its concomitant introduction of completely arbitrary constants and scaling factors, is central to the process, and may even seem to be the actual engine of discovery itself. The problem is that this process has become so familiar that it is entirely implicit, and creating representations through building models in ideal spaces, often with complex numbers and lurking infinites, before bringing them down to the observable with the luggage of scaling constants and normalizing functions, is an everyday activity that every scientist has become familiar with.

But if knowledge is generated in this way, then what do these ideal models actually represent? What do the terms within them actually mean? *They are not generated from the observable; they are a simulacrum of it.* To claim that the entities in the equations actually exist is to belie how they have been generated; indeed, as is now widely recognized, the fact that such a process can be used to model observable reality is perhaps the greatest mystery of all, and has been used to make quite general statements about the nature of man and his relation to the Universe.[8]

The Three Card Trick

Nowhere has this inversion in the way knowledge is generated had greater impact than in man's perception of man. For in the transition from perception to representation, man himself has been quite literally pushed out of the picture. Man as a causal agent, as knower and doer, creator and destroyer—the mind of man—seems to have no place in this idealized recreation of experience.

How this has come about reminds me of the famous three card trick that is played sometimes on unsuspecting passers-by in busy shopping streets. There are three cards laid out on a table and you are invited to bet with the player of the trick that you can follow the movements of a large denomination banknote that is placed under one of them. He then starts sliding the cards around, weaving them past one another; after a few seconds, the bet is placed and you choose the card whose movements you have been following; surely it is under there! It never is of course—the note has gone and with it your money.

In the same way, there has been a three card trick to remove mind from matter—to remove mind completely, in fact, so that it has gone like the banknote. The first card is the view of the ancients. The Greeks saw man as causally effective in a world of effective causes: a player among other players, if you like. His freedom was limited by considerations of natural harmony and economy, but the idea that purposive action was possible was a central theme of the underlying causal structures, which were codified as the notorious "final cause" of Aristotle's analysis.

But this sort of analysis caused tremendous problems when it was reintroduced to the Europe of Christendom. If man were causal in some sense, then what was the relation of that causal potency to God, who is the ultimate cause? For if man were made in God's image, and God were outside his creation in the sense of being able to miraculously intervene in its order, then was not man too in some sense beyond the surrounding structure of causes? Was not Homo sapiens—the thinking animal—somehow different in kind from all other living beings? Here the Christian view lay in direct contradiction with Greek knowledge, with its well articulated conception of the natural world with man firmly embedded within it. With the growing acceptance of Greek thought during the Renaissance, this ancient conception of man led to the widespread promulgation of a kind of atheism, perhaps better described as pantheistic naturalism, that began to seriously threaten the authority of the Church.

It is against this background that the second card of the three card trick was played—the absolute generalization of the Galilean supposition into a complete system by Descartes. Supported by (possibly even employed by) the Oratorian order of the Catholic Church, Descartes was the first to realize that the paradox presented between the law-like behavior of the creation and the creative freedom of both God and man could only be solved by the posit of a complete split between God and His creation. Such a split enabled him to describe a clear conception of law, that is, the mathematical properties by which the Godhead ordered the behavior of matter. This law God could change, if He wished, at any time from moment to moment; that it did not change allowed the possibility of knowledge to that most special being of His creation, man, for God would not knowingly deceive. Purposive action was a possibility only for man; for the rest lay only the following of law by brute matter.

Of course there was a demarcation problem as to where the machine stopped and the heavenly stuff began. Broadly speaking animals were seen as totally mechanical; indeed there was an extraordinary, almost obscene, out-working of this split in the science of Iatromechanics in which the workings of animals were modeled on hydraulic principles. And there was also the problem of so-called Magnetick phenomena: the influences of tides and weather on mood and health, the mysterious processes of germination and fertility, where there seemed to be ghostly "stuff" that was almost an intermediate between God and the mechanical world.

Then the third card was played. The mechanical explanations could be made total. As Laplace said, "I don't need God in this hypothesis . . ." This happened in the nineteenth century, although its roots were in the Enlightenment. People realized that their mechanical ideas could be made so comprehensive that they did not need God, and by default the mind of man, Descarte's "Cogito", at all. Mind as a causal agent was written out of the equation. Now instead of having material causes and mind, final cause, in a world ruled by natural law, mind had gone. We have inherited a world in which mind is not a natural category at all.

The Structure of Scientific Explanation

With this history as a background, I would like to look more closely at how scientific representations are made, and where any possible anomalies might lie.

The point is of course that we are born into a world that predates us; we arrive with the show going on, and so are faced with the task of inferring both what is actually there and how it might operate. Most notably, there are a succession of complex characteristics of the material world, complex properties if you like, which under scientific analysis reveal themselves to be the product of underlying mechanisms (processes). But they present themselves to our raw perceptions as a whole array, not broken up into convenient parcels for us to look at.

There is a two-fold rhythm to the process of scientific analysis: induction moves from the particular to the general; the general principles are then applied deductively to generate predictions which can be checked against experience. Thus representations which are generated by induction lead to novel interventions, and these, in turn, modify the representations. The process is self-referential, but the circle of referents grows; thus it can be seen as spiral rather than a circle.

All this is very well, and is an expression of the bed-rock intuition that our knowledge is advancing, progressing, even if we cannot measure it from any outside vantage point. Predictions get more and more accurate, and more and more phenomena are brought into articulation within an integrated structure, even though the cycle of representations based on and generating new interventions is not logically impervious.

This movement from the observed behavior of a thing to a description of "how it works" is the classic form of scientific explanation. Normally the process of induction proceeds by two stages. First the complex properties of things are broken down into an array of simpler properties. This is the process of reduction, often associated with special places where the reductive process takes place (laboratories) and involving all the schemata of classification. Reduction in this sense is really a methodological technique, as the original properties are too complex to analyze directly. But once clear descriptions of these simple properties are achieved, then they can be redescribed as the outworkings of mechanisms, processes. This is the second stage, through which the explanatory task is achieved.

But what lies behind this cycle? Are there any rules that can be discerned that might throw light on its operation overall? To do this I have made a map which endeavors to sum up how things are explained: how the special language of science is related to the observable world (see Diagram 1 page 142).

Take the ability to speak as an example. Here is a property of persons which requires explanation. As such it is too complicated a phenomenon, so it is reduced, via studies of language and human anatomy and physiology, to a property of an area of the brain; so one might say "I can talk to you now because of an area of my brain..." But even this is too complicated: studies seem to reveal that this ability is itself due to the firing of a whole array of cells in that brain area. So now we are getting down to a much simpler property with which to complete our explanation. For having got to that point, one can then redescribe the behavior of the array of cells in terms of the processes within them; the explanation is accomplished.

Looking at such a scheme, it is clearly an outworking of the original Galilean conception. Appearances are seen as misleading, in that the characteristic behavior of things are themselves composite and made up of simpler things; the behavior of these simpler things is itself the outworking of simple processes. Thus the multifarious appearance of the world is seen, explained—understood as caused by—the behavior of a small number of actual processes.

But how do we know that there are only a small number of such processes? Why, for example, should the arrow of explanation not cross from property to process higher up in the scale of complexity? Why, for example, can there not be complex and irreducible processes that generate complex properties?

The Need for Emergent Causes

Indeed, in following the arrow of cause from the properties of things to the processes that underlie those properties, it has been clear for some time that there are properties which cannot be totally described at the level of atomic forces or whatever. This realization has led to the concept of "emergent causes" to describe properties that are observed at higher levels of complexity. It is not a new concept; Bindra, in a critique of Sperry's concept of emergent causation, argues that the need for such a concept was first recognized in the early eighteenth century.[9] A simple example is the argument that the collective properties of water cannot be explained in terms of the properties of its individual constituents (in this case hydrogen and oxygen); something is added as they come into chemical relationship. The property of water emerges, and no complete explanation of water can be made at the simplest level without a statement of its behavior in terms of properties at a higher level of complexity.

But such emergent causes do not in themselves imply that there are processes operating at that level of complexity that are not based on the behavior of the constituent parts; what is being evoked is the idea that in those areas where the behavior of the parts is indeterminate, higher order causes can supervene. Thus, to give another example that is used by Roger Sperry in discussing this idea, an iron cartwheel may be comprised of iron atoms, but its behavior in rolling down a hill supervenes on all of them and cannot be predicted from any one of them individually. To use an anthropomorphic metaphor, the atoms "do not care" whether they are rolling collectively or not, so the possibility of that behavior emerges. But they would care if one tried to break the wheel into pieces and they would resist it; hence the property of the cartwheel in holding its particular form through time can be properly described at a lower level of analysis, as a property of the individual atoms that make it up.

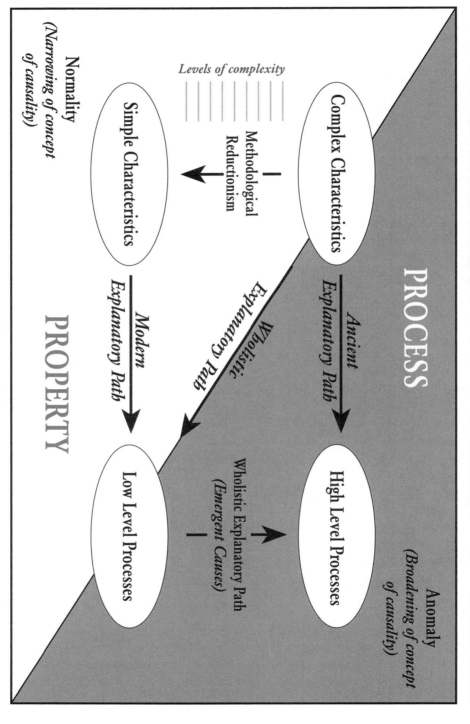

Diagram 1
Causality: Mapping "Explanatory Paths"

So this acts as a critique of reductionism, that first step in the analysis of phenomena into the simplest parts mentioned above. There are manifold examples where complete descriptions of the properties of things in terms of the processes that bring them into being cannot be made at a simple level; there is a nesting hierarchy of levels from the atomic through the chemical to the organismic, culminating perhaps in the psychological itself. Each one of these exploits areas that are indeterminate in the behavior of its constituents and the structures of which it is made.

States of Being

But are these emergent properties indicative of true causes? Can one, for example, follow in the footsteps of Galileo and Descartes and conclude from their existence that there must also be emergent states of being—"emergent processes", to use the terminology of my analysis? In other words, what ontological status do such causes have?

Take for example the quote from Marjorie Grene[10] used in her discussion of causation in biology. Having stated that "At least a two level ontology is needed for the interpretation of living things" she then goes on to say that "the higher level depends for its existence on the lower level, but the laws of the lower level, although presupposed by, cannot explain the existence of the higher . . ."

But the posit of a two level ontology has direct implications. How can one level be "dependent" on another in an ontological sense? Are we dealing here with names or with real entities?

This issue is clarified further by an inquiry into how such emergent causes might have their effect. In the first case, where analysis reveals that it is necessary to propose the operation of forces that cannot be predicted from the atomic or subatomic level—the emergent causes—the action of such forces is not direct but is mediated through the lower levels of activity; mediated, as was mentioned, through supervening in areas of indeterminacy in those lower levels. And as long as there is no conflict between the operation of the higher order causes and those of the lower levels of structure there will be no problem; in fact there can never be conflict, for in areas where there is determinate action in the lower levels there can never be supervening action from above; the emergent causes have no causal potency in this regard.

But the possibility exists, in theory at least, that there might be causes that are "true" causes at the level of complexity to which they refer; that is, causes which act directly rather than being mediated through lower levels. For example, if we apply this distinction to our map and ask whether there are complex processes in this second sense, then it is to areas such as psychokinesis or telepathy that one would look for answers. Here the action of mind on matter is direct rather than mediated through the volitional control of the body. An earlier version of this idea was the posit of a vital force inherent within living systems; that is, a force beyond the mere physical functioning of the organismic world. This is the ancient explanatory path; that of complex causation—the proposal of causal potency, arising directly from a high level of complexity rather than being mediated through lower levels of structure: like the person mentioned earlier, the causal potency arises directly from that level of complexity rather than emerging from below. (See Diagram 1, which shows causal arrows operating higher up the scale of complexity.)

Being and Knowing

It is this aspect of the idea of emergent causes that worries me most. What exactly are emergent causes? Do they refer to real things or are they just ways of looking? The problem is very simple. I have mentioned the nice image of the nesting hierarchy of levels rising from the atomic and perhaps culminating in the psychological, or perhaps even the spiritual. But now we know that the atomic level itself is an emergent form, emergent from the subatomic realm beneath it. And that realm, too, emerges from even more layers below. So, as was mentioned in the example of the cartwheel, each level operates in the gaps left by the level below, which in its turn relies on the level below it, and so on. What sort of ontology is this? It was Popper who first pointed out that epistemologically science is "driving piles into the mud";[11] now this metaphor seems to apply ontologically as well. The Galilean conception of complex appearances revealed as the operations of underlying processes—the idea that there is some bedrock of reality upon which we can rely—seems a total chimera.

If the behavior at every level is to be seen as emerging from the level below it, then it is clear that some novel conception is needed to fulfil the unique task of science, which is to give reasons and explanations that are not mere descriptions in other words.

Building Blocks for the Materialist

Of course the dominant form of this task of explanation has been materialism; materialism asserts the omnicompetence of science. Or, to be more precise, it asserts that a total statement of observable reality can be made using the interactions of a strictly limited number of categories of being. These categories provide the basic concepts that can be used in the explanation, and must be a given to it. As I have tried to explain elsewhere,[12] in this sense they are metaphysical to it, in that they are chosen prior to the process of represen-

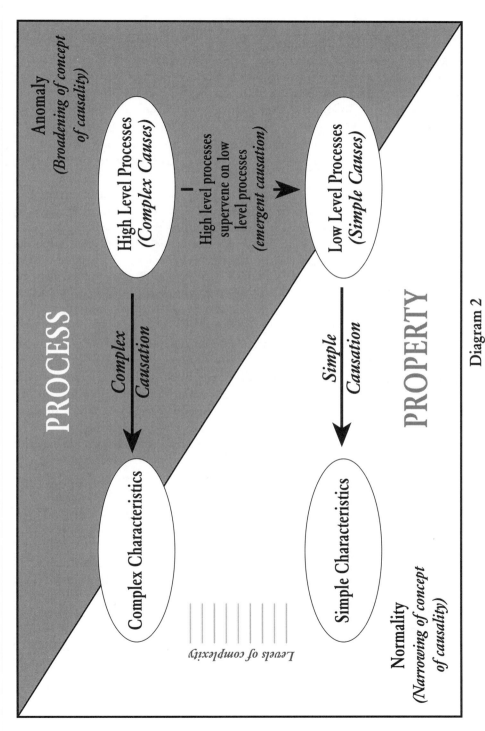

Diagram 2

Mapping the Operation of Causes

tation and intervention in which they are brought into relation with the observable world in all its complexity. It is in this context that the question must arise as to whether the set of categories presently in use, coupled with the idea of emergent causes arising at different levels in a hierarchy of structure, can provide a total statement of all there is; that is, a theory of everything.

Indeed the category set that is proposed by scientific materialism is surprisingly small. Materialism proposes that all that exists is matter and energy moving in space and time, which in turn can be described as a deformation of a space-time matrix. All other properties are proposed as emergent from this primal reality.

The problem is that matter and energy as such cannot account for the structures from which the other properties emerge. For even at the simplest level, matter and energy behave in predictable ways—they are law-like. How are we to account for that within the materialist category set? Here we see a trace of the three card trick, for in the Cartesian split between mind and matter, law-likeness was placed very firmly in the mind realm, as God's ordering of base matter. Without such ordering all would be chaos. *But with the Laplacian removal of the mind stuff altogether, the fact of law-likeness is left without any explanatory foundation at all.*

Matter and energy are fundamental quantities, and scientific materialism aims to make a comprehensive quantitative statement about physical reality. Qualitative statements were rejected along with final causes in the overthrow of scholasticism that began with Galileo and which was completed in the early nineteenth century. As Galileo pointed out to such devastating effect, qualitative statements are just names for types of behavior, rather than explanations of them; as exemplified in his wonderful description of the effects of morphine being due to its "dormative quality".

But law-likeness is a quality, not a quantity. Matter and energy may exist quantitatively, but laws qualify quantitative behavior. So it should be no surprise at all to find that modern statements of law-likeness, expressed in terms of the laws governing the behavior of subatomic particles, carry blatantly qualitative names such as "charm" and "up" or "down". In a sense such ascriptions are just indications of modern physicists coming clean about what has been true all along, namely that a totally quantitative science is just not possible.

So what of the possibilities that arise out of the indeterminate potential of the present day basement of scientific reality (soon to be further excavated, no doubt)? Such emergent properties also qualify the behavior of matter and energy in combination, but cannot be accounted for by them alone. If you like, to return to the causal map, scientific materialism has no category to account for its vertical axis—the axis of increasing complexity and increasingly qualified behavior—and so has no way of accounting for emergent causes at all.

Even further, following the arrow of complexity back down again in the causal map, it is clear that a science of quantities has no way of accounting for causes at all! This seemingly surprising conclusion was in fact pointed out by Hume in his examination of mechanical and volitional causes. In concluding that volitional causes are the only true causes that exist, he described mechanical causes as the mere succession of events, with no necessary linkage between them of any sort.[13]

Information

A scientific language that claims to accurately describe the world but cannot account for causes! Perhaps an overhaul of the category set is overdue. It seems that in the rejection of the dualist solution, in which all structuring resides in the mind stuff, the material remnant of the original pair is not up to its explanatory task.

One solution to this problem has received some attention of late. I refer to the widely canvassed idea that *information* might be the category that is missing. Instead of the duopoly of energy and matter, the trinity made by the addition of information to the ultimate category set offers a tremendous increase in explanatory potential. Its addition to the picture seems to offer the possibility of accounting for both causes and complexity, and so provide the vertical dimension on the causal map so obviously missing from a purely quantitative account.

To do this requires just one simple rule: the idea that information bound to matter and energy is determinative of causal action. At the most basic level, this means that there is information that determines the law-like behavior of matter, and as matter is arranged in more and more complex wholes, it is the bound information that accounts for its new properties.[14]

The reason that information can fill this role is that, unlike matter and energy, information is not subject to conservation law, even though, like matter and energy, it can be properly defined as a substance. A substance is defined as that which underlies manifestations, so in the new scheme there are three categories underlying manifestation—matter, energy and information—and although the amount of matter and energy may be a finite quantity in any system, the amount of information is potentially infinite. It is from this "information gain" that the hierarchy of increasingly qualified and complex behavior emerges.

With this simple concept, the otherwise inexplicable properties displayed by matter become open to analysis. For example, it is a well worn adage that "all there is" in a human body is a few glasses of chemicals dissolved in eight gallons of water. Now quantitatively that is true. But what is wrong with it as a statement is that it takes no account of the vast amount of information bound into those few glasses of chemicals, in the rising hierarchy represented by physics, chemistry, biochemistry, physiology, behavior, etc. This successive binding of information to matter and energy can be seen as the determinative factor in the complex behavior that so obviously emerges; so that emergent properties, instead of having to be accepted as the unaccountable ordering of the windows of indeterminacy left by the basic laws of physics, are now revealed as the consequences of information itself.

An Information Physics?

Recently, a fascinating attempt has been made to create a total science of information, in which information is related to entropy and so is incorporated into the basic laws of thermodynamics as a quantitative measure. I refer here to a recent book by Tom Stonier[15] which makes a persuasive case for this possibility. Having set up camp, so to speak, at the basic level, Stonier then attempts to derive a relationship between information and organization, and so establish a link to the difficult property of entropy. This established, he then goes on to look at the function such a concept could play in the physics of energy and the concept of work, deriving the concept of useful work in terms of the "structural information" that is bound into the matter of energy transducers, be they heat engines or living beings. He even succeeds in a derivation of the amount of information, measured in bits, that is contained in a molar weight of the enzyme trypsin. In this scheme, proteins, the basic stuff of the biological realm, are revealed as information systems, and life is redescribed in an enlarged conception of physics.

But the treatment of information that Stonier gives, and the more general ideas described above, still raise problems. For example Stonier draws out an analogy between information and energy. Energy, in pre-relativity physics, is the abstract quantity which, when added to matter, manifests as heat. In the same way, he considers information to be the abstract quantity which, when added to matter, manifests itself as structure. Then, following a purely quantitative treatment, Stonier endeavors to derive a relationship between energy and information, analogous to that between energy and matter.

Here, however, the argument begins to break down, for in many ways information is quite different from matter and energy. As has been pointed out above, while information can be measured, it is not subject to conservation laws. One way in which this difference can be highlighted is in terms of meaning, which can be defined as the extent to which information is conveyed. For example, if a book in English is translated into a foreign language, then to the reader who can only speak English it will convey little or nothing; although it contains the same amount of information as its English original, the information is not conveyed. The problem is that this sort of distinction breaks any simple equation between information and other quantitative measures. To give another example, if one broadcasts a message to a million people, the information that has been conveyed in total is far greater than if one merely speaks the same message to a single listener. However, the energy used in running the transmitters is the same whether the message is being received or not. Thus no simple equation between energy and information seems viable.

The Problem of Life

One of the major questions raised by theories such as Stonier's is whether a merely quantitative conception of information provides an adequate conception of life itself. For in providing a category of being for the observable property of complexity, information theories seem to open the way to describe all the hierarchy of sciences in the same terminology. Thus the development from the inert to the animate can now be redescribed in terms of the binding of information to matter. As such, this seems an idea that is absolutely congruent with the Darwinian evolutionary model, where it is the information expressed in the germ line that provides both the link and the motive for the passage of life from generation to generation.

This has the added benefit that the biosphere as well as the organisms within it can be re-analyzed in new terms. The daily activities of living beings inform their environment; thus this new perspective leads to the prediction that the behavior of the biosphere would be inadequately modeled by merely geological considerations, and new and emergent levels of behavior would be expected to appear once life had evolved. These ideas, made famous by the Gaia hypothesis of James Lovelock[16] now appear as a consequence of the outworking of natural law.

Indeed one can go further; such a conception provides an attractive approach to the old paradox of volitional versus mechanical causation. Living beings inform their environment, and nowhere is this more apparent than in the activities of man. Within this framework, the impact of man on the environment is just a further outworking of the informing of matter, a further development of the biosphere. Volitional causation is then seen as an emergent capacity of the structure of the brain, in which the new potentials of this, the most structured piece of matter on the planet, become expressed through the mediation of the body.

However, despite its attractiveness, this new scheme has a major weakness. The problem with it is the problem of meaning, in that a purely quantitative conception of meaning cannot achieve this explanatory task. This is because information requires a context in which to be conveyed. Just as in the analogy of the book, the information in the germ line requires all the apparatus of gene expression and control to convey its message, which otherwise lies dormant. Something in the cell recognizes the useful information from the useless and expresses it, and it is here that the crucial process occurs. Within the Darwinian explanatory scheme, both the storage of information and the process of recognition are understood to be products of historical development rather than purposive choice, but the two-fold nature of the transmission of information is usually totally overlooked when Darwinian explanations are elaborated. Whereas random mutations in the germ line provide one polarity in the transmission of information from generation to generation, the other, the creation of suitable contexts in which such information can convey its meaning, is totally ignored. But without this second polarity, which is the receptive aspect, the changes in the first transmissive polarity can have no result.

Consciousness: A Return to the Problem of People and Things

Nowhere is this problem more apparent that in the attempt to account for the sensibility and behavior of the animal realm. For example, it is often proposed that the process by which sense organs evolve proceeds via the chance development of areas of sensitive skin, which confer selective advantage and so provide the basis for the development of increasingly sophisticated structures. Richard Dawkins[17] uses this account to reconstruct how the eye developed in lower vertebrates. But again, the problem of meaning rears its head. In order for such an initial mutation, in this case light-sensitive skin, to confer any advantage at all, the potential information has to be processed and converted into appropriate behavior. So not only must there be the initial mutation, but there must also be an interlocking mutation of the nervous system so that the information is conveyed to the brain of the animal, and a simultaneous mutation in the processing of sensation to account for the new stimulus and change the behavior of the animal to respond to it appropriately. All this is required for the new information to become meaning: the new genetic information alone is not enough.[18]

A similar problem regarding the conveying of information can be found in the writings of Roger Sperry. Sperry argues that conscious states are both emergent and genuinely causal states of the brain, unlike the materialist model of brain function that sees consciousness as an epiphenomenon of neural process. Along with the materialists, however, Sperry represents consciousness as the patterning of the neural networks of the brain.[19] As such, these ideas represent a criticism of the notion that a complete description of behavior can be given without an appeal to the causal potency of states of consciousness, while at the same time avoiding positing a dualistic solution as to where the causal potency of such states comes from.

But can one have an emergent phenomenon which is genuinely causal, rather than merely expressing an emergent property as described above? Sperry's analysis of the perception of pain is instructive:

> What is critical is the unique pattern of brain excitation that produces pain instead of something else . . . (it) must be conceived functionally and operationally in terms of its impact on a living unanesthetized cerebral system. . . . To try to explain the pain pattern or any other mental quality only in terms of spatio-temporal arrangement of nerve impulses without reference to the mental properties and the mental qualities themselves would be as formidable as trying to describe any of the complex molecular reactions known to biochemistry wholly in terms of the properties of electrons, protons and neutrons.

But here is a problem: what is this "pain pattern" or any other mental quality? Sperry is quite specific in stating that such conscious states are the patterning of neural processes, but what recognizes and interprets these patterns? What makes them meaningful—some higher order pattern? Somewhere, something has to recognize itself, or the information that is potentially present will not be conveyed, and so cannot be posited as the origin of causal potency.

So what is becoming apparent here is a problem of causation. Sperry's analysis requires that the causal potency of states of consciousness is necessary to account for behavior. The Darwinian solution to this has been to propose that although such states may seem causal, they have arisen in a historical process of trial and error. But both explanations, even if elaborated with a quantitative conception of information to provide for the emergence of novel structures, take for granted that the information contained in those structures is effectively conveyed and made meaningful. Does this imply a yet higher source of order? Somewhere the causal buck has to stop.

The Nature of the Qualitative: A Recapitulation

At this point in a long argument, it is time for a recapitulation; and it seems entirely appropriate here to do so on a personal note, for in many ways the story that I have tried to tell follows the history of my own struggle with these problems. Having first been bewildered at the silence with which science greets issues which concern meaning, I finally realized that this silence was a byproduct of the use of the ideal in the analysis of nature that has been in progress since the seventeenth century. As a mere technique, such a procedure can raise no hackles; but if it is just a technique, scientific analysis is reduced to a merely operational procedure that tells us nothing about our world. But it is clear that Galileo and Descartes had far wider ambitions, and indeed, the role that science plays today in our culture belies this narrower conception. If one wants to preserve the truth claim of science—as against its operational counter-part that one might label the "fact claim"—the basis of this idealization must come in for some critical scrutiny.

From this basis, I have argued that matter and energy alone, as the postulated "building blocks" which underlie all phenomena, cannot adequately support the truth claim, and that another basic concept, that of information, must be added if one is to both predict and model the world as we experience it. But here we get into deep water, because with the concept of information the issue of meaning is recovered, but now it is recovered not only as an endproduct of science, as I mentioned in my introduction, but at the very basis of the structure of the world. Information requires a context in which to be conveyed, in which to become meaningful. That the context is critical is the lost face of scientific truth, hidden not so much by the original authors of ideal analysis as in the great mechanical dreams of our nineteenth century forebears. I believe our task is to get it back.

Back to the Medieval Research Program

Of course an argument of this sort could be used in defense of a two substance ontology, in which the ultimate source of meaning is a pre-existent and separate state of being from that of the physical, and which thus provides the context for the material structures to exert their effects. But the problem that utterly confounds such a model is a simple one, namely that at no place can the ground where such interactions take place be made explicit. If there are two separate states of being, then there is no reason why they should interact at all. Hence the question of angels and pinheads that has become a parody of medieval interests, for it does not seem worth enquiring how many angels can dance on a pinhead if angels and pins are seen to be entirely different things.

But there is another alternative to the dualist solution that I would like to examine in the last section of this chapter. Perhaps a science that included the qualitative, and hence at the outset starts with man himself, might be congruent with what we have discovered so far and yet be able to unify it within a greater conception of reality. Rather than being written out as an irrelevant qualitative phantasm on the edge of our hard conception of a world of quantities, perhaps man might be able to take rightful place in a new conception at its center.

The Experiential versus the Experimental

I made reference earlier to the idealized nature of scientific knowledge, and asked what meaning can be given to the terms of the equations created by it. The quantities of science are those terms. But has man not, in creating this idealized representation, created the illusion of a machine by acting himself as the context, the nexus, the point where all the information is brought together and analyzed? Just as the Darwinian explanation for the development of living beings takes for granted that they will exploit their environment, so man the repres-enter and intervener takes his own perspective as a given, and does not realize that without it his conception of the universe as a machine cannot be viable.

Indeed there is a fascinating remnant of the transition to idealized science embedded in the English language. It concerns the Latin word "experimentum" which in its medieval context meant both a recipe and a description, rather like a guide book to a foreign country that contains both transport schedules and personal descriptions of the countryside. So books of "experimenta" are to be found containing what to a modern reader appears to be a bewildering jumble of facts and reminiscence.

But it was this very same word that was taken up as the emblem of the "experimental philosophy" of the seventeenth century. It is almost certain that at that time it still had its old meaning, and that the experimental insights of the early tyros of modern science were to them as much explorations—journeys into the wonder of the creation—as they were catalogues of observation and fact; the deeply religious preoccupations of many of the great scientists of this period is an embarrassing historical reality that sits uncomfortably with modern precon-ceptions.

But as was mentioned above, by the time of Laplace a totally quantitative conception of reality was ascendant, and with it the word "experimental" gathered its modern meaning. Experience had been banished from science, and it took a poet, working at much the same time, to coin a separate word to express the lost personal dimension: Samuel Taylor Coleridge first defined the word "experiential" in the 1830s.

A Science of Experience

So could experience be a forgotten part of science? Should we be putting Man, the perceiver, in the middle of it all? Or would such a development lead to an inevitable collapse of the boundaries of demarcation, and lead to the ascendance of opinion over evidence and so destroy the whole structure? One can readily make the case that the logical apparatus of scientific analysis is as much an artifice as any other device made by man, whether it be a telescope or whatever. We use these devices to enlarge and correct the representations made by our unaided senses, the raw common sense that is itself interpreted through the perspective of ages of world culture and training. But by what right does the experiencer become irrelevant to this process?

In the epistemological sense, this idea will raise no hackles. Ever since Pierre Duhem first pointed out that theories cannot be distinguished on mere evidence alone, that the "good taste" of the scientist must be evoked as the ultimate reason why one theory gains ascendancy over another,[20] the idea that personal, social or even political considerations can play a part in the development of scientific ideas has been increasingly accepted. Scientists cannot be separated from their culture any more than artists can.

But in the concept of information, and the importance of the context within which it is received, there lies a far more exciting possibility—the possibility that man the perceiver might play a part in an *ontological* sense as well. As well as being the well educated observer who chooses models of reality based on his or her experience and taste, but who still models a reality which is outside of themselves, there might also be the possibility that that same reality is ultimately entwined with the consciousness of the chooser, and entwined, by necessity, from the very beginning. That is, from the very beginning, there is another aspect of reality as yet unexamined by science, the aspect of the receptive, the context giver, the aspect which gives the possibility of meaning to mere information. And that aspect, as it is evoked in the ascending levels of complexity from molecules to man, ultimately resides in consciousness itself.

This is not merely to say that by looking we give meaning; it is to say that because we are able to look, the meaning already exists, and that we are already part of it. And this realization does not have to be mystical or vague, as though it can only be approached at the edge of our normal experience; it is to claim that from the very heart of materialism a face looks back, and it is our own.

So would a system of knowledge that included the observer as a participant collapse into one of mere opinion? The fear is a very real one, and we must be very careful indeed to ensure that it does not. If consciousness participates in every sense, then we must carefully recreate a methodology that allows for it. And not only is it to be included in the categories of being from which we attempt to recreate our experience, as was discussed earlier in this chapter, the so-called category set, but whole new areas of our experience—the correlates generated by introspection—are there to be systematically included.

There are many examples in other cultures of how this latter task might be achieved, most notably from the cultures of the East, where whole systems of knowledge have been erected from such correlates. Far from being chaotic and disorganized as one might expect if such an idea is inherently unworkable, what one finds when one studies these systems is a remarkable uniformity of view, and in some of those cultures, the information is organized into formal structures that bear ready resemblance to our own.

The External World

I believe that the discovery of the external world is the greatest achievement of Western culture, and yet here I am arguing for the inclusion of correlates generated by introspection! The necessity for doing this arises because we ourselves are part of that external world, and yet it is as if, in science, we have tried to find some way of creating a valid picture of it without including ourselves as a component. It is time to start questioning this presumption that lies at the foundations of science. Rather than proposing that all causes are mechanical and that our own volition is an illusion, why should we not invert the proposition and argue that all causes are volitional and that meaning is a component of reality?

The arrow of causation would then be reversed again; in acknowledging our participation in the world as natural objects among other natural objects, the order and interrelationship that is perceived externally would be recovered as the mirror of our own. Far from being silent on such matters, such a conception of science sees man as a context giver surrounded by context givers. It is the rediscovery of the muse, that most wonderful metaphor of Greek culture, of the idea that all knowledge is a union between information and context, active and passive, male and female, and that inner and outer, fact and meaning are the two sides of one process. That is the true cause. Epistemology and Ontology unite in the ground of being. Do we discover or create? Perhaps it is both.

Notes and References

1. *Criticism and the Growth of Knowledge*, edited by I. Lakatos and A. Musgrave, Cambridge University Press, 1970.

2. See Karl Popper, *The Logic of Scientific Discovery*, Hutchinson, 1959.

3. With thanks to Ian Hacking for writing *Representing and Intervening*, Cambridge University Press, 1983.

4. See *Noetic Sciences Review*, Summer 1990, p. 7.

5. For a more detailed description of this history, see W. A. Wallace, *Prelude to Galileo: Essays on the Medieval and Sixteenth-Century Sources of Galileo's Thought*, Reidel, 1981, pp. 124-159.

6.This location of Galileo at the medical university of Padua, and the central role that debates about the medical uses of herbs played in his thought, is echoed by the much earlier events in Greece, in which it was Hippocratic medicine that preceded the development of the thought of Thales, often called the first scientist. Although it is endlessly repeated that where Physics leads the other sciences follow in the development of Western man's view of the world, the historical narrative tends to invert this conclusion. Medicine—or perhaps more generally man's view of man—may turn out to be the more fundamental science after all.

7. See for example Paul Churchland, *Scientific Realism and the Plasticity of Mind,* Cambridge University Press, 1979.

8. See *The Cosmological Anthropic Principle* by J. Barrow and F. Tippler, Oxford University Press, 1986.

9. Dalbir Bindra, *Psychological Review* 6 , 1970, pp. 581-584.

10. Marjorie Grene in *The Understanding of Nature: Essays in the Philosophy of Biology,* D. Reidel, 1974, p. 48.

11. K. R. Popper, *The Logic of Scientific Discovery,* Hutchinson, 1959.

12. See my earlier article in the *Noetic Sciences Review,* Autumn 1989.

13. David Hume, *Treatise of Human Nature,* 1739. See the standard modern edition edited by P. N. Nidditch, Clarendon Press, 1978.

14. For an excellent account of the basic ideas about information, see David Bakan's article in *Body And Mind, Past Present And Future,* edited by R. W. Reiber, Academic Press, 1980, pp. 117-130.

15. Tom Stonier, *Information and the Internal Structure of the Universe,* Springer Verlag, 1990.

16. See, for example, James Lovelock, *The Ages of Gaia,* W. W. Norton, 1988.

17. Richard Dawkins, *The Selfish Gene,* Paladin, 1978.

18. See the chapter by Brian Goodwin in this volume for a more detailed exposition of this argument.

19. Roger Sperry, *Science and Moral Priority,* Basil Blackwell, 1982.

20. Pierre Duhem, *The Aim and Structure of Physical Theory,* translated by P. P. Wiener, Athaneum, 1977.

The Spiritual Substance of Science

by Robert G. Jahn and Brenda J. Dunne

T he metaphysical foundations of modern science, despite their superficial secularity, remain undergirded and shaped by the primordial desire of human consciousness to comprehend and utilize the organizational principles of the natural world. Over the larger portion of man's scholarly history, these principles were explicitly attributed to some form of divine order, and this quest for comprehension inevitably entailed spiritual as well as technical dimensions. From ancient Greeks to medieval monks to renaissance astronomers, the primary scientific task was to bring the mind of the scholar into resonance with the source of being. Even the mighty Isaac Newton, unchallenged patriarch of the modern scientific tradition, has been aptly described as "the last of the magicians"[1] who regarded the ultimate mechanism of change in the universe to reside in "the mystery by which mind could control matter".[2] But since Newton's time, the Cartesian dichotomy between mind and matter, although itself derived from metaphysical principles, has steadily driven science to focus on matter far more than on mind, and on analytical applications of its empirical principles far more than on their ultimate origins. Consequently, the spiritual portions of its foundations have fallen into desperate disrepair.

In our age, however, as science and its derivative technologies press forward into increasingly abstract and probabilistic domains of quantum and relativistic mechanics, the role of spirit or consciousness—whether divine or human, individual or collective—in the structure and operation of the physical world inescapably returns to more pragmatic and theoretical relevance, and can no longer casually be set aside if the goal is a truly comprehensive understanding of nature. The watershed metaphysical issue facing science today is whether it has reached sufficient maturity to re-encompass within its contemporary methodologies those components of consciousness that have always been implicit in its observations and representations of reality.

PEAR Research

The Princeton Engineering Anomalies Research (PEAR) program was established in 1979 to study anomalous consciousness-related phenomena of possible relevance to basic physical science and engineering practice. The tactical approach of the program has been to apply state-of-the-art equipment and techniques to systematic investigation of anomalies arising in various random physical processes that appear to be correlated with the pre-recorded intentions of attending human operators. These studies have been designed, conducted, and analyzed by a broadly interdisciplinary staff drawn from several academic arenas, including psychology, physics, engineering, and the humanities.

A variety of simple random physical devices, typical of those commonly employed in modern data management systems, control machinery, and diagnostic equipment, are carefully designed, constructed and instrumented, and then extensively calibrated to establish their nominal performance. Each of these is capable of rapid generation of very large bodies of data with clearly defined statistical characteristics that can be transcribed into both on-line quantitative recordings and attractive analogue and digital feedback displays. Experimental protocols require the operators to generate data in three concurrent sequences—under pre-recorded intentions to shift the output distributions to higher values, to lower values, or to take undisturbed baselines—with all other conditions held constant. Thus, the primary variable in these experiments is the operator's *intention,* and effects are claimed only when statistically significant correlations between those intentions and changes in the output distributions are replicably observed. More than one hundred operators have participated in this program, all of whom have been anonymous, uncompensated volunteers, and none of whom claims any exceptional abilities in this regard; in fact, many have been self-proclaimed skeptics. The human/machine experiments have been complemented by a similarly extensive body of research data on a process termed "remote perception", wherein one participant acquires objective or subjective information about a geographical target scene far from his own location and inaccessible by known sensory means, where a second participant is stationed at an assigned time. In sum, the results of all of these experiments strongly indicate that within the fundamental processes by which it exchanges information with its environment, orders it, and interprets it, consciousness has the ability to bias probabilistic physical events, and therefore to avail itself of certain margins of reality.

Detailed presentations of these extensive experiments are available in numerous other publications.[3-13] Here we will present only a brief summary of the salient features of the empirical evidence drawn from one particular body of experiments involving a microelectronic random event generator (REG), although comparable results have been obtained with several other random and pseudorandom devices. This REG utilizes as its random source a commercial microelectronic noise diode, whose output is rendered by appropriate circuitry into a string of randomly alternating binary pulses. Simply stated, this device functions much like a very rapid automatic "coin flipper", producing trials of 200 binaries, or "flips", at a rate of 1000 *per second,* where the theoretical expectation for the mean of any given sequence of trials is 100. Exhaustive and ongoing calibration of this device confirms the conformance of its behavior to theoretical chance predictions.[5]

Over a twelve-year period, 91 different operators have generated a total of nearly 2.5 million trials, or approximately half a billion samples, on this device. All of these experiments have followed the same basic "tri-polar" protocol, wherein the operators attempt to shift the mean of this output distribution to higher or lower values, or to take an undistorted baseline in accordance with their pre-recorded intentions. These three strings of data, acquired under otherwise identical conditions and randomly interspersed, are then compared with each other and with the theoretically predicted outcome to establish the scale and character of any correlations with intention. All data are recorded automatically in indexed computer files, which are routinely compared with redundant hard-copy records produced on a strip printer. The device itself, as well as its supporting software, is equipped with numerous controls and failsafes to preclude any possibilities of technical malfunction or non-authorized operator intervention.

The overall results of this REG database indicate a small but persistent achievement in both the high and low directions of effort that are well beyond any chance fluctuations.[6] Although the scale of observed effects is quite marginal—equivalent to the correlated inversion of a few bits per ten thousand in the random string—these compound, over databases of this size, to highly significant statistical anomalies that not only challenge fundamental physical theory, but are well beyond the tolerance of many modern engineering control and information management systems, and thus have pragmatic implications for modern engineering practice.

In addition to the strongly significant results of this overall database, which is unlikely by chance to the order of 7×10^{-5}, there is evidence for distinctive individual "signatures" of achievement, suggesting operator-specific modes of interaction that entail differing responses to certain secondary parameters of the experimental protocol, such as whether the direction of effort is volitionally chosen or randomly assigned, the length of the experimental run, the mode of feedback employed, and others. There is also a marked tendency for stronger achievement in the high-going efforts than in the low, with 64% of the operators succeeding in producing positive correlations with their high intentions, compared to the 50% chance expectation, while only 46% produced positive correlations with their low intentions. Despite this inexplicable asymmetry in the performances and the varying sizes of the individual operator databases, the overall cumulative achievements correlate significantly with both directions of intention. Perhaps even more instructive is the finding that the individual effect sizes for all 91 operators are found to distribute normally around the slightly displaced mean value, with the majority of participants contributing to the overall effect.[13]

Other results worth noting emerge from of a body of "co-operator" REG experiments, where two operators interact with the device together with a shared intention. These were undertaken to determine whether the combined efforts of two operators, each of whom had established an individual pattern of achievement, would display evidence of an additive effect. Over a database of some 85,000 trials generated by 15 co-operator pairs, results were consistent with those of the single operator data, but showed no evidence of a significantly larger overall effect, and while there was some indication of repeatable patterns by given pairs, these bore no clear similarities to either of the individual efforts. What was surprising, however, was the observation that the same-sex operator pairs produced results that were opposite to intention in both directions of effort, while the opposite-sex pairs yielded significant positive results in both intentions, with average effect sizes 3.7 times larger than those of the single operators. When the opposite-sex pairs were "bonded" couples, their results had effect sizes nearly six times those of the single operators.[10]

As mentioned earlier, the PEAR human/machine experiments have been complemented by remote perception studies, where much of the data was obtained over distances of several thousand miles, and virtually all perceptions were reported many hours, or even days, before or after the targets were selected or visited. This attainment of anomalous yields over large intervening distances and times raised the question of whether the human/machine anomalies sketched above could similarly be demonstrated in remote and atemporal form. Such protocols have been developed for concurrent remote REG, and off-time remote REG experiments, and in all salient respects the character of these data is very similar to that of the local experiment.[9] In fact, one of the most fascinating features of all of this anomalous experimental evidence is its remarkable insensitivity to the magnitude of the distance separating the operator from the machine, or the remote percipient from his target. Within the high sensitivity of the equipment and data reduction procedures applied to these intrinsically stochastic data, no significant dependence of yield on intervening distance can be found, strongly suggesting that no traditional field-driven $1/r^2$ phenomena are involved.

Yet more striking is a similarly demonstrable independence of the anomalous results on the temporal separation of the operator's effort from the time of actual device activation, or of the percipient's visualization of the target scene from its actual time of visitation. In other words, the laboratory demonstrated operator-specific anomalies of the machine outputs can equally well be achieved by operators several thousand miles away, exerting their intentional efforts several hours, or even days, prior or subsequent to the machine operation. The remote percipients are equally successful in acquiring anomalous information about their intercontinental targets in cases where those locations will not be visited, or even selected, until several hours or days later. Again, the implications for any attempts to model such phenomena within the framework of existing physical theory are clearly quite severe.

Conceptual Model

Despite the philosophical resistance to such possibilities, we here face a large body of empirical data that not only entails unknown physical mechanisms, but also shows little regard for the most fundamental of physical coordinates: space and time. Intriguing as such systematic aberrations may be, without some complementary theoretical framework to guide their experimental iteration, progress toward basic understanding is unlikely, and it is that portion of our program which may be most relevant to this anthology. Thus, we offer here an illustration of one possible perspective for a rebalancing of the objective and subjective foundations of science, with full acknowledgment of its limitations, incompleteness, and speculative character.[1,14-16]

Before postulating any radical model, there is an obligation to search for more canonical explication of these consciousness-related anomalies, and indeed the literature abounds with attempts to apply various types of established physical formulation to this task. Many efforts to invoke existing representations of electromagnetic theory, statistical thermodynamics, geophysical mechanics, hyperspace properties, and other approaches have been made, but none has proven adequate to encompass all of the credible data. In particular, most are inconsistent with the lack of attenuation of the observed effects with distance, and all founder completely on the atemporal evidence. Clearly a more fundamental approach is required, one that explicitly acknowledges an active role for consciousness in the establishment of physical reality, and treats consciousness as the creator of its analytical metric, rather than as its servant.

In the contemporary secular Western view, consciousness is usually regarded as a centrally localized, functional entity immersed in a surrounding environmental sea that encompasses all physical, social, and cosmic properties, processes, and influences perceived to be exterior to consciousness itself (see Figure 1 next page). In this "particulate" view, reflecting the "I - not I" dichotomy of Cartesian philosophy, the interface between the individual consciousness and its environment is relatively sharp, and information about the environment is conveyed to each particulate consciousness via the physical senses and then assembled into experiential images. It is presumed that these images are indicative of correspondingly "real" features of the environment, much as optical images of physical objects may, by suitable lenses, be displayed on a screen. Conversely, the consciousness transmits, via other streams of information flowing outward across the interface, purposeful influences to produce effects within the environment, for example, by speaking, manipulating, or establishing other forms of disturbance. This particulate paradigm also allows the consciousness to engage in its own internal affairs, such as rumination, memory, emotion, etc., the study of which is the province of cognitive science and neurophysiology, and similarly permits the environment to proceed independently of consciousness with its own external exercises, which comprise the standard purview of the physical sciences.

If the sources, modes of transmission, and receptors of these inward, outward, internal and external information streams are well comprehended—or at least well catalogued—the particular processes involved are regarded as "normal". But if some aspect of the information generation, transmission, reception, or response is not readily accommodated within known scientific mechanisms, we label the process "anomalous". Such, for example, are the cases with the remote perception and human/machine anomalies described earlier. In the former, we are confronted with apparent acquisition of inward-flowing information, by means other than those of the physical senses, that allows the consciousness to form experiential images of physically inaccessible aspects of its environment. In the latter, information related to the intentions of the consciousness appears to radiate outward into the environment, palpably influencing it in ways that are inconsistent with known physical mechanisms.

The thesis we shall pursue from this point is that these anomalous effects are not so much consequences of shortfalls in our knowledge of physical and physiological mechanisms *per se,* as they are indicators of the inadequacy of this particulate, dualistic consciousness/environment model. In its place, we propose an alternative schema of the consciousness/environment dialogue, one that softens their mutual interface to a broader and more diffuse interpenetration. Although remaining centered at some specific point in the conceptual configuration (presumably defined by its host physical corpus), in this model consciousness is allowed to permeate outward into its surrounding environment to an extent consistent with its prevailing purpose. Conversely, the environment, however further specified, also extends its influence throughout

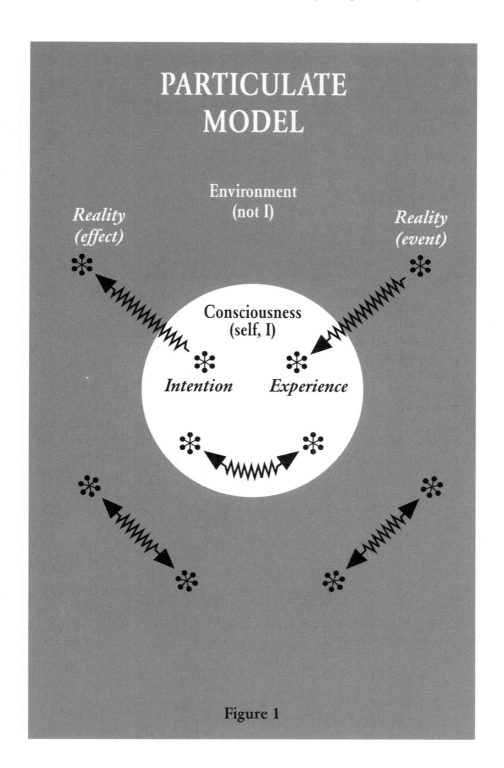

Figure 1

the consciousness entity, so that the interaction results in some proportion of each prevailing everywhere in the pattern. Thus, "experience" is viewed not so much as an image of "reality" as its subjective synonym; in fact, subjective "experience" and objective "reality" now merge into one holistic product of the consciousness/environment interpenetration. This model brings consciousness and environment into full partnership in the establishment of experience/reality or, at the very least, in its observation, articulation, and implementation.

In all of this, the term "consciousness" is intended to subsume all categories of subjective human experience (including perception, cognition, intuition, instinct, and emotion) at all levels, including those commonly termed "conscious", "subconscious", "superconscious", or "unconscious", without presumption of specific psychological or physiological mechanisms. The concept of "environment" includes all circumstances and influences affecting the consciousness that it perceives to be separate from itself, including, as appropriate, its own physical corpus and its physical habitat, as well as all the intangible psychological, social, and historical influences that bear upon it. In this interpenetration model consciousness and environment continue to engage in the "I/Not I" dialogue, but the interface between the two is now regarded as subjective and situation-specific (see Figure 2 next page).

This cooperative consciousness/environmental concept is, of course, far from new. Similar persuasions have been propounded by most of the major architects of modern science and philosophy throughout the history of Western scholarship. For example:

Francis Bacon:

. . . all the perceptions both of the senses and the mind bear reference to man and not to the universe, and the human mind resembles those uneven mirrors which impart their own properties to different objects.[17]

Arthur Schopenhauer:

. . . a consciousness without object is no consciousness at all . . . . Although materialism imagines that it postulates nothing more than this matter—atoms for instance—yet it unconsciously adds not only the subject, but also space, time, and causality, which depend on special determinations of the subject . . . the intellect and matter are correlatives, in other words, the one exists only for the other; both stand and fall together; the one is only the other's reflex. They are in fact really one and the same thing, considered from two opposite points of view.[18]

James Jeans:

The concepts which now prove to be fundamental to our understanding of nature . . . seem to my mind to be structures of pure thought . . . the universe begins to look more like a great thought than like a great machine.[19]

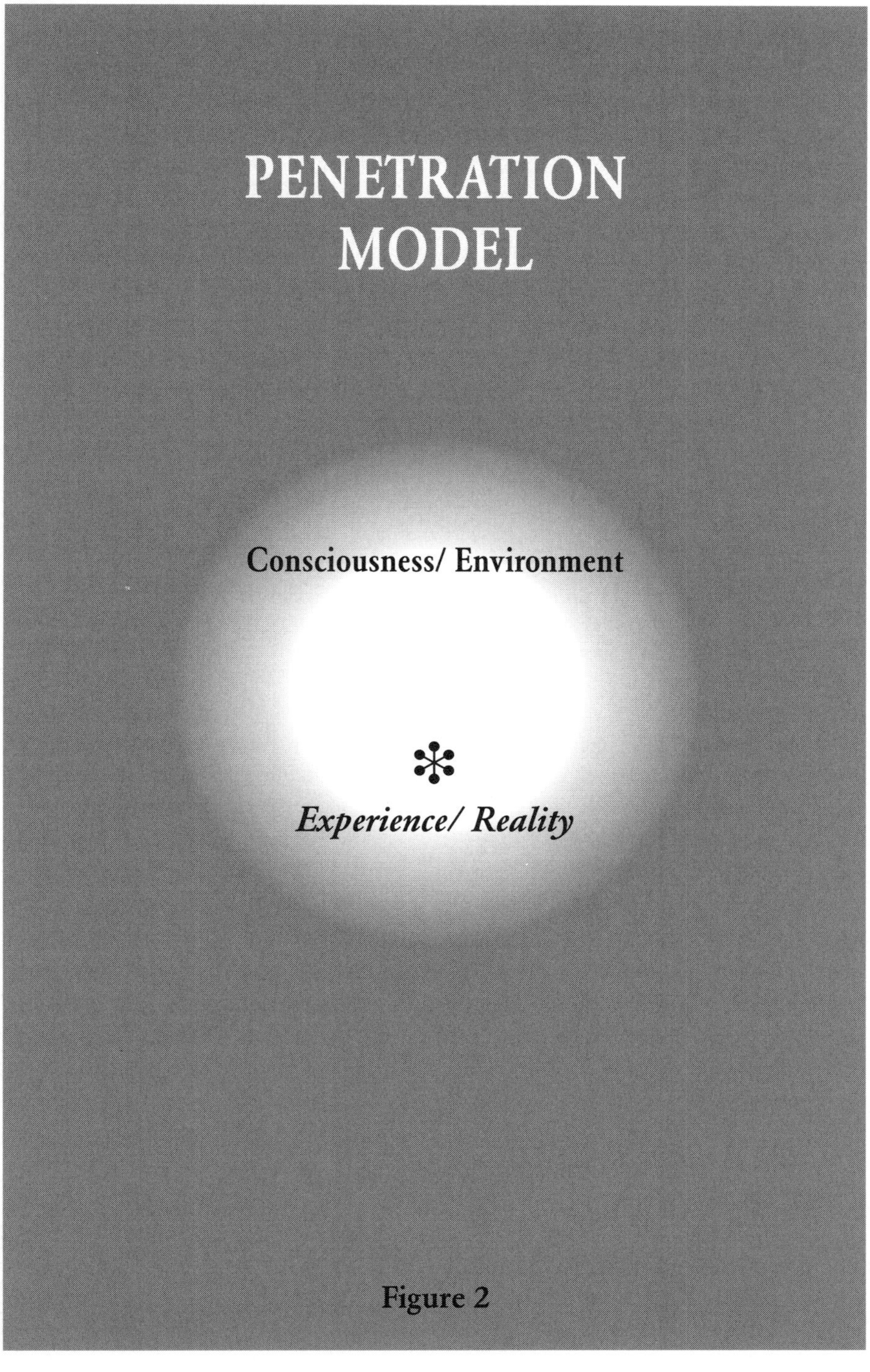

PENETRATION MODEL

Consciousness/ Environment

Experience/ Reality

Figure 2

Sigmund Freud:

The test of science is fully circumscribed if we confine it to showing how the world must appear to us in consequence of the particular character of our organization . . . [since] our mental apparatus . . . itself is a constituent part of that world which we are to investigate.[20]

Albert Einstein:

Concepts which have been proved to be useful in ordering things easily acquire such an authority over us that we forget their human origin and accept them as invariable.[21]

The system of concepts is a creation of man together with the rules of syntax, which constitute the structure of the conceptual systems. . . . All concepts, even those which are closest to experience, are from the point of view of logic freely chosen conventions, just as is the case with the concept of causality.[22]

Niels Bohr:

The impossibility of distinguishing in our customary way between physical phenomena and their observation places us, indeed, in a position quite similar to that which is so familiar in psychology where we are continually reminded of the difficulty of distinguishing between subject and object.[23]

Werner Heisenberg:

. . . in the Copenhagen interpretation of quantum theory we can indeed proceed without mentioning ourselves as individuals, but we cannot disregard the fact that natural science is formed by man. Natural science does not simply describe and explain nature; it is a part of the interplay between nature and ourselves; it describes nature as exposed to our method of questioning. This was a possibility Descartes could not have thought, but it makes the sharp separation between the world and the I impossible.[24]

All said, the issue reduces to this: consciousness and its total environmental surround are full partners in the establishment of experience—the literal parents of reality—and therefore both must be acknowledged in scientific experiment and theory.

The Wave Mechanics of Consciousness

To be of much pragmatic consequence, the consciousness interpenetration model of Figure 2 must be implemented with some form of mechanics that allows at least semi-quantitative computation of its consequences under specific circumstances. Of the several physical interpenetration analogies that might be invoked for this purpose, such as mass diffusion, thermal or electrical conduction, etc., the most propitious is the genre of wave propagation in a medium of non-uniform properties. Indeed, there is a suggestive similarity of the two views of consciousness illustrated in Figures 1 and 2 to the particle/wave dualities appearing in several historical and contemporary scientific contexts, and a brief review of this epistemology may prove instructive.

Actually, the conceptual distinction between the behavior of discrete, tangible blocks of matter and that of diffuse, undulating wave processes traces far back into human history, and has permeated virtually all attempts of human consciousness to represent the mechanics of its physical environment. Certainly early man encountered one portion of his pragmatic reality in particulate terms: his hand, his axe, and his cave; the trees, animals, and birds; the sun, moon, and stars were all sharply defined objects among which specific relationships could be visualized and implemented. Yet he doubtless noticed and pondered various wave-like processes as well: on the surface of a brook or ocean, in the cirrus patterns of the sky, or in the wind-driven vibrations of the leaves, and frequently represented these in his art and rituals, perhaps better to comprehend their mechanics as they bore on his day to day activities, or perhaps to invoke some of their aesthetic and mystical properties.

From these earliest impressions, the concepts of particles and waves have evolved to considerable philosophical and analytical sophistication as two modes of representation of a broad variety of physical phenomena. In numerous cases, one of these perspectives has remained dominant for some period, subsequently to be replaced by the other when proven inadequate to accommodate some new body of empirical evidence, and then again to be joined by the former in some dualistic compromise. Early Greek scholars were driven to propose a wave theory of sound to explain certain observations that were inconsistent with the prevailing atomistic perspectives. Many centuries later, a growing body of anomalous experimental data forced development of a wave theory of light to challenge, and eventually to displace, Newton's well-entrenched corpuscular model. Toward the close of the nineteenth century, the derivation from Maxwell's field equations of testable quantitative properties of electromagnetic waves subsumed particulate electrodynamics and unified much of prevailing physical theory in what then appeared to be a comprehensive philosophical fashion.

But particulate light, sound, and electricity were by no means dead and, conversely, particulate substance was soon to be challenged. Twentieth-century physics presented a plethora of new paradoxes, including the photon, the phonon, and the quantum, and, most perplexing of all, the wave nature of matter. Blackbody radiation and the photoelectric effect could not be explained by the wave theories of light; the Planck-Einstein frequency-quantized, particulate photon was essential to their explication. On the other hand, the particulate nature of matter was challenged as rationalization of the Bohr-Sommerfeld atomic energy levels and of the experimental data on electron diffraction required a monumental proposition from de Broglie and Schrödinger that particulate material objects could, in some situations, display wave-like characteristics.

To this day, these wave/particle paradoxes have not been fully resolved in any convincing physical model. For practical purposes, science uncomfortably concedes that under certain circumstances light and matter behave like discrete particles; under other circumstances they behave like waves. Analytically, we can derive useful and accurate predictions of their behavior if we can first guess which ethic will prevail in a given situation, and the relevant circumstances are themselves strongly influenced by the method of observation chosen by the experimenter. To a certain extent we can force some coherence of these perspectives by composing particle-like "wave packets" or waves of particulate probabilities, but philosophically the two formats must be regarded, in Bohr's profound terminology, as "complementary". In other words, the wave and particle perspectives are not mutually exclusive; rather, some mixture of both is necessary to represent the phenomena fully.

We propose that the interpretation of this enduring irreducible complementarity is that it is not the physical world *per se* that imposes the duality; it is our consciousness. More precisely, the complementarity arises in the process of consciousness interpenetrating with its physical environment, and it is therefore consistent to attribute to consciousness itself the option of wave-like as well as particulate character. In other words, the consciousness that has conceived both particles and waves, and found it necessary to alternate them in some complementary fashion for the representation of many physical phenomena, may find a similar complementarity necessary and useful in representing itself.

So long as the concept of a particulate consciousness is enforced as the sole option, effects like the remote influence on physical behavior or the acquisition of remote information observed in our experiments must remain inherently anomalous. But if consciousness allows itself the same wave/particle duality that it has already conceded to numerous physical processes, such situations become more tractable. For example, a wave-like consciousness could employ a host of interference, diffraction, penetration, and remote influence mechanisms to achieve normally most of the anomalies of its particulate counterpart. Most importantly, it could acquire the capacity to resonate, and to bond, with other wave-like consciousness, and, indeed, with any other wave-mechanical process in the physical world, and thereby to access a complementary spectrum of alternative experience.

Quantum Metaphors

To develop analytical and predictive capability, it is necessary to specify more precisely the mechanical character of the proposed consciousness wave system. In principle, virtually any established form of physical wave phenomena could be appropriated in metaphor, but the wave mechanics of contemporary quantum theory seems particularly apt for this purpose, for several reasons. First, physical quantum wave mechanics was itself developed to attend to a puzzling array of anomalies in the empirical base of modern physics. Second, it automatically acknowledges a wave/particle complementarity in its applications to specific situations. Third, in its "Copenhagen" interpretation, it concedes the influence of consciousness in the observation of physical effects. Fourth, the heuristic "principles" of quantum mechanics, such as "exclusion", "indistinguishability", "correspondence", "uncertainty", and "complementarity", each of them paradoxical within our cultural presumptions yet essential to the theoretical framework and thoroughly supported by experiment, readily lend themselves to generalization into the consciousness domain.

The development of this "quantum mechanics of consciousness" and its applications to particular experimental situations have been presented in detail elsewhere.[3,14] The essential strategy of the model is to represent consciousness in terms of quantum mechanical wave functions, and its environment by appropriate potential profiles. Schrödinger wave mechanics is then used to derive standing wave patterns (eigenfunctions) that can be associated with both the psychological and physical experiences of the consciousness/environment interaction. To bring this metaphor to pragmatic utility, it is necessary to relate certain mathematical aspects of the formalism, such as the coordinate system, the quantum numbers, and even the metric itself, with various impressionistic descriptors of consciousness, such as its intensity, perspective, approach/ avoidance attitude, balance between cognitive and emotional activity, and receptive/active disposition. With these in hand, not only the generic principles of quantum mechanics but a number of specific computational applications, such as the central force field and atomic structure, covalent molecular bonds, barrier penetration, and quantum statistical collective behavior, become useful analogies for representation and correlation of a variety of consciousness-related physical phenomena, both "normal" and "anomalous", and for the design of experiments to study these more systematically.

For example, it is possible to construct a "consciousness atom" wherein the probabilistic experiential states of the individual are represented by the allowed configurations of the given consciousness wave in the prevailing environmental profile. Although myriad and complex, these states may be quantized and indexed by specified subjective properties somewhat akin to physical quantum numbers, for example by the degree of investment or attention of the consciousness, the complexity of its state, the ratio of emotional to cognitive import, and an assertive/receptive indicator akin to the mystical yang/yin distinction. The requisites for transition among these states can then be specified in terms of incremental changes in such consciousness parameters.

Similarly, the resonance or bond between two consciousnesses, or between a consciousness and a physical process, may be represented in the form of a "consciousness molecule", wherein the surrender of individual identities yields alterations in the quantum states that can accommodate quite naturally the changes in behavior and experience that characterize the observed human/machine anomalies. The acquisition of information about targets remote in distance and time can be treated in terms of wave-mechanical "barrier penetration" formalism, wherein evanescent wave profiles can access domains forbidden to classical particles. Anomalous collective behavior of groups of individuals and/or physical systems may be represented via quantum statistical ensembles whose properties depart from classical experience.

Equally useful is the transposition of the physical quantum mechanical principles into consciousness analogies. The exclusion principle, for example, which in the physical domain relates to the spin pairing of half-integer spin particles, transposes into the ubiquitous masculine/feminine affinity. The correspondence principle allows wavelike consciousness behavior to translate into the more familiar particulate form under most common circumstances. The indistinguishability principle generalizes the consciousness bonds into any situation where surrender of individual identity results in collective behavior that cannot be fully reduced to the sum of its components. The uncertainty principle places limits on the simultaneous deployment of subjective and objective consciousness capacities, and so on.

Complementarity

Perhaps the most profound derivative of this model, however, is the broader interpretation of the concept of "complementarity", or the mutual compatibility of any two conjugate physical properties. Our common dualistic conceptualization interprets much of human experience in terms of a grid of polar opposites: high vs. low; hot vs. cold; positive vs. negative. Classical philosophy has developed the polarity concept to higher sophistication; mind vs. matter, thesis vs. antithesis, etc., but does not relieve the one-dimensional competition. In either form, the spectrum of options between the polar extremes remains essentially linear; enhancement of one property inescapably entails reduction in the other. But analytical science also recognizes a fundamentally different pairing of two properties, each independently definable and irreducible, but both needed for full specification of a physical state. Such conjugate pairs include, for example, all corresponding components of linear and angular momentum and position, or energy and time, and several important theorems of classical mechanics pertain to their interactive behavior. Indeed, one of the earliest formulations of quantum theory proceeded from the "quantum of action" which quantized the integrals of conjugate coordinates over bounded physical processes. In subsequently more sophisticated developments of quantum mechanics, the importance of this complementarity–this paradox of dependence and independence–became more pragmatically and philosophically crucial in defining two-dimensional conceptual spaces of combinatorial options.

In pondering various enigmas of quantum physics, Niels Bohr was driven to extend the complementarity principle into frankly philosophical and metaphysical dimensions that bore much more widely on human experience. He wrote:

> . . . we must, indeed, remember that the nature of our consciousness brings about a complementary relationship, in all domains of knowledge, between the analysis of a concept and its immediate application. . . . In associating the psychical and physical aspects of existence, we are concerned with a special relationship of complementarity which it is not possible thoroughly to understand by one-sided application either of physical or of psychological laws. . . . Only a renunciation in this respect will enable us to comprehend . . . that harmony which is experienced as free will and analyzed in terms of causality.[25]

> The real problem is: How can that part of reality which begins with consciousness be combined with those parts that are treated in physics and chemistry? . . . Here we obviously have a genuine case of complementarity.[26]

Bohr's equally philosophical student, Werner Heisenberg, clearly subscribed to such generalization:

> We realize that the situation of complementarity is not confined to the atomic world alone; we meet it when we reflect about a decision and the motives for our decision or when we have the choice between enjoying music and analyzing its structure.[27]

As did their colleague Wolfgang Pauli:

> On the one hand, the idea of complementarity in modern physics has demonstrated to us, in a new kind of synthesis, that the contradiction in the applications of old contrasting conceptions (such as particle and wave) is only apparent; on the other hand, the employability of old alchemical ideas in the psychology of Jung points to a deeper unity of psychical and physical occurrences. To us . . . the only acceptable point of view appears to be the one that recognizes both sides of reality–the quantitative and the qualita-

tive, the physical and the psychical—as compatible with each other, and can embrace them simultaneously. . . . It would be most satisfactory of all if physics and psyche could be seen as complementary aspects of the same reality.[28]

One of the major stimulations of this broader interpretation of complementarity was the same wave/particle duality discussed above. To Bohr and his colleagues, the dichotomy between particulate and wavelike behavior of light, sound, or atomic scale structures and interactions was not to be regarded as paradoxical, but as the proper response of "nature exposed to our means of questioning." Both forms of experience were needed to acquire the full essence of the situation. The extension of this complementarity concept to the wave/particle characteristics and operations of consciousness itself would thus also seem reasonable, and would vastly extend its capabilities to subsume comfortably many of its "particulate" anomalies.

The magnitude of this revision in our conceptual perspective should not be understated. In the Bohr/Heisenberg/Pauli view, it is not just our quantifiable tangible experience that needs to be more ambivalently represented, but our impressionistic capacities as well. Thus, for example, the aesthetic and analytical aspects of an experience may be compounded in arbitrary proportions, rather than necessarily being traded one for the other. Likewise, the structure and function of a machine need not be competitive, but may be elaborated to any complementary extent conceivable by the inventor. For our purposes, we follow further along this philosophical vein to propose that many states of consciousness are inherently complementary to one another in much this same sense. Without claim to completeness or uniqueness, a partial list of such "consciousness conjugates" might include:

- analysis/synthesis
- observation/participation
- structure/function
- goal/process
- logic/intuition
- doing/being
- objectivity/subjectivity
- sincerity/humor

In each case, the two components are functionally quite distinct, but may be compounded in arbitrary ratios to define a given experience. And, in each case, a certain association with particle-like vs. wave-like characteristics is evident.

Quantum mechanics imposes a second, equally profound relationship on its pairs of complementary properties. Despite their gross independence, they must conform to the uncertainty principle regarding the precision of their mutual specification; an attempt to be excessively sharp in the definition of one component inevitably blurs the identification or representation of the other. In quantum physics, high precision in measurement of a momentum inevitably blurs the identification of the corresponding position, or precise specification of time comes at the expense of definition of energy. In Bohr's broader interpretation, excessively precise analysis of a pattern obscures its holistic message; sharply structured reasoning clouds intuition; inordinate aesthetic demands confound structural integrity, etc. In each case there is an optimum balance or trade-off in the attention to each.

In mathematical terms, the uncertainty principle derives from the intrinsic inability of wave mechanics to represent a sharply localized object without employing a broad range of wavelengths or, equivalently, from the inability of a narrow-band wave function to be confined to a small region. The corresponding trade-off for consciousness patterns is that if a given concept or task is to be addressed with precision, a broad range of consciousness "wavelengths" must be deployed to assess its full set of characteristics, and the state of the consciousness itself cannot be fully specified. Conversely, if the consciousness is restricted to a single wavelength, that is, to a "pure state", it cannot establish details about the task it is contemplating. Such pure states of monotonic attention are sought in various meditation techniques and mystical practices, and are encountered in everyday experiences of "losing oneself" in a single activity, to the extent that it becomes impossible to describe precisely what one is thinking at the time.

The consciousness uncertainty principle may well define the most productive and fulfilling regimes of consciousness activity, namely where the doing and the being, or the analyzing and the synthesizing, are in some balance of focus. Consider the common examples of the person who "lives his job", of the actor, dancer, athlete, or skilled artisan whose mechanical skills are complemented by subjective immersion in the role, resulting in a transcendent performance or product. Testimony from such genius or artistry commonly speaks of the necessity for dynamic balance between the skills and the immersion, the doing and the being, if the highest creativity is to be attained; excessive attention to either proves counterproductive. Note also how we take greatest satisfaction in those technological devices in which structure and function are most harmoniously combined.

A similar complementarity/uncertainty situation may prevail in the controlled generation of anomalous phenomena and could be a useful criterion for the design of effective experiments to study the inter-relationships of mind and matter. If one surveys the assortment of laboratory programs that have attempted to generate and study consciousness-related anomalies in a systematic and productive manner, two routes to failure are apparent. On one extreme, many programs have been disqualified for a lack of scientific rigor, experimental sensitivity, and analytical sophistication that lead to suspect data and untrustworthy conclusions. But on the other extreme, there are programs that are so stringent in their experimental controls, or so pejorative in the treatment of their human participants, that the subtle effects sought are sterilized or suffocated before manifesting themselves in the data. The more productive laboratories are those that compound respect for both the scientific and aesthetic aspects of the process in a genuinely complementary fashion. In our own case, we have endeavored from the outset to blend sophistication of equipment and analysis with comfort of protocol, laboratory ambiance, and attitude of staff in a fashion that facilitates both the emergence of the desired effects and their capture in tangible formats.

The principle seems also to apply at the tactical level, for example our operators report that it is the blurring of identities and establishment of resonance between themselves and the machine that leads to realization of the desired behavior. In this, and many other respects, the phenomena display similarity to artistic, intellectual, or functional creativity, which are also clearly favored by environments wherein the requisite technical support is complemented by aesthetic ambiance and stimulation, where the creators can merge comfortably with their equipment and tasks. In this same spirit, the two forms of consciousness modeled in Figures 1 and 2 should not be regarded as mutually exclusive alternatives, but as complementary modalities that when functioning harmoniously in any form of human activity provide the most floribundant experiences of life.

Science and Spirituality

The powerful philosophical principle of complementarity extends its relevance even beyond these operational balances, to reach deeply into the metaphysical foundations of science and specifically into the question with which we began this chapter. In the ultimate sense, "science" in its neo-classical format, and "spirituality" in its loftiest definition, may themselves be regarded as two complementary ethics, fundamentally united by the yearning of human consciousness for understanding of its relationship to the cosmos and for participation in the creation of reality, yet sharply distinguished by the dualistic tactical approaches employed in pursuit of these goals. Science, launching itself from the primordial distinction of Self from Not-Self fostered by its Aristotelian and Judeo-Christian origins, relies on the ability of consciousness to discriminate, isolate, and represent the elements of reality via objective observation and dispassionate logic. Spirituality, in contrast, rooted in a primordial aesthetic passion for cosmic unity, employs the capabilities of consciousness for association and assimilation to achieve merger of Self and Not-Self in subjective identification with the mechanics of creation. The prevailing lack of compatibility of these objective and subjective capacities of consciousness lies at the base of the specific problem addressed by this volume, and indeed at the heart of the global philosophical impasse confounding the contemporary human condition. Einstein recognized the dilemma several decades ago, when he said:

> Science without religion is lame, religion without science is blind.[29]

> The cosmic religious experience is the strongest and noblest mainspring of scientific research.[30]

But he did not venture to offer a mechanics for integration of these two superficially contradictory modalities. Such resolution, we would submit, can only be via the very concept he long rejected—complementarity.

In the interplay of science and spirit we deal with the ultimate conjugate perspectives whereby consciousness triangulates its experience. The issue is whether these are deployed in mutually encumbering contradiction, or in mutually fulfilling complementarity. The desirability of the latter has, of course, long been recognized and propounded in abstraction, but never satisfactorily formulated in practical terms. Obviously, we are far from comprehensive understanding, let alone resolution, even now, but through experiments like those outlined above, we can at least rigorously demonstrate that human will, deployed in self-effacing resonance with its physical environment, or with another human consciousness, can condition experiential reality to significant extents, providing replicable correlations that can be systematically accumulated, codified and deployed within traditional scientific strategy. The challenge ahead is to expand and extend such controlled experimentation into many other scholarly sectors, and to develop more courageously responsive theoretical models from which to weave a new fabric of complementary science that respects and utilizes subjective quantities as much as objective, aesthetic techniques as much as analytic, and metaphysical experience as much as physical.

Clearly we face monumental obstacles of vocabulary, conceptualization, and measurability on our road to this holistic science, but we should be sustained by the recognition that scientific vocabulary of any era has always been only a subset of human linguistics; scientific observation and conceptualization have always drawn by metaphor from broader and less tangible human experience; and scientific logic has always been a special form of basic human reasoning. It is not unreasonable, therefore, to hope that the primordial consciousness that has so brilliantly conceived and refined its science of the objective, and that has so fully experienced and celebrated the spiritual dimensions of its subjective life, can now finally integrate these complementary perspectives into a super-science of the whole, wherein the human spirit stands as full partner with its cosmos in the establishment of reality.

References

1. J. M. Keynes, "Newton, the man" in G. Keynes, editor, *Essays in Biography*, W. W. Norton and Co., 1963, p. 311.

2. D. Kubrin, "Newton's inside out! Magic, class struggle, and the rise of mechanism in the West" in H. Woolf, editor, *The Analytic Spirit: Essays in the History of Science*, Cornell University Press, 1981, p. 113.

3. R. G. Jahn and B. J. Dunne, *Margins of Reality: The Role of Consciousness in the Physical World*, Harcourt Brace Jovanovich, 1987.

4. R. G. Jahn, B. J. Dunne and R. D. Nelson, "Engineering anomalies research", *Journal of Scientific Exploration* 1, 1987, pp. 21-50.

5. R. D. Nelson, G. J. Bradish and Y. H. Dobyns, "Random Event Generator: Qualification, calibration, and analysis", *Technical Note PEAR 89001*, Princeton Engineering Anomalies Research, Princeton University, School of Engineering/Applied Science, April 1989.

6. R. D. Nelson and Y. H. Dobyns, "Analysis of variance of REG experiments: Operator intention, secondary parameters, database structure", *Technical Note PEAR 91004*, Princeton Engineering Anomalies Research, Princeton University, School of Engineering/Applied Science, December 1991.

7. Y. H. Dobyns, "On the Bayesian analysis of REG data", *Journal of Scientific Exploration* 6, 1992, pp. 23-45.

8. R. G. Jahn, Y. H. Dobyns and B. J. Dunne, "Count population profiles in engineering anomalies experiments", *Journal of Scientific Exploration* 5, 1991, pp. 205-232.

9. B. J. Dunne and R. G. Jahn, "Experiments in remote human/machine interaction", *Journal of Scientific Exploration* 6, 1992, pp. 311-332.

10. B. J. Dunne, "Co-Operator experiments with an REG device", *Cultivating Consciousness: Enhancing Human Potential, Wellness, and Healing*, edited by K. Ramakrishna Rao, Praeger, 1993, pp. 149-163.

11. R. D. Nelson, B. J. Dunne and R. G. Jahn, "Operator related anomalies in a random mechanical cascade", *Journal of Scientific Exploration* 2, 1988, pp. 155-179.

12. B. J. Dunne, Y. H. Dobyns and S. M. Intner, "Precognitive Remote Perception III: Complete binary data base with analytical refinements", *Technical Note PEAR 89002*, Princeton Engineering Anomalies Research, Princeton University, School of Engineering/Applied Science, August 1989.

13. B. J. Dunne, R. D. Nelson and Y. H. Dobyns, "Individual operator contributions in large data base anomalies experiments", *Technical Note PEAR 88002*, Princeton Engineering Anomalies Research, Princeton University, School of Engineering/Applied Science, July 1988.

14. R. G. Jahn and B. J. Dunne, "On the quantum mechanics of consciousness, with applications to anomalous phenomena", *Foundations of Physics* 16, 1986, pp. 721-772.

15. B. J. Dunne and R. G. Jahn, "On the role of consciousness in random physical processes", in E. I. Bitsakis and C. A. Nicolaides, editors, *The Concept of Probability,* Klewer Academic Publishers, 1989, pp. 167-178.

16. R. G. Jahn, "The complementarity of consciousness", *Cultivating Consciousness: Enhancing Human Potential, Wellness, and Healing,* edited by K. Ramakrishna Rao, Praeger, 1993, pp. 111-121.

17. F. Bacon, "Idols of perception", in *Novum Organum,* quoted in G. B. Levitas, editor, *The World of Psychology, Vol. 1,* George Braziller, 1963., p. 161.

18. A. Schopenhauer, *The World as Will and Representation, Vol. II,* translated by E.F.J. Payne, Dover Publications, 1966, pp. 15-16.

19. J. Jeans, *The Mysterious Universe,* MacMillan Co., The University Press, 1948, pp. 166, 186.

20. S. Freud (1943), "The Future of an Illusion", quoted in Editor's Introduction, Sigmund Freud, *General Psychological Theory,* Collier Books, 1965, p. 9.

21. A. Einstein, in P. A. Schilpp, editor, *Albert Einstein: Philosopher/Scientist,* The Library of Living Philosophers, 1949, pp. 175-176.

22. Ibid., p. 13.

23. N. Bohr, *Atomic Theory and the Description of Nature,* Cambridge University Press, 1961, p. 15.

24. W. Heisenberg, *Physics and Philosophy,* Harper and Row, Harper Torchbooks, 1958, p. 81.

25. N. Bohr, *Atomic Theory and the Description of Nature,* Cambridge University Press, 1961, pp. 20, 24.

26. Ibid., p. 115.

27. W. Heisenberg, *Physics and Philosophy: The Revolution in Modern Physics,* Harper and Row, Harper Torchbooks, 1972, p. 179.

28. W. Pauli, "The influence of archetypal ideas on the scientific theories of Kepler" in C. G. Jung and W. Pauli, *The Interpretation of Nature and the Psyche,* Pantheon Books, Bollingen Series L1, 1955, pp. 208, 210.

29. A. Einstein, *Out of My Later Years,* rev. reprint edition, The Citadel Press, 1956, p. 26.

30. A. Einstein, in L. Barnett, *The Universe and Dr. Einstein,* rev. edition, Bantam Books, 1979, p. 108.

Toward an Indigenous Western Science:
Causality in the Universe
of Coherent Space-Time Structures

by Mae-Wan Ho

'Magister Ludi' and the 'Rainmaker': Two Ways of Knowing

Hermann Hesse's famous last novel describes the life of Joseph Knecht, Magister Ludi, or the supreme master of the Glass Bead Game.[1] The game is one of pure intellect directed at the synthesis of the spiritual and aesthetic abstractions in diverse disciplines of all ages, and it is the prerogative and *raison d'etre* of an entire spiritual institution, Castalia. Isolated within its enclaves and unsullied by reality, the chosen elite undertakes arduous scholastic studies, the sole purpose of which is to create ever more intricate themes and variations of the game. Castalia and the Glass Bead Game developed as antithesis to the philistine, superficial bourgeois society, intent on its own pursuit of conventional, establishment values. In the end, however, Joseph Knecht turns his back on Castalia, disillusioned with a life consecrated exclusively to the mind, recognizing not only its utter futility, but also its inherent danger and irresponsibility.

As addendum to the biography of Joseph Knecht, Hesse included the latter's posthumous writings: some poems and an account of three lives each set in a different age, but all dedicated to knowledge in different ways. The first interests me most of all. It is that of "The Rainmaker", also called Knecht, also a man of knowledge in his time. But there, the parallel ends. In contrast to the master of the Glass Bead Game, who excels in scholastic, intellectual knowledge, the rainmaker's knowledge comes directly from nature. Nature is the primary and only text: the waxing and waning of the moon, the disposition of the stars, the scent in the air, the wind in the trees, the call of birds, the chirring of insects, the spoor of animals and bits of fur left on their trails, are so many signs woven into the fabric of a mutually permeating, mutually defining reality which is nature. His predecessor and mentor taught him to experience nature until he too knew her with the same intimacy and sensitivity—until he could be one with her:

> He concentrated the very vibrations of the weather within himself, holding them within him in such a way that he could command the clouds and the winds—not, to be sure, just as he pleased, but out of the very intimacy and attachment he had with them, which totally erased the difference between him and the world, between inside and outside. At such times he could stand rapt, listening, or crouch rapt, with all his pores open, and not only feel the life of the winds and clouds within his own self, but also direct and engender it, somewhat in the way we can awaken and reproduce within ourselves a phrase of music that we know by heart. Then he needed only to hold his breath—and the wind or the thunder stopped; he needed only to nod or shake his head—and the hail pelted down or ceased; he needed only to express by a smile the balance of the conflicting forces within himself—and the billows of clouds would part, revealing the thin, bright blueness. There were many times of unusually pure harmony and composure in his soul when he carried the weather of the next few days within himself with infallible foreknowledge, as if the whole score were already written in his blood.[2]

This remarkable passage captures the intensely aesthetic and spiritual, and at the same time resolutely practical, orientation of a direct, participatory knowledge. The indigenous consciousness of undivided body and soul, feeling and intellect, permeates the whole of nature as nature holds him enthralled. This is the state of grace in which knower and known become mutually transparent and coherent; knowledge is both sacred and authentic because it comes from the source which is nature herself.

To those indigenous to nature—and I use indigenous in that sense because it is more fundamental than being indigenous to any particular culture or place—knowledge is also power; it is a matter of life and death, for a misreading of nature could end in famine and starvation. Indigenous knowledge is therefore effective where the knowledge of the Glass Bead Game is effete, divorced, as it were, from reality and from action. The rainmaker, by his knowledge, integrates the social life of his tribe to the order of nature's ways. Nature and culture are thus inseparable and in harmony one with the other.

We can see that indigenous knowledge is the active cause of things. By reading nature accurately and sensitively, the knower can engage in the happenings of her process, and create in partnership with her. It is the way of the *Tao* in Chinese philosophy—the effortless power of being and becoming with nature. How very different is our picture of nature viewed from the Newtonian framework, where cause is a blind extraneous force acting on a dumb indifferent object.

Traditional indigenous knowledge was closely and jealously guarded, not so much because it gave power, but because that power could be misused in the wrong hands. Along with power, therefore, also came responsibility. In the end, the rainmaker offered himself as sacrifice in an ultimate attempt to make rain.

What relevance has all this for us here and now, since the days of the rainmaker are irretrievably lost in the mists of time? Like many of his contemporaries and predecessors, Hesse was writing of the alienation of the human spirit in a society increasingly dominated by the reductionist, positivist science of the West, in which life no longer made sense. The only alternative seemed to be an outright rejection of that society for a life of intellectual contemplation or spiritual mysticism. Today, we live in the crisis of global ecological devastation that is the legacy of the same science and technology, which is spurred on by the Darwinian creed of ruthless exploitation of nature and of our fellow human beings. Yet out of the ruins of destruction, we see some glimmer of hope.

Western science was premised on the separation of the observer as disembodied mind from an objective nature observed. This was also the beginning of the demise of our natural being,[3] which I take to be the unfragmented consciousness wholly connected to nature. The mind-body dualism presupposes that we can know nature without experiencing her. More than that, we are told that our subjective experiences are unreliable, and must be denied at all cost in order to preserve the objectivity of science. Hence it is that generations of Western philosophers have been perplexed as to how we can know when the knowing being has been abstracted away from a reality which must be experienced to be understood.[4] It also follows that we can have no basis for linking cause and effect, nor for distinguishing good from bad, and the authentic from mere simulacrum.[5]

The history of Western culture since then is one of increasing alienation from nature and hence from our natural being, while nature becomes fragmented into atoms and fundamental particles. Yet when this reductionist, atomistic science is pursued to its logical conclusion and pushed to its very limits, it can only undermine the basis on which it was built. For everywhere, it reaffirms the unity of nature in which the knowing being is inextricably embedded,[6] compelling us toward a new knowledge system and a new way of knowing that is at the same time very old. It harks back to the universal indigenous wisdom that sees nature as she really is: the evolving plenitude that affords the existence of all things, the ultimate inspiration for the consciousness striving to know. I believe that the new science will come to resemble traditional indigenous science in many fundamental respects. To make the affinities explicit, I propose to call it the indigenous Western science; "indigenous" because it is premised on a direct experience of nature which is a unity embracing the knowing being. In this sense, indigenous knowledge is indifferent to time and place, but is the prerogative of the natural being of all ages. The natural being is the vehicle to authentic knowledge. Knowing involves the unfragmented indigenous consciousness—the natural being—communicating with nature, engaging her wholeheartedly without bounds or boundaries. There is hence no mismatch between knowledge and our experience of reality. For reality is not a flat impenetrable surface of common-sensible literalness. It has breadths and depths beyond our wildest imagination. The quality of our vision depends entirely on the extent our consciousness permeates and resonates within her magical realm. In this respect, there is complete symmetry between science and art. Both are creative acts of the most intimate communion with reality.[7]

As consistent with the character of indigenous science, it can be approached through many avenues: art, psychology, biology, ecology, sociology, linguistics, anthropology, philosophy, to name but a few.[8] In this essay, I would like to attempt an approach through contemporary physics and chemistry, especially of the organism, linking up with the philosophies of Whitehead and Bergson (though not claiming to be true to either), in order to outline what I hope to be a coherent and contemporary indigenous Western myth on the nature of reality.[9]

The Fall From Grace

The biblical account of the fall from grace is a parable of our exile as knowing beings from the magic kingdom of nature; it is a radical severing of form from content in that knowledge can no longer mean anything because it is unconnected to nature. In isolating the human consciousness from the reality which must be experienced to be understood, the content of knowledge is renounced at the outset. In turn, the imposition of an inappropriate form derived from the mechanical, materialistic worldview, led to the progressive erosion of the content of experience, resulting in the disenchantment of nature and of reality.[10]

A disjunction exists, therefore, between the quality of authentic experience and our description of reality in science. No one has written more vividly on the subject than Bergson.[11] He invites us to step into the rich flowing stream of our consciousness to recover the authentic experience of reality for which we have substituted a flat literal simulacrum given in language, in particular, the language of science.

In this language, words which represent our feelings—love and hate, joy and pain—emptied of their experiential content, are taken for the feelings themselves. They are then defined as individual psychic entities (or psychological states), each uniform for every occasion across all individuals, differing only in magnitude, or intensity. But should we, as Bergson suggests, connect our mind to our inner feelings, we discover that what we actually experience is not a quantitative increase in intensity of some psychological state, but a succession of qualitative changes which "melt into and permeate one another" with no definite localizations or boundaries, each occupying the whole of our being within this span of feeling which Bergson refers to as "pure duration".

Pure duration is our intuitive experience of inner process, which is also inner time with its dynamic heterogeneous multiplicity of succession without separateness. Each moment is implicated in all other moments. Thus Newtonian time, in which separate moments, mutually external to one another, are juxtaposed in linear progression, arises from our attempt to externalize pure duration, which is an indivisible heterogeneous quality, to an infinitely divisible homogeneous quantity. In effect, we have reduced time to Newtonian space, an equally homogeneous medium in which isolated objects, mutually opaque, confront one another in frozen immobility.

Bergson emphasizes the need for introspection in order to recover the quality of experience. Yet introspection divorced from external reality will only give a partial insight into the indigenous experience of our rainmaker. Thus, Bergson opposes an inner "succession without mutual externality" to an outer "mutual externality without succession".[12] He distinguishes two different selves, of which one is the external projection of the other, inner self, into its spatial or social representation. The inner self is reached "by deep introspection, which leads us to grasp our inner states as living things, constantly becoming."

> But the moments at which we thus grasp ourselves are rare, and that is just why we are rarely free. The greater part of the time we live outside ourselves, hardly perceiving anything of ourselves but our own ghost, a colorless shadow which pure duration projects into homogeneous space. Hence our life unfolds in space rather than in time; we live for the external world rather than for ourselves; we speak rather than think; we 'are acted' rather than act ourselves.[13]

This passage anticipates the sentiment of the existentialist writers such as Camus and Sartre. A similar sentiment pervades T. S. Eliot's poetry. The following lines from "The Hollow Men" evoke strong echoes of Bergson's projected being outside ourselves:

We are the hollow men
We are the stuffed men
Leaning together
Headpiece filled with straw. Alas!
Our dried voices, when
We whisper together
Are quiet and meaningless
As wind in dried grass
Or rats' feet over broken glass
In our dried cellar
Shape without form, shade without color,
Paralyzed force, gesture without motion . . .

The Fallacy of Misplaced Concreteness

Bergson's protestations were directed against one of the most fundamental assumptions underlying the modernist, scientistic culture of the West. This claims to express the most concrete, common-sensible aspect of nature: that material objects have simple locations in space and time. Yet space and time are not symmetrical. A material object is supposed to have extension in space in such a way that dividing the space it occupies will divide the material accordingly. On the other hand, if the object endures within a period of time, then it is assumed to exist equally in any portion of that period. In other words, dividing the time does nothing to the material because it is always assumed to be immobile. Hence the lapse of time is a mere accident, the material being indifferent to it. The world is simply made of a succession of instantaneous immobile configurations of matter, each instant bearing no inherent reference to any other instant of time. How, then, is it possible to link cause and effect? How are we justified in inferring by observation the great "laws of nature"? This was essentially the problem of induction raised by Hume.[14] The problem was created because we have mistaken the abstraction for reality—a case of the fallacy of misplaced concreteness.

Another case of the fallacy of misplaced concreteness concerns the nature of the qualities of objects. Ideal Newtonian objects are devoid of attributes except for location, mass or momentum. Yet the objects of our experience are saturated with qualities such as color, scents and sounds. How can this square with the science of physical reality? Locke attempted to solve this problem by elaborating a theory of primary and secondary qualities.[15] The primary qualities are the essential qualities of substances whose spatiotemporal relationships constitute nature. The occurrences of nature are apprehended by minds associated in some ways with living bodies. The mind, in apprehending, also experiences sensations which are qualities of the mind alone, but are projected by the mind to "clothe" the appropriate bodies in external nature. From henceforth, mind and nature (as inert matter) confront each other across an impermeable divide, and philosophers align themselves in each of three possible camps: the dualists who insist on the division, and the two varieties of monists—"those who put mind inside matter and those who put matter inside mind".[16] The most famous philosopher in the last category is Bishop Berkeley, who contends that natural entities exist only in the perception of the mind.

The Organism as Agent of Prehensive Unity

In order to transcend the philosophical ruin left in the wake of mechanical materialism, Whitehead attempted to return to a kind of native realism, not unlike the pan-psychism or pan-animism that is usually attributed to the so-called primitive mind by Western anthropologists. Whitehead, however, cites Francis Bacon as his source of inspiration, who not only attributed consciousness or perception to all bodies, including the "inanimate", but also endowed them with distinctive qualities, saying

> It is certain that all bodies whatsoever, though they have no sense, yet they have perception . . . and whether the body be alterant or altered, evermore a perception precedes operation; for else all bodies would be alike one to another.[17]

Whitehead substitutes for "perception" the word "prehension" in order to include "apprehension which may or may not be cognitive".[18] What follows from this in his own thought is not completely clear, and with due apologies to many excellent Whiteheadian scholars,[19] in my exposition below I shall inevitably be interpreting his ideas to suit my own purpose. A great part of the difficulty is that our language is quite unequal to the task of the organicist process philosophy that he is developing—the same difficulty continues to frustrate my own attempt here.

Whitehead rejects the existence of inert objects or things with simple locations in space and time. As all nature is process, there is only the progressive realization of natural occurrences. For mind, he substitutes a process of prehensive unification. The realization of an occurrence is, thus,

> the gathering of things (sic) into the unity of a prehension. . . . This unity of a prehension defines itself as a here and a now, and the things so gathered into the grasped unity have essential references to other places and other times.[20]

The focus of prehensive unification is the "event" which has individuated by the act of prehensive unification. (We shall see later that an organism is an event with enduring pattern.) Seen in this way, neither the event nor the prehensive unification of "things" gathered into a unity is subject to simple location, for

> each volume of space, or each lapse of time, includes in its essence aspects of all volumes of space, or of all lapses of time.[21]

The event, therefore, has a space-time structure of its own (although Whitehead did not use these terms).

Each event also possesses its own special qualities, which Whitehead refers to as "eternal objects", whereby the "interfusion of events" is effected. Furthermore,

> There is a reciprocity of aspects and there are patterns of aspects. Each event corresponds to two such patterns: namely the pattern of aspects of other events which it grasps into its own unity, and the pattern of its aspects which other events severally grasp into their unities. Accordingly, a non-materialist philosophy of nature will identify a primary organism as being the emergence of some particular pattern as grasped in the unity of a real event.[22]

In other words, the event, or the organism, and its environment of other events are mutually implicated and mutually constitutive. Realization depends on the act of prehension, which enfolds the environment consisting of others into a unity residing in a "self", while aspects of the self are communicated to others for their enfoldments. The realization of "self" and "other" are thus completely intertwined; the one does not occur without the other.

Toward a Theory of the Organism

Whitehead refers to a "primary organism" as the emergence of some particular pattern as grasped in the unity of a real event (see above). Defined in this way, the question is left open as to whether the fundamental particles of physics such as protons and electrons, or, at the other extreme, entire planets such as the Earth, are also organisms. As an event, the concept of an organism includes the concept of the interaction of organisms. The organism in its own prehension, however, is an achievement in its own right and for its own sake, because it has enfolded diverse entities into an enduring pattern which is uniquely itself. In its own realization, it also contributes to the realization of other organisms. But though each organism is necessary for the community of organisms, its "value" or contribution depends on something intrinsic to it—its endurance, and its ability to recover its self-identity or specific organization in the midst of the flux of reality. This does not mean that it necessarily maintains some constant shape or form. It may realize itself in the guise of an individual enduring entity which nevertheless undergoes a sequence of transformations that together constitute its life-history.[23]

An organism comes into being by its own activity out of a substrate which Whitehead refers to as the underlying, eternal "energy of realization". The analogy between Whitehead's view of nature and many traditional indigenous philosophies is obvious. The Ufaina Indians in the Colombian Amazon, for example, believe in a vital force called "fufaka" which is present in, and circulates among, all living things. The source of this vital force is the sun.[24] Similarly, traditional Chinese Taoist philosophy speaks of the "qi", the undifferentiated primal energy pervading the universe, which is the substrate for realizing the multiplicity of things. In turn, these philosophies are not so far removed from the biochemical ecology of the biosphere in Western science, in which the energy from the sun, trapped by green plants, is channeled into a cyclic web of biosynthesis and degradation involving all organisms. Material and energy flow link the entire planet together. We shall see later on that organisms are also linked by information flow.

Though consciousness is constitutive of the universe, located in organisms which are foci of prehensive unification, Whitehead perceived that the organisms differ in "value" or purposiveness in terms of their endurance of pattern in the flux of process. (This is related to the quality of organization which I shall presently introduce as its space-time structure.) Some form no more than a ripple on the surface of the energy substrate; the vast majority in the middle apparently "obey" the laws of physics; while at the other extreme are those who rise to conscious thought and are capable of exercising abstract judgments.

> The individual perception arising from enduring objects will vary in its individual depth and width according to the way in which the pattern dominates its own route. It may represent the faintest ripple differentiating the general substrate energy; or in the other extreme, it may rise to conscious thought, which includes poising before self-conscious judgment the abstract possibilities of value inherent in various situations of ideal togetherness. The intermediate cases will group round the individual perception as envisaging (without self-consciousness) that one immediate possibility of attainment which represents the closest analogy to its own immediate past, having regard to the actual aspects which are there for prehension.[25]

An individual consists of a distinctive enfoldment of its environment, therefore each individual is simultaneously delocalized over all individuals. There is another sense in which individuality is relative. An individual

> whose own life-history is part within the life-history of some larger, deeper, more complete pattern, is liable to have aspects of that larger pattern

dominating its own being, and so to experience modifications of that larger pattern reflected in itself as modifications of its own being. This is the theory of organic mechanism.[26]

An obvious situation where nested individualities occur is in a species or a society. Societies evolve slowly, their slowly changing variables defining parameters for the evolution of individuals within them. The picture of nested individuality and constitutive mutuality is also consistent with Lovelock's Gaia hypothesis,[27] which proposes that the Earth is one cybernetic system, maintained far from thermodynamic equilibrium in conditions suitable for life by the actions of the "organisms" (both physical and biological) within it.

In these examples, not only are individuals part of a larger organism, but the substance, the very essence of each individual, is constitutive of every other. There is a mutuality of enfoldment and unfoldment, of the implicate and explicate, between organism and environment. The organism, on individuating, enfolds the environment into itself simultaneously as it unfolds to the environment. Explicate order in the environment is implicate in the organism just as the organism's explicate pattern is implicate in the environment. This is precisely David Bohm's account of the quantum universe. In analogy to the hologram, the implicate order of an object is contained in an interference pattern of light distributed throughout space, in which it can be said to be enfolded. By an act of unfoldment, however, the original form of the object could once again be made explicate.

> Each separate and extended form in the explicate order is enfolded in the whole and . . . in turn, the whole is enfolded in this form.[28]

In the latest version of Bohm's theory, the universe is pictured as a continuous field with quantized values for energy, momentum and angular momentum. Such a field will manifest as both particles and as waves emanating and converging on the regions where particles are detected. This field is organized and maintained by the "superquantum potential" which is a function of the entire universe.

What we have here is a kind of universal process of constant creation and annihilation, determined through the superquantum potential so as to give a world of form and structure in which all manifest features are only relatively constant, recurrent and stable aspects of the whole.[29]

In summary, organisms are enduring patterns of activity, and concrescences of such activities, emerging from the underlying energy substrate. They are thus dynamic structures which evolve in the process of continual realization or becoming, ever enfolding from the environment to unfold to the next novelty of being.[30] In this light, causality is immanent to being and not external to it. Organisms are their own cause as well as the "cause" of other events or organisms in their environment.

Whitehead's organicism is in many ways a logical progression from the demise of mechanical materialism which began toward the end of the last century. The rise of thermodynamics introduced a new kind of conservation law—that of energy in place of mass. Mass was no longer the pre-eminent permanent quality. Instead, the notion of energy became fundamental, especially after Einstein worked out the famous mass-energy equation, and nuclear fission in the atomic bomb proved him right, with devastating consequences. At the same time, Maxwell's theory of electromagnetism demanded that there should indeed be energy, in the form of electromagnetic fields pervading throughout all space, which is not immediately dependent on matter. Finally, the development of quantum theory reveals that even the atoms of solid matter are thought to be composed of vibrations which can radiate out into space under certain circumstances. Matter loses solidity more and more under the steady scrutiny of relentless rationality.

Meanwhile, the Newtonian picture of homogeneous absolute time and space gives way to relativity. Each inertial frame of reference (associated with its own observer or prehensive organism) must be considered as having a distinct space-time metric. The organism has no simple location in space-time. Moreover, an organism can alter its space-time by its own motion or activity. It is possible that some organisms will no longer "endure" under changes of space-time. Thus, the organism's space-time metric, and perforce its internal space-time, cannot be regarded as given, but arises out of its own activities. The organization of these activities is also its internal space-time structure—its implicateness of individuation and its "value", which is not a quantity but a quality. Bergson's "pure duration" is a quality of the same cloth, and is akin to temporal organization in living systems.[31] The notion of internal space-time structure, introduced in the following sections, refers to that which is generated by the organism's own activities of prehension or enfoldment.

The Organism as a Space-Time Structure

a) The space-time catenation of living process

That organisms possess both spatial and temporal organization is so obvious as to hardly need belaboring. Spatial organization is the focus of investigation for developmental biologists, anatomists and histologists alike; while temporal organization, in terms of biological rhythms, has exercised physiologists for almost half a century now, with but little progress in their search for the biochemical mechanism of the "biological clock".[32] What I would like to address here is a somewhat different perspective on the "implicatedness", the "complicity" or "depth" of the organism's space-time structure.

The organism is a dissipative structure[33] in the sense that it is maintained in a steady state by a flow of energy and chemicals. As soon as that flow is interrupted, disintegration and death begins. However, that steady state is not a static bulk phase in a rigid unvarying container. Even a single cell has its characteristic shape and anatomy, all parts of which are in constant motion; its electrical potentials and mechanical properties similarly are subject to cyclic and non-cyclic changes as it responds to and counteracts environmental fluctuations. Spatially, the cell is partitioned into numerous compartments, each with its own steady states of processes that can respond directly to external stimuli and relay signals to other compartments of the cell. Within each compartment, microdomains[34] can be separately energized to give local circuits, and complexes of two or more molecules can function autonomously as "molecular machines". In other words, the "steady state" is not a state at all but a conglomeration of processes which are spatiotemporally organized; that is, it has a deep space-time structure, and cannot be represented as an instantaneous state or even a configuration of states. Relaxation times of processes range from $<10^{-14}$ seconds for resonant energy transfer between molecules to 10^7 seconds for circannual rhythms. The spatial extent of processes, similarly, span at least ten orders of magnitude from 10^{-10} meters for intermolecular interactions to several meters for nerve conduction and the general coordination of movements in larger animals.

The problem immediately arises as to how we can describe such a space-time structure, and, in particular, whether the thermodynamics of ordinary equilibrium processes have any relevance for the living system. The physical chemist R.J.P. Williams[35] has advocated a shift from a conventional thermodynamic approach to a dynamic approach. Williams proposes that the changes are catenated in both time and space: the extremely rapid transient flows (very short-lived pulses of chemical or of energy) are propagated to longer and longer time domains of minutes, hours, days, and so on into the "future" via interlocking processes which ultimately straddle generations.[36] These processes include the by now familiar enzyme activation cascades, which lead to the expression of different genes and morphological differentiation as cells respond to changes in their immediate environment—nerve cells on electrical or neurotransmitter stimulation; liver, pancreatic or gonadal cells on being activated by hormones. These are, in effect, projections into the future, consisting of an enfoldment of the present environment subject to past history. In total, they constitute that which is usually referred to as the system's memory, determining to some extent how the system unfolds and enfolds in future. Simultaneously, the locus of change propagates spatially to the rest of the cell or organism, stimulating other processes to take place which then feed back on the earlier process to dampen or amplify its effects. (It may lead, for example, to the organism altering its environment.) Physiologically, therefore, every volume of space has reference to every other volume, just as each lapse of time is implicated in all other lapses of time.

The dynamism of the living system is such that each single cell is simultaneously crisscrossed by many circuits of flow, each with its own time domain and vectorial direction specified by local pumping, gating and chemical transformation, such that classical equilibrium constants are quite irrelevant.

> In such a system there are no fixed constants such as equilibrium constants or solubility products, as each such constant, defined relative to a convention standard state, is a continuous function of variables.[37]

The variables which make up the "constants" include the flow rates, the electrical and mechanical field strengths and so on. Furthermore, since the products of reactions alter the chemical potentials of all the components by altering the variables, the equilibrium "constants" will also be functions of time. All is flux: there is indeed no holding nature still and looking at it.[38]

The above biochemical description also gives considerable substance to Bergson's intuition of "pure duration" as a succession of qualitative changes melting into and permeating one another, which is the essence of living process.

b) The thermodynamics of living systems

The question alluded to above is whether living systems violate the laws of physics. Our present knowledge of biochemistry already shows how inadequate the laws of thermodynamics are—at least, as we now understand them to be. But there is a deeper problem.

The physical world runs down, according to the second law of thermodynamics, such that useful energy continually degrades into heat, or random molecular motion. Concomitantly, order dissolves into disorder, the measure of which is entropy. The biological world, by contrast, seems capable of going in the opposite direction—of increasing organization by a flow of energy and matter. Many physicists and chemists feel that as all biological processes require either chemical energy or light energy and involve real chemical reactions, both the first and second law of thermodynamics must apply to living systems (the first law of thermodynamics is the law of conservation of energy). Yet chemical reactions within organisms have efficiencies that greatly exceed those occurring outside. For example, motor cars convert only 10 to 20% of the energy available in petrol into work. Energy conversion in animal muscles, by contrast, is between 66% and 98% efficient[39]; in other words, little of the available energy is degraded into entropy.

So what is the secret of the organism? One answer is that because living systems are open, they can create a local decrease in entropy at the expense of the rest of the universe, so that the entropy of living systems plus the universe always increases in all real processes.[40] But a more fundamental reason may have to do with the formulation of the second law itself.

The second law of thermodynamics, as usually formulated, is a statistical law which can only be applied to a system consisting of a large number of particles, that is, a bulk phase system. As is clear from the previous description, living systems do not have a bulk phase. Instead, they consist of compartments and microdomains, each with its own steady state, and complexes of a few molecules can act as efficient cyclic molecular machines with no immediate reference to the steady state of its surroundings. This implies that if thermodynamics is to apply to living systems, it must apply to single individual molecules, as contended by McClare.[41]

In order to formulate the second law of thermodynamics so that it applies to single molecules, McClare introduces the key notion of a characteristic time interval. Consider a system at equilibrium at temperature θ within an interval of time τ. The energies contained in this system can be partitioned into stored energies versus thermal energies. Thermal energies are those that exchange with each other and reach equilibrium in a time less than τ (so technically they give the typical Boltzmann distribution characterized by the temperature θ. Stored energies are those that remain in a non-equilibrium distribution for a time greater than τ, either as characterized by a higher temperature, or such that states of higher energy are more populated than states of lower energy. So, stored energy is any form which does not thermalize or degrade into heat in the interval τ.

McClare goes on to restate the second law as follows: useful work is only done by a molecular system when one form of stored energy is converted into another. In other words, thermalized energy is unavailable for work and it is impossible to convert thermalized energy into stored energy. But in my view, this is unnecessarily restrictive, and possibly untrue, for thermal energy *can be* harvested to do useful work in a cooperative system (see below). It is only necessary to recognize that useful work can be done by a molecular system by a transfer of stored energy in a time less than τ.

The major consequence of McClare's formulation arises from the explicit introduction of time. For there are now two quite distinct ways of doing useful work: slowly according to conventional thermodynamic theory, and quickly, in which case conventional thermodynamics does not apply. Both of these are reversible and operate at maximum efficiency as no entropy is generated. (This is implicit in the classical formulation, $dS \geq 0$, for which the limiting case is $dS=0$.) Let us consider the slow process first.

A slow process is one that occurs at or near equilibrium. By taking explicit account of characteristic time, a reversible thermodynamic process merely needs to be slow enough for all thermally exchanging energies to equilibrate, that is, to spread evenly throughout the system. In other words, it needs to be slower than τ, which can in reality be a very short period of time. So high efficiencies of energy conversion can still be attained in thermodynamic processes which occur quite rapidly, provided that equilibration is fast enough. This may be where spatial partitioning and the establishment of microdomains is crucial for restricting the volume within which equilibration occurs, thus reducing the equilibration time. This means that local equilibrium may be achieved at least for some biochemical reactions in the living system.

At the other extreme, there is the quick process, where an exchange of energy occurs so fast that it, too, is reversible. In other words, provided the exchanging energies are not thermal energies in the first place, but remain stored, then the process is limited only by the speed of light. Resonant energy transfer between molecules is an example of a fast process. As is well known, chemical bonds, when excited, will vibrate at characteristic frequencies, and any two (or more) bonds which have the same intrinsic frequency of vibration will resonate with one another. More important, the energy of vibration can be transferred through large distances (theoretically infinite, if the energy is radiated, as electromagnetic radiations travel through space at the speed of light, though in practice it may be limited by nonspecific absorption in the intervening medium). Resonant energy transfer occurs typically in 10^{-14} seconds, whereas the vibrations themselves die down, or thermalize, in 10^{-9} seconds to 10^1 seconds. The process is 100% efficient and highly specific, being determined by the frequency of the vibration itself, and resonating molecules (like people) can attract one another. By contrast, conventional chemical reactions depend on energy transfer that occurs only at collision; they are inefficient because a lot of the energy is dissipated as heat, and specificity is low, for non-reactive species could collide with each other as often as reactive species.

Does resonant energy transfer occur in the living system? McClare suggests it occurs in muscle contraction,[42] where it has already been shown that the energy released in the hydrolysis of ATP (the immediate source of chemical energy supply for the muscle) is almost completely converted into mechanical energy. This is, in effect, the molecular machine, which can cycle autonomously without equilibration with its environment. The reaction has been reinvestigated by Hibbard et al.,[43] using much more sophisticated techniques to monitor the chemical-mechanical energy transduction. Their results suggest that the formation of the myosin-actin complex is coupled to the release of inorganic phosphate from ATP in a reaction that is readily reversible; in other words, this is a reaction that generates no entropy. Similarly, in photosynthesis, whereby green plants convert light energy into chemical energy, charge separation occurs when a quantum of light is absorbed by the chlorophyll molecules in the antenna complex. Recent work[44] shows that the first step of the charge separation is a readily reversible reaction that takes place in less than 10^{-13} seconds, again implying a fast process that generates no entropy.

Thus, the living system may use both means of efficient energy transfer: slow and quick reactions, always with respect to the relaxation time, which is itself a variable according to the processes and the spatial extents involved. This insight is offered by taking into account the space-time structure of living systems explicitly.

Another important insight is the fundamental quantum nature of important biological processes. McClare[45] defines a "molecular energy machine" as one in which the energy stored in single molecules is released in a specific molecular form and then converted into another specific form so quickly that it never has time to become heat. It is also a quantum machine because it sums the effects produced by single molecules. Muscle contraction is the most obvious example. A muscle is a sum of many fibers, each of which is, in turn, a sum of many individual molecules; the action of all in concert produces a muscle contraction. Even in the field of conventional enzyme kinetics, more and more quantum mechanical effects are being recognized. Electron tunneling is already well-known.[46] Now it appears that hydrogen transfer reactions also involve tunneling across energy barriers via an overlap of quantum mechanical wave functions between substrates and products. They do not occur by thermal activation as conventionally conceived.[47]

The existence of molecular quantum machines immediately raises the question as to how the astronomical numbers of individual quantum machines can be coordinated over the macroscopic distances that are characteristic of biological functioning. This is the fundamental problem of biological organization. Just as bulk phase thermodynamics is inapplicable to the living system which consists of quantum molecular machines, so, perforce, some new principle is required for the coordination of quantum molecular machines. This principle is quantum coherence, which will be developed later on.

For now, we would like to address the question of the nature of space and time. In particular, we would like to give substance to the idea, as consistent with a process ontology, that they are constructed by the actions of organisms—organisms interpreted widely as in the sense of Whitehead's philosophy.

Space-Time Structure and Quantum Theory

The nature of space and time is fundamental to our theory of reality. The mismatch between the Newtonian universe and our intuitive experience of reality hinges on space and time. In fact, all subsequent developments in Western science may be seen as a struggle to reinstate our intuitive, indigenous notions of space and time, which deep within our soul we feel to be more consonant with authentic experience. But there has only been limited success so far.

Einstein's theory of special relativity substitutes for absolute space and absolute time a four-dimensional space-time continuum which is different for each observer in its own inertial frame. Space and time have become symmetrical to each other, but they remain definite quantities. In quantum theory, on the other hand, space coordinates lose definiteness in becoming operators, and hence statistical quantities, but time remains a simple parameter as in classical mechanics.

Another problem in connection with time is that the laws of physics in both classical and quantum mechanics, as well as in relativity, are time-symmetric, that is, they do not distinguish between past and future. Yet real processes seem to have an "arrow of time". So time ought to be related to real processes. If so, it would have the quality that Bergson refers to as pure duration. In other words, it would have a structure. Schommers,[48] like both Whitehead and Bergson, argues for the primacy of process, and in an interesting reformulation of quantum theory shows how time and space are tied to real processes.

He begins from a consideration of Mach's principle, which eliminates absolute space-time from the causal system of mechanics. According to Mach, particles do not move relative to space, but to the center of all the other masses in the universe. In other words, absolute space and time coordinates cannot be determined empirically. Any change in position of masses is not due to the interaction between coordinates and masses, but entirely between the masses. However, neither relativity nor quantum mechanics have incorporated Mach's principle in their formulation.

If one takes account of Mach's principle, space-time must be considered as an auxiliary element for the geometrical description of real processes. In other words, real processes are projected to space-time or "(r,t)-space" from perhaps a more fundamental space—that which represents reality more authentically in terms of the parameters of interactions, that is, momentum and energy, the "(p,E)-space". The two spaces are equivalent descriptions and are connected by the mathematical device of a Fourier transformation. (Intermediate spaces can also be formed which are similarly connected.) The result is that time, as much as space, takes the form of an operator in (p,E)-space where momentum and energy are parameters and take on definite values.

Hence the wave function for space-time ψ (r,t) leads to probability distributions for both space and time. Processes consisting of matter interacting—that is in (p,E)-space—generate space-time structures. In other words, space-time structures are caused by action, and in the limiting cases of a stationary process and a free particle, that is, the wave function $\psi(r,t)=0$, no time- or space-structures are defined.

In Schommer's scheme, energy and time representations are complementary, and for non-stationary processes an uncertainty relationship exists between them which is of the same form as that between position and momentum in conventional quantum theory. The consequence is that both energy structure and the internal time structure are different for different systems when compared to an external reference time structure such as a clock.

In fact, space-time forms a non-absolute continuum depending on the reference mass. In turn, mass is nothing but a quality of action, represented perhaps somewhat inadequately as energy and momentum.

So far, nothing has been said concerning the interaction between space-time structures, such as occurs in perception or prehension between "subject" and "object", which may have very different space-time structures. Before I venture into this territory, it is necessary to introduce the idea of coherence, which I believe to be the key to biological organization.

Coherence and Biological Organization

What is the basis of the remarkable spatiotemporal organization in all living systems, a pattern that is stably maintained in the face of a constant flux of energy and matter? How does this organization enable them to transform energy so rapidly, and with such high efficiency? How do organisms react so promptly and sensitively to specific cues from the environment? Despite great advances in molecular biology within the past 50 years, we have as yet no satisfactory explanation for any of these distinguishing characteristics of living systems. Nobel laureate biochemist Szent-Györgyi was one of the first to suggest that we can only begin to understand the characteristics of living systems if we take into account the collective properties of the molecular aggregates, such as those observed under special conditions in solid state physics.[49]

The molecules in most physical matter have a high degree of uncoordinated or random thermal motion. But when the temperature is lowered to beyond a critical level, all the molecules may condense into a collective state, and exhibit the unusual properties of superfluidity and superconductivity. In other words, all the molecules of the system move as one, and conduct electricity with zero resistance (by a coordinated arrangement of conducting electrons). Liquid helium, at temperatures close to absolute zero, was the first and only superfluid substance known, and various pure metals and alloys are now known to be superconducting at liquid helium temperatures. Recently, technology has progressed to superconducting materials which can work at much higher temperatures, above absolute zero.

The solid-state physicist Herbert Fröhlich[50] points out that something like a condensation into a collective mode of activity may be occurring in living systems such that they are, in effect, superconductors working at physiological temperatures. He suggests that metabolic energy, instead of being lost as heat, is actually stored in the form of collective modes of electromechanical and electromagnetic vibrations that extend over macroscopic distances within the organisms. He calls these collective modes "coherent excitations". The collective modes can vary from a stable or metastable highly polarized state (resulting from mode softening of interacting frequencies toward a collective frequency of zero), to limit cycle oscillations, to much higher frequencies when the energy supply exceeds a certain threshold. Each collective "mode" can in effect be a band of frequencies, with varying spatial extents as consistent with the spatiotemporal structure of the living system. Nevertheless, the frequencies are coupled together so that energy fed into any specific frequency is readily communicated to other frequencies. (Conceptually, Fröhlich achieved energy exchange via a "heat-bath", though, as we shall see later, this energy coupling may have a more fundamental origin.)

Coherent excitations are responsible for long-range order in the living system, as well as for efficient energy transfer. Under those conditions, the organism will also be very sensitive to external electromagnetic fields, and weak signals will be greatly amplified. Fröhlich's theory of coherent excitations involves classical mechanisms and offers a plausible explanation for the biological effects of electromagnetic fields which have increasingly become the focus of public attention.

For instance, Presman[51] reviewed observations suggesting that diverse organisms are sensitive to electromagnetic fields of extremely low intensities: of magnitudes that are similar to those occurring in nature. These natural electromagnetic sources, such as the Earth's magnetic field, provide information for navigation and growth in a wide variety of organisms, while major biological rhythms are closely attuned to the natural electromagnetic rhythms of the Earth, which are in turn tied to periodic variations in solar and lunar activities. In many cases, the sensitivity of the organisms to electromagnetic fields is such that they detect signals below the level of thermal noise. This indicates that the electromagnetic field cannot be acting on the biological system by conventional energy transfer, but by informational transfer. Moreover, it points to the existence of amplifying mechanisms in the organisms receiving the information (and acting on it). Specifically, the living system itself must also be organized by intrinsic electrodynamical fields, capable of receiving (and transmitting) electromagnetic information in a wide range of frequencies—rather like an extraordinarily efficient and sensitive, and extremely broad-band, radio receiver and transmitter, much as Fröhlich has suggested. In my own laboratory, we have just completed a study showing that brief exposures of early fruitfly (*Drosophila*) embryos to weak magnetic fields result in a high proportion of characteristic body pattern abnormalities in the larvae hatching 24 hours later.[52] As the energies involved are below thermal threshold, there can be no significant effect unless there is a high degree of cooperativity or coherence in the pattern determination processes reacting to the external field. A wide-ranging review of many similar observations since the 1970s is in a recent book by Becker.[53]

Fröhlich's hypothesis of coherent excitations in living systems has received independent support from research on light emission carried out by Popp and his colleagues.[54] They show how the characteristics of light emitted from diverse organisms point to the existence of a coherent photon field which underlies living organization. In a very real sense, we are all beings of light. "Light" here refers to electromagnetic radiation in the entire spectrum, from the optical region (that which we normally call light) to electromagnetic fields of one hertz and below. Not only are organisms fields of coherent light waves which organize their activities, but they are literally immersed in a sea of light consisting of the cosmic radiation background, the sun's radiant energy and the Earth's fields—to which they are attuned and through which they receive electromagnetic signals from and transmit signals to other organisms, possibly to all other organisms. This vision is completely consonant with that presented by Whitehead and Bohm described earlier. But I am jumping ahead.

Quantum Coherence

A key notion in this new perspective of living organization is coherence. So I shall start from first principles and try to explain what it is.

Coherence in ordinary language means correlation, a sticking together, or connectedness, also, a consistency in the system. So we refer to people's speech or thought as coherent if the parts fit together well, and incoherent if they are uttering meaningless nonsense, or presenting ideas that don't make sense as a whole. Thus, coherence always refers to wholeness. However, in order to appreciate its full meaning, it is necessary to make incursions into its quantum physical description, which gives us some insights that are otherwise not accessible from a common-sensible, literal description.

Let us begin with Young's two-slit experiment, in which a source of monochromatic light is placed behind a screen with two narrow slits. (Figure 1.)

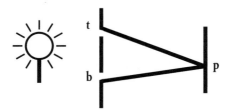

Figure 1: The Two-Slit Experiment

As is well known, light behaves as either particles or waves according as to whether one or both slits are opened. When both slits are opened, even single photons behave as waves in that they pass through both slits at once, and, falling upon a photographic plate, form a characteristic interference pattern. The intensity or brightness of the pattern at each point depends on a "probability" that light falls on to that point.

The "probability" is placed between quotation marks because it is not probability in the ordinary sense. One way of representing those probabilities is as correlation functions consisting of the product of two complex amplitudes. Light arriving at the point p on the photographic plate has taken different paths, tp and bp. The intensity at p is then given as the sum of four such correlation functions:

$$I = G(t,t) + G(b,b) + G(t,b) + G(b,t)$$

where $G(t,t)$ is the intensity with only top slit opened, $G(b,b)$ the intensity with only bottom slit opened, and $G(t,b)+G(b,t)=2G(t,b)$ is the additional intensity when both slits are opened. At different points on the photographic plate, the intensity is

$$I = G(t,t) + G(b,b) + 2G(t,b)\ cos\ \theta$$

where θ is the angle of the phase difference between the two light waves.

The fringe contrast in the interference pattern depends on the magnitude of $G(t,b)$. If this correlation function vanishes, it means that the light coming out of t and b are uncorrelated; and if there is no correlation, we say that the light at t and b is incoherent. On the other hand, increase in coherence results in an increase in fringe contrast, that is, the brightness of the bands. Since $cos\ \theta$ is never greater than one (when the two beams are perfectly in phase), then the fringe contrast is maximized by making $G(t,b)$ as large as possible and that signifies maximum coherence. But there is an upper bound to how large $G(t,b)$ can be. It is given by the so-called Schwarz inequality:

$$G(t,t) \, G(b,b) > |G(t,b)|^2$$

The maximum of $G\,(t,b)$ is obviously obtained when the two sides are equal:

$$G(t,t) \, G(b,b) = |G(t,b)|^2$$

Now, it is this equation that gives us a description of quantum coherence. A field is coherent at two space-time points, say, t and b, if the above equation is true. Furthermore, we have a coherent field if this equality holds for all space-time points, X_1 and X_2. This coherence is referred to as first-order coherence because its refers to correlation between only two space-time points, and we write it more generally as

$$G_{(1)}(X_1, X_1) \, G_{(1)}(X_2, X_2) = |G_{(1)}(X_1, X_2)|^2$$

This equation tells us that, paradoxically, the correlation between two space-time points in a coherent field factorizes, or decomposes, neatly into the self-correlations at the two points separately, and that this factorizability or decomposability is a sufficient condition for coherence. What it means is that any two points in a coherent field behave statistically independently of each other. If we put two photon detectors in this field, they will register photons independently of each other.

Coherence can be generalized to arbitrarily higher orders, say, to n approaching ∞, in which case we shall be talking about a fully coherent field. If nth order coherence holds, then all of the correlation functions which represent joint counting rates for m-fold coincidence experiments (where $m<n$) factorize as the product of the self-correlations at the individual space-time points. In other words, if we put n different counters in the field, they will each record photons in a way which is statistically independent of all the others with no special tendency toward coincidences, or correlations.[55]

A coherent state is thus one of maximum global cohesion and also maximum local freedom! Nature presents us a deep riddle that compels us to accommodate seemingly polar opposites. What she is telling us is that coherence does not mean uniformity, where everybody must be doing the same thing all the time. An intuitive way to think about it is in terms of a symphony orchestra or a grand ballet, or, better yet, a jazz band where every individual is doing his or her own thing, but is yet in tune or in step with the whole. This is precisely the biochemical picture we now have of the living state: microcompartments and microdomains, right down to molecular machines, all functioning autonomously, doing very different things at different rates, yet they are in step with the whole organism.

Factorizability optimizes communication by providing an uncorrelated network of space-time points which can be modulated instantaneously by specific signals. Furthermore, it provides the highest possible fringe contrast (or visibility) for pattern recognition, which may account for the great specificities in response of organisms to diverse stimuli. The factorizability of coherent fields may also underlie the efficiency of bioenergetic processes in two respects. First, it concentrates the highest amount of energy of the same field as well as creating effectively field-free zones within the field (by destructive interference). Second, since the higher order correlations (correlations of many points) are the smallest in a completely coherent field, the tiniest possible amount of energy is subject to correlated transfer between an arbitrarily large number of space-time points in the field with minimum loss.[56]

One of the ways of achieving coherence is to occupy only one mode, which is precisely the sort of thing that happens in superconductivity and superfluidity. That "mode" does not have to be a single frequency, it can be a broadband of frequencies, such as are found in biological organisms. But as mentioned above, in order to constitute one "mode", these frequencies have to be coupled together or intercommunicating. It means energy fed into one frequency must be capable of being propagated to all the frequencies. Another characteristic of the coherent field is that it is fluctuationless or noiseless, the sort that any communication engineer working at radio-frequencies, for example, would say is coherent.

In summary, quantum coherence is capable of explaining many of the most distinctive properties of living systems. In the next section, I review some of the evidence for coherence from work on biophotons and other areas of research.

Biophotons and Coherence in Living Systems

Practically all organisms emit light at a steady rate which varies from a few photons per cell per day to several photons per organism per second[57]. The emission of biophotons, as they are called, is strongly correlated with functional states of the organisms, and responds to many external stimuli or stresses (see below). It shows a highly nonlinear response to temperature which is characteristic of many physiological processes. Spectral analyses of the emitted light reveals that it typically covers the entire range of optical frequencies, with an approximately equal distribution of photons throughout the range. Such a distribution deviates markedly from the equilibrium Boltzmann distribution—and is never found in non-living systems. It also suggests that the different frequencies are in fact intercommunicating, so that energy fed into any frequency is rapidly distributed to all other frequencies, precisely as predicted for a coherent state.

Biophotons can also be studied as rescattered emission after a brief exposure to light of different spectral compositions. It has been found without exception that the rescattered emission decays not according to an exponential function characteristic of non-coherent light, but according to a hyperbolic function which is a sufficient condition for a coherent light-field. The hyperbolic function takes the general form,

$$x = A(t + t_o)^{-1/\Delta}$$

where x is the light intensity, A is a constant and t is time after light exposure. The light intensity is inversely proportional to time, which points to the existence of memory in the system and, hence, of time-measure.

This phenomenon can be intuitively understood as follows. In a system consisting of non-interacting molecules emitting at random, the energy of the emitted photons is lost completely to the outside, or converted into heat, which is the ultimate non-coherent energy. If the molecules are emitting coherently, however, the energy of the emitted photons is not completely lost. Instead, part of it is coherently coupled back or restored to the system. The consequence is that the decay is delayed, and follows typically a hyperbolic curve with a long tail. Other non-linear forms of delayed decay kinetics can be predicted from a coherent field, such as oscillations, which are also frequently observed.

The typical hyperbolic and nonlinear decay kinetics is uniform throughout the visible spectrum, as evidenced both by the rescattering of monochromatic light, or light of restricted spectral compositions, and by the spectral analysis of the rescattered emission. The rescattered emission also covers the same broad range of frequencies, and its spectral distribution may be maintained even when the system is perturbed to such an extent that the emission intensity changes over several orders of magnitude—suggesting that all the frequencies are in effect coupled together. Such observations are consistent with the idea that the living system is one coherent photon field far from equilibrium, with coherence simultaneously in the whole range of frequencies that are nonetheless coupled together to give a single degree of freedom *as a statistical average*.

As is made clear in the description of quantum coherence above, coherence does not mean uniformity, or that every part of the organism must be doing the same thing or vibrating with the same frequencies. There can indeed be domains of local autonomy such as that we know to exist in the organism. Furthermore, as argued in preceding sections, organisms have a space-time structure, hence any measurement of the degree of freedom performed within a finite time interval will deviate from the ideal of one, which is that of a fully coupled system with little or no space-time structure. Another source of variation may arise because some parts of the system are in fact temporarily decoupled from the whole, and hence the degree of coherence will also reflect changes in the functional states of the system. Such a variation in the degree of coherence appears to be associated with the development of malignancy in cells (see below).

Evidence for Coherence from Other Areas of Research

Evidence for various aspects of coherence come from many areas of biological and biochemical research, although the researchers themselves do not recognize them as such. Frequency coupling has long been observed for biological rhythms,[58] which often show harmonic relationships with one another, as, for example, the relationship between respiratory rhythm and heartbeat frequency. Similarly, the phenomenon of sub-harmonic resonance is well-known in metabolic oscillations, where entrainment of the metabolic oscillators is obtained to external driving frequencies which are approximately integer multiples of the fundamental.[59] Recently, a gene has been isolated in *Drosophila*, mutations of which alters the circadian period. Remarkably, the wing-beat frequency of its love-song is correspondingly speeded up or slowed down according to whether the circadian period is shortened or lengthened.[60]

A high degree of coherence or coordination exists in muscle contraction, as already pointed out. Insect flight muscle oscillates synchronously with great rapidity, supporting wing beat periods of milliseconds.[61] Many organisms, tissues and cells show spontaneous oscillatory contractile activities that are coherent over large spatial domains with periods ranging from 10^{-1} seconds to minutes. Similarly, spontaneous oscillations in membrane potentials can occur in a wide range of "non-excitable" cells as well as in cells traditionally regarded as excitable, that is, neurons, and these range in frequencies from 10^{-3} seconds to minutes, again involving entire cells or tissues (such as the stomach and the intestine).[62] Finally, recent applications of supersensitive SQUID magnetometers to monitor electrical activities of the brain have revealed an astonishing repertoire of rapid coherent changes (in milliseconds) which sweep over large areas of the brain.[63] These and the observations on synchronous firing patterns (40 to 60 hertz) in widely separated areas of the brain recorded by conventional electrodes[64] are compelling neurobiologists to consider mechanisms which can account for such long range coherence. The authors suggest that the synchronization of oscillatory response in spatially separate regions may serve as "a mechanism for the extraction and representation of global and coherent features of a pattern", and for "establishing cell assemblies that are characterized by the phase and frequency of their coherent oscillations".[65]

At the molecular level, muscle contraction is shown to occur in definite quantal steps that are synchronous over entire muscle fibers, and measurements with high speed ultrasensitive instrumentation suggest that the contraction is essentially fluctuationless[66] (as characteristic of a coherent quantum field, see above). Similarly, the beating of cilia in mussels and other organisms also occurs in synchronized quantal steps with little or no fluctuation.[67]

One consequence of coherence that can be mentioned here has to do with energy storage. Coherence is associated with a time and a volume over which phase correlation is maintained. The coherence time for a quantum molecular process is just the characteristic time interval τ over which energy remains stored in McClare's formulation of the second law referred to above. This has the consequence that, in conformity with the second law of thermodynamics, the longer the coherence time, τ, the more extended is the timescale over which efficient energy transfer processes can take place provided that they are much less than τ or in the quasi-equilibrium approximation if they take place slowly with respect to τ. In other words, efficient energy transfer processes can in principle occur over a wide range of timescales, depending on the coherence times in the system, which we shall return to later.

Long Range Communication Between Cells and Organisms

In considering the possibility that cells and organisms may communicate at long range by means of electromagnetic signals, Presman[68] points to some of the perennial mysteries of the living world: how do birds in a flock, or fish in a shoal, move so effortlessly and simultaneously as one? During emotional mobilization, the speed and strength of action of the organism are much greater than the normal working level. The motor nerve to the muscle conducts at 100 times the speed of the vegetative nerves, which are responsible for the activation of processes leading to the enhancement of the contractile activity of the muscles required in a crisis: adrenaline release, dilatation of muscular vessels and increase in the heart rate. Thus, it appears that the muscle receives the signals for enhanced coordinated action long before the signals arrive at the organs responsible for the enhancement of muscle activity! This suggests that there may be a system of communication that sends emergency messages simultaneously to all organs, including those not directly connected with the nerve network. The speed with which this system operates rules out all conventional mechanisms (see Ho[69] for a similar assessment of the visual system). Furthermore, there are grounds for believing that electromagnetic signals are involved. Animals are highly sensitive to electromagnetic fields, which can also act as conditional stimuli for the elaboration of conditioned reflexes. Special electromagnetic receptors are present in animals, including humans. And electromagnetic signals of various frequencies, other than visible biophotons, can be recorded in the vicinity of isolated organs and cells, as well as close to entire organisms. In my laboratory, we have indeed recorded profuse electrical signals from fruitfly embryos (from about 1 hertz to 30 hertz) during the earliest stages of development.[70] Thus, long range communication between cells and organisms is a distinct possibility, given that they both emit and are sensitive to weak electromagnetic fields.

Schamhart and van Wijk[71] investigated the photon-emission characteristics of normal and malignant cells. They found that while normal cells exhibit decreasing light re-emission with increasing cell density, malignant cells show a highly non-linear increase with increasing cell density, suggesting long-range interactions between the cells which are responsible for their differing social behavior: the tendency of disaggregation in the malignant tumor cells as opposed to attractive long range forces between normal cells. The difference between cancer cells and normal cells may lie in their communicative capability, which in turn depends on their degree of coherence. The parameter $1/\Delta$ in the hyperbolic decay function (see p. 202) can be taken as a measure of incoherence, as it is directly correlated with the inability of the system to reabsorb emitted energy coherently. This value was shown to increase with increasing cell density in the malignant cells, whereas that of normal cells decreased.

Similar long range interactions between organisms have been demonstrated in *Daphnia*[72] where the emission rate varies periodically with cell number in such a way as to suggest a relationship to average separation distances which are harmonics of the body size.

In synchronously developing populations of early *Drosophila* embryos, we have recently discovered the remarkable phenomenon of super-delayed luminescence in which intense prolonged flashes of light are re-emitted with delay times of 20 minutes to eight hours after a single brief light exposure. These may result from cooperative interactions among embryos within the entire population, such that all the embryos re-emit in synchrony.[73] The long delays in re-emission also imply that coherence times for the process range from minutes up to eight hours.

Organisms as Coherent Space-Time Structures

We can now see that organisms are coherent space-time structures, and, furthermore, that this is the essence of biological organization. Such an understanding also provides a solution to one of the perpetual riddles of life: what constitutes an individual or a "self"? The answer is that an individual is simply a field of coherent activity. Defined in this way, it readily opens the way to the sort of nested individualities of which Whitehead speaks, but with the added insight that individualities are spatially and temporally fluid entities, in accordance with the extent of the coherence established. Thus, in long range communication between cells and organisms, the entire community may become one when coherence is established and communication occurs without obstruction or delay. This is the ideal coherent society,[74] which maximizes both global cohesion and individual freedom. Within the coherence time there is no space separation: that is, the usual spatial neighborhood relationship becomes irrelevant. Similarly, within the coherence volume, there is no time separation, hence instantaneous (faster than light) communication can occur. Feelings can indeed spread "like wildfire", and people everywhere can get caught up simultaneously in a sudden fervor.

Coherence is also a solution to the Einstein-Rosen-Podolsky paradox in which two originally correlated particles become spatially widely separated and yet seem able to communicate instantaneously. This solution is already implicit in Einstein's remarks:

> If the partial systems A and B form a total system which is described by its psi-function $\psi\,(AB)$, there is no reason why any mutually independent existence (state of reality) should be ascribed to the partial systems A and B viewed separately, *not even if the partial systems are spatially separated from each other at the particular time under consideration.* The assertion that, in this latter case, the real situation of B could not be (directly) influenced by any measurement taken on A is therefore, within the framework of quantum theory, unfounded and (as the paradox shows) unacceptable.[75]

In other words, if the particles remain coherent, then they must be considered effectively as one system, despite spatial separation.

Within the living system, coherence times and coherence volumes are themselves determined by the relaxation times and volumes of the processes involved. We may envisage biological rhythms as manifesting a hierarchy of coherence times that define the time-frames of the processes within the organism. This fits with Bergson's concept of pure duration, which we may now identify as the time taken for the completion of a process. A heartbeat requires a full cycle of contraction and relaxation before we recognize it as such, that is, the duration of a heart beat, which is about one second in external reference time. In the brain, neurobiologists have recently discovered an endogenous 40 hertz rhythm that is coherent over the entire brain;[76] it is possible that this may define the duration of primary perception. Within that duration, which we can regard as the coherence time in that level of the nested hierarchy of time structure, processes coherent with it will generate no time at all. A similar argument should apply to the corresponding coherence volume.

This representation of individuals as coherent space-time structures implies that space and time, in terms of separation and passage, are both generated, perhaps in proportion to the incoherencies of action. Thus, a coherent sage may well be living in a truly timeless-spaceless state, which is beyond our comprehension. I believe some of us get glimpses of this in a particularly inspired moment, or during an aesthetic or religious experience, not unlike that achieved by the rainmaker.

In ordinary perception, on the other hand, the organism interacts with the environmental object, a perturbation propagates within the organism and is registered or assimilated in its physiology (enfolded). This results in time generation. The greater the wave function $\psi(r,t)$ changes, perhaps the more time is generated. Conversely, the more match or transparency there is between object and subject, the less time is generated.

Another consequence is that coherent states encompass regimes of simultaneity within which instantaneous communication can take place and spatial separation becomes irrelevant. This can occur within individuals, and, as we have seen, also between members of a population. Whole societies can, in principle, match coherent space-time structures and achieve instantaneous communication over long distances, transcending ordinary, common-sensible space-time. Perhaps unusual states of consciousness such as clairvoyance, telepathy, so-called extrasensory perception are due to such matching of coherent space-time structures.

But something further may be required for the emergence of what I have referred to as a coherent society, that is, a society which maximizes both global cohesion and local freedom, in accordance with the definition of quantum coherence. From the foregoing discussion, it is obviously a society where social spacetime structure matches both natural space-time and individual private space-time. This has considerable relevance for Illich's idea of convivial scales of machinery as well as communities and institutions.[77]

Causality in a Universe of Coherent Space-time Structures

The primary implication of the organicist view as represented by both Bergson and Whitehead is that causation is immanent to process, embodied in organisms. Causation is coextensive with being; it is both local to the organism and distributed in the community of other organisms in a mutuality of enfoldment and creative unfolding. It is not mediated by so many external forces acting on so many indifferent objects. This has deep implications for the issue of freewill as opposed to determinism which I can only touch upon here.

First of all, the positing of "self" as a domain of coherent space-time structure implies the existence of active agents who are free. Freedom in this context means being true to self, in other words, being coherent. A free act is thus a coherent act. Of course not all acts are free, since one is seldom coherent. Yet the mere possibility of being unfree affirms the opposite: that freedom is real. As Bergson expressed it,

> . . . we are free when our acts spring from our whole personality, when they express it, when they have that indefinable resemblance to it which one sometimes finds between the artist and his work.[78]

Since self is distributed, as it is implicated in a community of other entities, being true to self does *not* imply acting against others. On the contrary, sustaining others sustains the self, so being true to others is also being true to self. It is only within a mechanistic Darwinian perspective that freedom becomes perverted into acts against others.[79]

According to John Stuart Mill,[80] to be free "must mean to be conscious, before I have decided, that I am able to decide either way." So defenders of free will claim that when we act freely, some other action would have been equally possible. Conversely, proponents of determinism assert that given certain antecedent conditions, only one resultant action was possible.

The problem itself is posed on the mechanistic assumptions of immobility and mutual externality of events. This gives rise to two equally unacceptable alternatives: either that an immobile configuration of antecedents "determines" another immobile configuration of resultants, or that, at any frozen instant, to be or not to be are equally likely choices for a consciousness that is external to itself–a process which immediately leads us back to Cartesian mind-matter dualism, which makes us strangers to ourselves. In the reality of process, where the self is ever becoming, it does not pass like an automaton from one frozen instant to the next. Instead, the quality of experience permeates the whole being in a succession without separateness in "a self which lives and develops by means of its very hesitations, until the free action drops from it like an overripe fruit."[81]

One might represent consciousness as a wave function that evolves, constantly being transformed by experience as well as overt acts. The issue of quantum indeterminism is a very deep one, but the picture of a wave function– a pure state–consisting of a total interfusion of feelings, each of which occupies the whole being, is precisely what Bergson describes. Such a pure state cannot be resolved or factorized into a mixture of states, except under certain conditions. Thus, the overt act, or choice, does follow from the antecedent, but it cannot be predicted in advance. One can at best retrace the abstract "steps" and represent the evolution of the consciousness as having followed a "trajectory". In truth, the so-called trajectory was traced out by one's own actions, both overt and covert up to that point.

Moreover, when one reinstates the full quality of our consciousness, we can see that there can be no identical or repeatable states, which, when presented again at any time, will bring about identical resultant states. The "wave-function" that is consciousness is always changing and always unique, as it is "colored" by all the tones of our personality. Thus each of us loves and hates in different ways, yet language makes no distinction from one to the other. Only by the efforts of the great novelists and artists can we recover the plenum that is life and reality.

Gibson, a chief exponent of a process ontology in perception, has this to say on consciousness:

> The stream of consciousness does not consist of an instantaneous present and a linear past receding into the distance; it is not a 'travelling razor's edge' dividing the past from the future. Perhaps the present has a certain duration. If so, it should be possible to find out when perceiving stops and remembering begins. But it has not been possible. . . . A perception, in fact, does not have an end. Perceiving goes on.[82]

Nature is ever-present to us, as we are to ourselves. This ever-present is structured, as we have seen. Our experience consists of the catenation of events of different durations, which propagates and reverberates in and around our being, constantly being registered and recreated. What constitutes memory of some event is the continuing present for the over-arching process of which the event is part.[83]

The universe of coherent space-time structures is thus a nested hierarchy of individualities and communities which come into being through acts of prehensive unification. Just as the organism is ever-present to itself during its entire life history, and all other individualities are ever-present to it, the universe is ever-present to itself in the universal duration where creation never ceases by the convocation of individual acts, which are now surfacing from the energy substrate, now condensing to new patterns, now submerging to re-emerge in another guise.

Reality is thus a shimmering presence of infinite planes, a luminous labyrinth of the active now connecting "past" and "future", "real" with "ideal", where potential unfolds into actual and actual enfolds to further potential through the free action and intentions of the organism. It is a sea awash with significations, dreams and desires. This reality we carry with us, an ever-present straining toward the future. The act is the cause; it is none other than the creation of meaning, the realization of the ideal and the consummation of desire.

Notes and References

1. H. Hesse, *Magister Ludi: The Glass Bead Game*, translated by R. and C. Winston, Bantam Books, 1943, 1970.

2. Hesse, 1943, 1970, ibid., pp. 433-434.

3. See M-W. Ho, "Natural being and coherent society" in *Social and Natural Complexity* (special issue of *The Journal of Social and Biological Structures*), edited by E. L. Khalil and K. E. Boulding, 1992a.

4. M-W. Ho, "Reanimating nature: the integration of science with human experience", *Beshara Magazine* 8, 1989a, pp. 16-25; reprinted with minor modifications in *Leonardo*, 24 (5), 1991, pp. 607-615.

5. M.-W. Ho, "A quest for total understanding" in *Learning without Limits: The Dilemma of Knowledge*, transcript, Saros Seminars, Saros Publications, 1990a, pp. 47-66.

6. See Ho, 1989a, ref 4.

7. See Ho, 1989a, 1990a, refs 4 and 5.

8. This is done in my book, *The Rainbow and the Worm: The Physics of Organisms* (1993).

9. Others have gone before me in this venture: Ilya Prigogine on the physics of becoming (see ref 33); David Bohm on *Wholeness and Implicate Order*, Routledge and Kegan Paul, 1980; and, more recently, R. B. Jahn and B. J. Dunne, "On the quantum mechanics of consciousness, with application to anomalous phenomena" in *Foundations of Physics* 16, 1986, pp. 721-772. See also Jahn and Dunne in this volume.

10. See Ho, 1992a, ref 3.

11. H. Bergson, *Time and Free Will: An Essay on the Immediate Data of Consciousness*, translated by F. L. Pogson, George Allen & Unwin, Ltd., 1916.

12. Bergson, 1916, p. 227.

13. Bergson, 1916, p. 231.

14. See A. N. Whitehead, *Science and the Modern World*, Fontana Books, 1925, p. 68.

15. Ibid.

16. Ibid., p. 73.

17. Ibid., p. 87.

18. Ibid., p. 88.

19. For example, D. Emmet, *The Effectiveness of Causes*, MacMillan, 1984.

20. Whitehead, 1925, p. 88, ref 14.

21. Whitehead, 1925, p. 90, ref 14.

22. Whitehead, 1925, pp. 128-129, ref 14.

23. See M-W. Ho, "How rational can rational morphology be? A post-Darwinian rational taxonomy based on a structuralism of process", *Rivista di Biologia* 81, 1988, pp. 11-55.

24. P. Bunyard, *The Colombian Amazon: Policies for the Protection of the Indigenous Peoples and Their Environment*, The Ecological Press, 1989, p. 68.

25. Whitehead, 1925, pp. 131-132, ref 14.

26. Whitehead, 1925, p. 132, ref 14.

27. J. E. Lovelock, *Gaia: A New Look at Life on Earth*, Oxford University Press, 1979; also J. E. Lovelock, *The Ages of Gaia*, Oxford University Press, 1988.

28. D. Bohm, "Hidden variables and the implicate order" in *Quantum Implications. Essays in Honor of David Bohm,* edited by B. J. Hiley and F. D. Peat, Routledge and Kegan Paul, 1987, pp. 33-45.

29. Bohm, 1987, p. 43.

30. See Ho, 1988, ref 23.

31. B. C. Goodwin, *Temporal Organization in Cells,* Academic Press, 1963.

32. See D. S. Morse, L. Fritzand J. W. Hastings, "What is the clock? Translational regulation of circadian bioluminescence", *TIBS* 15, 1990, pp. 262-265.

33. I. Prigogine, *Introduction to Thermodynamics of Irreversible Processes,* Wiley, 1967.

34. R.J.P. Williams, "On first looking into nature's chemistry. Part I. The role of small molecules and ions: the transport of the elements. Part II. The role of large molecules, especially proteins", *Chem. Soc. Rev.* 9 (3), 1980, pp. 281-324; 325-364.

35. Williams, 1980, p. 311.

36. See Ho, 1988; also M. W. Ho, "Where does biological form come from?", *Rivista di Biologia* 77, 1984, pp. 147-79.

37. Williams, 1980, p. 363, ref 34.

38. A. N. Whitehead, *Concept of Nature,* Cambridge University Press, 1920.

39. M. H. Kushmerick, R. E. Larson and R. E. Davies, "The chemical energetics of muscle contraction. I. Activation heat, heat of shortening and ATP utilization for activation-relaxation processes", *Proc. Roy. Soc. Lond.* B, 1969, pp. 174, 293-313.

40. E. Schrödinger, *What is Life?,* Cambridge University Press, 1944.

41. C.W.F. McClare, "Chemical machines, Maxwell's demon and living organisms", *J. Theor. Biol.* 30, 1971, pp. 1-34.

42. C.W.F. McClare, "A 'molecular energy' muscle model", *J. Theor. Biol.* 35, 1972, pp. 569-575.

43. M. G. Hibbard, J. A. Dantzig, D. R. Trentham and V. E. Goldman, "Phosphate release and force generation in skeletal muscle fibres", *Science* 228, 1985, pp. 1317-1319.

44. G. R. Fleming, J. L. Martin and J. Breton, "Rates of primary electron transfer in photosynthetic reaction centers and their mechanistic implications", *Nature* 333, 1988, pp. 190-192.

45. McClare, 1971, p. 14, ref 41.

46. See Williams, 1980, ref 34.

47. J. Y. Klinman, "Quantum mechanical effects in enzyme-catalyzed hydrogen transfer reactions", *TIBS* 14, 1989, pp. 368-373.

48. W. Schommers, "Space-time and quantum phenomena" in *Quantum Theory and Pictures of Reality,* edited by W. Schommers, Springer-Verlag, 1989, pp. 217-277.

49. A. Szent-Györgi, *Introduction to a Submolecular Biology,* Academic Press, 1960.

50. H. Fröhlich, "The biological effects of microwaves and related questions", *Advances in Electronics and Electronic Physics* 53, 1980, pp. 85-152.

51. A. S. Presman, *Electromagnetic Fields and Life,* Plenum Press, 1970.

52. M-W. Ho, T. A. Stone, I. Jerman, J. Bolton, H. Bolton, B. C. Goodwin, P. T. Saunders and F. Robertson, "Brief exposure to weak static magnetic fields during early embryogenesis cause cuticular pattern abnormalities in Drosophila larvae", *Physics in Medicine and Biology,* 37, 1992, pp. 1171-1179.

53. R. O. Becker, *Cross Currents: The Promise of Electromedicine, The Perils of Electropollution,* Jeremy P. Tarcher, Inc., 1990.

54. F. A. Popp, K. H. Li, W. P. Mei, M. Galle and R. Heuroh, "Physical aspects of biophotons", *Experientia* 44, 1988, pp. 576-585.

55. This account is based on R. J. Glauber, "Coherence and quantum detection" in *Quantum Optics,* edited by R. J. Glauber, Academic Press, 1969.

56. This insight is due to Popp, in F. A. Popp and M-W. Ho, *Light and Life* (in preparation), 1991.

57. For a fuller description of the characteristics of biophotons, see F. A. Popp, "On the coherence of ultraweak photoemission from living tissues" in *Disequilibrium and Self-Organization,* edited by C. W. Kilmister, Reidel, 1986. For a detailed analysis of hyperbolic decay kinetics in different parts of the light spectrum, see also F. Musumeci, M. Godlevski, F. A. Popp and M-W. Ho, "Time behavior of delayed luminescence in Acetabularia acetabulum" in *Advances in Biophoton Research,* edited by F. A. Popp, K. H. Li and Q. Gu, World Scientific (in press), 1992.

58. H. Breithaupt, "Biological rhythms and communications" in *Electromagnetic Bio-Information, 2nd ed.,* edited by F. A. Popp, R. Warnke, H. L. Konig and W. Peschka, Urban & Schwarzenberg, 1989, pp. 18-41.

59. G. Hess, "The glycolytic oscillator", *J. Exp. Biol.* 81, 1979, pp. 7-14.

60. C. B. Kyriacou, "The molecular ethology of the period gene", *Behavioral Genetics,* 20, 1990, pp. 191-211.

61. O. Sotavalta, 1947, cited in McClare, 1971.

62. See articles in *Cellular Oscillators, J. Exp. Biol.* 81, edited by M. J. Berridge, P. E. Rapp and J. E. Treherne, Cambridge University Press, 1979.

63. U. Ribary, A. A. Ioannides, K. D. Singh, R. Hasson, J.P.R. Bolton, F. Lado, A. Mogilner and R. Llinas, "Magnetic field tomography (MFT) of coherent thalamocortical 40hz oscillations in humans", *Proceedings of the National Academy of Science* 88, 1991, p. 11037.

64. C. M. Gray, P. Konig, A. K. Engel and W. Singer, "Oscillatory responses in cat visual cortex exhibit inter-columnar synchronization which reflects global stimulus properties", *Nature* 338, 1989, pp. 334-337.

65. Gray et al., 1989, p. 336-337.

66. H.L.M. Granzier, J. A. Myers and G. H. Pollack, "Stepwise shortening of muscle fibre segments", *J. Muscle Research and Cell Motility,* 8, 1987, pp. 242-251; T. Iwazumi, "High speed ultrasensitive instrumentation for myofibril mechanics measurements", *American Journal of Physiology* 252, 1987, pp. 253-262.

67. S. A. Baba, "Regular steps in bending cilia during the effective stroke", *Nature* 282, 1979, pp. 717-772.

68. See Presman, 1970, ref 51.

69. See M-W. Ho, "Coherent excitations and the physical foundations of life" in *Theoretical Biology,* edited by B. C. Goodwin and P. T. Saunders, Edinburgh University Press, 1989b, pp. 162-176.

70. See M-W. Ho, S. Ross, H. Bolton, F. A. Popp and K. H. Li, "Electrodynamic activities and their role in the organization of body pattern", *Journal of Scientific Exploration,* 1992, pp. 59-77.

71. S. Schamhart and R. van Wijk, "Photon emission and degree of differentiation" in *Photon Emission from Biological Systems,* edited by B. Jezowska-Trzebiatowski, B. Kochel, J. Slawinski and W. Strek, World Scientific, 1986, pp. 137-150.

72. M. Galle, R. Neurohr, G. Altman and W. Nagl, "Biophoton emission from Daphnia Magna: A possible factor in the self-regulation of swarming", *Experientia* 47, 1991, pp. 457-460.

73. M-W. Ho, F. A. Popp, X. Xu, S. Ross and P. T. Saunders, "Light emission and rescattering in synchronously developing populations of early Drosophila embryos—evidence for coherence of the

embryonic field and long range cooperativity" in *Biophotons Research and Coherence in Biological Systems,* edited by F. A. Popp, World Scientific, 1992.

74. See Ho, 1992a, ref 3.

75. Cited in Jahn and Dunn, 1986, p. 746, ref 9.

76. See Ribary et al., 1991, ref 63.

77. E. Illich, *Tools for Conviviality,* Fontana, 1973.

78. Bergson, 1916, p. 172, ref 11.

79. See Ho, 1992a, note 7, ref 3.

80. J. S. Mill, *Examination of Sir W. Hamilton's Philosophy 5th ed.,* 1878, pp. 580-583, cited in Bergson, 1916, p. 174.

81. Bergson, 1916, p. 176, ref 11.

82. J. J. Gibson, *The Ecological Approach to Visual Perception,* MIT Press, 1966.

83. M-W. Ho, "The role of action in evolution: Evolution by process and the ecological approach to perception" in *Evolutionary Models in the Social Sciences,* edited by T. Ingold, Cultural Dynamics, 1991, pp. 336-354.

Toward a Science of Qualities

by Brian C. Goodwin

Biology, the study of life, has always presented a particular problem to anyone seeking insight into that quality of organisms that we intuitively recognize as the state of being alive. Clearly living beings have some property of dynamic order that is elusive but insistent: a kind of presence that speaks to us at a deeply intuitive level since we share the condition. The very closeness of the experience makes description and analysis difficult. The structure of our language encourages the identification of "life" as a separate thing, a force or a substance that is in some sense added to the material matrix with which it is associated. This gives rise to a form of vitalism, which assumes an ontological distinction between the nature of the life force (spirit or soul) and the matter which it animates. This type of Cartesian dualism sits comfortably with our theological traditions, but it also inhabits areas of biological thought from which the original spirit/matter dualism was believed to have been exorcised.

For example, there is an interesting ghost that haunts contemporary biology, arising from the metaphoric use of the software/hardware dualism of programs and computers. It is generally assumed that each species is defined by a "genetic program" which contains all the information required to make a complex organism of characteristic form and behavior, starting from simple beginnings, such as an egg or a bud. This can be likened to the view that the plans for making a house contain all the information required for its construction. There is no harm in the metaphor so long as it is not taken literally; its limitation is that it ignores all the cognitive processes (or their biological equivalents) required for turning instructions into activities, and all the tacit knowledge required to organize these into coherent processes.

Nevertheless, there is a very strong tendency in biology to invest genetic instructions with the full generative power to create an organism. This results in an essentialism (genes = essence of life) that is vitalistic: a part of the organism is regarded as the source of its distinctive qualities and is given powers it does not really possess. I shall be discussing this at greater length later, since clarification of the issues involved touches a whole range of questions concerned with the nature of a science of qualities, and how this would differ from the quantitative science with which we are so familiar and which has been so successful. What will emerge is that varieties of vitalistic essentialism, whether reductionist (as in the genetic program) or spiritual (a vital essence of the organism), are equally unsatisfactory for the kind of understanding that characterizes a holistic science of qualities of the type I shall explore in the last sections of this chapter.

The overall plan of this essay is to examine first the meaning of a science of qualities in the context of biology. This involves a consideration of the explanatory scheme used in contemporary biology, especially its causal form. The difficulties encountered by this scheme will be discussed and an alternative described. The particular focus of this enquiry will be the problem of biological form, since variety of form is one of the distinctive qualities of the living realm. What will emerge from this is a holistic theory of form generation (morphogenesis) which provides a basis for a theory of the organism. The implications of this perspective in biology will then be extended to a broader cognitive context, involving a theory of knowledge that is identified with Goethe's approach to scientific understanding, and Polanyi's epistemological views. Those ideas are intimately linked to structuralist thinking as it has developed in different contexts during this century. Together these provide a basis for a holistic science of qualities.

Divide and Conquer: Separating Heredity from Development

Faced with the apparently intractable complexity of whole organisms, biologists have long found it an effective strategy to divide them into parts that can be analyzed separately. There are many different ways in which this can be done, and the traditions of thought within a culture often dictate the initial moves in the division, of which the subsequent conquest then bears the imprint.

Darwin's own way of formulating the major problems of biology, for instance, reflected a previous culturally influential pattern of thought about the natural world, that of Natural Theology. This tradition, best known through Paley's treatises (1803), sought evidence of God's existence as the purposeful creator and designer in the remarkable adaptation of organisms to their habitats. From this, Darwin inherited adaptation as the major biological phenomenon requiring explanation. He also accepted the historical mode of description and analysis that became prevalent during the nineteenth century, giving rise to descent or inheritance as a primary explanatory principle of evolution. As we shall now see, the way the organism was divided into manageable parts followed yet another aspect of our theological traditions—that which separates body from soul or matter from spirit.

Our analysis starts with Darwin's evolutionary mechanism for generating adapted species. His proposition was that populations of self-reproducing organisms with hereditary variation change in the direction of fitter variants under the action of natural selection. The great power and attractiveness of this description is that it provides an explanation of evolutionary phenomena in terms of natural causes located both within and external to organisms. The internal causes are growth potential in populations due to self-reproduction of organisms and hereditary transmission of variant characters. The external causes are differential survival of the more successful variants arising from interactions with the environment.

Darwin's own theory of inheritance was in fact inconsistent with his principle of natural selection. He was a Lamarckist, believing that adaptive modifications acquired by organisms during the course of their lifetimes were transmitted to their progeny. If this were true, then every individual in a population would have the potential to undergo adaptive change and to pass this on to its offspring. There would then be no need for the selection of fitter variants that arise randomly by chance variation of the hereditary material.

This inconsistency in Darwin's theory was resolved by the German zoologist August Weismann, whose clarifications appeared during the last two decades of the nineteenth century (1882, 1883). Weismann was initially, like Darwin, a Lamarckist. However, his experimental and theoretical work convinced him that this view of heredity was wrong, and it eventually led him to a theory that was consistent with natural selection and excluded the possibility of the inheritance of acquired characters. His studies of reproduction in insects led to the discovery that there is a particular part of the egg which forms the reproductive organs and hence is specifically involved in inheritance. He called this the "germ plasm", that part of the cytoplasm which generates the germ cells during development. In the fruitfly–*Drosophila*–for example, this special cytoplasm is located at the posterior pole of the egg and it is here that the pole cells are produced (see Figure 1 next page) at an early stage of development (1.5 hours after egg deposition, at 25° C). These pole cells generate the gametes or reproductive cells (eggs or sperm). The rest of the egg Weismann called the somatoplasm; it gives rise to the main body of the organism (the soma) other than the gametes.

Weismann generalized this observation to all organisms, proposing that all species have germ plasm that is distinct from the somatoplasm. Germ plasm is potentially immortal, since it gives rise to eggs which themselves contain germ plasm and so on from generation to generation, *ad infinitum*; whereas the rest

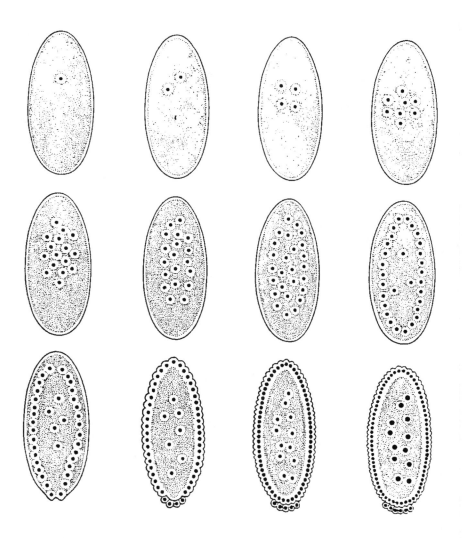

Figure 1:

The early development of *Drosophila* showing the pole cells, which contain the germ plasm, separating off at the posterior pole of the embryo. These pole cells produce the gametes from which the next generation derives.

of the organism is mortal and dies. The result is Weismann's dualism, shown schematically in Figure 2, in which the germ plasm carries the hereditary material from one generation to the next. Weismann knew from the work of other biologists who had made detailed cytological studies of the cell division process that the chromosomes are the most likely physical vehicles of the hereditary material because of their exact partitioning to progeny cells. So he identified the chromosomes within the nuclei of cells containing germ plasm as the potentially immortal carriers of inheritance, undergoing, as we now describe it, replication and passing on copies of themselves to subsequent generations.

Weismann deduced that this hereditary material carries instructions for making an organism of a particular kind, and that these instructions are present in the chromosomes of every cell in the body. He had a theory about the way these instructions are distributed to different parts of the body, directing the

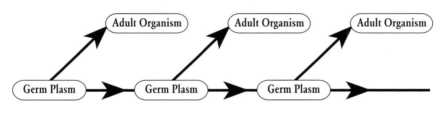

Figure 2:

A schematic description of the continuity of the germ plasm from generation to generation, and the formation of the mortal adult organism under the direction of information from the germ plasm.

production of different structures in different regions of the developing organism, but this is not our main concern at the moment. The important point is that Weismann introduced the proposal that information flows only one way—from the hereditary material in the chromosomes to the cytoplasm. The cell then differentiates in accordance with chromosomal instructions, and can also be modified by environmental influence. However, the differentiated cell does not alter the species-specific instructions coded in the hereditary material in the nucleus. Hence Lamarckian inheritance is impossible, since no somatic cell changes acquired during the lifetime of the organism can affect the hereditary material. The possibility of a return influence from soma to germ plasm is prevented by Weismann's barrier.

Within Weismann's theory, evolutionary change is dependent on changes in the hereditary information located in nuclei within the germ plasm, since this is the only hereditary path from generation to generation. These instructions are not altered by environmental influence, and only random variations can occur. These generate random variants in the characters of the organisms, on which natural selection operates. So here was a theory of inheritance consistent with natural selection.

The primacy of the germ plasm as the vehicle of inheritance relevant to evolutionary change in Weismann's theory had the immediate implication that hereditary change could be studied independently of development. Development was simply the process, directed by the hereditary material, that resulted in an organism of a particular type, whose important part for evolutionary change was the germ cells that would produce the next generation. The rest of the organism is mortal, of secondary interest as far as evolution is concerned.

When Mendel's work on inheritance was rediscovered in 1900, the conceptual scheme worked out by Weismann provided the perfect context for the development of a science of genetics that could concentrate exclusively on hereditary principles and ignore development. There were those who opposed the substitution of chromosomal factors for developmental processes, recognizing that they are not equivalent. William Bateson, who introduced the term "genetics" into biology, was one of those opponents. But the momentum of genetic studies that gathered during the first three decades of this century was such that all such objections were swept aside by the flood of discoveries that laid the foundation for the crowning achievement of biology in the twentieth century: the Modern Synthesis. This offered an explanation of the evolutionary process in terms of three basic principles which I express here in their current molecular descriptions:

1) the transmission of hereditary instructions from generation to generation via self-replicating DNA;

2) random variations in the instructions by modifications in the DNA; and

3) natural selection of the fitter variants in the organisms produced by the altered instructions.

In this view, the organism is only a vehicle for the DNA replicators which can be described as groups of "selfish genes" (Dawkins, 1976) whose sole goal is to leave more copies of themselves. So organisms disappear from biology as real entities, reduced to the hereditary instructions that generate them. The generative process is described as the result of a genetic program, defined as the set of instructions contained in a genome that codes for the molecules out of which an organism is made, and which specifies the time and place of their production in the developing embryo. Hence one gets statements of the type made by Delisi (1988):

> This collection of chromosomes in the fertilized egg constitutes the complete set of instructions for development, determining the timing and details of formation of the heart, the central nervous system, the immune system and every other organ and tissue required for life.

From Weismann's conception of organisms and their heredity has emerged the dramatic revelations of twentieth century biology such as the discovery of the self-replicating properties of DNA, the genetic code, and the way genetic instructions are translated into proteins. These are startling achievements, constituting detailed molecular manifestations of the conceptual structure that Weismann introduced into biology at the end of the last century.

The Causal Structure of Weismannism and Neo-Darwinism

Weismann recognized that the problem of inheritance has to be resolved in terms of the control of growth and development: the task is to "trace heredity back to growth" (Weismann, 1883). Hence reproductive invariance is to be understood in terms of invariant developmental, or generative, processes. But having recognized this, Weismann then reintroduced into biological thinking an Idealist conception of the organism which was a transformed concept of an "Idea" or a "Soul". He argued that offspring resemble parents because both are the "effects" of identical processes of growth and development. Constant effects imply constant causes—a classical empiricist conception of causality (see Bhaskar, 1978). Weismann located these causes in the germ cells, which contain a specific substance with a "highly complex structure"—the germ plasm—"with the power of developing into a complex organism". As we have seen, this complex substance was later identified as DNA, the molecular vehicle of inheritance. Weismann described it as a historically given agent which can change its nature during the course of history and which is not really a part of the material and visible organism it produces. He was here reflecting the influence of German idealism, wherein such an agent was a non-material Idea or plan. Weismann materialized the Idea, but the germ plasm remained in a separate realm. The germ plasm and the substance of the body, the somatoplasm, occupy different spheres (Weismann, 1882).

So the visible organism is the expression of an idealist "central directing agency" or a material "Idea". This is now described as a genetic program, analogous to computer software which is also a set of ideas, instructions, or algorithms, quite distinct from the hardware that implements these instructions (see for example Webster and Goodwin, 1982, for a further elaboration of this analysis).

Before engaging in a critical examination of Neo-Darwinism, it is of interest to take a sideways look at the metaphorical aspects of the theory. One of the clearest expositions of the Neo-Darwinian perspective is to be found in the books by Dawkins (1976, 1982, 1986), who identifies himself as a Neo-Weismannist. These popular works present both the conceptual structure of the evolutionary paradigm and its metaphors. They can be summarized as follows:

1) Organisms are epiphenomena of groups of genes whose goal is to leave more copies of themselves. The hereditary material is basically "selfish".

2) The inherently "selfish" qualities of the hereditary material are reflected in the competitive interactions between organisms that result in survival of fitter variants, generated by the more successful genes.

3) Organisms are constantly striving to climb up local peaks in a "fitness" landscape, always trying to increase their capacity to survive but, like Sisyphus' stone, always rolling down again (in this case because the landscape keeps changing).

4) Paradoxically, humans can develop altruistic qualities that contradict their inherently selfish nature, by means of educational efforts.

The first three propositions can be cast in mathematical form and constitute the analytical foundations of population genetics, wherein interbreeding populations of organisms are reduced to gene frequencies. The fourth contains an interesting logical *non sequitur*, since it is difficult to understand how an organism, all of whose properties are determined by selfish genes, can escape their basic influence. However, this proposition does express with uncanny fidelity the doctrine of salvation. This gives the key to the metaphorical origins of the other three assumptions, which all reflect the vulgar form of fundamentalist Christian beliefs:

1) Humanity is born in sin; we have a base inheritance (coded in base pairs, actually, since the structure of the DNA double helix depends upon bonding between pairs of biochemical elements called nucleotide bases, though the pun was not intended by the biochemists).

2) Humanity is therefore condemned to a life of conflict and

3) Perpetual toil

4) But by faith and moral effort humanity can be saved from its fallen, selfish state.

The power of metaphors is that they live substantially in the unconscious realm. Most biologists who accept some form of the first set of propositions would vehemently reject the second. An analysis of the subtle factors that have contributed to the extraordinary success of Darwinism in our culture is beyond the scope of this essay. Here, I want to simply acknowledge this important dimension of scientific theory, which is examined in greater depth in other essays in this volume. (See particularly Nelson, Maso and Laughlin.)

Returning to Weismann and Neo-Darwinism, it is necessary now to ask if the conceptual structure that has been so successful in generating fruitful hypotheses, whose investigation has uncovered the molecular foundations of living organisms, is consistent with the evidence about organismic properties. This is the task of the next section.

Flaws in the Foundations of the Modern Synthesis

Weismann's conception of heredity was completely compatible with the principles of Mendelian genetics when these were rediscovered at the turn of the century. Genetics defined the rules according to which Weismann's hereditary determinants behaved during their transmission between generations in sexually reproducing species. Together with Darwin's principle of evolution by natural selection, this defined Neo-Darwinism. With subsequent developments in molecular biology, what has emerged is a highly successful theory of inheritance, described in terms of the self-replicating properties and recombinant behavior of DNA macromolecules, which are the carriers of hereditary instructions; and an equally successful theory of how DNA generates the molecular composition of an organism during its development—that is, via the genetic code, the processes of transcription and translation, and the mechanisms of gene regulation. These theories of inheritance and the molecular composition of organisms are among the most impressive fruits of Weismann's theory as it has flowered during the course of this century, providing the molecular foundations for the modern synthesis.

However, this synthesis is based upon a number of factual and conceptual limitations that now need to be examined in detail.

1) The proposition that morphogenesis is the result of a genetic program, and statements such as that of Delisi (1988) above—that the chromosomes contain the complete set of instructions for development—is incorrect. A genetic program can define the molecular composition of the developing organism at any moment in its development, but this is insufficient to explain the processes that lead to a heart, a nervous system, or other morphological features of the organism.

The reason is that molecular composition is not, in general, sufficient to determine form or morphology. This follows from basic physics, familiar to us all. The simplest examples are polymorphic crystals such as those of carbon and sulphur. Knowing that a crystal is made of carbon does not tell us its form; it could be graphite, diamond, or one of the Buckminster Fullerines (for example C_{60}). Liquids provide further examples. Knowing that a liquid is made of H_2O or C_2H_5OH or C_6H_6 does not explain its form, as when it flows with spiral motion down a drain or forms waves under the action of air passing over its surface. To explain such forms we need to know a) the principles according to which the system is organized, as expressed in the Navier-Stokes equations describing the properties of fluids, and b) the particular conditions to which the system is exposed.

Organisms are no exceptions to these physical principles. If we want to describe their most basic properties, such as how they are generated, we have to understand the principles according to which they are organized. Knowing their molecular composition may be very useful in helping to describe these principles, but describing organisms in terms of a catalogue of gene activities and molecular composition will not tell us what kind of physical system we are dealing with, nor what its spatial forms are. This is why genetic programs, which specify the molecular composition of an organism at every stage of its development, are unable to explain morphology.

Since evolution is all about organisms and how they change, if we don't understand how they are generated and what kinds of transformation they can undergo, we are going to have trouble understanding what evolution is about.

2) The DNA of an organism is not a self-replicating entity, a "replicator". The only way in which prokaryotic or eukaryotic genomes can be accurately and completely replicated is within the context of a growing and dividing cell, that is, it is the cell that reproduces. The importance of this recognition is that the cell is an organized entity that embodies principles of order that are not reducible to the set of hereditary instructions in the DNA. Cell division also involves morphogenesis, the formation of the mitotic apparatus and the changes of shape that occur during cell division. These again arise from cytoplasmic organization that is not reducible to the activity of DNA, either as a "replicator" or as a "genetic program". The genome as an autonomous replicator is an abstraction that does not conform to biological reality. What is true is that the DNA is the only molecular constituent of the cell that is precisely duplicated (within a small error tolerance) and distributed to the daughter cells during the process of cell reproduction.

3) Weismann's dualism is wrong. In all unicellular organisms, all plants, and many animal taxa, including mammals, there is no separation of germ plasm from somatoplasm. What reproduces is organisms via their lifecycles, not a special part that is distinct from the rest of the reproducing body. Weismann's generalization from his studies of insects was simply a gross biological error that has been generally overlooked, presumably because his theory fitted the neo-Darwinian scheme so well. Buss (1987) recognized this error and has written a

very interesting and thoughtful book that attempts to reformulate Neo-Darwinism without Weismann's dualism. However, he uses natural selection as an explanatory principle.

4) Natural selection does not explain the phenomena of biology. In particular, it does not explain species morphologies. The reason for this is again perfectly simple and straightforward. Natural selection is about persistence: the capacity of members of a particular species to continue their lifecycles in specific habitats. It tells us nothing about existence: why species morphologies are possible as part of the repertoire of biological forms or how they are generated. Given a particular morphology, it is possible to study how different aspects of the form contribute to species survival—that is, in what ways the structures that constitute morphology, such as limbs, are adapted to life in specific habitats. This is a study of dynamic stability, the stability of the lifecycle of the species.

But examining how a character contributes to the survival of a species (its stability) does not explain why the character is possible or how it comes into existence. That can be done only by studying the generative process whereby the character is produced, and understanding the range of transformations that are compatible with the process. For example, studying the aerodynamic stability of the bat's wing can tell us how well it serves the purpose of flight, allowing these mammals to make their living in the air. This is an important aspect of lifecycle analysis. But stability studies are basically tautologies: the forms that persist are stable forms. The value of stability analysis is that it allows us to generate hypotheses about the ways in which organismic forms (morphology and behavior) contribute to the stability of the lifecycle, and then to test these by various means.

Organisms as Fields

Our analysis so far shows that the structure of the living realm is not to be understood solely in terms of hereditary essences (germ plasms, genomes, or replicators) that undergo selective change determined by the reproductive success of the organisms they produce. What evolves is whole organisms, which are dynamic entities that reproduce and have hereditary properties. What is the nature of these entities? They are particular kinds of fields. A field is a domain of relational order in which the state of any part is a defined function of the states of neighboring parts (the neighborhood can be local, or extend over the whole organism). The field concept is absolutely fundamental in all physical theories. Electrical, magnetic, electromagnetic, electrodynamic, hydrodynamic, gravitational fields—all these have distinctive properties and are defined by specific equations, but they all share the property of relational order in space and (in general) changes in time.

Organisms are extended in space and change in time. Hence any theory of the organism must be a field theory of some kind. What I shall do in this section is, first, describe some observations that illustrate the field properties of organisms, and then consider a particular mathematical description that makes precise the nature of the organization that underlies field behavior. This will give us a particular insight into organisms as self-organized wholes. The causal structure of this organization will then be examined.

The field concept entered biology as a result of a classical experiment performed by the German zoologist Hans Driesch, who was a contemporary of Weismann. Driesch (1892) separated the two cells produced by the first cleavage division of a fertilized sea urchin egg and observed that each of these, which would normally have produced half of an organism, actually produced a complete pluteus larva, the initial free-living form of the species. Each of these larvae was half the size of a normal pluteus, but was complete in every detail and grew into perfectly normal adults. This capacity of parts to produce wholes is called regulation. Driesch's observation actually invalidated Weismann's initial hypothesis about the nature of hereditary determinants that instruct the development of the embryo, for he (Weismann) believed that these were partitioned to different parts so that the left half of the embryo, say, receives different instructions to the right half. Driesch's experiment showed that each half of an egg divided by the first cleavage plane (which corresponds roughly to the plane of bilateral symmetry dividing the future organism into right and left halves) has the potential to develop into a whole organism. As we would now say, each cell receives a complete set of genetic instructions, carried in the nucleus. But how is the system organized so that when these two cells remain part of one embryo each produces half the future organism, but when they are separated, each produces a whole?

Driesch compared the phenomenon with the magnetic field of a bar magnet, with north and south poles and a magnetic field in the space between them. Divide the magnet into two and each half produces a whole magnetic field, with north and south poles, rather than two half fields with separated poles. Thus was the field concept introduced into biology. Driesch's ponderings on the implications of his own and related findings in embryology form the content of an extremely interesting book entitled *The Science and Philosophy of the Organism* (1929). Here Driesch breaks with the tradition of developmental mechanics in which he grew up, founded by Wilhelm Roux. Roux regarded development as the expression of a particular type of physiochemical organization that resulted in the phenomenon of regulation, that is, the capacity of parts of living organisms to produce wholes. But according to Driesch, anyone who has properly grasped the idea of embryonic regulation must be taken beyond mechanics. Accordingly, he proposed that the capacities of organisms to self-organize, and to re-organize after disturbances such as spatial separation of parts, is a quality that comes from a domain beyond matter, space, and time. Following Aristotle, he called it the "entelechy". So once again we encounter a familiar dualism in theories of the organism—the invocation of a directing and organizing agency that is distinct from the body of the organism.

The capacity of parts of organisms to make wholes is of course the basis of reproduction, and so is fundamental to the living process. The egg cell is a part of the adult body with the capacity, when activated, of producing a whole which then generates parts with the same property. A bud forms in the budding zone of a mature hydroid and develops into a whole new organism which, when mature, also produces buds. Regeneration is an expression of the same property: from a limb stump, a newt regenerates a complete replica of the lost limb; a cutting of a plant regenerates roots and develops into a new individual. These phenomena reveal distinctive qualities of living organisms: the capacity to maintain themselves as dynamic forms, to restore their dynamic order after disturbance, and to generate their characteristic forms from parts. But these parts are not "essences", like the germ plasm or the DNA. They are parts of the organism that share with the whole the dynamic spatio-temporal organization I shall call a developmental field. The part can be a limb stump of a newt, a fragment of the body of a hydroid, or a single cell—the egg—but all share the same dynamic order of the developmental field.

Reproduction always involves replication of the genetic material, usually DNA, which is an integral component of a reproducing organism. Inheritance is the stable repetition of the developmental process in successive generations, resulting in organisms of similar form. The genetic material is involved in this process, but it does not control and direct it in the sense of acting as the sufficient cause of the developmental process. It is necessary now to examine more closely how "sufficient cause" is to be defined in this context.

Developmental Dynamics

Consider the lifecycle described in Figure 3 (next page). The organism is the marine alga, *Acetabularia acetabulum*, inhabitant of shallow waters around the shores of the Mediterranean. Isogametes (there is no sexual differentiation) fuse in pairs, conjugating to form a zygote. A growing tip is generated that extends to form a stalk, while at the base a root-like rhizoid develops, the nucleus remaining in one of its branches. As the stalk grows, rings of delicate, branching structures (bracts or verticils) that make up whorls are produced periodically and then, when the stalk has reached a length of 2-3 cm, a cap is initiated (see Figure

4 next page). This grows into the beautifully sculptured structure which gives the species its common name: the Mermaid's Cap. The whorls drop off and the single giant cell assumes its adult form (see Figure 5 page 230) with rhizoid (containing the nucleus), a stalk 2-4 cm in length, and a cap with a diameter of 0.5-1 cm. The whole developmental period, from zygote to mature form, takes about 3 months. The mature cell remains in a stable state for several months and then enters reproductive mode with a sequence of divisions of the nucleus, producing thousands of haploid nuclei that are carried by the streaming cytoplasm into the cap, where they differentiate into gametes enclosed within cysts. The cell wall of the cap then dissolves, releasing the cysts into the sea-water. Little "trap-doors" open in the cysts, releasing the gametes, which again fuse in pairs to re-initiate lifecycles.

How are we to understand such a process? Why, for example, are whorls produced? They develop and then drop off, apparently serving no function in the adult. We know that the algae can grow without producing whorls (Goodwin et al., 1983), and there are instances in which caps are produced without the prior production of whorls. When faced with such an anomaly, the Darwinist seeks explanations in history. Just as our appendices were useful in our ancestors and we retain them out of a kind of inertia, so the story goes, it is likewise suggested that whorls were useful in an ancestor of *Acetabularia* and have persisted in this species because of hereditary inertia and a failure of natural selection to eliminate these useless structures. Evidence in favor of this hypothesis comes from the observation that other species of Dasycladales, to which *Acetabularia* belongs, have no caps while the whorls serve as gametangia, the structures where the gametes are produced.

However, there are serious limitations to this view. First, it fails to explain how whorls are generated in the first place, and so it gives no insight into why whorls are possible consequences of growth and morphogenesis in algal cells. Second, the assumption that natural selection stabilized whorls when they first appeared and were used as gametangia, but failed to eliminate them from the developmental process when they were no longer required, is of virtually no explanatory value since the reasoning is ad hoc and arbitrary; it simply redescribes what is observed. Finally, and most seriously, there is no way in which the hypothesis of the historical/functionalist framework of explanation can be investigated systematically and put to direct test. It is story-telling of a genre that is unfortunately all too common in biology.

The alternative is to attempt to model the generative basis of growth and morphogenesis, to identify the main variables involved in the dynamic process, and then to deduce experimentally testable hypotheses to evaluate the validity of the model. This is the conventional procedure in the exact sciences, and there is no reason why it should not work in biology. Indeed, there are many areas of

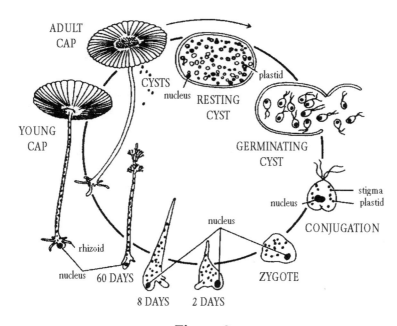

Figure 3:

The life cycle of *Acetabularia acetabulum.*

Figure 4:

Formation of a cap primordium, after three whorls.

Figure 5:

The structure of the adult *Acetabularia* cell.

biological study where this is precisely how investigations are conducted, and there is a sound tradition of morphogenetic modeling that proceeds in this manner. D'Arcy Wentworth Thompson's (1942) classic volumes *On Growth and Form* are celebrated instances of this tradition. A recent contribution is *Mathematical Biology* by J. D. Murray (1989), which contains a wealth of examples of morphogenetic modeling. The application of these principles of analysis to the problem of morphogenesis in *Acetabularia* is described in detail in other publications (Goodwin and Trainor, 1985, Brière and Goodwin, 1988, Goodwin, 1990), so I shall confine myself here to the essentials, and extract the relevant causal inferences.

There are thousands of genes in an organism such as *Acetabularia*, and hence thousands of different types of protein that make up its molecular composition. If the function of all of these had to be known in detail before the developmental process could be modeled in terms of their interactions, biologists would have a hopeless task on their hands, and an appeal to an entelechy or a special central directing agency to organize the whole into a coherent process would be an understandable, if desperate, measure. However, there is a more satisfactory procedure available. This is to identify those aspects of cell structure and organization that are primarily involved in changes of shape, to describe their properties in mathematical terms, and then to analyze their behavior by analytical or computer simulation studies.

We (Trainor, Brière, and I) reduced the complexity of the cell to three components: the cell wall, the cytoplasm, and the central vacuole which contains fluid and salts and exerts an osmotic pressure on the wall, giving the cell its turgidity. The cytoplasm is the most complex of the three. Its dynamic behavior was described in terms of mechanical properties arising from a network of filaments (the cytoskeleton) that constitutes a major aspect of its spatial organization, and the effect of calcium on these filaments. The physiological regulation of calcium within the cell and the effect of changes of mechanical state of the cytoplasm on calcium concentration were also specified, resulting in coupled equations that described the developmental field. These were then shown to have the property of spontaneous change of state starting from spatially non-uniform patterns. Technically this is known as bifurcation, which involves symmetry-breaking in the system; that is, spatial (and temporal) order can arise spontaneously from an initially uniform state. Thus the system can become more complex as a result of its own intrinsic dynamic organization. Bifurcation is also what underlies the phenomenon of deterministic chaos, which is complex behavior in time arising as a result of a sequence of bifurcations (symmetry-breakings) in a dynamical system. These are the recognized dynamic elements whereby complex order can emerge in systems organized according to relatively simple rules. Our concern is primarily with spatial order, but space and time belong together in fields, and patterns generally arise in both dimensions simultaneously, as we shall now see.

Having produced a working model of *Acetabularia* in the sense that we could describe the whole in terms of basically three spatially extended, interacting components (wall, cytoplasm, and vacuole), the next step was to explore its behavior and see if anything like the morphogenetic patterns observed during development could be produced. Although biologically very simple, our model was mathematically complex and only computer simulation could be used to study its behavior. Given this complexity (no less than 26 parameters!) it seemed that we were in for a very protracted search of parameter space before we found anything resembling an actual morphogenetic sequence such as tip formation, growth, and whorl formation. After all, the story goes that organisms have had millions of years to search randomly for combinations of genes that produce viable organisms. The effects of genes in our model were defined by parameter values: such quantities as the mechanical properties (elastic modulus) of the cell wall, the concentration of calcium required to change the mechanical state of the cytoplasm, and the osmotic pressure exerted by the vacuole. All these are subject to change with genetic mutation, which alters the properties of the molecules which constitute the various structures of our model cell (cell wall, cytoskeleton, calcium regulatory molecules, etc.).

However, we didn't have evolutionary time periods at our disposal. We selected parameter values that gave localized morphogenetic changes, such as initiation of tip growth, and then let the model follow its own devices. It could grow according to simple rules; and it could make patterns spontaneously, as previously described, though the range of possible patterns for fixed parameters was restricted by the intrinsic wavelengths that characterized the spatial modes available to the morphogenetic field. So the system was quite constrained. However, whatever patterns emerged did so as a result of the intrinsic dynamic organization of the system, which was distributed over the whole field describing the cell. The results surprised us.

The simulation began with a uniform state over the cell, which then spontaneously bifurcated to generate a tip. This grew and then changed in a manner we had not anticipated, because it was so similar to what the living cell does. Just before a whorl is produced, the growing tip flattens. We had never understood why. But this is what the model did, and by looking at the variables involved we could see why.

The concentration of calcium spontaneously changed its pattern during growth in such a way that the mechanical state of the cytoplasm and its effects on the cell wall resulted in a flattened tip and a region of maximum curvature where the ring of bracts constituting a whorl would be produced next. Would the model then generate the whorl pattern? It did. And furthermore, it spontaneously went through a sequence in which whorl formation was followed by the reinitiation of a tip, which then again flattened and underwent the whorl bifurcation. So we got the elements of a morphogenetic sequence virtually for nothing! Once parameters were set (genes specified) so as to give localized growth (a condition required for increase in complexity), the morphogenetic field produced a systematically changing geometry and dynamics that mimicked what the actual cell does. Experimental observations support the changing calcium patterns observed in the model.

It appears that the organism is simply doing what comes naturally to its state of spatial, dynamic organization (its field properties), following a trajectory that is a spontaneous expression of its order, just as the spiral pattern of water flowing down a plug-hole is a spontaneous expression of the order of the liquid state. The difference, of course, is that living organisms have available to them a much greater range of patterns than liquids do. However, it is not unreasonable to propose that a systematic study of morphogenetic fields will actually reveal the major patterns of spatial order available to organisms, and the sequences in which they occur, as in *Acetabularia*. There is already evidence for this from the work of other morphogenetic modelers such as Odell et al. (1981), Oster et al. (1988), and Murray (1989), who have shown the power of mechano-chemical models of the type just described for *Acetabularia* to generate a range of fundamental morphological patterns in animals. These include limb and skin structures, basic embryonic events such as gastrulation and neurulation, and pigment patterns such as the leopard's spots and the zebra's stripes. Equivalent modeling of basic patterns of leaves and flower elements in plants arises from the work of Paul Green (1987, 1989).

It may seem unreasonably ambitious to propose that there are common generative principles that underlie the full range of biological forms, but explaining this possibility is precisely the structuralist enterprise in biology (see for example Goodwin, 1990, Ho, 1989). It is analogous to the proposition that there are common generative principles underlying all human languages, despite their apparent diversity. From this perspective the great diversity of biological forms may become intelligible within the unity of a system of transformations resulting from change of parameters (genes) in developmental fields. The regularities of the biological realm—which make taxonomy possible and inspired Linnaeus to contemplate the possibility of discovering the laws of biological order through systematics—would then be seen to arise from common generative principles operating over the whole of the living domain. Such an intelligible unification in biology would shift the emphasis from the historical reconstruction of life on Earth—which was Darwin's goal and that of current evolutionary theory—to the construction of the system of transformations that define the range of biological forms, making a rational taxonomy possible. Evolution is then an exploration of this realm of the possible, and each species has the status of a "natural kind"—an entity with an inner necessity—rather than that of an individual resulting from historical accident, which is how it appears in Neo-Darwinism (see Hull, 1984). The shift of values resulting from this perspective will be examined later. Let us now look at the causal implications of a view of organisms as developmental fields.

Immanent Causation and Causal Powers

Fields are domains of relational order, the parts relating to one another in a manner particular to the field in question. Organisms have the additional distinctive property that their fields constitute a regulative whole defined by a logical property of closure. This means that insofar as circumstances allow, the organism completes itself, restoring missing parts and returning to the normal operating condition of its dynamic variables. This stability is not homeostatic but homeodynamic, or homeorhetic as Waddington (1957) put it. It is self-completing and self-generating (autopoietic, the term used by Maturana and Varela, 1987). Organisms depend upon an external environment, a habitat, whose particular qualities influence its state but they do not determine it. *Acetabularia*, for example, requires that calcium be within a certain range of its usual value in sea-water (10mM) in order to develop normally. If this range is exceeded, abnormalities of development and morphology occur (Goodwin et al., 1983). The organism also alters its environment; electrical currents can be measured around a developing *Acetabularia* cell (O'Shea et al., 1990). But the basic situation is that organisms express their natures as autonomous entities through the dynamics of their lifecycles. What kind of causation is involved here?

Neo-Darwinism attempts to locate the causes of organisms in their genes and in the effects of the environment, as expressed in natural selection. The causality invoked is atomistic, that is, one entity acts upon another, producing a change, as when billiard balls collide. Gene products interact to produce the organism; the organism interacts with the environment and either succumbs or survives.

But such a view ignores the nature of living organization. When this is defined, as in field equations, the role of the genes becomes perfectly clear; they define parameter values. Different parameter values can produce different organismic forms, as can different (mutant) genes. But parameters do not define dynamics. The dynamics of developmental fields must also be known if we are to understand lifecycles, which are ordered, repetitive patterns of transformation that recreate wholes from parts. Genes as parameters stabilize a particular cyclic trajectory, defining the distinctive lifecycle of a species. But they do not cause it, because they do not determine its dynamic order.

The whole organism is in fact both the cause and effect of itself; it is pure self-sustaining activity. There is no separation of cause and effect in a lifecycle, which is equivalent to the recognition that organisms have closed, causal loops or cycles that account for their autonomy, their power of regulation and of reproduction. This type of causation is called immanent, as distinct from transeunt causation (compare Emmet, 1984) where cause and effect can be distinguished (the familiar example being colliding billiard balls, where the entity identified with the cause is external to that on which it has an effect). This distinction goes back to Aristotle (Metaphysics):

> When the result is something apart from the exercise (of producing it), the actualizing is in the thing that is being made, e.g. the act of building is in the thing that is being built. . . but when there is no product apart from the actualizing (in the producing), the actualizing is in the agent, e.g., the seeing is in the seeing subject and theorizing in the theorizing subject, and the life is in the soul.

In medieval philosophy, there was a similar distinction between making (facere), in which the activity is transferred to something external, and doing (agere), where the activity and its effect remain within the agent. Neo-Darwinism describes the organism as the effect of a separable cause, which is the genetic program; in Monod's (1972) phrase, the phenotype (the collection of characters that define the organism) is the revelation of the genotype. This involves an atomistic causality in which causes and effects are distinguished, and entities (genes, molecules) take precedence over relationships. This is a science of quantities, of substances interacting mechanically, the overall result of whose aggregate of activities defines the organism as a sum of interactions.

I am not denying that within the overall totality of the organism itself it is possible to identify processes that conform to the principle of transeunt causation. An enzyme acting upon a substrate and generating a product can be usefully described in these terms. Thus within the context of a process whose causation is immanent, such as an organismic lifecycle, constituent processes can be isolated conceptually or materially (as are enzyme and substrate in a test tube) and analyzed in terms of separable causes and effects. However, the simple sum of such processes does not describe the lifecycle itself, whose logical closure and autonomy arise from an immanent or cyclical self-completing causation. The words "closure" and "autonomy" here must not be taken to mean isolation and independence. As emphasized earlier, the dynamic of an organismic lifecycle includes environmental variables and a flux of matter and energy through the organism as an open system—a "dissipative structure" in Prigogine's phase. But the emphasis I am placing here is on structure rather than dissipation; all open systems, of which organisms are paradigmatic examples, are dissipative, so this term gives no distinctive quality to the living state. Structure, on the other hand, does—at least in the context of structuralism, as I shall shortly make clear.

The organism as a process manifesting immanent causation adds a distinctive quality of self-completion, self-definition, to its constituent processes, which obey transeunt causation. But even the latter must be re-conceptualized in order to escape fully from the empiricist view of causation that still traps matter in a mechanistic model of causal sequence. The route out is indicated by Harré and Madden (1975) who question the very basis of atomistic causality as conceived by Hume, saying: "There can be no doubt that the Humean conception of Causality . . . must be wrong". To remedy its inadequacies, they actually go back to Faraday's (1857) definition of force in terms of powers:

> What I mean by the word [force] is the source or sources of all possible actions of the particles or materials of the universe, these being often called the powers of nature when spoken of in relation to the different manners in which their effects are shown.

Harré and Madden (1975) develop this view of causal agency in terms of the concept of "powerful particulars", which they summarize as follows:

> Causality is to be understood on the model of the active production of effects by powerful particulars, such as magnets, falling stones, compressed gases, stressed metals, and the like. The model for causal concepts thus shifts from the essentially inert items of the billiard ball paradigm to the essentially active items of the set of paradigms listed above.

This process in nature is to be understood in terms of the transformations of active entities that embody powerful particulars, that is, distinctive types of causal power. This is in contrast to the view that matter is inert, acted upon by external forces.

Applying this within the context of field theory, with the notion of potential, they continue, developing on Faraday's conception:

> The 'lines of force' then picture the directional structure of powers or potentials, distributed in space. The fundamental entity then becomes a single, unified field, in perpetual process of change as its structure modulates from one distribution of potentials of a certain value to another. (Harré and Madden, 1975, p. 175)

Organismic lifecycles involve powerful particulars that are organized into logically self-completing dynamic structures. We have seen that in order to describe an organismic process such as morphogenesis, it is necessary to define the relational order that exists in a developmental field. This involves a distributed causality that closes on itself in space and expresses its nature through an ordered sequence of states that also closes in time, completing a lifecycle. An organism is a dynamic form engaged in process, becoming other in order to remain itself, as Brady (1987) has aptly expressed Goethe's insight into biological nature. For Goethe was one of the first to grasp and articulate the nature of organisms as dynamic wholes undergoing transformation.

The dialectical union of organism and environment in a continuously changing evolutionary dynamic has been very clearly described by Levins and Lewontin (1985), by Ho and Saunders (1979) and by Oyama (1986). The present description of organismic lifecycles as dynamic structures fully endorses this view, while stressing the quality of immanent order that characterizes the living process. Since this dynamic process includes relevant aspects of the environment, its stable states are precisely those lifecycles that persist (are stable in, or "adapted to", the habitat). Thus natural selection is automatically included as the stability aspect of organism as process, taking account naturally of functionalist considerations which on their own fail to provide explanations of biological form (morphology and behavior).

To make these arguments concrete, the lifecycle of *Acetabularia* involves genes and their products, organized in space and changing in time, including electrical currents which flow across the visible boundaries of the organism and unite it with the marine environment on which it depends. No part of this being constitutes its essence. The distinctive self-copying property of the DNA provides the means whereby many crucial parameter values are transmitted to the progeny, in order that they start their lifecycles in the neighborhood of the same state as the parent at the beginning of its development, and follow similar trajectories. This is inheritance, which involves both the parameter values (genetic and environmental) and the condition of dynamic space-time order of the developmental field. Evolution involves the exploration of the potential developmental trajectories of the organism, which are generated both by genetic variation and change of environment (arising from both external change and organismic activity). Some genetic change is random, as in conventional Neo-Darwinism; some appears to be directed, as described by Cairns et al. (1988) and by Hall (1988), revealing an essentially Lamarckist evolutionary process. But the resulting transformations of organismic lifecycles are not random, whatever may be the nature of the genetic change. They belong to the constrained set of possibilities that constitute the realm of biological form. The very existence of a systematic classification scheme of organismic morphologies, as in a Linnaean taxonomy of biological species, is evidence of this logical unity of the biological realm, despite its diversity. The nature of this biological order has been a focus of intense scrutiny and debate, as in the famous encounter between the great French rational morphologists, Cuvier and Geoffroy St. Hilaire, in 1821, in whose outcome Goethe was passionately interested.

A major point at issue in this debate was whether biological forms are to be understood as members of discrete logical categories, which Cuvier maintained to be four in number for all animal species (vertebrates, molluscs, arthropods, and radiolaria), each with a distinct body plan; or whether, as Geoffroy fervently declared,

> there are no different animals. One fact alone dominates; it is as if a single
> Being were appearing.

Geoffroy's position anticipated Darwin's unification of life, though he belonged to the pre-evolutionary era of biology. However, there is a sharp distinction between Geoffroy's focus and Darwin's. The former was seeking the logical principles that unite the great diversity of organismic forms as transformations of one another, just as the physical elements are united by principles of logical order and transmutation in the periodic table. Whereas Darwin's vision was of the continuity of biological forms in time, and he assumed that organisms have no necessary principles of internal order and organization other than those that conform to the ultimate necessity of successful performance and survival. Goethe provided a way of resolving these in a dynamic theory of biological form and transformation which provides the basis for a new biology and a science of qualities.

Qualities and Values

Quantitative science and its goals took explicit form in the seventeenth century, with Francis Bacon exercising a decisive influence. One of the historical influences to which Bacon reacted negatively was what he perceived to be the unbridled, undisciplined expression of the imagination in such charismatic figures as Giordano Bruno, who was burned for his alleged sorcery by the Catholic Church in 1600. However, Bruno's real threat to the Establishment was his advocacy of a vast moral reform and liberation that invoked the full range of being—terrestrial, celestial, and super-celestial—which constituted the unified cosmology of the Renaissance magian worldview (Yates, 1964, 1979). We continue to encounter this vision in Shakespeare's plays, where music, the harmony of the spheres and the world of qualities unfold before our eyes, bewitching us with nostalgic glimpses of a totally connected world of meaning and significance. The science of the Renaissance magi as represented in the works of towering figures such as Pico della Mirandola, Francisco Giorgi, Ficino, Reuchlin, John Dee, and Bruno himself, was a Science of Qualities based on the Dignities of God such as Bonitas (Goodness), Magnitudo (Greatness), Eternitas (Eternity), Potestas (Power), Sapientia (Wisdom), and so on. Within this cosmic scheme the imagination played a significant part in exploring the possible ways of making the world—both the occult and the overt—intelligible. Bacon perceived much of this as excessively subjective and arbitrary, and sought to discipline the imagination by greater attention to natural phenomena. The natural sciences then developed during the seventeenth century with the goal not only of understanding natural phenomena in themselves—that is, objectively—but of using this understanding to gain control over natural processes and exploit them for human use; to subdue nature and harness her powers to human needs. The various branches of natural science are still called "disciplines", reflecting Bacon's injunction to discipline the imagination, and we are living in an age where the officially sanctioned forms of scientific enquiry are primarily those that increase the quantity of goods and currency.

Goethe's response to Bacon's view was:

> . . . he still has an excellent influence, so long as we appreciate that his doctrine is one-sided and allow the mind to exert its influence also.

Goethe's vision of science proposed to combine the disciplined observation of natural science with particular qualities of mind. He followed Kant in distinguishing between "Verstand" or intellect, with its separating, analytical tendencies, and "Vernunft", reason, with its capacity to comprehend diversity in an intelligible unity.

> The Intellect [Verstand] cannot reach up to her [Nature]; a man must be able to rise up to the highest plane of Reason [Vernunft] in order to touch the Divine, which reveals itself in archetypal phenomena—moral as well as physical—behind which it dwells, and which proceed from it.

Goethe's language sounds Idealistic and Transcendental, and he is often classified with the movement of Idealist Morphology that attempted to identify a particular morphological type as the ideal model on which all variants are based. This was the position of the English comparative morphologist Richard Owen, who was severely critical of Darwin on the grounds that he (Darwin) saw all biological forms as contingent and functional, not expressions of ideal archetypes. However, Darwin did in fact use precisely this form of typological reasoning, but he located types in a historical rather than an ideal context. His archetypes were "common ancestral forms", the historical "givens" on which were based all subsequent variants, adapted to different purposes.

Goethe avoided both of these forms of idealism. For him, the archetype is not a defined form but a set of possible forms, united under transformation. We would now describe it as the common generative principles that underlie the various manifestations of a form, such as tetrapod limbs, or the leaves and the flowering parts of plants. Goethe saw the archetype, the generator, as immanent in the expressed forms. It is not transcendental, living in another realm, as does Driesch's entelechy. So Goethe is fully dynamic in his conception of form, as expressed in "Gedichte, Eins and Alles":

> First it must stir in self-creation
> Shaping itself for transformation,
> And merely seems at moments still.
> The Eternal energizes all;
> Each into nothingness must fall
> If preservation be its will.

The organism must change in order to realize itself; hence the dynamics of lifecycles.

But how does the mind enter into the apprehension and understanding of these forms? Are they not just given by nature? According to Goethe, there is a "Bildung", a cultivation of cognitive faculties in association with the phenomena in order to arrive at the perception of intelligible unity in natural processes. In an extremely illuminating article on Goethe, Zajonc (1987) quotes Hiebel's (1961) description of Goethe's conception of this process:

> The faculties of man fully and unconsciously combine the acquired with the innate through practice, teaching, reflection, successes, failures, chal-

lenge and opposition and always again reflection, so that they bring forth a unity which astounds the world.

Zajonc also quotes from a letter to Jacobi in which Goethe expresses his sense of awe at the task:

> To grasp the phenomena, to fix them in experiments, to arrange the experiences and know the possible mode of representation of them—the first as attentively as possible, the second as exhaustively as possible and the last with sufficient many-sidedness—demands a moulding of man's poor ego, a transformation so great that I never should have believed it possible.

This conception of life as ordered transformation thus carries over to our own cognitive activities, and our acquisition of knowledge. Just as organism and environment constitute a dynamic whole, each being influenced by the other, locked in a process of mutual transformation in which the nature and potential of each is expressed in ways appropriate to the circumstances, so the individual seeking knowledge is locked in an embrace with the world. Out of this union emerges a generated reality that bears the imprint of both natures involved in the process. Polanyi (1958) has written with great clarity and insight on the transcendence of the subject/object duality in the development of knowledge:

> Yet personal knowledge in science is not made but discovered, and as such it claims to establish contact with reality beyond the clues on which it relies. It commits us, passionately and far beyond our comprehension, to a vision of reality. Of this responsibility we cannot direct ourselves by setting up objective criteria of verifiability—or falsifiability, or testability, or what you will. For we live in it as in the garment of our own skin. Like love, to which it is akin, this commitment is a 'shirt of flame', blazing with passion and, also like love, consumed by devotion to a universal demand. Such is the true sense of objectivity in science.

It is this commitment of the whole person, heart, soul, and mind, in the search for intelligibility that results in a "perceived coherence", as Polanyi calls it, based upon "tacit knowledge" which grows into the very fibers of our "organs of the mind", using Goethe's phrase. The deep relationships between organisms and minds become obvious in these metaphors—relationships that have been recognized and developed by many biologists, among whom Piaget's (1980) work stands out as a particularly significant example. This leads to the recognition that the whole of biology can be cast in a cognitive mode, resulting in the description of deep similarities between biological processes and cognition (Goodwin 1976, 1978, Maturana and Varela, 1987). Among other properties, the cognitive enterprise shares with organisms the quality of generating coherent wholes that undergo transformation. Included in these are our scientific theories, which never stay still but change in ways that express the nature of mind as well as that of nature, constituting the "necessary unity" that Bateson (1976) spoke of. The explicit recognition that the properties of wholeness (completion), regulation, and transformation are qualities that identify the activities of mind in seeking to make sense of phenomena (to make it intelligible) has been articulated in a systematic way only in this century, through the development of structuralism (Piaget, 1971, Caws, 1988). Caws in fact calls structuralism "The Art of the Intelligible":

> . . . for something to be intelligible, then, would be for it to lend itself to 'interbinding', that is, to understanding in terms of connecting links that hold things in place with respect to one another. (Caws, 1988, p. 7)

Understanding how things hold together puts the emphasis on relational order rather than on the substances out of which the system is made, though substantial properties must also be taken into account. This then leads to the identification of the inherent unity of whatever system is being studied, its properties of wholeness and the set of transformations which it can undergo while conforming to its internal rules of relational order. These are the properties that define a structure: wholeness, regulation, and transformation (Piaget, 1971). The most familiar examples of structuralist analysis are those that have come from the study of language and myth: de Saussure's (1916) classic studies leading to the work of Harris (1968) and Chomsky (1957, 1968), and Lévi-Strauss' comprehensive examination of the structure of myths (1958, 1966). But there is a large body of structuralist analysis dealing with the objects of other human sciences besides those of linguistics and mythology: psychology, anthropology, economics, politics, literature, and philosophy. The structures generated in these areas have the status of intentional objects, so structuralism is also a theory of significance and meaning. It therefore rejects the restrictive prescriptions of positivism and behaviorism, which seek to eliminate human qualities and mental (subjective) states from the human sciences. The objects studied in the human sciences relate simultaneously to human intentions and to external reality, as language or myth combine both subjective qualities and objective reality. So structuralism provides a methodological basis for a holistic science of qualities that includes values and intentions.

The application of the structuralist method to biology is presented in detail in a number of other publications (Webster and Goodwin, 1982, Webster 1984, 1989, Goodwin 1989, 1990, Ho and Fox, 1988, Ho, 1984, 1989, Hughes and Lambert, 1984). Biology falls into that difficult, ambiguous space between the natural and the human sciences, sharing qualities of both; hence the possibility of a cognitive biology in which organisms are seen as intentional agents, whose actions have significance in relation to their activities. These in turn are understood as expressions of their natures as autonomous, self-organizing, self-generating wholes that undergo ordered transformations in response to internal and external parameter change, as previously stated. Piaget (1980) took the view that

> the organism is, in a way, the paradigm structure. If we knew our own organism through and through it would, on account of its double role of complex physical object and originator of behavior, give us the key to a general theory of structure.

Organisms are themselves structures, with the properties of wholeness, regulation, and transformation that have been previously described. It was argued earlier that the program of rendering the biological realm intelligible requires an understanding of species as transformations of one another within the set of forms consistent with their basic generative principles. This is similar to Chomsky's program in linguistics, which aimed to uncover the generative principles (deep structure) that underlie the diversity of languages at one level and the diversity of sentences within any particular language at another level. Thus he wanted to unite the diversity as manifestations of a common generative structure which originates in deep properties of the human mind, understood as a product of social relationships (Ingold, 1990). Chomsky emphasizes syntax at the expense of semantics, whereas in the study of organisms I want to keep meaning and value clearly in view. To see how this may be done we return again to Goethe.

Goethe used the empirical method of science—the detailed observation of the phenomena of nature—but he was not an empiricist. In fact, he made a claim about the discovery of truth through scientific investigation that goes significantly beyond what is generally accepted as the legitimate process of hypothesis formulation and test in the search for scientific truth. Goethe's fundamental assumption is that intelligibility in science involves not simply bringing phenomena into a systematic structure, but incorporating them into a system of relationships—a whole—that discloses the necessary connections between them. He believed that a system of this kind is not described simply by formal logic or the mathematical domain of pure quantities, but involves also qualities and an inner necessity that gives the structure an apodeictic property (the quality of a necessary truth). In relation to his theory of plant form and metamorphosis, his conviction was that the understanding that he had achieved in relation to what he called the "primal plant" ("Urpflanze") allowed him to

> go on forever inventing plants and know that their existence is logical; that is to say, if they do not actually exist, they could, for they are not the shadowy phantoms of a vain imagination, but possess an inner necessity and truth. (Hegge, 1987)

Truth is thus itself the result of a generative process. It is neither given in the empirical evidence, nor is it the result of pre-existing forms of intuition and understanding in the Kantian sense. Goethe acknowledged that there are *a priori* aspects of our cognition, but he claimed that it is possible to develop "organs", through experience and directly linked to observation, that widen and extend innate cognitive capacities. Whereas current science results from developed cognitive capacities that describe primarily the substantial, quantitative aspects of nature, Goethe aimed to develop corresponding capacities for qualitative properties. As described by Hegge (1987) in a very perceptive article, Goethe's notion of "direct apprehension" of true and necessary relationships

> is in principle nothing other than what we would call in, say, mathematics the 'capacity to grasp' mathematical connections.

She then goes on to quote Goethe: "Mathematics is . . . an organ of the higher inner sense . . . ", something that is developed by systematic use. Likewise the capacities for a science of qualities need to be systematically developed through a committed study of the phenomena. Goethe provided examples of this both in his theory of plant form and his theory of color, which is holistic and explicitly qualitative since it is concerned with color experience. This latter is fundamentally different from Newton's theory of color, which has been the accepted view for over 300 years. However, recent studies of color vision have shifted decisively away from Newton and toward Goethe (see for example Varela and Thompson, 1990). And his theory of plant form and transformation is essentially the same as the structuralist theory of biological form that I described earlier. Modern science seems to be catching up with this remarkable figure. Let me now draw out some implications of a holistic science of qualities as it applies to our view of the biological realm.

A New Biology

As described earlier, in relation to the structuralist enterprise in the human sciences, the structures generated by human activity have the status of intentional objects, incorporating qualities, significance, and meaning. What is the status of structures identified in biology? We have seen that organisms are themselves structures. Whether or not the whole realm of biological form is also to be identified as a structure at a different level is an open question—a matter of research—dependent upon the identification of dynamic principles that can meaningfully (that is not trivially) generate the full range of biological forms. Cuvier may have been right in the sense that it may not be possible to use the same basic dynamical system to simulate morphogenesis in all species simply by changing parameter values. This remains to be seen. However, the position

I am adopting is that as structures, organisms of a particular type (constituting a morphological species) have the status of natural kinds, states of "organic stability" in Bateson's (1894) phrase. Another way of putting this is to say that the morphogenetic process of a particular species is intrinsically robust (Goodwin, Kauffman and Murray, 1993), that is, it constitutes an attractor in the dynamical system whose alternative stable pathways or trajectories define different lifecycles.

The most familiar examples of natural kinds in science are the elements, which are the dynamic states of constellations of protons, neutrons, and electrons, described by quantum mechanics. Natural kinds have qualities as well as quantities. Organisms as coherent entities that "possess an inner necessity and truth" express their natures through their qualities of form, color, and behavior patterns, which can change with changing quantities of genes and their products, that is, qualities and quantities are linked. Organisms cannot be explained as solutions to problems of survival posed by the environment, or as products of selfish genes whose goal is to increase in quantity. Organismic lifecycles must be dynamically stable in particular habitats, to be sure. But as we have seen, stability and function do not explain lifecycles, since they tell us nothing about the underlying generative dynamics. The example of *Acetabularia* described earlier in terms of a developmental field illustrates these basic ideas. This organism generates whorls not because they are useful but because they are natural—an expression of the "inner necessity and truth" that is immanent in this dynamic form.

This view of the biological realm suggests solutions to some of the major puzzles that have arisen in the study of evolution. A primary example is the phenomenon of evolutionary stasis. On the whole, species don't change during their lifetimes (millions of years); they just persist. Darwinism, with its emphasis on adaptation, leads to the expectation that there will be continuous change as species adapt to changing environmental conditions. But the plethodontid salamanders of North America are morphologically the same now as they were 100 million years ago, despite very extensive environmental alteration. What holds a species in such a stable morphological state? The answer suggested by a structuralist biology is that basic salamander morphology is an expression of a biological natural kind, a particularly robust attractor in morphogenetic space that has not altered significantly despite extensive parameter changes. This type of robustness is called "structural stability" in the jargon of dynamical systems, a term used by Thom (1972) for the stability of the seven catastrophes that described generic singularities in the space of smooth mappings in four dimensions. It is an extended concept of structural stability that is appropriate in the present context, since there are in general more than two levels to the hierarchical dynamics of development. However, the same basic concepts apply, and what we may be seeing in evolutionary stasis such as the plethodonts is precisely such an extended notion of structural stability. This is a dynamic whose attractor remains generically unchanged in spite of parameter modifications that are reflected in the unexpectedly large differences in the DNA of different species of this salamander group, even though they all share the same body form.

It is now recognized that the classical, Darwinian picture of the taxonomic relationships between species as a branching tree of related forms has to be extensively modified. The anticipated missing links that were expected to reveal the adaptive continuity between the branches and their twigs are still largely missing from an extensively searched fossil record, and the notion of primary punctuated equilibrium (Eldridge and Gould, 1976), or saltation, is generally acknowledged as a phenomenon, though without any agreed explanation. The view of species as natural kinds leads one to expect precisely this; as random and/or directed variations occur in parameter space, the wave of evolutionary exploration (not progression) will hit basins of attraction of the morphogenetic field, resulting in new biological forms. If these are stable, they will persist until parameter changes result in their extinction. The duration of the species depends upon the structural stability of the attractor. Small, unstable attractors represent transient species; large, stable attractors represent persistent species— like the plethodontid salamander and the horseshoe crab, which have altered very little from their fossil ancestors. In this view, species come and go not because they successfully solve, for a period of time, survival problems as adapted forms in a particular habitat. That is a truism, not an explanation. The deeper reason may be that species are natural kinds, dynamic attractors in a morphogenetic space that is necessarily and fundamentally quantized, with discrete, separated basins of attraction. It is the distribution of these basins and their sizes that need to be studied by appropriate dynamic models, in order to see whether it is possible to match the known patterns of species stability to a model of evolution as a holistic dynamic process.

Another aspect of evolution which has remained a puzzle is the phenomenon of parallelism, wherein different but related lineages develop similar forms in quite distinct environments. The phenomenon is most familiarly known in the parallel evolution of the marsupials of Australia and placental mammals in other parts of the world. Striking species similarities emerge in these different lines: wolf, cat, jumping and ordinary mice, flying and non-flying squirrels, moles. In terms of adaptation to the external environment, there is no good explanation for this. The Australian habitat is distinct, and the evolutionary process is an infinitely plastic one that can generate an immense diversity of adapted forms, according to Darwinian theory. But it doesn't do so, preferring to generate species that are strikingly similar in their morphologies on different continents. This is to be expected in a structuralist view, since the marsupial and the placental mammals have very similar embryologies. Since their morphogenesis is basically the same, they fall into similar attractors in morphospace during their evolution—hence the observed parallelism.

There are many other aspects of evolution that similarly yield easily to a structuralist analysis, but with difficulty and implausibly to a purely functionalist interpretation. However, to elaborate on them here would detain us too long. Let me just mention a recent book by Robert Wesson (1991) called *Beyond Natural Selection* where many of these problems are described. Wesson's solution is to propose the existence of "genetic attractors" in biological space. This doesn't quite work, because genes vary between morphologically similar species. But "morphogenetic attractors" is a plausible solution with a realistic research program. Each of these attractors reveals a distinct constellation of biological qualities of morphology and behavior, each species a natural biological kind.

The spectacle that we perceive in the panoply of living beings is an expression of the creative potential of the living state, a dance of life that has no goal, no purpose, and no cause external to itself. But it has meaning, which is two-fold. Within the organism, relational order gives coherence to the whole, creating a domain of intrinsic meaning and significance particular to the organism. There is also relational order over the biological realm as a whole (including the dynamic relationships with the environment), giving meaning and significance at this level.

At the level of the organism, the coherent behavior of a self-causing process results in a kind of boundary between self and other that sharpens, as sensory modalities become more clearly defined, into those of sight, touch, pressure, warmth, cold, hearing, taste, etc., that emerge during evolution. This increasing intensity of the inner/outer distinction is associated with the inner states we refer to as subjectivity and consciousness, and the outer patterns we describe as objective reality. The evolution of life is continuous with the evolution of consciousness. Awareness of meaning, relevance, significance, arise from the experience of coherent order both within and without. Although the inner and the outer are distinguished by different qualities, they constitute a unity, a whole. One of the features of our present-day state of consciousness is that our experience and awareness now extend in an immediate, experiential sense to the planet as a single meaningful totality.

It is here that we encounter Gaia, the intuitive insight expressed by Lovelock (1979, 1988) in terms of the dynamic stability of the geo-biosphere, the mutually dependent relational order that defines the coherent state of this living planet. This "organism" is also expressing its nature. We are a part of this planetary order—a part that is now anxiously seeking a balanced relationship with other species and the total environment that will allow for sustainable development, that is, a state of dynamic order in which our nature is expressed within a context of relational order, of planetary community, which provides meaning and heals alienation. The Neo-Darwinian view encourages us to believe that, because we are a product of selfish genes that result in a propensity to conflict and violence, we will go on consolidating our position as a dominant species by eliminating others, following instinctive tendencies that we have great difficulty controlling even when we see that they have become self-destructive. Bacon's solution was for humanity to join forces in an assault on nature:

> Nor is mine a trumpet which summons and excites man to . . . quarrel and fight with one another; but rather to make peace between themselves, and turning with united forces against the Nature of things, to storm and occupy her castles and strongholds, and extend the bounds of human empire, as far as God Almighty in his goodness may permit.

We have been all too successful in this, and now we blame it on our genetic inheritance!

But there is another perspective that gives some grounds for optimism. This comes from a different reading of organisms, including human beings. As previously described, organisms are structures, self-regulating, transforming wholes generated by the distributed causal agency immanent in developmental fields that include genes and relevant aspects of the environment as part of its dynamic order. Each species is a distinct expression of this living order, a natural kind that reveals particular qualities of color, morphology and behavior as well as specific quantities of various substances. Organisms are also intentional agents, engaged in expressing their natures, which are intrinsically holistic and dynamic.

Human nature is grounded in this holistic biology of the organism. But in addition we engage in a level of activity we call culture. The products of this activity are also structures—self-organizing wholes such as linguistic, mythological, kinship and artistic systems. These intentional objects are the result of the engagement of humans with the world, having the effect of bringing the complexity of human nature into a dynamic equilibrium with its environment in structures of meaning. It is in our deepest nature to make wholes out of parts, to heal by ordered transformation. We are perhaps now engaged in the later stages of creating a global culture with a shift of emphasis from the part to the whole, and a recognition that meaning comes from local participation in the relational order of a new level of integrated planetary being.

The process of creation is always precarious and unpredictable, involving jumps to new levels of order with their emergent qualities. We can at present only intuit the outlines of a holistic global culture, but it is clearly necessary that this go beyond humanism, that great rallying cry of Modernity that rightly insisted on human values but emphasized their expression in individuals and had an anthropocentric focus. What is now developing is an extended sense of community that grows out of the perennial mythological roots that link our culture to all others. This is the sense of the sacredness of nature, a recognition of the intrinsic value of every being because all share in the creative process. Nature imposes values simply because it is creation, an expression of qualities for their own sake. A new biology that emphasizes the qualities of life and the creative potential of relational structures helps this difficult but urgent transformation of cultural perspective. (These ideas are developed further in Goodwin [1994].)

Acknowledgements

I have involved many people in my attempt to clarify the ideas in this paper. I would particularly like to acknowledge, with much gratitude, correspondence and discussions with Cor van de Weele, Arno Wouters, Gerry Webster and Mae-Wan Ho. But my deepest debt is to Willis Harman for asking me to write it in the first place, which otherwise I would not have attempted, and for his continual promptings and encouragement with the task.

References

G. Bateson, *Mind and Nature: A Necessary Unity*, Bantam, 1976.

W. Bateson, *Materials for the Study of Variation*, Cambridge University Press, 1894.

R. Bhaskar, *A Realist Theory of Science*, Harvester, 1978.

R. H. Brady, "Form and cause in Goethe's morphology" in *Goethe and the Sciences: A Reappraisal*, edited by F. Amrine, F. T. Zucker, and H. Wheeler, D. Reidel, 1987, pp. 237-300.

C. Brière and B. C. Goodwin, "Geometry and dynamics of tip morphogenesis in *Acetabularia*", *Theoret. Biol.* 131, 1988, pp. 461-475.

L. W. Buss, *The Evolution of Individuality*, Princeton University Press, 1987.

J. Cairns, J. Overbaugh, and S. Miller, "The origins of mutants", *Nature* 335, 1988, pp. 142-145.

P. Caws, "Structuralism : The Art of the Intelligible", *Contemporary Studies in Philosophy and the Human Sciences*, Humanities Press International, 1988.

N. Chomsky, *Syntactic Structures*, Mouton and Co., 1957.

N. Chomsky, *Language and Mind*, Berkeley University Press, 1968.

R. Dawkins, *The Selfish Gene*, Oxford University Press, 1976.

R. Dawkins, *The Extended Phenotype*, Oxford University Press, 1982.

R. Dawkins, *The Blind Watchmaker*, Longmans, 1986.

C. Delisi, "The Human Genome Project", *Amer. Sci.* 76, 1988, pp. 488-493.

H. Driesch, "The potency of the first two cleavage cells in the development of echinoderms" (1892) in *Foundations of Experimental Embryology*, edited by B. H. Willier and J. M. Oppenheimer, Prentice-Hall, 1964.

H. Driesch, *The Science and Philosophy of the Organism,* 2nd edition, Black, 1929.

D. Emmet, *The Effectiveness of Causes,* Macmillan, 1984.

M. Faraday, *Experimental Researches in Electricity,* London, II, 1859, p. 284.

B. C. Goodwin, *Analytical Physiology of Cells and Developing Organisms,* Academic Press, 1976.

B. C. Goodwin, "A cognitive view of biological process", *J. Social. Biol. Struct.* 1, 1978, pp. 117-125.

B. C. Goodwin, "A structuralist research programme in developmental biology" in *Dynamic Structures in Biology,* edited by B. C. Goodwin, A. Sibatani, G. Webster, Edinburgh University Press, 1989, pp. 49-61.

B. C. Goodwin, *How the Leopard Changed Its Spots: The Evolution of Complexity* (MacMillan, 1994)

B. C. Goodwin, "Structuralism in biology", *Science Progress Oxford* 74, 1990, pp. 227-244.

B. C. Goodwin, J. C. Skelton, and S. M. Kirk-Bell, "Control of regeneration and morphogenesis by divalent cations in *Acetabularia mediterranea*", *Planta* 157, 1983, pp. 1-7.

B. C. Goodwin and L.E.H. Trainor, "Tip and whorl morphogenesis in *Acetabularia* by calcium-regulated strain fields", *J. Theoret. Biol.* 117, 1985, pp. 79-106.

B. C. Goodwin, S. A. Kauffman, and J. D. Murray, "Is morphogensis an intrinsically robust process", *J. Theoret. Biol.,* 163, 1993, pp. 135-144.

P. B. Green, "Inheritance of pattern: Analysis from phenotype to gene", *Amer. Zool.* 27, 1987, p. 657.

P. B. Green, "Shoot morphogenesis, vegetative through floral, from a biophysical perspective" in *Plant Reproduction: From Floral Induction to Pollination,* edited by E. Lord and G. Bernier, Am. Soc. Plant Physiol. Symp. Series, Vol. 1, 1989, pp. 58-75.

B. C. Hall, "Adaptive evolution that requires multiple spontaneous mutations", *Genetics* 120, 1988, pp. 887-897.

R. Harré and E. H. Madden, *Causal Powers: A Theory of Natural Necessity,* Basil Blackwell, 1975.

Z. S. Harris, *Mathematical Structures of Language,* Interscience, 1968.

H. Hegge, "Theory of science in the light of Goethe's science of nature" in *Goethe and the Sciences: A Reappraisal,* edited by F. Amrine, F. J. Zucker, and H. Wheeler, D. Reidel, 1987, pp. 195-218.

F. Hiebel, *Goethe,* Francke, 1961.

M-W. Ho, "Where does biological form come from?", *Rivista di Biologia* 77, 1984, pp. 147-179.

M-W. Ho, "An exercise in rational taxonomy", *J. Theor. Biol.* 147, 1989, pp. 43-57.

M-W. Ho and P. T. Saunders, "Beyond Neo-Darwinism: An epigenetic approach to evolution", *J. Theor. Biol.* 78, 1979, pp. 573-591.

M-W. Ho and S. W. Fox, editors, *Evolutionary Processes and Metaphors,* Wiley, 1988.

M-W. Ho and P. T. Saunders, "How to segment generically and reliably", *J. Theor. Biol.* (submitted 1992).

A. J. Hughes and D. M. Lambert, "Functionalism and structuralism: Alternative 'Ways of Seeing'", *J. Theor. Biol.* 111, 1984, pp. 787-800.

D. L. Hull, "Historical entities and historial narrative" in *Minds, Machines and Evolution,* edited by C. Hookey, Cambridge University Press, 1984.

T. Ingold, "An anthropologist looks at biology (Curt Lecture 1989)", *Man* (NS) 25, 1990, pp. 208-209.

R. Levins and R. Lewontin, *The Dialectical Biologist,* Harvard University Press, 1985.

C. Lévi-Strauss, *Anthropologie Structurale,* Plon, 1958.

C. Lévi-Strauss, *The Savage Mind,* University of Chicago Press, 1966.

J. Lovelock, *A New Look at Life on Earth,* Oxford University Press, 1979.

H. R. Maturana and F. J. Varela, *The Biological Roots of Human Understanding,* New Science Library Shambhala, 1987.

J. Monod, *Chance and Necessity*, Collins, 1972.

J. D. Murray, *Mathematical Biology,* Springer-Verlag, 1989.

G. Odell, G. F. Oster, B. Burnside, and P. Alberch, "The mechanical basis of morphogenesis", *Devel. Biol.* 85, 1981, pp. 446-462.

P. O'Shea, B. Goodwin, and I. Ridge, "A vibrating electrode analysis of extracellular ion currents in *Acetabularia acetabulum*", *Cell Science* 97, 1990, pp. 505-508.

G. F. Oster, N. Shubin, J. D. Murray, and P. Alberch, "Evolution and morphogenetic rules: The shape of the vertebrate limb in ontogeny and phylogeny", *Evolution* 42, 1988, pp. 862-884.

S. Oyama, *The Ontogeny of Information,* Cambridge University Press, 1986.

W. Paley, *Natural Theology; or Evidences of the Existence and Attribution of the Deity, collected from the Appearances of Nature,* 5th edition, 1802, printed for R. Faulder, 1803.

J. Piaget, *Structuralism,* Routlege and Kegan Paul, 1971.

J. Piaget, *Adaptation and Intelligence: Organic Selection and Phenocopy,* University of Chicago Press, 1980.

P. Polanyi, *Personal Knowledge: Towards a Post-Critical Philosophy,* University of Chicago Press, 1958.

Ferdinand de Saussure, *Course in General Linguistic,* 1916, edited by C. Bally and A. Sechehaye, New York Philosophical Library, 1959.

R. Thom, "Structuralism and biology" in *Towards a Theoretical Biology, Vol. 4,* edited by C. H. Waddington, Edinburgh University Press, 1972.

D'Arcy W. Thompson, *On Growth and Form,* 2nd. edition, Cambridge University Press, 1942.

F. J. Varela and E. Thompson, "Color vision: A case study in the foundations of cognitive science", *Revue de synthèse* IV°5, Nos 1-2, 1990, pp. 129-138.

C. H. Waddington, *The Strategy of the Genes,* Allen and Unwin, 1957.

G. C. Webster, "The relations of natural forms" in *Beyond Neo-Darwinism,* edited by M-W. Ho and P. T. Saunders, Academic Press, 1984, pp. 193-218.

G. C. Webster, "Structuralism and Darwinism: Concepts for the study of form" in *Dynamic Structures in Biology,* edited by B. Goodwin, A. Sibatani, G. Webster, Edinburgh University Press, 1989, pp. 1-15.

G. C. Webster and B. C. Goodwin, "The origin of species: A structuralist approach", *J. Soc. Biol. Struct.* 5, 1982, pp. 15-47.

A. Weismann (1882), reprinted in T. S. Hall, editor, *A Source Book in Animal Biology*, Hafner, 1964.

A. Weismann (1883), reprinted in J. A. Moore, editor, *Readings in Heredity and Development*, Oxford University Press, 1972.

R. Wesson, *Beyond Natural Selection,* MIT Press, 1991.

F. A. Yates, *Giordano Bruno and The Hermetic Tradition,* Routledge and Kegan Paul, 1964.

F. A. Yates, *The Occult Philosophy in the Elizabethan Age,* Routlege and Kegan Paul, 1979.

A. G. Zajonc, "Facts as theory: Aspects of Goethe's philosophy of science" in *Goethe and the Sciences: A Reappraisal,* edited by F. Amrine, F. J. Zucker and H. Wheeler, D. Reidel, 1987, pp. 219-245.

On the Relationship Between Science and the Life-World:

A Biogenetic Structural Theory of Meaning and Causation

by Charles D. Laughlin

All we can do is to gaze dimly at the infinitude of things, which lies beyond our finite apprehension. Words are inadequate for experience, and experience is inadequate to grasp the infinitude of the universe. Of course, this is a commonplace; but it cannot be repeated too often.

—Alfred North Whitehead

The worldview of Euro-American society is both shaped by and is active in shaping our life-world—that is, our individual world of immediate experience[1]. This is as true for scientists as it is for everyone else in society. And it is true for everyone on the planet, regardless of sociocultural background. One of the characteristics of our life-world is that we experience events that require comprehension. The most dramatic of these events include such things as aging and death, the origin of things, conception and birth, destruction, disease, transpersonal experiences of one sort or another, astronomical events, seasonal cycles, malevolence, catastrophes, etc.—the sorts of events that Tillich (1963) called "matters of ultimate concern". Of course everyday events also require comprehension, including events like planning a meal, getting to work, mowing the lawn, etc. Without comprehension, death remains a terrifying enigma and planning a meal forever beyond our capacity.

In other words, our life-world is always meaningful.[2] It is so thoroughly meaningful that we take its elements and relations for granted as "the way the world is". Our natural attitude (as Edmund Husserl, 1977, pp. 152-153, put it) toward our own life-world is one of uncritical acceptance. This is why my position in this chapter is by necessity a phenomenological one, for along with Husserl (1931, 1970, 1977) I would contend that a mature understanding of science requires a kind of "stepping back" (Husserl called this a "reduction") into consciousness to find out how much meaning is pre-given in the act of experiencing.

Hidden Forces

When one contemplates one's own consciousness, or when one studies the worldviews of non-Euro-American societies, one is struck by the fact that meaning in the life-world often requires that the hidden forces that produce or relate phenomena in experience be revealed in some way to consciousness. By being revealed, these hidden forces may be anticipated and perhaps controlled and "matters of ultimate concern" may be psychologically resolved. In "stepping back" into our own consciousness, we notice immediately that not all of the ingredients of meaning in our everyday experiences are perceptually apparent. Anthropologists have noticed that all human societies espouse a worldview which, often dramatically, reveals the more important hidden forces behind events. The hidden forces are given symbolic expression as animated, often anthropomorphic, characters that play an epiphanic role in myths, mystery plays, and other forms of ritual performance.

The Problem

Science has had a major impact on events both for Euro-Americans and for people in more traditional societies that have intensive contact with Euro-American society. As John Cove (1987) notes, an absolute distinction between science and traditional worldviews may be more apparent than real. However, there are differences between the two that have relevance to the problem being addressed by this volume (see the chapter by Vine Deloria). It is interesting that, whereas modern science is, like traditional worldviews, in the business of explaining phenomena by revealing hidden forces, science usually does not secure an integrated, meaningful life-world for most people influenced by its worldview. Of course, the conceptual and technological by-products of science influence our life-worlds, and have done so for three centuries or more. But science typically usurps the cultural position of traditional worldviews and thereby exacerbates a general sense of anomie or alienation from the kind of worldview that makes a totally integrated and meaningful life-world possible.

When we pause to ponder this failing on the part of science, we quickly come to consider the metaphysical foundations of science and how these may differ from the foundations of traditional views. And when we examine these foundations in a cross-cultural, comparative way, we are led to the crucial question of the relationship between meaning and causation in experience. What exactly is causation, as contrasted with meaning, and why is it possible for science to produce models of the former without enriching the life-world of people by enhancing the latter in any deep or integrating way? How do the fundamental assumptions about the nature of the world and how we come to know the world differ in science compared with traditional worldviews?

In order to answer these questions, let us first examine how the brain constitutes its world of experience from a biogenetic structural[3] perspective, and then consider within that context the relationship between meaning and causation and how this relationship reflects the metaphysical differences among systems of knowledge. We will then discuss some of the problems encountered in changing the metaphysical foundations of science, and will end the discussion by addressing the essential tension between creative science and the life-world.

A Biogenetic Structural Model of Cognition

The principal function of the human nervous system at the level of the cerebral cortex[4] is the construction of a vast network of models[5] of the world. Models are comprised of the organization of constituent cells and their patterned interaction, and this organization expressed as activity is "information"—literally that which results from the cells "in-forming" themselves (see Varela, 1979, Young, 1987, p. 27, Klopf, 1982). We call this entire network of models an individual's cognized environment. This term contrasts with an individual's operational environment which is the actual nature of that individual and its world.[6] Entities and events in the operational environment are called "noumena" (singular, noumenon).[7]

The cognized environment develops during the course of life by means of the entrainment[8] of networks of cells that become active, that grow, that interconnect and interact, and that become progressively hierarchized into more complex organizations (Bruner, 1974). The prime function of the cognized environment is the adaptation of systems of knowledge and response to ever changing noumena in their internal and external operational environment (Laughlin and d'Aquili, 1974, Neisser, 1976, E. J. Gibson, 1969, J. Gibson, 1979, Popper, 1972, Piaget, 1971, 1985). "Adaptation" in this sense means the development of models whose operations and motor responses assure the continued survival of the organism.

The Transcendental and the Zone of Uncertainty

The emphasis upon adaptation is important, for we make the fundamental metaphysical assumption that the operational environment is transcendental relative to the capacity of any individual or society to comprehend it. We do not mean by this that the operational environment is unknowable, but rather that knowledge is always intentional, developing, incomplete, and limited by the capacities of the brain doing the knowing (see Michael Scriven in this volume). The cognized environment is a system of points of view, and there is always more to know about the operational environment, or any noumenon within it, than can be known.

The brain does not take passive snapshots of the world. The operational environment is modeled in an active and adaptively isomorphic[9] way. This means there must always exist a set of boundaries to knowledge, a zone of uncertainty[10] (d'Aquili et al., 1979, pp. 40, 171), formed by the limits to spatial discernment and to the capacity of the individual or species to apprehend temporal and causal relations. The zone of uncertainty is the directly experienceable junction between the transcendental nature of the actual self and world, and the limits of an individual's or culture's understanding (see Elster, 1984, Chapter 4).

Neurognosis

The networks comprising the cognized environment have their developmental origin in initial neurognostic[11] structures that are present before, at, or just after birth, and that have an organization that is largely genetically determined. The evidence for the neurognostically organized, cognitive and perceptual competence of older fetuses and newborns is now overwhelming (Bower, 1989, Chamberlain, 1987, Spelke, 1988a, 1988b, Laughlin, 1991).

The development of these initial structures is neurognostically regulated as well; that is, the course of much of neural development is genetically charted. Development of neural models involves a great deal of selectivity among alternative entrainments (Changeux, 1985, Edelman, 1987, Varela, 1979). Some potential organizations deteriorate, others become active and are augmented, and still others remain relatively latent and undeveloped.

Empirical Modification Cycle (EMC)

The cognized environment and its models are self-constructing and self-regulating in the interests of adaptation to the polar demands of environmental press and organic integrity (see Brian Goodwin, this volume; see also Piaget, 1971, 1985). This requires that models interact with the operational environment in a feedforward manner. This feedforward, cognitive anticipatory-sensory fulfillment process we have called "the empirical modification cycle", or EMC (Laughlin and d'Aquili, 1974, pp. 84ff; see also Pribram, 1971, Neisser, 1976, Arbib, 1972, Powers, 1973, Gray, 1982, Varela, 1979, for consonant views). The role of behavior (motor activity) within the activity of the cognized environment is also a feedforward one; that is, behavior operates to control perception so that the sensory aspects of the anticipated experience are fulfilled (Powers, 1973).

The developmental interaction between neural models and the operational environment tends to routinize functional processes relative to particular noumena in the operational environment (see Ogden and Richards, 1923, pp. 56-57). Using C. H. Waddington's term, neural models become relatively fixed in organization and structure, and thus produce "creodes", that is, become regularized, recursive and predictable in organization, content, function, response and interaction relative to the object of consciousness (Waddington, 1957; see also Piaget, 1971, 1985).

Intentionality

The ongoing, moment-by-moment operation of the cognized environment is essentially intentional in organization. This fact is very important to our understanding of meaning and causation. Neural networks tend to organize themselves, both spatially and temporally, about a phenomenal object as a process. The focal object is also mediated by a neural network and is, for the moment, the nexus of cognitive, affective, metabolic and motor operations for the organism (Neisser, 1976, pp. 20ff).

Intentionality probably derives from a characteristic dialogue between the prefrontal cortex and the sensory cortex of the human brain. This interaction is neurognostic and thus ubiquitous to human consciousness, regardless of cultural background (Laughlin, 1988, Laughlin, McManus and d'Aquili, 1990, p. 105). Subsidiary structures entrained as a consequence of the dialogue between prefrontal and sensory cortical processes may be located over a wide expanse of cortical, subcortical and endocrinal areas. The intentional organization of neural processes mediating experience has a lot to do with our sense of causation.

Experience and the Life-world

Experience[12] is a function of this intentional dialogue, and consists of the construction of a phenomenal world within the sensorium. This latter is a field of neural activity that arises and dissolves in temporally sequential epochs and which is coordinated with cognitive processes that associate meaning and form in a unitary frame (Laughlin, 1988, Laughlin, n.d.). A point to emphasize here is that both the sensory and the cognitive-intentional aspects of experience are active (never static!) products of neurological functioning, and are exquisitely ordered in the service of abstract pattern recognition in experience (Gibson, 1969). The natural motivation of the human brain is toward an "effort after meaning", rather than an "effort after truth".[13] The brain at every moment of consciousness imposes an order in experience. Part of that order is an interpretation of the relations among objects and events—the essence of meaning. We can schematize this interaction as a kind of Two Hands Clapping Model of experience (see Figure 1).

The total field of experience—the life-world—arising each moment is mediated by what we call the conscious network, a continuously changing field of intentional neural entrainments that may include any particular neural network one moment and disentrain it the next (Laughlin, McManus and d'Aquili, 1990, pp. 94-95).

The Symbolic Function and Meaning

To summarize, the life-world is the unfolding stream of direct experience mediated by the individual's conscious network. The cognized environment is the entire "library" of potential entrainments from which the actual conscious network mediating each moment of consciousness may be entrained. In other

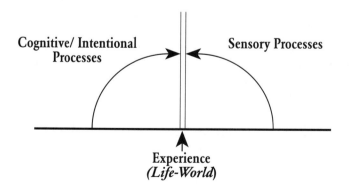

Figure 1:

The Two Hands Clapping Model of the Construction of Experience. Sensory and cognitive/intentional processes rise to meet in the construction of the life-world in each moment of consciousness.

words, the cognized environment is a system of potential neural transformations within the individual's nervous system, while the conscious network is the actual transform in each moment, experienced as the life-world.

We can see, therefore, that the life-world is inherently symbolic. Every aspect of the life-world is a construction mediated by models of noumena and intentional associations with those models provided from within the "library" of potential information. The relative veridicality of these models and associations depends upon a continuous EMC dialogue between relatively pliant neural structures and noumena in an ever changing operational environment. As implied by our Two Hands Clapping Model of experience, each moment of consciousness is a unitary field within which sensory form and meaning merge in an exquisitely ordered process of pattern recognition and signification (Gibson, 1969, Grossman, 1987). This field is renewed in each subsequent epoch in a fluid stream of form and meaning.[14]

Belief, Meaning and the Cycle of Meaning

Most of the meaning that informs experience is, as we have seen, made up of tacit knowledge, that is, creodized entrainments that operate below the level of awareness. Knowledge only becomes belief[15] when it takes a relatively abstract conceptual or imaginal form and the truth value of the knowledge somehow comes into question (see Rokeach, 1960, pp. 31-53). In other words, belief requires some awareness of propositional knowledge and some practical or affectively loaded evaluation of the knowledge to be made (Goodenough, 1990). There is also a social and conversational aspect of belief, and perhaps, as Peter du Preez (1991, pp. 193-208) suggests, it is generated by rhetoric, both in external conversation between people and in the internal dialogue between different parts of the being.

Belief, on this account, refers to a model or set of models formed at the conceptual/imaginal level of cortex and which are consciously held to be true (disbelief, of course, refers to the opposite). Belief usually refers to knowledge mediated at the cortical level of neurocognitive association and at the highest order of abstraction from experience. We become affectively attached to a belief either because it works well within our frame of reference, or because our frame of reference requires its truth. There may be an identification between the cognized self ("ego") and the belief: "I know that Jesus lives!" In fact, the ego may become thoroughly entrained as a system of beliefs and disbeliefs. This is one way of understanding an individual as a "culture-bearer" insofar as the process of forming beliefs is produced by enculturation.

Belief and Evidence

As we have seen, the human brain and its cognized environment are conservative systems. The brain regulates the adaptation of the organism by stabilizing the organism's models of the operational environment via the EMC and routinizing its interpretations and responses to events in the world. This feedforward conservatism does not magically cease at the level of belief. Although there is at least a modicum of awareness involved in belief, nonetheless actions taken in the operational environment as a consequence of a belief operate as tests of the truth value of that belief.

But there is no such thing as "pure" data upon which to base a test of belief.[16] Evidence of the truth or untruth of belief is always an interpretive process, especially within the everyday life-world of people. Belief leads to affirmative or exploratory action in the world, and that action then produces phenomenal feedback which is interpreted in terms of the belief that gave rise to the action in the first place. Experience, as we have seen in the Two Hands Clapping Model, is meaningful precisely because of the intentional projection of knowledge upon sensory events. Experience only becomes evidence when it is recalled (a cognitively selective process in itself) and interpreted relative to the belief in question. In a very real sense, we see what we want to see, and we want to see because of what we have seen.

Thus belief, action, and experience interpreted as evidence, participate as phases in a cycle of meaning[17] in which beliefs result in experiences that either cognitively operate to verify (confirm) and vivify (bring to life) them, or disconfirm—and thus to either transform or annul—them (see Figure 2).

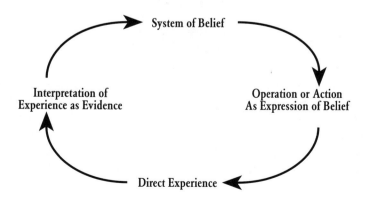

Figure 2:

The Operation of Belief within the Cycle of Meaning. The system of belief leads to activity in the world, which in turn leads to experiences interpreted as evidence of the truth or untruth of the belief system.

The Conservatism of Belief Systems

As we have seen, intentionality devoted to constructing belief structures also produces constraints upon the range of experiences we will "allow in" as evidence. Barriers to anomalous evidence are very common in culture, and are quite lawful in their operation (Rokeach, 1960, pp. 54-70). Because the cycle of meaning is fundamentally conservative, and exerts an "effort after meaning", rather than a pursuit of truth, anomalous experiences are either not allowed to arise, or if they arise are usually either interpreted in such a way as to confirm the belief[18] or are held in memory without being assimilated into the belief structure until a pattern of anomaly is cognized over time (see Rubinstein, Laughlin and McManus, 1984, p. 77).

Cosmology

There is an important distinction to be drawn between systems of belief encountered in traditional societies and those found in Euro-American industrial societies. Traditional worldviews tend to be cosmological in organization, whereas modern Euro-American worldviews are usually not cosmological (see Vine Deloria, this volume; see also Laughlin et al., 1986, Laughlin, McManus and d'Aquili, 1990, pp. 214-233). Despite the ethnocentric and ethnographically inappropriate use of the word "cosmology" by some physicists (for example Wheeler, 1983, Barrow and Tipler, 1986) and philosophers (Toulmin, 1982, Lucas, 1989) to refer to what I would call "quasi-cosmologies", science does not actually produce a living cosmology for most people, not even for most scientists themselves. A quasi-cosmology is a theory of the universe as a system, perhaps even a purposeful system, but the theory does not–perhaps cannot–relate to matters of ultimate concern and life-world of people. Indeed, science was largely responsible for the demise of the cosmological worldview that once prevailed in our culture three centuries ago (Burtt, 1932, pp. 4-11).

A (real) cosmology is a culturally patterned and socially transmitted cognized environment which is systemic in organization, is divided into multicameral domains, and is populated with entities that may be either visible (for example horned toad, coyote, the sun, etc.) or normally invisible (souls, radiant deities, subterranean worlds, divine messengers, etc.) to perception. Furthermore, a cosmology is dynamic (it develops or evolves) through time and constitutes an organic whole. It is often experienced as a space filled with objects and features (rocks, trees, mountains, rivers, stars, sun and moon, etc.) conceived to have both an outer (physical) and an inner (spiritual) nature. A cosmology is an account of all the significant elements and relations that make up the universe, and defines the position of an individual, the group, or all of humanity within that universe. A cosmos is a living totality which provides a frame of reference for all meaning, and the sacred source of all meaning. Not only is meaning a living reality, but so too is the cosmos a palpable, living fact of existence, made manifest in every moment of the individual's unfolding life-world.

Cosmologies are typically somatocentric.[19] That is, the human body is conceived as a microcosm that is placed at the very center of the cosmos (Neumann, 1963, p. 41; see Burtt, 1932, pp. 6, on the loss of this motif in the Euro-American worldview). The body is often appropriately oriented relative to the cardinal directions of the universe. Anatomical parts such as organs and joints may signify features in the greater cosmos. The *axis mundi* (axis of the world) may be equated with the spinal column, and dismemberment of the body at the joints may be associated with fragmentation of the cosmic relations.

A cosmology will frequently offer an explanation for the origin of the world, as well as its significant elements and relations. It may also predict the future course of the world (Eliade, 1963, pp. 54-74). Explanations of matters of ultimate concern are couched in mythological terms. That is, they are encoded within a set of stories with highly symbolic, even archetypal characters, features and events.

The closest one can come in most traditional societies to what Euro-American philosophy means by "metaphysics" is an account (usually highly symbolic) of the cosmos, and the (usually highly ritualized) procedures by means of which one may directly experience the reality (perhaps even meta-reality) of that account. In other words, "metaphysics" for most people on the planet is a process of integrative interpretation of the individual life-world within the society's cosmological frame of reference. This interaction between the socially defined and transmitted cosmology on the one hand, and the direct experience of the reality of that cosmology by individual members of society on the other hand, is modeled as a cosmological cycle of meaning in Figure 3.

The interdependence of cosmology and direct experience in traditional societies cannot be overemphasized, for it is the crux of the solution to the problem posed at the beginning of this chapter. It suggests that there is an the operative difference between traditional, cosmological "metaphysics" and scientific "metaphysics" with respect to the everyday life-world of people. The operative difference is that the traditional life-world arises as a consequence of what we might call cosmological consciousness in which the cosmos "comes alive" in direct experience (see Eliade, 1959, pp. 116-117). Cosmological consciousness is at once grounded in, and appreciative of, the sacred nature of the life-world. And the sacred nature of experience derives in part from an integrative interpretation of the life-world and its features and aspects as the production of normally hidden, but intuitively adumbrated "divine" forces.

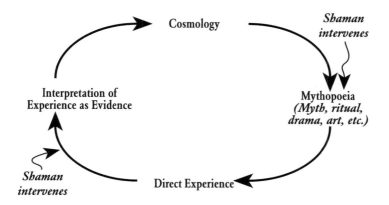

Figure 3:

The Cosmological Cycle of Meaning. The cosmology as symbolically expressed through a society's mythopoeia leads to activity in the world that in turn leads to experiences interpreted as evidence of the existence of the cosmology. The shaman, or adept, structures the conditions leading to, and the context of, the interpretation of experience.

Scientific Explanation

Were human beings actually rational automatons who were able to automatically drop or transform their beliefs in response to anomalous evidence, then science would no doubt conform to the logical positivist program. But in this post-Kuhnian era, no one who is familiar with the history and philosophy of science holds this fictional account of science to be anything like an accurate picture of how science is actually carried out (see Suppe, 1977, Feyerabend, 1975, Lakatos, 1970, Toulmin, 1972, Giere, 1984).[20]

Science and the Cycle of Meaning

After all, scientists are human beings, and they are thus naturally, and largely unconsciously, culture-bearers. Science itself is a Euro-American socio-cultural institution. Theories may become socially favored and take on the status of belief, and because they are found to be useful, or because they become affectively charged and evaluated within an institutional cycle of meaning, they are frequently the very devil to change or supplant. Theories are influenced by the rest of knowledge in the scientist's cognized environment, and egos can become so thoroughly associated with theories and the procedures for verifying those theories that anomalies are disregarded or missed altogether. Just as cosmological systems produce creodes in the individual cognized environment, so too do scientific theories. Scientific theories, in other words, are involved in a cycle of meaning, and thus contribute to and are influenced by their own cultural content (see Figure 4 below).

Realizing all of this, Paul Feyerabend (1975) has argued for a proliferation of competing theories and against the establishment of exclusive methodologies in scientific disciplines. He has done so in recognition of the inevitable narrowing effect that theories, methodologies and techniques exercise upon clear and unobstructed exploration of the world. Methodologies and observations derive their meaning in part from the theories that originally give rise to them and which they continue to serve. In that respect, theories are analogous to traditional worldviews and methodologies are analogous to rituals.

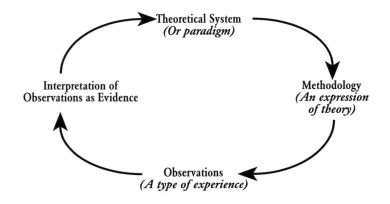

Figure 4:

The Operation of Scientific Theory Within a Cycle of Meaning. The system of theoretical belief leads to methodological activity in the world that in turn leads to observations interpreted as evidence of the truth or untruth of the theoretical system.

Science and the Zone of Uncertainty

However, I do not wish to imply that science is just another worldview among many. In many respects science is unique as an institutionalized system of inquiry (see Michael Scriven in this volume on this issue). What makes science progress, when it does progress, is a socially enhanced importance of evidence in producing and evaluating knowledge. Science exhibits more ritualized reverence for the zone of uncertainty than do most of the planet's traditional epistemologies. However, even with this institutionalization of the importance of direct, observational evidence, the tacit, unconscious, pre-scientific processes that produce the cognized environment and its systems of belief continue to operate in the scientific consciousness, and may significantly obstruct the quest for truth. Indeed, so much has this been the case in the history of science that some rather more self-aware researchers and philosophers have come to consider the anomalies produced by theories to be far more valuable to the progress of science than the theories themselves (see for example Kuhn, 1970, Pribram, 1971).

Causation

At the heart of most scientific theorizing is some model of causation—that is, some view about the necessary interconnections among events in the world. It would be well, therefore, to look into the attributes of models of causation and the role they play in scientific explanations and meaning.

There are four attributes of this classic description of causation that are particularly worth noting:

1) the cause and the effect are usually conceived to be distinct events

2) the cause and the effect are conceived as occurring in time with the cause always preceding the effect

3) the cause and its effect must either occur within the same location in space, or have a trajectory of interaction traceable within space

4) teleological, or purposeful, causation in nature is often considered at best to be normatively suspect, and at worst to be blatantly "religious" or "metaphysical" (see Suppe, 1989, pp. 284-285).

The view of cause and effect as distinct events occurring at two points in time forms part of the natural attitude of science because it is the common sense view of causation held in Euro-American culture (Jaspars, Hewstone and Fincham, 1983, p. 4). Reference to processes is lost in this delineation of temporal location, and thus ideas like that of "backward causation" are considered absurd (Faye, 1989, p. 9).

Of course, there are models of causation in science that are more complex than this simple lineal notion, and that conceive of simultaneous reciprocal causation among different parts of a system (see Roger Sperry in this volume; see also Ackoff and Emery, 1972, Blalock, 1969, 1985). However, even this more complex view of causal reciprocity does not abrogate the natural attitude among Euro-American thinkers that the different parts of a system are discrete, or that an effect occurring earlier in time than its cause is absurd.

The idea of "causation-at-a-distance" (or "non-local causation") is also considered absurd, for, like "backwards causation", it runs counter to our materialistic natural attitude about the possible relations that may obtain among events in the world (see Jahn and Dunne on this issue, this volume). A scientific model in which this type of causation-at-a-distance is successfully introduced is to be found in David Bohm's (1980) theory of the implicate order. Bohm suggests that the world of phenomena (the "explicate order") unfolds out of and enfolds back into a reality (the "implicate order") that is essentially whole, a-temporal, and admitting of causal relations outside of observable explicate order spacetime.

The historical trend in science has been to separate models of causation from anything approaching a philosophy or theory of purpose. Of course there have been exceptions to this trend. For example, the inclusion of an "anthropic principle" in astrophysical theory suggests that the essential organization of the universe in its first moments of existence necessitated the eventual evolution of our kind of sentience (see for example Carr and Rees, 1979, Barrow and Tipler, 1986). Also, recent reformulations of evolutionary theory away from neo-Darwinism and toward a structuralist account of phylogenesis often include a teleological conception of causation (see for example Brian Goodwin, 1989, 1990, also this volume; Lima-de-Faria, 1988, van der Hammen, 1988). But generally speaking, unless a theory is able to stipulate the mechanism of causation, teleological conceptions of the causal relations among events are considered suspect. They are suspect because they are reminiscent of divine plans and "written in the Great Book" metaphysical and religious accounts of the universe to which institutional science is an epistemological reaction.

Causation, the Life-world and the Brain

Most scientific models of causation fall unwittingly into what Alfred North Whitehead (1964) called the fallacy of misplaced concreteness; that is, they reify rational conceptions of causation upon a process that is essentially transcendental. Contrary to the classical view of David Hume (1960), causation is demonstrably an attribute of the organization of perception (Whitehead, 1947, 1964, Michotte, 1963, Mandelbaum, 1977, Jaspars, Hewstone and Fincham, 1983), and is such from the earliest stages of childhood development (Piaget, 1974). In other words, causation is "already there" to perception prior to any rational reflection upon it.[21] Causation is, as Whitehead (1947, 1978, pp. 175-177) rightly taught, an "aboriginal", or primitive aspect of the organization of perceptual awareness.[22] If one turns to the exploration of one's own stream of consciousness, one may quickly ascertain that causation is an essential element in the construction of experience.

The Phenomenology of Causation

Perhaps the most complete phenomenological account of causation in the Euro-American philosophical literature is to be found in Part Two of Maurice Mandelbaum's book *The Anatomy of Historical Knowledge* (1977, pp. 49-142). In that work, Mandelbaum demonstrates that the apprehension of causation in the everyday life-world involves an inherent awareness of interrelations among elements and phases of a process, and not the rational attribution of a cause-effect covariation among distinct events. These interrelations may occur simultaneously, as when the interaction between two opposing football players during the course of a "play" results in a "tackle" and the end of the "play". The interaction between the players causes the tackle, but is simultaneous within a single process. In actual experience, the interaction is the tackle which is the end of the play. Or, the sense of causation may derive from adumbrating a pattern of regularity in a sequence of events—"adumbration" in this case being a kind of intuitive leap from experience to recognized pattern.

The interweaving of movements among objects within a single process is what Michotte (1963, p. 217) termed "ampliation". What we are aware of is both objects and their interrelated movements within a contextual perception of a process. Moreover, because consciousness is essentially intentional, in some moments of consciousness it is the object awareness that is predominant and in other moments of consciousness it is the overall movement ("kinematic integration" in Michotte's terms) that predominates. In the latter case, it is the awareness of the covariation of the different phases and elements comprising a movement that is of essence.

Of course, upon reflection we may interpret the covariation of phases within a movement, or the adumbration of regularity in a sequence of phases, in an analytical way (Mackie, 1974, p. 230). Abstract patterns of causal relations encountered concretely in perception may be projected upon experience in the absence of actual ampliation or adumbration—a process Whitehead (1955, pp. 101-109) called "extensive abstraction". We might say that x occurred and then y occurred as a consequence, or that every time x occurs, y also occurs. But this abstraction derives, whether consciously or unconsciously on the part of the abstractor, from direct apprehension. And the process of extensive abstraction may result in an over-simplification of the model of causation. Where there are multiple types of causation in direct experience (Hart and Honore, 1959, p. 17), perhaps a single pattern becomes abstracted and elevated to the status of a logical necessity. Among other things, failure to recognize the roots of causation in experience may result in ignoring the precise contextual variables that must be considered in order for an explanation to successfully account for an actual event (see Scriven, 1958).

Our perceptual system is neurognostically organized to perceive the entire movement as an integrated process—to re-cognize the process as both a complex of interacting parts and a whole. "Taking a sip of coffee" is not normally experienced as a series of distinct, causal events (although it can be rationalized as such after the fact). It is rather an integrated whole which may involve phases of movement occurring simultaneously (lifting the cup and opening the lips) or over time (lifting and then tipping the cup).

The awareness of objects within an integrated process, involving kinematic integration, ampliation and adumbrated significance of covariation and regularity, is fundamental to human consciousness. The weight of evidence suggests that this is so from or near birth.[23] Moreover, there exists an important literature in the neurosciences pertaining to the possible structures mediating causation. Some of this work involves the structures of internal time consciousness and there remains a good deal of controversy on findings and interpretations in this field. Nonetheless, this research is suggestive of the neurophysiological substrate of perceptual epochs and processual/causal relations across bundles of epochs.[24] There is substantial evidence for some sort of central temporal processing mechanism based upon a minute perceptual unit within which temporal discriminations cannot be made (see Sanford, 1971, Harter, 1967, Steriade and Deschenes, 1985, Efron, 1970 and Childers and Perry, 1971 for relevant reviews). Stimuli of different durations that appear to be phase-locked to cortical rhythms and presented within an epoch will be perceived as simultaneous, whereas stimuli presented across epochs will be perceived as sequential, continual and processual (Varela et al., 1981), or in apparent motion (Ramachandran and Anstis, 1986). The duration of an epoch seems to average around 100 msec (1/10 of a second) and is equivalent to the wavelength of the EEG cortical alpha rhythm (Childers and Perry, 1971).

The more abstract interpretations of causation informing the life-world involve many of the very processes that mediate the intentionality of conscious experience. In fact, the adult human brain seems to be uniquely[25] capable of abstracting causal relations from perceptual experience and is thereby able to model relations among objects and events experientially distant in both space and time.[26] The ability to track causal processes over lengthy durations was clearly significant in the evolution of the hominid line and is probably due to the remarkable advance in the relative size and complexity of the prefrontal lobes of the cerebral cortex.[27]

The "causal operator", as my friend and colleague Eugene d'Aquili (see d'Aquili and Mol, 1990, pp. 142-146) likes to call it, is the complex entrainment of various parts of the cortex that mediates the continuity of long-term processes and temporal sequencing of neurocognitive operations. There is considerable evidence that the "causal operator" in its most rational, conceptual, conscious guise is mediated by the reciprocal interaction between the left hemisphere prefrontal lobe and the inferior parietal lobule located in the left parietal cortex, an area that mediates the formation of concepts (Luria, 1966, Pribram and Luria, 1973, Mills and Rollman, 1980, Swisher and Hirsch, 1971, Fuster, 1980, Stuss and Benson, 1986).

Causation and Meaning

From all that has been said above, it should be obvious that we cannot answer our central questions concerning science and the life-world by drawing a simple distinction between scientific causal explanation on the one hand and non-causal meaning in the lifeworld of people on the other hand. This tactic will not work because, as we have seen, scientific models of causation are rooted, however unconsciously on the part of scientists, in the essential, neurognostic structure of the life-world. The sense of causation is "already there" in the acts of perception, intuitive adumbration of perceptual regularities, intentional cognition and action. Causation is already an essential ingredient in the cognition of "plans" and in the ampliation of motion. Thus, causation is an inherent ingredient in the construction of meaning for all people, regardless of cultural background. In a word, we operate upon (usually tacit) causal relations all the time in our everyday lives.

So, why do scientific explanations not produce integrative meaning in the life-world of people, even when causation is a primary ingredient of both? And what is it about the metaphysical assumptions behind scientific explanations that so effectively inhibit the production of integrative meaning in the life-world of people?

We have already come far in answering these questions. Scientific explanations usually incorporate models of causation that are both limited to the products of conceptual abstraction and alienated from their experiential roots in the primordial sense of causation. As such, explanations usually isolate objects and events, including the observer from the observed. Causation within its context of process is ignored. Moreover, scientific causation and life-world causation are mediated differently by the brain, the former by left hemisphere conceptual structures, and the latter by various areas throughout the entire structure of the conscious network. Causation in the life-world is largely a pre-rational perceptual and intentional primitive mediated by a number of structures over wide areas of neural tissue, while scientific models of causation are mathematical-linguistic propositions produced by the structures mediating conceptualization and symbolic communication.

Fragmentation of the Cycle of Meaning

However, there is more to the schism between scientific explanation and the life-world than just differences in views of causation. Scientific explanations often pertain to domains of experience not encountered by people in their everyday life-world. Scientists become interested in things like the dynamics of ice flow in the Arctic, the migration patterns of hummingbirds, and the interactions among subatomic particles. Any such interest leads to a history of experiences on the part of the scientist that is divorced from the normal life-world of people around the scientist—perhaps even divorced from the scientist's own everyday life-world.

This is especially true for explorations that involve experimentation rather than naturalistic observations. Experiments amount to artificial experiential domains that by their very nature distort the natural flow of the life-world. Experimental psychologists may close themselves off from the natural world and spend hours running rats through mazes. Chemists may spend hours ensconced in a laboratory mixing chemicals and reading computer outputs. These activities produce experiences for the scientists that are removed from the flow of life-world experiences unfolding for most people all the time, and for the scientists themselves when they are not in their labs. These factors tend to produce what Whitehead (1978, p. 289) called a "bifurcation of nature"—a discrepancy between the life-world and the world according to science. This bifurcation of nature is attended by a fragmented cycle of meaning; or, perhaps more accurately, multiple cycles of meaning. One system of knowledge is related to experiences in the everyday life-world, another system of knowledge to experiences in the field or experimental lab. My hunch would be that the fragmentation for the naturalist may be less severe than that for the experimental physicist or rat-running psychologist, but that is an empirical question beyond the scope of this inquiry.

Technology and Fragmented Cognized Environments

Science presents views of the world that counter the universal motifs of traditional cosmologies. We are taught that the universe is not somatocentric, that things are not interdependent, that hidden, anthropomorphized forces do not in fact exist, and that there is no purpose behind the evolution of the world. Meanwhile, science produces technological changes in the operational environment which in turn result in changes in the life-world of people. Technology, after all, is the expression of knowledge, in this case the artifacts of scientific knowledge. And technology as an expression of knowledge produces life-world experiences for people.

The disparity between new experiences and the lack of comprehension may disrupt the natural cycle of meaning to the extent that the traditional worldview of people may be seriously called into question, and even eradicated. Yet scientific knowledge contributes little or nothing in the way of a replacement. Much less does science address the "matters of ultimate concern" at the roots of traditional belief systems. It is the understanding of the disruptive influence of technology upon traditional worldview that underlies the anti-scientific, anti-technological attitudes of such communities as the Amish, Mennonites and Christian Scientists who resist the encroachment of scientific technology upon their lives and cultures.

Our Answer in Brief

Science, by virtue of its own historical and metaphysical blinders, is therefore rarely able to produce comprehension relative to matters of ultimate concern, and is thus usually unable to produce cosmology in the traditional sense. Moreover, science is rarely reflexive (Ihde, 1990, p. 22). Scientists—even really creative ones—rarely look as closely at the processes of their own observation as they do at the object of their scrutiny. In short, scientific knowledge is too fragmented, linked to experiences far too esoteric, too unrelated to the matters that concern people the most, and too unreflexive, for such knowledge to effectively produce integrative meaning in the life-world. In addition, scientific models of causation tend to be alienated from life-world meaning. Scientific models of causation are often mechanical and isolate phenomena, whereas life-world causation is inherently processual and holistic. Combined, these factors give us most of the answer to our root question, and suggest the directions that must be followed in the future for the bifurcation between the scientific worldview and the life-world to be bridged.

Shall We Eliminate Science?

As understandable as the anti-scientific attitudes of the Amish or Christian Scientists may be in terms of effective cultural and religious conservatism, the facile rejection of science will not resolve the bifurcation problem. There are a number of good reasons for this.

Science Works!

In the first place, as Edmund Husserl (1970) noted in *The Crisis of European Sciences and Transcendental Phenomenology,* science has gained its history of success because it works. Despite flaws in its metaphysical assumptions, its alienation from its roots in experience, its bifurcation of nature, and its disruptive influences upon the culture that spawned it and other traditional cultures that embrace it, science does what it does better than any other such social institution in human history. The reason why it works so well is not hard to fathom as long as we keep in mind that science progresses, when it actually does progress, by applying an "effort after truth", rather than the traditional "effort after meaning". The essence of creative science is attention to paradox and the truth-value of views.

Science opens up the world to a mind-boggling array of explorations. Only science has allowed us to see the reconstructed face of a 2500-year-old mummy; to put people in space and to send probes to Mars; to understand the genetic processes that produce our body; to build up a picture of the age of the dinosaurs; to develop an effective treatment for diabetes; to see the inner workings of our brain; and to light our houses with electricity. Science does what it does well, and that is to open up the transcendental operational environment to exploration, explanation and utilitarian control.

Mind-Body Dualism is Pre-Scientific in Origin

In the second place, the roots of the bifurcation are grounded in the pre-scientific mind-body dualism of Euro-American culture. That is, Euro-American culture's separation of things mental and things physical derives from the reified conceptual rift between the largely rational mental faculties and the body. This derives historically from both the Hebraic and post-Socratic Greek cultures, and became elaborated in Cartesian philosophy. The schism between mind and body, so much a part of the Euro-American "natural attitude", characterizes the entire human condition and finds its way into such absolute theoretical distinctions as mind vs. brain, culture vs. nature and the notion of cultural dominion over nature. Even scientific disciplines are split into the "physical" sciences like chemistry, biology and physics, and the "social" sciences like psychology, anthropology and economics. Knowledge is hierarchized and the highest level is considered to be rational knowledge (rather than say intuitive or imaginative knowledge). The pre-eminent value of causation in explanation is usually the "control" of the data (that is, prediction and retrodiction via specified causal links), this being the equivalent of the mind exercising control over the body and the physical world, and the domination of nature by culture—all hallmarks of Euro-American cultural values (Burtt, 1932, p. 307).

And in philosophy, the mind-body schism occurs in distinctions such as free will (associated with rational decision making and choice) vs. determinism (associated with the body, instinct and necessity). It is difficult for Euro-American philosophers to resolve the question of free will without alienating the mind from the body (Searle, 1984). The body may be determined, but the mind is potentially free. Even the traditional bifurcation of metaphysics into "epistemology" (the mental question: how do we come to know what we claim to know about the world?) and "ontology" (the physical question: what is the world like "out there" apart from our knowing of it?) reproduces this schism.

In theology, of course, the distinction is elevated further to a dualism between body and soul: the body may die but the soul lives on. It is my opinion that mind-body dualism represents Euro-American culture's own distinct adaptation to the fundamental problem described so eloquently by Ernest Becker (1973) in *The Denial of Death,* that being the problem inherent in coming to terms with the awareness of our own "creatureliness". As Becker notes, the existential problem faced by all human beings everywhere is the recognition that we are creatures that apparently die. Different societies have developed different bodies of knowledge to resolve this dilemma. The resolution usually involves in one way or another the denial of, or reassuring interpretation of, the empirical fact of death. Some societies, such as most Euro-American societies, resolve the existential problem of death by separating an immortal aspect of mind from the obviously mortal body. Such societies posit the existence of a normally hidden, but essential, attribute of being (the "soul") that is in one sense or another immortal.

Naturally the metaphysics of any such society will be tainted by this fundamental schism. A familiar theme in Euro-American metaphysics, reflected for example in Cartesian metaphysics, has been the divorcing of rational conceptions of the world from the data of raw experience. In various ways knowledge is said to exist as mathematical and linguistic propositions about the world, not in the life-world itself. Truth is to be found through the exercise of reason, not from meditation upon the "nature of the things themselves". In some idealist metaphysical systems, reality or sense data are considered to be a kind of chaos that only becomes ordered with the application of the rational mind. In other systems, such as naive realism, the mind is considered to be independent of the reality being observed. No matter how solipsistic, skeptical, or realistic these and other more complex versions of the relations between mind and reality (including even the phenomenology of Husserl) are, they nonetheless tend to be conditioned by different transformations of the same mind-body dualism that also informs Euro-American theological and scientific views. It should be obvious that as long as scientific views are unconsciously conditioned by this dualism, there is no possibility of eliminating its divisive effects upon research, explanation and models of causation, and the impact these have on the life-world of people.

The Continuum of Empirical Commitment

In placing the significance of science both as a social institution and as an enterprise within the context of cross-cultural approaches to knowledge, it helps to realize that all healthy humans everywhere on the planet are to some extent empirical in evaluating their beliefs. This is an important consideration, for it was once the vogue of generations of social theorists to consider "primitive" thought to be fundamentally different from "civilized" thought (see for example Levy-Bruhl, 1923, Levi-Strauss, 1966). This view is no longer tenable in the face of modern ethnographic research to the contrary (see Horton and Finnegan, 1973, Cove, 1987). Rather, it is more accurate to focus attention upon the relationship between belief and evidence in human thought, whatever the sociocultural background.

It perhaps may help our understanding of the relationship of science to traditional worldviews to imagine all approaches to knowledge, whether they be individual or social, or whether they be directed toward "inner" reality (knowledge of being and consciousness) or "outer" reality (knowledge of events in the phenomenal world), on a single continuum defined by their relative openness to evidence; that is, by the importance of empirical verification to the construction of beliefs (Rokeach, 1960, pp. 54-70; see Figure 5 below).

Openness to empirical input into models of self or world inevitably results in paradox. Paradox may be kept at bay by at least partially closing belief systems to empirical modification. At the left hand extreme of the continuum (#1) are to be found beliefs about the self and the world relatively closed to empirical modification. These are the ones that will interpret any potentially disconfirming experiences so that they either verify the beliefs or are deemed irrelevant. The balance point of the continuum (#3) represents those belief systems that remain both confident of the truth of their views of the world and open to dynamic

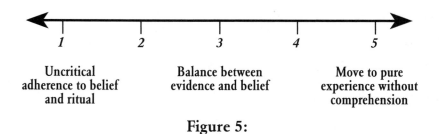

Figure 5:

The Continuum of Empirical Commitment. Human approaches to knowledge, whether personal or cultural, and whether of inner being or the outer world, may be distinguished by the extent of their openness to evidence and commitment to empirical verification. Approaches lying between 1 and 3 tend to be "efforts after meaning", while those between 3 and 5 tend to be "efforts after truth".

modification relative to changing evidence about the self and the world. Such systems may indeed be changed by novel experiences and apparent paradox. A.F.C. Wallace (1966) called this process of culture change "revitalization", especially when it affected the worldview and religion of a society.

Between these ideal types lie most of the planet's traditional worldviews. These are systems of belief and practice that are relatively conservative of meaning, and that are characterized by their heavy reliance upon ritualized procedures for assuring experiences that verify and vivify the system. And because they concern themselves most with matters of ultimate concern that rarely change, paradoxical experiences may have little effect upon the innermost core symbolism upon which the integrity of the system depends. Yet, when required by novel circumstances, these systems do "revitalize" themselves by rearranging their symbolism and standard interpretations in order to accommodate the new circumstances.

Approaches to knowledge lying between the balance point (#3) and the right hand extreme of the continuum (#5) are systems that value empirical exploration as much as, or more than, they do conservation of meaning. Creative science lies somewhere between the balance point and #4, where the evaluation of the truth of beliefs is ideally being tested in the crucible of empirical observation. The area between #4 and #5 is intended to represent those rare phenomenological traditions that require mature contemplation[28] and that eventually drop the reliance upon belief systems altogether and pursue the nature of "pure" experience.[29]

And obviously the range of conservatism and empirical commitment varies enormously among individual scientists. When I place science between #3 and #4, I am generalizing about creative scientists, and not about the numerous members of the scientific community who call themselves "scientists" but who merely do what they were taught to do and are not actually creative. It is my impression that most of the creative science is carried out by only a fraction of the individuals that call themselves "scientists". As Kuhn (1977) and others have pointed out, creative science proceeds as well as it does only against the resistance visited by the inherent cultural natures of the people making up the scientific community. Indeed, the dialectic that produces creative science depends upon the tension between the "effort after meaning" and the "effort after truth". Merely creative science respects the zone of uncertainty inevitably generated by any system of knowledge. Leading edge creative science seeks to expand the zone of uncertainty so as to generate the maximum amount of paradox and question.

Can Science Better Inform the Life-World?

In conclusion, assuming what I have said about the metaphysical foundations of science is an accurate picture, let us now ask if this ironic situation may be minimized or eliminated by future science? In my opinion, the answer is a qualified "yes". After all, the limitations I have discussed are largely tacit cultural loadings upon the metaphysical foundations of scientific explanation. And culture can be changed. Within the limitations suggested by a biogenetic structural theory of knowledge, it is entirely possible for the schism between scientific explanation and the life-world of people affected by science to be greatly reduced—under certain conditions, of course.

There are numerous signs that some disciplines within science and philosophy are tending in that direction. Apart from the obvious concern of the contributors to this volume, the signs include an increasing emphasis upon interdisciplinary approaches to knowledge: an expanding reflexiveness on the part of disciplines and self-reflection on the part of many scientists; a return to the concerns of cosmology and systematic philosophy; a greater appreciation of the role of phenomenology; and a growing transpersonal movement. For example, developments in the philosophy of science continue to be away from ideological views of science (represented by logical positivism) and toward empirical studies of how science and scientists actually operate (see Suppe, 1989, Toulmin, 1982, Rubinstein, Laughlin and McManus, 1984). Elsewhere in philosophy there is both a return to a serious consideration of systematic metaphysics and cosmology (for example, in the process metaphysics of Whitehead; Lucas, 1989) and an increasing interest in phenomenology (Ihde, 1986).

In science itself there is a greater awareness that the act of observation influences the results of experimentation and field research (see Michael Scriven in this volume). This is notable in quantum mechanics (Zurek, van der Merve and Miller, 1988) and the more recent chaos theory (Gleick, 1987) in the physical sciences, and in the postmodern critique of the social sciences (Woodiwiss, 1990, Lash, 1990). And there is a small, but growing and significant interest in transpersonalism in the sciences, that is, in what extraordinary states of consciousness have to teach us about ourselves, the world, and our accrual of knowledge (Wilber, 1980, 1983, Laughlin, McManus and d'Aquili, 1990, Harman, 1988, 1991). There are also indications that science is producing new, more holistic and experientially accurate models of causation (for example see Willis Harman, this volume, and Roger Sperry, 1987, this volume; see also Bohm, 1980).

Toward a Self-Aware Science

Science has not been particularly reflexive over the course of its history. Science has progressed, when it has progressed at all, more from the inherent creative drive of human sentience than from any real understanding of how creativity operates. In other words, like intentionality, ampliation of movement, internal time consciousness and other such essential attributes of consciousness, creativity in the production of knowledge is "already there" for consciousness. Creativity is inherent in the neurognostic structure of the nervous system. Indeed, if Whitehead (1978, Rapp and Wiehl, 1990) is correct, creativity is ubiquitous to the nature of the universe. A fundamental error that scientists have made for generations is to reify their conceptual models of the "scientific method" upon their experience of the transcendental fact of their creativity.

Bringing awareness to bear on scientific consciousness and activity can only help to alleviate the conditions that produce the bifurcation of nature. Therefore, any activity that increases the self-awareness of people qua scientists will have the inevitable effect of decreasing the gap between scientific knowledge and the life-world. Any disciplined approach to self-awareness inevitably brings the contemplative in direct touch with their own life-world and its essential structures—including the truth of totality. A good example here is Arne Naess' (1989, p. 28, Devall, 1985, pp. 65-77) distinction between the fragmentary worldview produced by the "shallow ecology" movement in science, with its concern for solving particular problems (such as pollution, erosion, resource deprivation, food distribution, etc.), and the "deep ecology" movement marked by the intuitive awareness of the totality of existence and the transformation of consciousness and lifestyle produced by that intuition. The former focuses on rational problem-solving, the latter on a radical transformation of the individual life-world.

If disciplined contemplation is carried out over the course of years, a process of maturation may occur in self-awareness not unlike that of the "seasoning" that occurs in any other occupation (cooking, carpentry, atomic physics, philosophy, etc.). The awareness of the structures of one's own experience involves the interpenetration of sensory and cognitive networks within conscious network, just as does any other act of intentionality. Let us remind ourselves of this fact with the Two Hands Clapping Model (see Figure 6 next page):

The overall effect of contemplation upon scientific consciousness is signified by the ancient motif of the snake eating its own tail—the *uroboros*. Self-awareness alters the neural entrainments in the brain of the self-aware. We must always remember that the nervous system is made up of living cells, not microchips. The living cells that comprise neural networks will reorganize

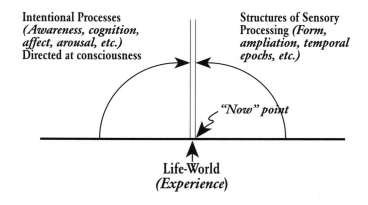

Figure 6:

The Two Hands Clapping Model of Self-Awareness. The contemplative grows in self-knowledge as a result of studying the structures of experience operating in each moment of consciousness. Maturing self-knowledge changes the life-world, even as it is being studied.

themselves around any new tasks placed before them. To redirect the intentional processes of the brain toward their own activities is to set a new and challenging adaptation before the society of cells comprising these processes, and they will eventually reorganize themselves in order to master the demands of the inquiry. In becoming self-aware, one transforms that process within one of which one is aware, including eventually the intentional structures themselves.

The Advantages of a Contemplative Scientist

Because we have elsewhere discussed the various advantages of, and resistances to, incorporating mature contemplation into science (see Laughlin, 1989, Laughlin, McManus and d'Aquili, 1990, pp. 296-333), I will only briefly suggest here a few advantages as they relate to the topic of this volume. I predict that there will continue to be an increasing incorporation of mature contemplation into science, and that this merger of contemplation and science will have at least the following general effects:

1) Pre-scientific mind-body dualism will be alleviated.

Direct experience of the totality of one's being tends to eliminate views of an absolute distinction between the mind and the body. Direct experiences of the unity of being produce dramatic and paradoxical data before a consciousness conditioned by a natural attitude characterized by mind-body dualism. As the natural attitude changes to become harmonious with experience, beliefs and scientific theories based upon that natural attitude become perceived as "unreal" and untenable.

2) Consciousness will be understood to be transcendental.

The contemplative can no longer take consciousness for granted. Consciousness is directly experienced as having a determining influence upon phenomena, their context and their relations. How one views the world depends upon the state of consciousness within which the world arises for the subject. What the contemplative understands by concepts like "objective", "observe", "empirical", etc. may undergo considerable shift in meaning. Any notion that naive realism is an accurate representation of the real world apart from our observation of it becomes self-evidently absurd. Consciousness itself (and its cognized environment) becomes an indispensable ingredient of any theoretical stance relative to the operational environment.

3) Causation will be understood to be transcendental.

As the contemplative experiences the dissolution of the mind-body schism and gets more "in touch" with their transcendental being, and as the contemplative comes to appreciate the integral part played by consciousness in the construction of the life-world, the contemplative's understanding of causation becomes likewise changed. The contemplative's model of causation comes to more and more approximate that encountered in the life-world. Indeed, causation itself may become the object of study. In some contemplative traditions, the adept is given a set of exercises specifically designed to develop awareness of causation (see Kalupahana, 1975, on Buddhist practice).

4) The discrepancy between scientific models of causation and life-world causation will be eliminated, as will be the fiction of the independence of objects.

When awareness of causation by the contemplative sufficiently matures, two transformations of comprehension may occur. In the first place, there will no longer exist for the contemplative qua scientist a serious discrepancy between models of causation in scientific explanations and meaningful causation as encountered in the life-world. The former becomes the result of adumbration of, and extensive abstraction from, the latter. The contemplative qua scientist ceases to reify abstract models of causation that are disharmonious with causation experienced in the life-world.

In the second place, the contemplative qua scientist no longer takes as true the naive realist's belief that objects exist independently of each other, and that causation only occurs among spatio-temporally proximate objects. In keeping with the lesson of quantum physics, the lesson of mature contemplation is that the process of experiencing a noumenon involves causation at multiple levels between the observer and the observed, and may occur over considerable distances and durations (on this issue, see Arthur Zajonc in this volume).

5) The insights and findings of contemplation qua science will become grounded in the neurosciences instead of traditional ideology.

With the rapid development of interdisciplinary neuroscience, there now exists the possibility of combining phenomenological explorations and insights with what we are coming to know about the structures and functions of the nervous system. As I have argued elsewhere (Laughlin, McManus and d'Aquili, 1990, pp. 13-14), contemplative discoveries about the essential structures of consciousness and neuroscientific discoveries about the structures of the nervous system may be considered as two views of the same transcendental reality. My prediction is that when mature contemplation becomes combined with the neurosciences, the resulting neuro-phenomenology will constitute the most powerful approach yet to the study of consciousness.

Conclusion

I have given a qualified "yes" to the question of whether the dualism between scientific explanation and the life-world of people can be bridged. But as we have seen, the cycle of meaning operating to produce meaning in the life-world, and that operating to produce creative science, are not grounded on the same principle. The former is the result of the "effort after meaning" and the latter the result of the "effort after truth". In some respects the requirements for creative science are antithetical to the conservative nature of belief systems. Indeed, creative science often requires a welter of paradox and anomaly. Thus, as Thomas Kuhn, Paul Feyerabend, Imre Lakotos and others have so ably shown, the production of creative science is inherently a revolutionary process. Creative science really depends upon the maintenance of an "essential tension" (Kuhn, 1977, pp. 225-239) between the conservative need for certainty and meaning in peoples' life-worlds on the one hand, and the radical demands of the pursuit of truth on the other hand.

An example of the kind of paradox that eventually results in paradigm-transforming theory in science is that produced by the lengthy series of experiments carried out by Robert Jahn and Brenda Dunne (1987, this volume) on the influence of consciousness upon the performance of machines. The results of these experiments appear to demonstrate both causation at a distance and backwards causation. No current general theory of spacetime can fully explain these paradoxical data. These data thus stand as a challenge to our understanding of both mind and world.

As long as human beings inherently struggle for meaning in their lives, and continue to cling to their worldviews in order to maintain a meaningful life-world, there will always be some bifurcation and tension between the world according to science and the life-world of people—even among scientists. As I have argued, the human brain tends to creodize its comprehension and responses to the operational environment; it tends toward the "hardening of the categories", if you will pardon a trite phrase. As I have taken pains to show, novelty challenges creodic acts, and is thus threatening to conservative systems of knowledge.

This tension can be (and I predict will be) alleviated by eliminating some of the unconscious aspects of the pre-scientific natural attitude of scientists, and thus some of the tacit cognitive underpinnings of the metaphysical foundations of science. But as long as some humans insist upon pushing outwards into the zone of uncertainty, beyond the point where knowledge readily produces comfy, conservative meaning in the life-world, there will always exist some tension between these polarized fulfillments of intentionality and their institutional expressions in culture and society.

Notes

This paper was condensed from an earlier monograph commissioned by the Institute of Noetic Sciences (Laughlin, 1992). I wish to thank Willis Harman for his help and encouragement during this project. As always, I owe a debt to my fellow biogenetic structuralists, especially to Gene d'Aquili, John McManus and Robert Rubinstein. I also wish to thank Earl Count and Ven. Tarchin for sharing their ideas. And, of course, I am grateful to the other authors in this volume with whom I had the opportunity to discuss matters during the Asilomar conference sponsored by the IONS in November 1991.

1. The concept of the life-world, or Lebenswelt, originates with the last major work of Edmund Husserl (1970, pp. 103-189), and was later developed in works by Merleau-Ponty (1964), and Schutz (Schutz and Luckmann, 1973, 1989); see Spiegelberg (1982, p. 144). It means the "reality that is lived", including knowledge about the world that is pregiven in experience.

2. I do not mean "meaning" in the usual, quite limited linguistic or semiotic sense (for example Schiffer, 1972, Savigny, 1988), but rather in the broadest possible sense (as in Ogden and Richards, 1923, Hill, 1971) to include knowledge operating at every level of the constitution of the life-world, from perception and somesthesis through abstract thought and imagination.

3. Over the years I have worked with a group that has developed a body of theory we call biogenetic structuralism and which explains the relationships among neurological structures, consciousness and culture; see d'Aquili, Laughlin and McManus, 1979, Laughlin and d'Aquili, 1974, Laughlin, McManus and d'Aquili, 1990, and Rubinstein, Laughlin and McManus, 1984.

4. The cortex is the evolutionarily newest part of the nervous system and forms a corrugated layer of tissue on the top of the brain. Part of its function is the internal depiction of the being and its environment to and for itself (Laughlin and d'Aquili, 1974, Jerison, 1973, 1985). We agree with Doty (1975) that conscious processing of experience is largely a cortical function.

5. When we speak of a model, we do not refer either to an ideal type or to a description of a theory. A model is an actual organization of tissue, the function of which is to mediate some aspect or aspects of the world before the mind.

6. We borrowed the concepts of cognized and operational environments from Rappaport (1968), but have changed their meaning substantially from his usage. For further elaboration of these concepts, see Laughlin and Brady (1978, p. 6), d'Aquili et al. (1979, pp. 12ff), Rubinstein et al. (1984, pp. 21ff), and Laughlin, McManus and d'Aquili (1990).

7. "Noumena" is a Kantian term, but I do not wish to imply by my use of the concept that the operational environment and its constituent noumena are fundamentally unknowable. Quite the contrary, the human brain is the product of millions of years of evolution for an organ that comes to know its being and its world. The brain more or less accurately depicts its operational environment within the biological constraints of its capacity to interact with its own being and its world, and the demands of the organism's efforts to conserve the integrity of its internal organization (Piaget, 1971, 1985). As Whitehead (1938, p. 121) so succinctly put it, ". . . we experience the universe, and we analyze in our consciousness a minute selection of its details".

8. "Entrainment" is a technical term in neurophysiology that means the linking of neural systems into larger configurations by way of dendritic-axonic-endocrinological interconnections. As the term implies, the process is like building up a train from a selection of railroad cars. Entrainments may be momentary or enduring. A change in a pattern of entrainment is termed "re-entrainment".

9. We have given a technical definition of "adaptive isomorphism" in d'Aquili et al. (1979, p. 17). The term implies that models are partially isomorphic to at least the extent required for survival. "Isomorphic" means that the elements and relations comprising the neural model are not the same as those of the noumenon in the being or the world being modeled. And just as there is more to a real airplane than there is to a model airplane, so too is there "transcendentally" more to the noumenon than there is to the model—unless, of course, it is the neural network comprising the model that is itself the noumenon.

10. Edmund Husserl's (1931) term for this is "horizon".

11. The concept of neurognosis is complex and refers to the essential genetical component producing universal patterns of activity within the nervous system, and the experiential and behavioral concomitants of that activity; see Laughlin, 1991, Laughlin and d'Aquili (1974, Chapter 5), Laughlin, McManus and d'Aquili (1990, Chapter 2) and d'Aquili et al. (1979, pp. 8ff).

12. We mean by experience "that which arises before the subject" in consciousness (see Dilthey, 1976, Husserl, 1977). This includes perception, thought, imagination, intuition, affect, somesthesis and sensation.

13. I am indebted to Earl W. Count (personal communication) for this distinction which he attributes to I. A. Richards.

14. In the interests of clarity, let me be more explicit about the relationship between "meaning" and "information". Meaning is information that participates in organizing the life-world. Information is the literal "in-forming" (a la Varela, 1979), or entrainment of neural networks mediating any regulatory or control function of the nervous system, whether that function participates as meaning or not.

15. In normal English parlance; see Black (1973) on the anthropological use of the term.

16. As both Popper (1972) and Northrup (1947) have amply shown, evidence cannot prove a belief or a theory to be absolutely true, for any piece of evidence may be explained by more than one belief. But evidence can go a long way in disproving (or falsifying) a belief.

17. Our cycle of meaning is somewhat like Paul Riceour's "hermeneutic circle".

18. An entire body of psychology exists dealing with this issue (see Festinger, 1957).

19. I am indebted to George MacDonald for this concept.

20. Kuhn (1977) has argued that scientific disciplines function to regulate knowledge much as do cultures. Other authorities believe that scientific theories evolve much like societies or biological species (Giere, 1984, Campbell, 1974, Toulmin, 1972).

21. By "already there", I mean that it is given in perception after being "constituted", that is, as a consequence of the activity of the neurognostic structures mediating perception (see Ihde, 1990, p. 29 on this issue).

22. Whitehead (1947, 1978, pp. 175-180) taught that consciousness exhibits two modes: the mode of presentational immediacy and the mode of causal efficacy. He argued that Hume considered the world of perception as arising in only the former mode, to the wrongful exclusion of the latter mode.

23. For a review of the neuro-cognitive evidence for causation in infant perception and adult psychology, see Laughlin, 1991, Laughlin, McManus and d'Aquili, 1990.

24. These epochs are variously termed "perceptual moments", "temporal frames", "excitability cycles", "central intermittency" and "perceptual frames" (see, for example, Varela et al., 1981).

25. There is evidence that chimpanzees and other anthropoid apes are capable of rudimentary causal abstraction beyond relations given to perception (see for example Premack, 1976). If so, it seems likely that the emergence of the importance of our human-like "causal operator" occurred at some point after the divergence of the hominoids from the rest of the primate order.

26. Elsewhere we have called the evolution of this abstractive ability the "cognitive extension of prehension" (see Laughlin and d'Aquili, 1974, pp. 76-99).

27. The lateral or "granular" prefrontal cortex has exhibited greater allometric development than most other areas of the hominid nervous system (Nauta, 1971, Passingham, 1973).

28. For example, Zen Buddhist insight meditation, and transcendental phenomenology.

29. A word of caution must be interjected here. Some traditional "shamanic" traditions actually encourage individual practitioners to transcend the society's worldview (for example in Ridington and Ridington, 1970, Cove, 1987). Such systems may appear on the surface to be conservative of meaning and, for most of the society's members, they undoubtedly would fall between #2 and #3 on the continuum. But hidden in the folds of the system may be found adepts that have matured as contemplatives and who would appear further right on the continuum. The ethnographic data are frequently poor with reference to levels of maturation recognized by traditional worldviews.

References

Russell L. Ackoff and Fred E. Emery, *On Purposeful Systems*, Aldine-Atherton, 1972.

M. A. Arbib, *The Metaphorical Brain*, Wiley, 1972.

J. D. Barrow and F. J. Tipler, *The Anthropic Cosmological Principle*, Clarendon, 1986.

E. Becker, *The Denial of Death*, Free Press, 1973.

M. Black, "Belief systems" in *Handbook of Social and Cultural Anthropology*, edited by J. J. Honigmann, Rand McNally, 1973.

H. M. Blalock, *Theory Construction*, Prentice-Hall, 1969.

H. M. Blalock, editor, *Causal Models in the Social Sciences*, Aldine, 1985.

D. Bohm, *Wholeness and the Implicate Order*, Routledge and Kegan Paul, 1980.

T. G. Bower, *The Rational Infant: Learning in Infancy*, W. H. Freeman, 1989.

J. S. Bruner, "The organization of early skilled action" in *The Integration of a Child into a Social World*, edited by M.P.M. Richards, Cambridge University Press, 1974.

E. A. Burtt, *The Metaphysical Foundations of Modern Physical Science: A Historical and Critical Essay* (2nd edition), Harcourt Brace, 1932.

D. T. Campbell, "Evolutionary epistemology" in *The Philosophy of Karl Popper,* edited by P. A. Schilpp, Open Court, 1974.

B. J. Carr and M. J. Rees, "The anthropic principle and the structure of the physical world", *Nature* 278, 1979, pp. 605-612.

D. B. Chamberlain, "The cognitive newborn: A scientific update", *The British Journal of Psychotherapy* 4 (1), 1987, pp. 30-71.

J. P. Changeux, *Neuronal Man: The Biology of Mind,* Oxford University Press, 1985

D. G. Childers and N. W. Perry, "Alpha-like activity in vision", *Brain Research* 25, 1971, pp. 1-20.

J. J. Cove, *Shattered Images: Dialogues and Meditations on Tsimshian Narratives,* Carleton University Press, 1987.

E. G. d'Aquili, C. D. Laughlin and J. McManus, *The Spectrum of Ritual,* Columbia University Press, 1979.

E. G. d'Aquili and H. Mol, *The Regulation of Physical and Mental Systems,* Edwin Mellen Press, 1990.

B. Devall, *Deep Ecology,* Gibbs M. Smith, 1985.

W. Dilthey, *Selected Writings,* edited by H. P. Rickman, Cambridge University Press, 1976.

R. W. Doty, "Consciousness from matter", *Acta Neurobiol. Exp.* 35, 1975, pp. 791-804.

P. Du Preez, *A Science of Mind: The Quest for Psychological Reality,* Academic Press, 1991.

G. M. Edelman, *Neural Darwinism: The Theory of Neuronal Group Selection,* Basic Books, 1987.

R. Efron, "The minimum duration of a perception", *Neuropsychologia* 8, 1970, pp. 57-63.

M. Eliade, *The Sacred and the Profane: The Nature of Religion,* Harper and Row, 1959.

M. Eliade, *Myth and Reality,* Harper and Row, 1963.

J. Elster, *Ulysses and the Sirens,* Cambridge University Press, 1984.

J. Faye, *The Reality of the Future: An Essay on Time, Causation and Backward Causation,* Odense University Press, 1989.

L. Festinger, *A Theory of Cognitive Dissonance,* Harper, 1957.

P. K. Feyerabend, *Against Method,* Verso, 1975.

J. M. Fuster, *The Prefrontal Cortex: Anatomy, Physiology, and Neuropsychology of the Frontal Lobe,* Raven, 1980.

E. J. Gibson, *Principles of Perceptual Learning and Development,* Appleton-Century-Crofts, 1969.

J. J. Gibson, *The Ecological Approach to Visual Perception,* Houghton Mifflin, 1979.

R. N. Giere, "Toward a unified theory of science" in *Science and Reality: Recent Work in the Philosophy of Science,* edited by J. T. Cushing, C. F. Delaney and G. M. Gutting. University of Notre Dame Press, 1984.

J. Gleick, *Chaos,* Penguin, 1987.

W. Goodenough, "Evolution of the human capacity for beliefs", *American Anthropologist* (in press, 1990).

B. C. Goodwin, "A structuralist research programme in developmental biology" in *Dynamic Structures in Biology,* edited by B. C. Goodwin, A. Sibatani, G. Webster, Edinburgh University Press, 1989.

B. C. Goodwin, "Structuralism in biology", *Science Progress Oxford* 74, 1990, pp. 227-244.

J. A. Gray, *The Neuropsychology of Anxiety,* Oxford University Press, 1982.

S. Grossman, *The Adaptive Brain,* North-Holland, 1987.

W. W. Harman, "The transpersonal challenge to the scientific paradigm: The need for a restructuring of science", *Revision* 11 (2), 1988, pp. 13-21.

W. W. Harman, *A Re-examination of the Metaphysical Foundations of Modern Science. Causality Issues in Contemporary Science*, Research Report CP-1, Institute of Noetic Sciences, 1991.

H.L.A. Hart and A. M. Honore, *Causation in the Law*, Clarendon Press, 1959.

M. Harter, "Excitability cycles and cortical scanning: A review of two hypotheses of central intermittancy in perception", *Psychological Bulletin* 68, 1967, pp. 47-58.

T. E. Hill, *The Concept of Meaning*, Humanities Press, 1971.

R. Horton and R. Finnegan, *Modes of Thought: Essays on Thinking in Western and Non-Western Societies*, Faber and Faber, 1973.

D. Hume, *A Treatise of Human Nature*, Oxford University Press, 1960 (originally published 1739).

E. Husserl, *Ideas: General Introduction to Pure Phenomenology*, MacMillan, 1931.

E. Husserl, *The Crisis of European Sciences and Transcendental Phenomenology*, Northwestern University Press, 1970.

E. Husserl, *Cartesian Meditations: An Introduction to Phenomenology*, Martinus Nijhoff, 1977.

D. Ihde, *Consequences of Phenomenology*, State University of New York Press, 1986.

D. Ihde, *Technology and the Lifeworld*, Indiana University Press, 1990.

R. G. Jahn and B. J. Dunne, *Margins of Reality: The Role of Consciousness in the Physical World*, Harcourt Brace Jovanovich, 1987.

J. Jaspars, M. Hewstone and F. D. Fincham, "Attribution theory and research: The state of the art" in *Attribution Theory and Research: Conceptual, Developmental and Social Dimensions*, edited by J. Jaspars, F. D. Fincham and M. Hewstone, Academic Press, 1983.

H. J. Jerison, *Evolution of the Brain and Intelligence*, Academic Press, 1973.

H. J. Jerison, "On the evolution of mind", *Brain and Mind*, edited by D. A. Oakley, Methuen, 1985.

D. J. Kalupahana, *Causality: The Central Philosophy of Buddhism*, The University Press of Hawaii, 1975.

A. Harry Klopf, *The Hedonistic Neuron*, Hemisphere, 1982.

T. S. Kuhn, *The Structure of Scientific Revolutions* (2nd edition), University of Chicago Press, 1970.

T. S. Kuhn, *The Essential Tension*, University of Chicago Press, 1977.

I. Lakatos, *Criticism and the Growth of Knowledge*, Cambridge University Press, 1970.

S. Lash, *Sociology of Postmodernism*, Routledge, 1990.

C. D. Laughlin, "The prefrontosensorial polarity principle: Toward a neurophenomenology of intentionality", *Biological Forum* 81, 1988, pp. 245-262.

C. D. Laughlin, "Transpersonal anthropology: Some methodological issues", *Western Canadian Anthropologist* 5, 1989, pp. 29-60.

C. D. Laughlin, "Pre- and perinatal brain development and enculturation: A biogenetic structural approach", *Human Nature* 2 (3), 1991, pp. 171-213.

C. D. Laughlin, *The Mirror of the Brain: A Neurophenomenology of Mature Contemplation* (manuscript, n.d.).

C. D. Laughlin, *Scientific Explanation and the Life-World: A Biogenetic Structural Theory of Meaning and Causation*, Institute of Noetic Sciences, Causality Project, Report No. CP-2, 1992.

C. D. Laughlin and E. G. d'Aquili, *Biogenetic Structuralism*, Columbia University Press, 1974.

C. D. Laughlin and I. A. Brady, editors, *Extinction and Survival in Human Populations*, Columbia University Press, 1978.

C. D. Laughlin, J. McManus and E. G. d'Aquili, *Brain, Symbol and Experience*, Columbia University Press, 1990.

C. D. Laughlin, J. McManus, R. A. Rubinstein and J. Shearer, "The ritual control of experience", *Studies in Symbolic Interaction, Part A,* edited by Norman K. Denzin, JAI Press, 1986.

D. M. Levin, *The Open Vision: Nihilism and the Postmodern Situation*, Routledge, 1988.

C. Levi-Strauss, *The Savage Mind*, University of Chicago Press, 1966.

L. Levy-Bruhl, *Primitive Mentality,* 1966 edition, Beacon Press, 1923.

A. Lima-de-Faria, *Evolution Without Selection: Form and Function by Autoevolution,* Elsevier, 1988.

G. R. Lucas, *The Rehabilitation of Whitehead: An Analytical and Historical Assessment of Process Philosophy*, State University of New York Press, 1989.

A. R. Luria, *Higher Cortical Functions in Man*, Basic Books, 1966.

J. L. Mackie, *The Cement of the Universe: A Study of Causation*, Clarendon, 1974.

M. Mandelbaum, *The Anatomy of Historical Knowledge,* Johns Hopkins University Press, 1977.

M. Merleau-Ponty, *The Primacy of Perception,* Northwestern University Press, 1964.

A. Michotte, *The Perception of Causality*, Basic Books, 1963.

L. Mills and G. B. Rollman, "Hemispheric asymmetry for auditory perception of temporal order", *Neuropsychologia* 18, 1980, pp. 41-47.

A. Naess, *Ecology, Community and Lifestyle: Outline of an Ecosophy*, Cambridge University Press, 1989.

W.J.H. Nauta, "The problem of the frontal lobe: A reinterpretation", *Journal of Psychiatric Research* 8, 1971, pp. 167-187.

U. Neisser, *Cognition and Reality*, Freeman, 1976.

E. Neumann, *The Great Mother*, Princeton University Press, 1963.

F.S.C. Northrup, *The Logic of the Sciences and the Humanities*, Macmillan, 1947.

C. K. Ogden and I. A. Richards, *The Meaning of Meaning* (8th edition), Harcourt Brace Jovanovich, 1923.

R. E. Passingham, "Anatomical differences between the neocortex of man and other primates", *Brain Behavior Evolution* 7, 1973, pp. 337-359.

J. Piaget, *The Biology of Knowledge,* University of Chicago Press, 1971.

J. Piaget, *Understanding Causality*, Norton, 1974.

J. Piaget, *The Development of Thought*, The Viking Press, 1977.

J. Piaget, *The Equilibration of Cognitive Structures,* University of Chicago Press, 1985

K. R. Popper, *Objective Knowledge: An Evolutionary Approach,* Oxford University Press, 1972.

W. T. Powers, *Behavior: The Control of Perception*, Aldine, 1973.

D. Premack, *Intelligence in Ape and Man*, Lawrence Erlbaum, 1976.

K. H. Pribram, *Languages of the Brain*, Prentice-Hall, 1971.

K. H. Pribram and A.R. Luria, *Psychophysiology of the Frontal Lobes*, Academic Press, 1973.

V. S. Ramachandran and S. M. Anstis, "The perception of apparent motion", *Scientific American* 254 (6), 1986, pp. 102-109.

F. Rapp and R. Wiehl, *Whitehead's Metaphysics of Creativity*, State University of New York Press, 1990.

R. A. Rappaport, *Pigs for the Ancestors*, Yale University Press, 1968.

R. Ridington and T. Ridington, "The inner eye of shamanism and totemism", *History of Religions* 10 (1), 1970, pp. 49-61.

M. Rokeach, *The Open and Closed Mind*, Basic Books, 1960.

R. A. Rubinstein, C. Laughlin and J. McManus, *Science as Cognitive Process*, University of Pennsylvania Press, 1984.

J. A. Sanford, "A periodic basis for perception and action" in *Biological Rhythms and Human Performance,* edited by W. Colquhuon, Academic Press, 1971.

E. von Savigny, *The Social Foundations of Meaning*, Springer-Verlag, 1988.

S. R. Schiffer, *Meaning*, Clarendon Press, 1972.

A. Schutz and T. Luckman, *The Structures of the Life-World,* Northwestern University Press, 1973.

A. Schutz and T. Luckmann, *The Structures of the Life-World: Vol. II*, Northwestern University Press, 1989.

M. Scriven, "Definitions, explanations, and theories" in *Minnesota Studies in the Philosophy of Science, Vol. II: Concepts, Theories, and the Mind-Body Problem,* University of Minnesota Press, 1958, pp. 99-195.

J. Searle, *Mind, Brain and Science,* British Broadcasting Corporation, 1984.

E. S. Spelke, "Where perceiving ends and thinking begins: The apprehension of objects in infancy" in *Perceptual Development in Infancy,* edited by A. Yonas, Erlbaum, 1988a.

E. S. Spelke, "The origins of physical knowledge" in *Thought Without Language*, edited by L. Weiskrantz, Clarendon Press, 1988b.

R. W. Sperry, "Structure and significance of the consciousness revolution", *Journal of Mind and Behavior* 8 (1), 1987, pp. 37-66.

H. Spiegelberg, *The Phenomenological Movement: A Historical Introduction, 3rd edition,* Martinus Nijhoff, 1982.

M. Steriade and M. Deschenes, "The thalamus as a neuronal oscillator", *Brain Research Reviews* 8, 1985, pp. 1-63.

D. T. Stuss and D. F. Benson, *The Frontal Lobes*, Raven, 1986.

F. Suppe, editor, *The Structure of Scientific Theories, 2nd edition,* University of Illinois Press, 1977.

F. Suppe, *The Semantic Conception of Theories and Scientific Realism*, University of Illinois Press, 1989.

L. Swisher and I. Hirsch, "Brain damage and the ordering of two temporally successive stimuli", *Neuropsychologia* 10, 1971, pp. 137-152.

P. Tillich, *Systematic Theology*, University of Chicago Press, 1963.

S. E. Toulmin, *Human Knowledge*, Princeton University Press, 1972.

S. E. Toulmin, *The Return to Cosmology: Postmodern Science and the Theology of Nature*, University of California Press, 1982.

L. Van der Hammen, *Unfoldment and Manifestation*, SPB Academic Publishing, 1988.

F. J. Varela, *Principles of Biological Autonomy,* Elsevier North Holland, 1979.

F. J. Varela et al., "Perceptual framing and cortical alpha rhythm", *Neuropsychologia* 19 (5), 1981, pp. 675-686.

C. H. Waddington, *The Strategy of the Genes*, George Allen and Unwin, 1957.

A.F.C. Wallace, *Religion: An Anthropological View*, Random House, 1966.

J. A. Wheeler, "Law without law" in *Quantum Theory and Measurement*, edited by J. A. Wheeler and W. H. Zure, Princeton University Press, 1983 .

A. N. Whitehead, *Modes of Thought*, Cambridge University Press, 1938.

A. N. Whitehead, "Uniformity and contingency" in *Essays in Science and Philosophy*, Philosophical Library, 1947, pp. 132-148.

A. N. Whitehead, *An Enquiry Concerning the Principles of Natural Knowledge,* Cambridge University Press, 1955.

A. N. Whitehead, *Concept of Nature*, Cambridge University Press, 1964.

A. N. Whitehead, *Process and Reality: An Essay in Cosmology* (the corrected edition by D. R. Griffin and D. W. Sherburne), The Free Press, 1978.

K. Wilber, *The Atman Project: A Transpersonal View of Human Development*, The Theosophical Publishing House, 1980.

K. Wilber, *Up From Eden*, Shambhala, 1983.

A. Woodiwiss, *Social Theory after Postmodernism,* Pluto, 1990.

P. Young, *The Nature of Information*, Praeger, 1987.

W.H.A. Zurek, A. van der Merwe and W. T. Miller, *Between Quantum and Cosmos*, Princeton University Press, 1988.

If you think about it, you will see that it is true

by Vine Deloria Jr.

The movement toward a "science of wholeness" depends in large measure on the ability of philosophers and scientific thinkers to move beyond their comfortable and presently accepted categories of arranging and interpreting data to glimpse and grasp new unities of experience and knowledge. In order to do this, we must first ask fundamental questions about the goals of science. Do we wish to predict or describe? At what level do we wish to do either of these things? What does it mean to have knowledge that is applicable to the world around us and to have it arranged in a systematic manner? What systems are applicable to the different kinds of data derived at the different levels at which scientific inquiry can be conducted? How are data derived from a causative-dominated methodology to be combined with insights or information created by simple observation or intuitive visions?

Some Western thinkers have recently begun to examine the knowledge and insights which non-Western peoples had about the natural world. Part of this movement is a popular fad which romanticizes the primitive and his relationship to his pristine environment, but part is also a sincere attempt to reach out and gain new insights and perspectives. Even with the flexible scientific paradigm of relativity and indeterminacy, there are strong indications that we have reached a dead end in many sciences and perhaps need new insights derived from other sources. So why not tribal knowledge?

Most recent efforts have been limited to gathering specific information: plant knowledge, fishing practices, forms of pottery making, and irrigation and forest management burning techniques. In psychoanalysis, the Jungians are exploring similarities between Western archetypal figures and tribal legends and folk-heroes. More recent efforts have been made to gain knowledge of the use of plants which have certain curative powers. Jurisprudence is examining new kinds of mediation techniques and different victim compensation theories for minor offenses to replace retribution as the theoretical basis for criminal law, thereby even modifying the concept of the social contract itself. Many approaches are being taken to incorporate tribal values and knowledge into Western thought systems, but as yet no systematic comparison of tribal and scientific knowledge of the natural world has been made.

One reason that scientists examine non-Western knowledge on an *ad hoc* basis is the persistent belief held by Western intellectuals that non-Western peoples represent an earlier stage of their own cultural evolution—often that tribal cultures represent failed efforts to understand the natural world (the Incas had wheels, why didn't they make cars?). Non-Western knowledge is believed to originate from primitive efforts to explain a mysterious universe. In this view, the alleged failure of primitive/tribal man to control nature mechanically is evidence of his ignorance and his inability to conceive of abstract general principles and concepts. Tribal methodologies for gathering information are believed to be "pre-scientific" in the sense that they are pre-causal and incapable of objective symbolic thought. This belief, as we shall see, is a dreadful stereotypical reading of the knowledge of non-Western peoples, and wholly incorrect.

In fact, tribal peoples are as systematic and philosophical as Western scientists in their efforts to understand the world around them. They simply use other kinds of data and have goals other than determining the mechanical functioning of things. A good way to determine the relevance of tribal knowledge and illustrate its potential for providing insights for the present body of scientific knowledge is to examine some of the knowledge of a particular tribe and discuss what they knew and how they gathered this information. I would like to take a few selections from a historical report on the philosophy of the Western Teton Sioux to illustrate my points.

I. The Indian Perspective

In late August of 1919, A. McG. Beede, a missionary on the Standing Rock Sioux reservation in North Dakota, sent Melvin Gilmore, the Curator of the State Historical Society, a manuscript which discussed the beliefs of the Western Teton Sioux. This paper is regarded as an early and accurate account of the knowledge of the Western Sioux and Chippewa Indians. Beede's discussions with the Indians reveal their basic attitude regarding the knowledge they possessed and their response to the scientific knowledge which Beede and his friend Harry Boise discussed with them. The conversations have a startlingly modern ring to them. Beede wrote:

The Western Sioux believed that each being, a rock for instance, is an actual community of persons with ample locomotion among themselves, and such locomotion not regarded as circumscribed or restricted, save as the maker (oicage) of the whole gives to each species his own sphere. And, they reasoned, this limitation is merely in body (tancan), the mind, intelligence, and spirit of each is privileged to range through and blend with totality by gaining a right attitude toward Woniya (Spirit).[1]

And, I should have said, the fact of a rock, or any object, being a community of locomotive persons, was based, or concomitant with, the belief that not a few of their people actually had the ability to *see into and through* a rock discerning its make-up, similarly as we look into a community or grove of trees. I have known many Indians believing they possessed this ability—and not regarding it as anything remarkable—and there was no occasion for doubting their sincerity.[2] (Emphasis added)

Of course, the history of any people contains mythology (which is, perhaps, not quite so simple or invaluable as many a 'scientist' might assume), but is such a mythology composed entirely of myths added one to another, or is there beneath all and through all and in all an all-compelling something unexplained by our 'scientific' 'force and energy' which the Western Sioux thought of, sincerely claimed to know of, as Woniya (Spirit)? It does not bother the old Indians to understand, in an elementary way, what we mean by 'the modern scientific attitude' . . . [3]

There is no difficulty in leading an old Teton Sioux Indian to understand the 'scientific' attitude, and that the processes that give rise to phenomena may be more and more known by man and may be, to some extent, controlled by man, and that in this way the forces of nature may become a mainspring of progress in the individual and in the human race. The idea of atoms and electrons is easy and pleasing to an old Indian, and he grasps the idea of chemistry. Such things make ready contact with his previous observation and thinking.[4]

In the Turtle Mountains, North Dakota, Harry Boise . . . was with me eight months. At his request I allowed him to teach the old Chippewa and Cree Indians there the modern scientific attitude with its view of things. . . . The chief among his pupils was old Sakan'ku Skonk (Rising Sun) . . . . But Rising Sun, speaking the conclusion of all, pronounced 'the scientific view' inadequate. *Not bad, or untrue, but inadequate to explain, among many other things, how man is to find and know a road along which he wishes and chooses to make this said progress unless the Great Manitoo by his spirit guides the mind of man, keeping human beings just and generous and hospitable.*[5] (Emphasis added.)

The Similarity of Conclusions

These passages give something of the flavor of the knowledge of the old Indians, people who had known the life of freedom before they were confined to the reservations and subjected to Western religious and educational systems. Substitute "energy" for "spirit" in some of these passages, and we have a modern theory of energy/matter. But the similarity, although profound, hides a deeper truth which we must examine. For these two groups, the old Indians and the modern scientists, reach their conclusions in entirely different ways, using data that are completely incompatible if placed together.

The old Indians, as Rising Sun noted, were interested in finding the proper moral and ethical road upon which human beings should walk. All knowledge, if it was to be useful, was directed toward that goal. Absent in this approach was the idea that knowledge existed apart from human beings and their communities, and could stand alone for "its own sake". In the Indian conception, it was impossible that there could be abstract propositions that could be used to explore the structure of the physical world. Knowledge was derived from individual and communal experiences in daily life, in keen observation of the environment, and in interpretive messages which they received from spirits in ceremonies, visions and dreams.

In formulating their understanding of the world, Indians did not discard any experience. Everything had to be included in the spectrum of knowledge and related to what was already known. Since the general propositions which informed the people about the world were the product of generations of tradition and experience, people accepted on faith what they had not experienced, with the hope that during their lifetime they would come to understand.

The Nebraska poet John Neihardt interviewed Black Elk, the Oglala Sioux medicine man, about the beliefs and practices of the old days. During their conversations Black Elk told Neihardt how the Sioux received the sacred White Buffalo Calf Pipe, the central religious object of the Plains Indians. The story involved the appearance of a woman who instructed the people in moral, social, and religious standards and showed them how to communicate with the higher powers through the use of the pipe in ceremonies. After finishing his story, Black Elk paused, was silent for a time, and said:

> This they tell, and whether it happened so or not, I do not know; but if you think about it, you can see that it is true.[6]

This is not only a statement of faith: it is a principle of epistemological method.

If the Western Sioux obtained their knowledge by accepting everything they experienced as grist for the mill, Western science has drawn its conclusions by excluding the kinds of data which the Western Sioux cherished. Western science holds that ideas, concepts, and experiences must be clearly stated, and be capable of replication in an experimental setting by an objective observer. Any bit of data or body of knowledge that does not meet this standard is suspect or rejected out of hand. Thus most emotional experiences of human beings are discarded as unsuitable for the scientific enterprise, or are pushed to the periphery of respectability and grudgingly given a bit of status.

Science further limits itself by insisting that all data fall within the reigning interpretive paradigm of the time. According to Thomas Kuhn, a paradigm primarily enables scientists to classify data and verify whether or not it falls within the acceptable mode of interpretation. One of the things a scientific community acquires with a paradigm, Kuhn explains,

> is a criterion for choosing problems that, while the paradigm is taken for granted, can be assumed to have solutions. To a great extent these are the only problems that the community will admit as scientific or encourage its members to undertake. Other problems, including many that had previously been standard, are rejected as metaphysical, as the concern of another discipline or sometimes as just too problematic to be worth the time.[7]

If science works within this severely restricted arena in which statements have such limited validity, how can we have faith that it is presenting to us anything remotely approaching a reliable knowledge about the world? And why do scientists, knowing these limitations, act so dogmatically about what they know?

Scientific knowledge also has the problem of internal politics, in which prominent scholars can force acceptance or rejection of theories based on wholly extraneous considerations, often a matter of personal preference or the desire for professional status. New research on the relationship between Charles Darwin and Alfred Wallace, for example, shows that it is quite possible that Darwin simply stole Wallace's idea of natural selection and had the right political connections within the English scientific establishment to make good his theft.[8] Such revelations would indicate that there is considerable reason to be skeptical about the findings of Western science, since it excludes a substantial amount of data and allows cliques to determine what is acceptable theory and doctrine.

But how do we explain the Indian perspective on knowledge, which saw no need to engage in the process of developing interpretive frameworks, producing many anomalies, creating *ad hoc* theories, and finally formulating new explanations? How do Indians handle anomalies? For there surely must have been anomalies in a worldview of such relative simplicity?

Indians believed that everything that humans experience has value and instructs us in some aspect of life. The fundamental premise is that we cannot "mis-experience" anything; we can only misinterpret what we experience. Therefore, in some instances we can experience something entirely new, and so we must be alert and not try to classify things too quickly. The world is constantly creating itself because everything is alive and making choices which determine the future. There cannot be such such a thing as an anomaly in this kind of framework: some things are accepted because there is value in the very mystery they represent.

Since, in the Indian system, all data must be considered, the task is to find the proper pattern of interpretation for the great variety of ordinary and extraordinary experiences we have. Ordinary and extraordinary must come together in one coherent comprehensive storyline. Sometimes this narrative will deal with human behavior and sometimes with the behavior of higher powers. But it will have a point to it and will always represent a direction of future growth. Finally, with the wisdom which old age brings, there will be time for reflection and the discovery of unsuspected relationships which make themselves manifest in consciousness and so come to be understood.

The Moral Universe

The real interest of the old Indians was not to discover the abstract structure of physical reality but rather to find the proper road along which, during the duration of a person's life, individuals were supposed to walk. This colorful image of the road suggests that the universe is a moral universe, that is to say, that there is a proper way to live in the universe; there is a content to every action, behavior, and belief; the sum total of our life experiences has a reality. There is a direction to the universe, empirically exemplified in the physical growth cycles of childhood, youth and old age, with the corresponding responsibility of every entity to enjoy life, fulfill itself, and increase in wisdom and the spiritual development of personality. Nothing has incidental meaning and there are no coincidences.

The wise person will realize their own limitations and act with some degree of humility until he or she has sufficient knowledge to act with confidence. Every bit of information must be related to the general framework of moral interpretation since it is personal to them and their community. No body of knowledge exists for its own sake outside the moral framework of understanding. We are, in the truest sense possible, creators or co-creators with the higher powers and what we do has immediate importance for the rest of the universe.

This attitude extends to data and experiences far beyond the immediate physical environment, including the stars, other worlds and galaxies, the other higher and lower planes of existence and the places of higher and lower spiritual activities. If many Indian legends appear to be geocentric, to be restricted to the conditions existing on this Earth, it is because they are formulated in this manner to make the transmission of information easier. But there are many accounts of people traveling to other worlds, of people becoming birds and animals, living with them, and experiencing the great variety of possible modes of existence. In the moral universe all activities, events, and entities are related, and consequently it does not matter what kind of existence an entity enjoys, for the responsibility is always there for it to participate in the continuing creation of reality.

The Teton Sioux and Chippewa knew, for instance, that spirit or energy was the primary mode of physical existence and they had experienced it as having personality, purpose, and moral substance. If we compare their understanding with modern efforts to describe the ultimate physical ground of the universe, we find that Werner Heisenberg suggested that

> the elementary particles of modern physics can be transformed into each other exactly as in the philosophy of Plato. They do not themselves consist of matter, but they are the only possible forms of matter. Energy becomes matter by taking on the form of an elementary particle, by manifesting itself in this form.[9]

Heisenberg, following Einstein, described an implied equation in which energy equals matter. In the Platonic philosophy to which he refers, however, the forms and ideas themselves have an active function in determining shape, content and mode of manifestation, implying that mind undergirds everything else. Heisenberg did not take Plato's hint that the identity of matter and energy is only the beginning of understanding; there is a subsequent path to follow which links knowledge of the natural world with a realm in which human activities have content and meaning. Consequently, although modern physics is greatly admired for its description of physical reality, in fact it is only confronting the boundaries of possible knowledge of the physical world and in doing so has surrendered—for the time being at least—its ability to link its knowledge with other human concerns.

What the Western Sioux sought was the moral content of entities and relationships; they tried to understand their role and function in the natural world, and to come to an understanding, often revealed by the entities themselves, of the actual physical composition of things. Coming from the opposite ends of the spectrum of knowledge and methodology—the Indian representing perhaps the extreme of subjectivity and the Western scientist the extreme of objectivity—these views suggest a middle meeting-ground where contradictions can possibly be resolved. But the content of whatever configuration may exist in the middle would seem to be, following the Western Sioux and Plato, a knowledge of the physical universe arranged or understood in such a manner as to call forth some form of moral response.[10]

This conclusion is anathema to most scientists, whose fear (well-justified considering the history of warfare between sacred and secular forces in Western civilization) is that if such ethical dimensions are admitted, it would once again allow ecclesiastical authorities to gain control of social and political institutions and so prevent or inhibit investigative scientific activities. Thus introducing purpose and morality suggests for many people the existence of a higher entity which can become an object of worship, and thereafter a source of continuing social conflict.

In fact, the old Indians did not see a specific higher personality who demanded worship and adoration in the manner in which we find deity portrayed in the traditions of the Near East. Rather they saw and experienced personality in every aspect of the universe and called it "Woniya" (Spirit), looking to it for guidance in a manner quite similar to Socrates obeying his daemon. I do not believe this perspective is pantheistic in the traditional sense that frightens scientists and religious peoples alike. Even those tribes who projected from the experiences of birds, animals and plants and personified these experiences did not make any particular entity a deity alone and apart from everything else. Most of the tribes were content to stop their description with a simple affirmation of the existence of Spirit. The Sioux, in fact, simply said the "Great Mysterious". Only later, when Christian missionaries attempted to link Sioux traditions to their own religious systems, did this mysterious presence begin to take on human forms and demand a groveling, flattering kind of worship.

II. The Structure of the Tribal Universe

The Plains Indians arranged their knowledge in a circular format, which is to say, there were no ultimate terms or constituents of their universe, only sets of relationships which sought to describe phenomena. No concept could stand alone in the way that time, space, and matter once stood as absolute entities in Western science. All concepts not only had content but were themselves composed of the elements of other ideas to which they were related. Thus it was possible to begin with one idea, thoroughly examine it by relating it to other concepts and arrive back at the starting point with the assurance that a person could properly interpret what constituted the idea and how it might manifest itself in concrete physical experiences.

The purpose of such an arrangement was to be certain that all known aspects of something would be included in the information that people possessed and considered when making decisions and reaching conclusions. There were, therefore, almost limitless ways of describing snow, rain, wind or other natural phenomena, since each particular manifestation of the general concept needed to be described accurately and placed properly within a spectrum of the possibilities of realization. Indian languages, and the Dakota/Lakota language which the Western Sioux used, had a very large vocabulary which enabled people to be specific in remembering and describing the ways that a concept could be realized within human experience.

In the rest of this section, we will try to unravel some aspects of the Sioux circle of knowledge, and make a list of the most important components of the Indian universe. When we do so, we find the following major elements:

1) The universe is alive

2) Everything is related

3) All relationships are historical

4) Space determines the nature of relationships

5) Time determines the meaning of relationships

Other interpreters of the Sioux worldview may differ considerably in the emphasis they place on certain concepts. I feel certain, however, that these principles would emerge if a consensus of the interpreters was achieved.

The Universe is Alive

It cannot be argued that the universe is moral or has a moral purpose without simultaneously maintaining that the universe is alive. The old Indians had no problem with this concept because they experienced life in everything, and there was no reason to suppose that the continuum of life was not universal. The belief in a living universe raises hackles among many scientists today because it raises the spectre of subjectivity and calls to mind the religious perspective, in which the universe is seen as divine. On the other hand, within the Western religions, the idea of the "living universe" is often dismissed as "merely pantheism", as if labeling a belief could thereby explain it.

It has never been clear to me how and why modern science discarded the idea of a living universe so easily. Granted that parts of Western culture require a dead, objective universe in order to avoid the moral questions raised by the wasteful exploitation of resources, and granted that other cultures have gone to extremes in devotional activities in worshiping a living universe, what real basis does science have for maintaining that the universe is largely composed of dead, inert, and personless bits of matter/energy?[11] The fact that, in practice, we treat other parts of the physical world as if they were inert does not, in itself, provide proof that we are correct. What is objectionable about the idea of the universe being alive, and at what point or level of complexity can we say with any assurance that it is dead or devoid of life?

Recent controversy over the living universe has been particularized within science in the debate over the "Gaia Hypothesis", which I consider in detail in the final section of this paper. James Lovelock and a bevy of colleagues, admirers, and followers have raised the question of whether it is helpful to view the planet as a living organism.[12] But the debate has often centered on false arguments, with both the advocates and opponents of the theory restricting the definition of "life" to reactive organic phenomena that are observed primarily in the higher organisms.

Traditional Indians are quite amused to see this revival of the debate over whether or not the planet is alive. Long ago in ceremonies and visions Indians came to experience this truth. The practical criterion that is always cited to demonstrate its validity is the easily observable fact that the Earth nurtures smaller forms of life—people, plants, birds, animals, rivers, valleys and continents. For Indians, both speculation and analogy end at this point. To go further and attribute a plenitude of familiar human characteristics to the Earth is unwarranted. It would cast the planet in the restricted clothing of lesser beings, and we would not be able to gain insights and knowledge about the real essence of the Earth.

Nor was there any reason to suppose that other forms of life did not have the same basic intelligence as humans. The Sioux, as well as other tribes, interpreted the scheme of life as leading eventually to the production of human beings. Unlike Western religion and philosophy, however, the fact that man had been the final product of the purposeful life force did not make him the crown of creation. Coming last, humans beings were the "younger brothers" of the other life forms and therefore had to learn everything from these creatures. Thus human activities resembled bird and animal behavior in many ways and brought the unity of conscious life to an objective consistency.

This idea that everything in the universe is alive, and that the universe itself is alive, is knowledge as useful as anything that Western science has discovered or hypothesized. When understood and made operative by serious and sensitive individuals, it is as reliable a means of making predictions as anything suggested by mathematical formulas or projected by computer programs. There are, however, substantial differences in the manner in which predictions are made. Because the universe is alive, there is choice for all things and the future is always indeterminate. Consequently predictions are based on the knowledge of the "character" of an entity. Statements about how an entity will behave have almost the same probabilities as the educated speculations made at the subatomic level in physics.

Here the Indian knowledge has an edge over Western scientific knowledge. A truly wise and gifted individual can appear to "cause" things to happen because he can participate in the emerging event in a way that rarely occurs in Western science.[13] Thus it is that people are said to have "powers", which is another way of saying that their understanding of natural process and their ability to enter into events is highly developed and sophisticated. The living universe requires mutual respect among its members and this suggests that a strong sense of individual identity and self is a dominant characteristic of the world as we know it.[14] The willingness of entities to allow others to fulfill themselves, and the refusal of any entity to intrude thoughtlessly on another, must be the operative principle of this universe.[15] Consequently self-knowledge and self-discipline are high values of behavior. Only by allowing innovation by every entity can the universe move forward and create the future. This creative participation is always personal and has an aspect of novelty.

Some human cultures, it is true, have exaggerated the idea of respect, transforming it into worship, and have created customs and behaviors that appear very strange to us. The Hindu reverence for all life and the subsequent adoration of cows in the midst of starving human beings strikes us as absurd and unnecessary. But this kind of behavior is not found within the American Indian experience. Respect in the American Indian context does not mean the worship of other forms of life, but involves two attitudes. One attitude is the acceptance of self-discipline by humans and their communities to act responsibly toward other forms of life. The other attitude is to seek to establish communications and covenants with other forms of life on a mutually agreeable basis. Developing responsible self-discipline is not difficult, but it cannot be done in a society in which equality is perceived as sameness and conformity. Sitting Bull, looking with disdain at the white man's educational style, remarked that "it is not necessary that eagles be crows." We would do well to cast a critical glance at our ideas and expectations of democracy, brotherhood, and equality in the light of the demand for self-discipline.

We want to have certain benefits from the physical world. In seeking something for ourselves, we must recognize that obtaining what we want at the expense of other forms of life or of the Earth itself is short-sighted and disrupts the balance which the whole fabric of life requires. Instead of the predatory jungle which the Anglo-Saxon imagination conjures up to analogize life, in which the most powerful swallows up the weak and unprotected, life is better understood as a tapestry, or as a symphony in which each player has a specific part or role to play. We must be in our proper place and we must play our role at the appropriate moment. Mutual respect in many ways is a function of a strong sense of personal and communal identity, and it is significant that most of the tribes described themselves as "the people", a distinct group with clearly defined values and patterns of behavior.

The idea of the covenant, clearly articulated in the Old Testament theology of the prophets, is an early and important concept for tribal peoples. Stories explaining how the people came to hunt the buffalo, how the salmon came to be the major food supply, how bird feathers were incorporated into ceremonial costumes and medicine bundles, all derive from early interspecies communications in which other forms of life agreed to allow themselves to be used in ceremonial and economic ways. A covenant places responsibilities on both parties and provides a means of healing any breach in the relationship. Thus it was that while Indians hunted and fished wild game, they made it a rule that unless they were starving and needed food for survival, they would not take the animals and birds until these creatures had enjoyed a full family life and reproduced their kind. Even today when taking eagles, the Apaches restrict the hunt to late summer or autumn to ensure that the eagles have the chance to mate, raise a family and go through the major cycles of life experiences.

Everything is Related

A living universe within which events and actions have moral content necessarily suggests that all things are related. Not only is everything related, but it also participates in the moral content of events, so responsibility for maintaining the harmony of life falls equally on all creatures. This principle of relatedness appears most often in the religious realm in the phrase "All My Relatives" which is used as an opening invocation and closing benediction for ceremonies. "All My Relatives", believed by many people, including many Indians, to be a merely devout religious sentiment, also has a secular purpose which is to remind us of our responsibility to respect life and to fulfill our covenantal duties. But few people understand that the phrase also describes the epistemology of the Indian worldview, providing the methodological basis for the gathering information about the world.

Western science uses various methods for determining its truths. One of the most common methods is the experimental application of previously derived theories to new kinds of phenomena and the subsequent verification or modification of the theory. But modern science is interested primarily in the physical world and its structure, the search for the ultimate material constituent of the physical universe having been a constant quest since Democritus developed his theory of the atom.

American Indians, understanding that the universe consisted of living entities, were interested in learning how other forms of life behaved, for they saw that every entity had a personality and could exercise a measure of free will and choice. Consequently Indian people carefully observed phenomena in order to determine what relationships existed between and among the various "peoples" of the world. Their understanding of relationships provided the Indians with the knowledge necessary to live comfortably in the physical world and to not unduly intrude into the lives of other creatures.

Some tribes divided the world into specific classifications, initially using obvious criteria, such as the distinction between the "two-leggeds" and "four-leggeds" used by the Plains Indians.[16] Once a class was identified, continued observation enabled people to derive a set of commonalities which the entities of each classification shared and a specific body of information became available. Within the classification of the "two-leggeds" were birds, humans, and the bear. Since the Indians were interested in behavior, they observed what kinds of actions and skills these three groups of peoples had in common. Not only did they learn about bird and bear behavior in a wide variety of circumstances, but recognizing certain kinds of behavior in other species also enabled them to become introspective about their own actions in different settings.

Thus, the bear was the only two-legged creature that hibernated, and so they thought that if the bear did not have to rid his body of wastes and toxins periodically, he must have some powers of self-healing. Consequently much of the observation of the bear was directed toward his diet; whatever the bear ate, people considered edible for human beings also. Herbs and plants which the bear ate or applied to his body were used by the Indians for the same purposes. This knowledge was cumulative, required precise constant observation, and involved the development of a memory with almost computer-like retrieval capability. To discover a plant that the bear used for a skin disease, for example, people might have to recall instances substantially separated in time and space in which they had seen a bear with a deteriorating coat rubbing himself in a specific bush. Scientists today could not make such acute observations because they would not credit the bear with either intelligence or knowledge about the world.[17]

Similarly, the birds were regarded as messengers of the higher spiritual forces, and when they made an appearance people paid close attention to their behavior. Depending on what kind of bird arrived, the time of year and how he behaved, the message might vary considerably. People believed that birds understood the proper behavior for stable family relations because they saw the bird parents sharing responsibility for raising the chicks. Unlike many other young, young birds in their helplessness greatly resembled human babies, and so the connection between birds and humans was seen to be quite comparable in terms of the family. Many tribal social codes and communal customs were derived from watching the birds build nests, feed their young, and teach them. Again, whatever the birds ate was carefully noted and often the same seeds and fruits were gathered and used for similar purposes.

Almost all the medicinal plants used were originally received in one way or another from birds. These plants were made into teas and broths or were crushed for poultices to be applied to parts of the body. Plants could only be used in that manner; to consider "breaking down" the plant into its constituent chemical element parts and producing aspirin or Bufferin as modern scientists do would have been regarded as a violation of the spirit of the plant and prohibited. People would have been afraid that although the derived medicine was helpful, in violating the integrity of the plant a harmful by-product might have been produced. Indians assumed that elements of a plant were supposed to be together and consequently they did not venture to try to get at the "essence" of a thing and produce an artificial product.

People would sometimes have dreams in which the spirit of the bird, plant or animal would appear and provide information on the use which these creatures made of plants and herbs. The person to whom the dream or vision came then was authorized to gather the plants and herbs and use them medicinally. There are many stories about the way that the plants called attention to themselves and offered to show how they should be used. People say that the cottonwood tree taught the people how to make tipis when they first went on the plains and that proper tipi robes, when laid out on the ground, formed the outline of the cottonwood leaf.[18]

If we could imagine a world in which human concerns were not the primary value, and we observed nature in the old Indians' way, we would observe a plant (or a bird or animal) for a prolonged period of time. We would note what time of year the plant began to grow and green out; when it blossomed; when it bore fruit; how many fruits or seeds it produced; what animals and birds ate the fruit and when during the maturation process they appeared; what colors its leaves and fruits took on during the various parts of the growing season; whether it shed its leaves and needles and what birds and animals made use of them; and many other kinds of behavior of the plant. From these observations we would come to understand both the plant and its life stages. By remembering the birds and animals who made use of the plant—and when they did so during the calendar year and when in terms of their own growth cycles—we would have a reasonable idea of how useful the plant would be for us.

This knowledge, however, would still be general and would need further refining. At certain times some men and women would receive, either in dreams or in visions, very precise knowledge on other ways in which the plant could be used by humans—information which could not have been obtained through experiment or trial and error use. Some knowledge was so precise that it might only be needed once in a human lifetime.[19] And of course tribes often shared their knowledge of plants or even traded medicinal plants back and forth across large distances so that the knowledge of plants took on an encyclopedic aspect.

In general, women were more likely to have plant knowledge than men, because it was the women who gathered the food from plants and because, at least in the eastern part of the continent, they owned the lands and gardens, and so had to establish their own relationship with the plants. Among the Six Nations, for example, there was a very large body of plant knowledge dominated by three domestic plants: Squash, Beans, and Corn. These plants were called the "Three Sisters" and the stories tell that, being siblings, they grew better if planted together. The fact that we now know that these plants make a natural nitrogen cycle demonstrates that Indian plant knowledge had accurate results comparable to modern scientific explanations.

All Relationships are Historical

Part of the experience of life is the passage of time, the fact of personal growth, and the understanding of oneself produced by reflective memory processes. Since the universe was known by the Indians to be alive, it followed that all entities had some memory and enjoyed the experience of the passage of time. Thus relationships were understood as enduring in time and were characterized by the same kinds of disruptive historic events as we see in human history. All covenants wore out and changes seemed to occur in the same way as they do in human experience. Thus plants might gather together for a long time but then suddenly disappear, beginning to grow in different areas or adapting themselves to new lands and climatic conditions. We call this kind of change evolution today, but the old Indians did not see it that way. They knew that any changes that occurred were already inherent in the creature, or within its potentiality for change—a possibility which some Western scientists are now beginning to accept.

The historical dimension of relationships is very useful for the purposes of understanding Indian psychology and religion. Succeeding generations of a family will have the same medicine birds, animals and plants, even though each generation may encounter these animal helpers in entirely different ways and in contradictory circumstances. When these medicine helpers are known, it is possible, without knowing any family member personally, to give an accurate description of the personalities of each generation and something of their knowledge, role in the tribe, and accomplishments. This knowledge has been kept reasonably intact in most tribes and figures in contemporary politics and education as much as other considerations. And the knowledge can be used to predict how living members of the family will act in any given situation. A recent article on multiple personality therapy performed on an Indian suggests that it is possible to tap into these unsuspected family relationships with other forms of life.[20]

Knowledge of the historical relationships can be exceedingly useful in modern science in providing guidance for ecological restoration projects. The appearance or disappearance of a certain plant can be used to predict similar behavior by related plants and animals. We must note, however, that the relationships established by the Indians are personal relationships between and among other forms of life, and therefore they do not necessarily follow the definitions established by Western scientific systems of classifications. Thus the characteristics that modern botanists and biologists use to define species and genera are not comparable in many respects to the Indian classification by personality types.

A good judgment of the accuracy of Indian knowledge and Western scientific knowledge might be made by allowing Indians and scientists to restore similar tracts of land according to different conceptions of what kinds of life can be sustained on the land. In recent years, for instance, the near-extinct prairie chicken has made a comeback in areas where it had not been seen for decades and some Indians attribute this re-emergence to a change in plants to more traditional varieties on lands that produced wheat and imported grains for many years.

Space Determines the Nature of Relationships

Although the preliminary discussion of the living universe has emphasized spiritual/personality values, the idea that everything is related has definite space/time relevance. Here perhaps we begin to speak mysteriously and vaguely when we try to explain concepts. For most forms of life there appears to be a definite pattern of spatial existence. With plants it is not difficult to see that they are restricted to certain locations, although in fact they can move if they so desire. Most locations of plants can be easily explained by reference to soil, climate, and availability of water. But many medicine men spoke of the places which the various entities were destined to occupy, and of the beginning of a world age as a time when everything was in its proper place. Some of the language appears to be quasi-Aristotelian in that they attributed a sense of purpose to an entity without having evidence of it. But since each entity has a set of relationships with other entities, all of these relationships were established in a particular geometric pattern and manifested themselves in spatial arrangements. Thus people became concerned when a plant or animal was found in a place where it should not be.

There were basically three major manifestations of space in the Sioux universe: the ceremonial directions; the sacred places which define meaning for the life around them; and the particular place which each species, including particular groups of humans, comes to occupy and live in.

1) The Ceremonial Directions

These were the most abstract expression of the idea of space. Each entity, and by extension each place, was the center of the universe—thinking which fits well with scientific relativity theory. In ceremonies the object was to draw into participation all the powerful elements of the cosmos. So the sacred pipe was offered to the four directions, to the sky and the Earth, and acknowledgment was made that at every ceremonial the center of the ritual action is the seventh direction—which is the "here and now". Since distance was not regarded as a meaningful obstacle when spiritual powers were invoked, each ceremony began with a representation of the whole cosmos, whether it was a vision quest pit, a sweat lodge, the bowl of the pipe itself, or a Sun Dance arbor.

The object of ceremonial is to make whole again what has now become disassociated and chaotic. In order to accomplish this goal, all possible elements of the universe must be brought within a harmony; sacrifices must be made to heal the injuries of each party, and a new beginning must be made. Some observers are correct when they describe a ceremony as "world-renewing", since the object of ceremony is to cleanse the participants and offer them a new beginning. But they are wrong when they interpret renewal as simply symbolic in the Western sense of representation. Without the four directions, in the Sioux understanding, the world would not have its physical structure; sky and Earth are necessary for human and animal existence, and the center itself represents all possible times taking place simultaneously. In practical terms relationships are renewed and restored and must be conducted in accordance with the structure of the human universe of the directions once again.

2) Sacred Places

The Sioux also understood the Earth to have special places of power and significance and these places were regarded as sacred in the sense that they required respect and human self-discipline. The Black Hills, for example, were sacred because they were at the center of the Sioux universe (as represented by Bear Butte on the eastern edge of the Hills) and because they were set aside by the higher powers as a sanctuary for the birds and animals.[21] Scattered in many different locations throughout the Sioux lands were certain other places where revelations had been given to the people or they had experienced a spiritual presence. Today people try to see if the stories that are told about these places have any basis in historical fact because each generation seems to know the places—even though, in many instances, the people are not allowed to go there because they are owned by private parties or are on federal and state lands from which Indians are often excluded.

Every tribe admitted the existence of these holy places and there was a general amnesty in warfare that allowed people to visit sacred places undisturbed. The Pipestone Quarry in Minnesota, for example, was used by a large number of tribes to gather stone for ceremonial pipes, even though the Yankton Sioux were universally regarded as the spiritual guardians of the spot. Information going back beyond human memory held that as people approached this place thunder would rumble and a wind would blow sprightly.[22] Human behavior, as well as the behavior of other forms of life, was significantly changed at these places and therefore continuing relationships were subject to the superior spiritual power of these places.

3) Particular Places

Finally there was the idea that particular places were designed for particular species, and, in human terms, for particular peoples. Long ago, even before kinship relations were established, a Sioux man had a dream about the great island hill[23] toward which the people were supposed to migrate. In the course of tribal history the people wandered through the southeastern United States, into Pennsylvania and west toward the Great Lakes, until finally they came to the Black Hills where they were destined to live. After finding the proper place, migrations ceased and the people took on ceremonial duties for particular locations.

The importance of finding the proper living space is illustrated by plants and animals. Will and Hyde note that there were different varieties of corn for each climate belt along the Missouri River and consequently tribes living along the river could trade the corn they grew for other corn as goods.[24] In the Pacific Northwest, tribes would share a river and catch salmon at a bewildering variety of locations, from the mouth of the river to the final spawning grounds. Since the chemistry of the salmon was changing as the fish went upstream, different ways of preserving the catch were used at each location. Each place determined the various life forms it would support and these creatures then worked cooperatively at their chosen location.

The implications for Western science of the idea of a special place are tremendous. Knowing the sets of relationships between the various plants and animals enables one to predict what kinds of species will be present in a healthy environment, and so failure to locate a species in a particular location will alert people about the condition of the place. Within that place, however, one will also find the most precise examples of species since the place itself affects things. An understanding of particularity might have helped Darwin reach a different conclusion about species of birds in the Gallapagos. Most important, however, for cultural and philosophical understanding is the recognition that species adapt themselves to the Earth and within limits do not change it without suffering the consequences.

Time Determines the Meaning of Relationships

Time is a complicated concept in a living universe. The basic pattern seems to be that of growth processes, which is to say that time has qualitative packets of quanta that are regulated by the amount of time it takes an organism or entity to complete a step in maturation. Thus all entities are regulated by the seasons and their interaction has a superior season of its own which encompasses their relationship and has a moral purpose. Tribes broke human patterns down into several steps: pre-birth, babies, children, youth, adults, mature adults, and elders.[25] The idea of the "seven generations" was commonly used by the Plains tribes to describe the relationships existing within a genetic family. If a family was respectable and responsible, its members would be granted old age and a person could live long enough to see and know his great-grandparents and his great-grandchildren. Thus generations, and not decades, were the measure of human life.

Since there was interspecies communication between humans and other forms of life, people also became aware of larger cycles of time which can be described as the time jointly shared by all forms of life within a geographical area. This time line seems to have been dominated by the idea of vocation and/ or the idea of the fullness of time. In some undetermined manner, the universe had a direction to it: every entity had a part to play in the creation of the future, and human beings had a special vocation in which they initiated, at the proper time, new relationships and events. In the experience of the Vision Quest people were given the basic outlines of their lives, but not specific predictions as to when, in chronological time, certain events might occur.[26] During the ceremonial experiences, as the years passed, humans would be told when and how the larger cosmic time was moving and would at times be urged to hurry—or counseled to wait until conditions were right for them to play their particular role.

There was a profound sense of determinacy within this aspect of time, but there was also flexibility, so that sequences of action which people knew were to take place did not necessarily have to occur in a manner that people understood or could anticipate. This sense of a determined sequence of specific future actions was seen as evidence that the Earth was a living being and that smaller entities were her children and subject to the larger motions of the universe.

On more everyday levels, there was the recognition that over a long period of time human behavior itself changed as the people perceived, or had revealed to them through ceremonials, the occasional behavior of other life forms which indicated the depth of power contained within them. Thus a people could live on a tract of land for generations without suspecting or perceiving that a certain plant was edible or could be used for medicinal purposes. As the special cases began to accumulate, additional knowledge was gained about the location and its life forms and the full meaning of the relationship became apparent. This increased knowledge was important because it enhanced the precision with which humans used the plants and animals and increased the respect paid to certain other life forms. So, in general, it was recognized that not all information is available to us immediately; some things may simply come into being during the course of time.

Also, because of the passage of time, plants, birds, and animals sometimes withdrew from their relationship with people, or uses changed and they did not reappear for several generations. Or humans abused a relationship and found that the creature withdrew from its role in the environment. Medicine men taught that plants and animals do not become extinct—they go away and do not come back until the location is being treated properly. This belief is being verified today in ecological restoration projects. Lands abused for generations, if treated properly and with respect, will see a flowering of plants which once lived there and which were believed to be extinct, and the birds and animals related to those plants will return. It is worth noting that the plants return first, then the animals, and finally the birds. (Thus antelope have returned to some portions of the Dakota plains but prairie chickens have still not made a complete return.)

Western science is committed to the doctrine of evolution and consequently sees changes in plants, birds, and animals as responding to the passage of time and changes in the environment. While science cannot adequately explain the mechanism of evolution, it regards changes as permanent. The Sioux traditional people say that the important thing is the spirit of the creature; that it can and does change aspects of its physical shape in order to deal with change, but that basically it remains the same entity. Since the Indian interest is in the spirit or soul of the other creature and not in its morphology, some substitutions can be made in ceremonial objects providing the substituted materials have the same spiritual relationship to people that the former objects had.[27]

In outlining the Sioux knowledge of the physical universe, and attempting to demonstrate the principles which govern it, we are able to see new applications and interpretation of our existing knowledge. In the next section, I shall consider how these ideas could become accessible to contemporary scientists, and what kind of barriers stand in the way of this happening.

III. The Conversation with Modern Science

There are some obvious difficulties in the exchange of ideas when this traditional Indian perspective is asked to speak to the modern Western scientific mind. The Indian's knowledge has to be accorded some credibility until it can be demonstrated in its proper context, for, in a fundamental sense, Indian knowledge is much too "practical" for Western science. That is to say, its applicability to the world around us is primarily as a part of daily living. Only with great difficulty can it be translated into scientific doctrines or philosophical statements that have any relevance for understanding our world in a general, objective way. Since its basis is personal relationship, Indian knowledge is perfectly suited to people living in a predominately natural environment; to the degree that the environment reflects the technological industrial society of today, it is increasingly ineffective since it is based on mutually beneficial participation and not the desire for control of nature.

The best avenue we can pursue at present is to identify the areas in which attitudes can be softened and efforts to translate meanings initiated. Thus, although I have entitled this section of the paper "the conversation", what I really mean is that if we can make some changes in attitude and perspective among scientists in certain areas, roadblocks will be removed which will enable us to begin serious conversations across cultural lines. I do not project direct communications back and forth, although some very constructive conversations are being held today. But the context in which these conversations are being held is on an individual, face-to-face basis between Western peoples willing to cast aside their presuppositions and Indians who feel a need to communicate some of their ideas. Unfortunately these encounters are more isolated than we would suppose, with the result that few consistent transfers of ideas are occurring in a context which would ensure that the conversations continue.

I will therefore highlight a number of topics which I believe should be placed on the agenda of Western science for serious consideration. Several of them involve general cultural attitudes which transcend the field of science and represent the general posture of Western culture toward other peoples. As such they may be too politically difficult to resolve. But they have been present from the beginning of cultural encounter and will continue to color efforts to exchange ideas.

Racism

Racial attitudes have almost totally precluded any meaningful discussion of important topics between American Indians and Western scientists and thinkers. At best American Indians are regarded as "quaint" (if not poetic and noble) creatures, but rarely have Indians been understood as intelligent beings. The major attraction of the Indian has been the exotic nature of his way of life and the strange beliefs which he appears to represent. Part of this sense of the strange is generated by the orientation of the tribal peoples toward the objects of the natural world, which to many non-Indians appears to be childish.

One of the problems with communication is that Indians assume that their counterparts in the conversation speak from a holistic point of view. Therefore their statements are direct and specific, and while phrased in simple terms, they are to be taken literally. Questions are always answered with a great deal of specificity. Thus the question "What do you know about the stars?" may not elicit any response at all, or it may call forth a fable or legend which seems to avoid the question altogether. The reason is that this question is altogether too general; it asks that the speaker choose from his understanding some item that might be of interest to the questioner. A much better way of handling this situation might be to ask "What can you tell me about the stars?"

Let us examine what this new question means. The query is phrased to allow the Indian to respond specifically because it identifies a limit which he can understand and immediately apply. He can respond by telling what he knows—understood as revealing the extent of his knowledge—or he can tell what he is allowed to tell to outsiders without revealing specific knowledge that is prohibited to them. A third possible context exists; it may be the wrong time of year to speak of stars at all, as most tribes do not speak of the stars during the summertime. What the Indian could never do, under any circumstances, is to tell everything he knows about the stars, because that would involve having the outsider around from then on so that when occasions arose in which specific knowledge could be passed on, the questioner would be present and available to be told the information.

None of these contexts are present in the mind of the non-Indian questioner. He always approaches the Indian expecting to hear great and wondrous tales. If nothing important is forthcoming, he decides that the Indian knows nothing at all about the subject—a conclusion for which cultural and racial stereotypes have already prepared him. The further assumption made by non-Indians is that the Indian understands the question and strongly desires to provide the non-Indian with the truth—since that is the expectation of the non-Indian. But the answer, regardless of the question, must fall within the categories and classifications already established in the mind of the non-Indian.

Often, the Indian begins his exposition with a statement that has great validity at many levels of communication within his own cultural context. To respond to a question about plants or animals with the statement that "they were created that way" only invokes rejection from the non-Indian, for whom evolution is the only acceptable explanation of the origins of life. Yet what the Indian is really saying is that the plant or animal behavior has been consistent since Indians have been observing them and that it therefore at minimum represents something permanent which cannot be taken lightly.

Western science also requires certification in order to recognize expertise. Consequently the Indian possessor of information is always submerged by the crowd of non-Indians who have "studied" a tribe or custom, and who have their own interpretation of data and a vital interest in maintaining their control over its interpretation. I know many instances in which Indian experts have been denied any status within the non-Indian world, whereas white scholars who have spent a minimal period of time with the community, who have no roots in it and who do not speak its language, follow its customs or attend its ceremonies, are acceptable articulators of the tribal way.

I personally have doubts about whether this barrier can be overcome. A visit to any bookstore will reveal shelf after shelf of books written by non-Indians claiming to represent various aspects of Indian traditional knowledge. The trend seems to be one of taking the knowledge and religion of the Indians and recasting it in comforting terms for non-Indian consumption. Although many Indians complain about the theft of ideas and symbols, my concern is much deeper. How can non-Indians ever learn any of these things if they rush to print and practice before they really understand what symbols and beliefs mean?

Is Philosophical Perspective Racially Grounded?

The difference between Indians and other peoples in the way they process their information is so profound that one must ask whether philosophical perspectives are not racially grounded; that is to say, is there some fundamental element of human personality inherited in the genes that determines the way that different peoples interpret data? This question is important because we already have studies showing certain groups of people to be more susceptible or vulnerable to different viruses and illnesses than others. Who can give a good explanation for Indian vulnerability to diabetes, or African-American suscepti-bility to sickle-cell anemia? In the kindest way, we have allowed our findings about the health of different groups to become part of medical science without exploiting the race question (although some sociobiologists and conservative politicians have made white supremacy a theme to be exploited—usually based on IQ tests which highly favor affluent whites).

The question now is whether or not we will allow the recognition of differences in how the world is perceived. Lucien Levy-Bruhl, in *How Natives Think*, made the following observation:

> One specially noticeable form of the memory so highly developed in natives is that which preserves to the minutest detail the aspect of regions they have traversed, and this permits their retracing their steps with a confidence which amazes Europeans. Among North American Indians this topographical memory is something marvellous; *it is quite enough for them to have been in a place only once for them to have an exact image of it in their minds*, and one which will never be lost. However vast and untraveled a forest may be, they cross it without losing their way, once they have got their bearings.[28] (Emphasis added).

It might seem that Levy-Bruhl was exaggerating, but in fact a very high percentage of American Indians, even those people who have grown up in the urban areas and not experienced the openness of reservation lands, can immediately learn rural and wilderness landscapes as if they were seasoned woodsmen.[29] It would be comforting to believe that it is simply a case of resocialization, but the phenomenon seems to be much deeper than that. Carl Jung toyed with the idea of a racial unconsciousness somewhere within the collective unconscious and it seems to me that the racial question needs to be examined at this depth.[30]

With the tensions created by the five centuries of Western exploitation of the planet and non-Western peoples, this topic can only be discussed with extreme delicacy. Yet reflecting on these kinds of differences instead of passing them off as ethnic quirks might lead us to an examination of the possibility of psychic genetics as a real phenomenon of the natural world which we have not previously suspected. Since differences between species is so easily noted in the other forms of life, we should not immediately discard such a possibility. In the traditional knowledge of the Indians, for instance, many tribes had perceived fundamental differences in people, and attempted a classification, dividing their population into summer and winter people, sky and Earth people, etc. It was believed that these distinctions represented something more than social convenience.

Traditional elders have told me that certain tribes have a particular knowledge or skill. They liken this knowledge to the different species of birds building different kinds of nests and animals preparing different burrows or dens. In scientific terms, this analogy between human beings and animals might be rejected, since species are not supposed to be able to mate successfully and human ethnic and racial groups can all successfully intermarry. But the barrier to understanding here is the adoption of the scientific method of classification as the absolute standard and the expectation that all data will fall within its parameters.

Clearly, races and ethnic groups should be treated impartially by social and political institutions, but we should also be prepared to recognize that there are some real differences in behavior, temperament, and capability represented in racial and ethnic groups. One difference might be the basic response to and understanding of the physical world since this attitude would be derived from the group's historical experiences. Recognizing such inherent differences in perspective should provide us with a much larger philosophical context within which to examine fundamental questions.

The Critique of Absolutism

There must be a radical, critical self-examination of the doctrines of Western science. Science must turn into itself and rework many of its basic premises. It must identify, admit to, and discard the accommodations it has made to non-scientific factors and correct the misdirections and misplaced emphases which presently color its findings and beliefs. We must admit that there are vast areas in which we have virtually no real knowledge beyond our own limited ability to manipulate phenomena or definitions.

Quite often we find prominent scientists declaring that everything that can be known will be discovered within a short time because science has discovered the final principles underlying the physical universe. Science is built upon the premise that we can reach ultimate understanding, and implies that we really do know what nature and its processes are. We therefore engender an attitude of absolutism, even though intelligent, practicing scientists know that the conclusions they are reaching about the world are often tentative. A familiar anecdote concerns the head of the government patent office at the end of the last century who wanted to abolish the job because everything had already been invented—and this shortly before the great technological explosion of this century!

The change we need to make to combat absolutism, therefore, is two-fold: we must develop the humility to admit that even our present sophisticated knowledge does not encompass the many ways we can understand the world. And we must recognize the real limitations of language, mathematics, and theory in describing the world as it really is, in totality. Narrative storylines, epigrams, the sequence of dreams and ancient legends must be accorded the same status as $E = mc^2$ when they are seen within their proper area of knowledge. We must once again stand in awe of the universe emotionally as well as intellectually. While we may purport to understand and control some natural processes, there is no doubt that we are subject to the operation of all natural processes; we are within, not above nature.

It seems unlikely that this proposition could be sold to the public of the Western world, which devoutly believes in technology and science and relies on the application of scientific theories to solve all human problems. One way of side-stepping the political overtones of abandoning the idea of possessing absolute knowledge might be to demand that scientific theories become increasingly inclusive. That is to say, we should not restrict theories to the explanation of pre-selected phenomena but insist that they encompass the widest possible sets of data. Rather than a few clear ideas explaining a limited field of information, we should seek comprehensive narratives that cover a much larger field of data but are phrased in language that has great emotional impact and less rationality.

IV. The Gaia Hypothesis as a Model

The barriers to communication and cooperation are, I believe, insurmountable if we pretend that we can transmit ideas and concepts directly across cultural and social boundaries. If we wish to move beyond mechanical causality and create a comprehensive "whole" science, we must find a new model of physical reality which does not have the mechanistic connotations of Western science, and which enables us to hold anomalies within the framework of information until we are able to fit them into the interpretive scheme. The recent exposition of the Gaia hypothesis offers us an opportunity to rearrange some of our existing knowledge in an organic model in which processes have as much status as identifiable physical structures or motions. I conclude this paper, therefore, with some comments on the Gaia hypothesis, and some suggestions as to how it could be developed further.

1. The Earth as Living Organism

James Lovelock, after developing computer models to determine whether or not Mars had ever supported organic life, or could do so in the future, suggested that in some areas it was useful to conceive of the Earth as a living organism and describe its processes as if it were a single functioning entity. He then combined observations about the rate of rock and soil erosion, the existence of algae in beach and lagoon pools and linked these things with concentrations of sulphur and bacterial organisms in the ocean. This network functions as if it was an organic process, even though only part of the chain is regarded by science as organic in any way. Lovelock then made successful predictions about the content of the oceans and was able to suggest that the Earth has a resiliency comparable to a biologically living entity.

This model has been misunderstood by Lovelock's critics, who are inclined to project human-sized behavioral and mental processes onto the larger planetary screen. Unfortunately, when working on a planetary level, Lovelock has been forced to admit that natural geologic and climatic changes in the past had visited destruction far surpassing present levels of environmental degradation on the Earth and it had been able to maintain a life-support system in spite of the catastrophes. Thus the model can be used by both supporters and opponents of environmental legislation, rendering the model neutral for political discussions and maintaining an abstract distance between the Earth and our species.

The Sioux, as well as most other tribes, had a sense of Earth as a living being, and they developed a structure in which all facets of planetary existence were included. The mountains were the bones of Mother Earth, the rivers her veins, the water her blood, the rain her tears, the trees and grasses her hair, the wind her breath, and the various species her organs.[31] Each of these entities was a complete person in and of itself, but it was also a functioning part of a larger whole which incorporated the full living functions into a greater organic unity. Within the larger unity/identity of Mother Earth, without the Western distinction of animate and inanimate, were the many processes that maintained a life-support system for wholly organic entities.

The Sioux model and the Lovelock model are reasonably close to each other, in that both recognize that what we call inanimate objects and processes may in fact provide an important link in the support system whereby increasingly complex organic entities are able to live, reach maturity, and reproduce themselves. In addition, however, the Sioux see the universe as having a moral balance which has to be included in any equation describing the physical world. The Sioux would never see environmental degradation, for instance, as neutral, but would perceive in human and/or other large creatures' moral failings the cause of the physical disorder.

From this point of view, it is clear that Lovelock and his followers have not asked the proper questions about the animate-inanimate relationship, and consequently the Gaia model has not been able to produce startling insights into other processes. The Sioux were comfortable with the notion that what we call inanimate entities can be brought into relationship with humans in particular events—some of which furthered the human ability to live on the Earth. Two lengthy examples can be used to demonstrate this recognition. Luther Standing Bear, recounting memories of his life, told about an incident involving Last Horse, a Sioux medicine man:

> Some of my band, the Oglalas, went to visit the Brule band and by way of entertainment preparations were made for a dance and feast. The day was bright and beautiful, and everyone was dressed in feathers and painted buckskin. But a storm came up suddenly, threatening to disrupt the gathering, so of course there was much unhappiness as the wind began to blow harder and rain began to fall. Last Horse walked out of his tipi and disrobed, coming out wearing only breechcloth and moccasins. His hair streamed down his back and in his hand he carried his rattle. Walking slowly to the center of the village he raised his face to the sky and sang his Thunder songs, which commanded the clouds to part. Slowly but surely, under the magic of the song, the clouds parted and the sky was clear once more.[32]

In Western scientific terms, this event would be a happy coincidence; in the Sioux tradition, it is a case of special medicine power, and if we place it within a new realm in which we are combining non-Western and Western scientific insights into the natural world, it is an example of human power to control and direct what are thought to be inanimate entities.

We assume a prior relationship between Last Horse and the Thunders which makes this event possible but it cannot be explained as simply coincidence or be attributed to the idea that Last Horse was simply a clever fellow.

Beede, writing about the Western Sioux veneration of a sacred stone on the Standing Rock reservation, observed:

> Why is a holy rock used to aid the suppliant, especially when praying in great anxiety or distress, rather than some other object? A rock is selected for this purpose upon which pictures prophetic of events to come are supposed to appear, sometimes, without human agency, and disappear later. A rock of this kind was formerly on Medicine Hill near Cannon Ball Sub-Station. Some years ago we were assembled, three hundred tents, for a religious gathering at St. James Church, half a mile from this rock. Old Indians came to me, at about 9 o'clock a.m., and said that the lightning would strike some-body in camp that day, for a picture had appeared while the dew was on the rock (as such pictures do always appear, if at all), but they did not tell me until 9 o'clock. And the lightning did strike a tent in camp and nearly kill a woman (whose name I now forget), at about 4 o'clock p.m. . . . I have known several similar things, equally foretelling events to come. I can not account for it. A strict 'scientist' will disbelieve it. What's the use to dispute?[33]

In this example the communication moves from the non-human to the human to forecast events, the animate and inanimate mixing precisely and with inanimate taking the initiative. A survey of the literature on Indians would reveal that these examples were sufficiently common as to command people's faith in the process. It could even be argued that these events are replicable providing the proper interpreters are present.

2. Species as Organs of the Earth

The idea that each species represents a particular organ of the planet is also worthy of consideration. Science already acknowledges the role which birds and animals play in spreading seeds and fertilizing the ground. Species are expected to thrive and rely on other creatures for their support, and in turn they perform functions which enable their related species to prosper also. The complex of the whole set of organisms apparently works to produce a life-support system for regions and these regions linked together constitute the living planet. We might break the analysis into two parts: the species directly supports other life and the various relationships of species linked together support the planet.

Accepting this definition of species might enable science to redirect its investigations with the goal of discovering the real linkages between and among birds, plants and animals. A weak overture has already been made in this direction by ecologists using a particular species as an "indicator" to gauge the environmental health of a region. But, as with the buffalo and ground beetle, the relationships are hidden and unsuspected and to understand more about them requires close observation, coupled with the attitude that creatures are doing purposeful things. Relativity and indeterminacy have taught us that the observer really is a part of the experiment–not simply as an intruder but as an active participant. Since there is an admitted observer relationship to the data, we need only to affirm that this relationship be deliberately personal to make the change to an organic model.

A note of caution must prevail. When Lovelock began to articulate his hypothesis, his naive followers suggested that with computers we, human beings, had become the nervous system of the planet.[34] This idea may have been comforting to the well-educated affluent people in the West, but when we include in the picture the billions of human beings in starvation and near-starvation conditions, lacking not only computers but food and clothing as well, the idea that humans beings are now in command of the planet is plainly absurd. Consequently, modeling the Earth as a mother does not mean cutting down rain forests because a bald headed person can survive as well as one with hair, nor is re-channeling our water into irrigation projects to grow unneeded crops and commodities a means of "purifying Mother Earth's blood". We cannot accept the model and continue to abuse the identifiable parts of the Earth. Similarly with the species of plants and animals; if we recognize their work as "organs" of the Earth, we must ensure that they prosper as well as ourselves.

3. Symbiotic Relationships as Indicative of Mind

In the biological sciences, there is a concept of the symbiotic relationship in which two or more species have an intimate relationship with each other. Often it is observed that if their connection is broken, both species perish. The idea suggests a cooperative enterprise of great magnitude, and could be used as a model to argue against the traditional idea of "nature red in tooth and claw". Studies have shown, for instance,[35] that many vertebrate species regulate their own population and that, except in unusual circumstances, predators have little or no effect on populations.

The Sioux and Cheyenne have an old story that at the beginning of this world there was a great race to determine whether the four-leggeds would feed on the two-leggeds or vice versa. The race was held in the Black Hills of South Dakota and the first circle of foothills, an eroded part of this geologic uplift, was the racetrack. The two-leggeds, represented by human beings, birds, and bears (who often stand on their hind legs), won the contest when magpie rode part way on the buffalo's horn and then quickly flew across the finish line. In exchange for being the provider of food for the two-leggeds, the four-leggeds required the two-leggeds to allow their bodies to turn to dust and form the grasses that would in turn feed the grazing animals.

The story illustrates a symbiotic relationship that was established on a covenantal basis. It was taught to Indian children to ensure that they treated the four-legged animals well. The rule was that, if at all possible, no animal should be killed for food unless and until it had completed a life cycle—married and had children and had experienced something of the adult life. By extension of the human parallel, hunters would often not take obviously old buffalo, elk and deer in homage to their old age and wisdom. This relationship between human beings and animals is not symbiotic in a strictly biological sense, but if we began to understand that as organisms become more complex they have an increasing ability to take care of themselves and develop some control over the way that relationships are structured, these networks could be included within the scope of the symbiotic relationship.

V. Conclusion

It is comforting to believe that we can transpose concepts and ideas from one cultural context to another and thereby gain new ways of understanding the world. But each cultural context has a unity of its own which gathers information into a particular set of interpretations. Removing an idea from one context to another is therefore a doubtful process because the methodologies by which each culture gathers information are different.

In contemplating the conditions under which a coherent conversation between the Western and tribal forms of knowledge could take place, it quickly becomes clear that Western science is neither unified nor homogenized. It lacks a systematic exposition of its basic tenets, and can perhaps be best described as an informal agreement among educated people to work within very restricted fields and accord standing and status to others in similarly situated groups. A further barrier is the fact that Western epistemological methodology is one of reductionism, and consequently the structure of human knowledge appears as a pyramid in which physics and mathematics form the apex and other fields of knowledge are placed below them along the remainder of the pyramid according to their similarities to, and use of, physics and mathematics. Even the social sciences, which should be observational, now feel a great need to become more mathematical—with results which are sometimes ludicrous.

It is widely agreed that a massive paradigm shift is necessary now within science. The idea that the world is an animated being introduces the concept of purpose into the scientific enterprise—an idea which is already inherent in DNA/RNA research. Even so, scientists have been unwilling to give status to the idea that life includes intelligence and knowledge even on the highest and lowest levels of identifiable existence. Plato's effort to move beyond form to link human values and emotions with the realities of the physical world shows an apprehension of morality very similar to that which formed the basis of the Western Sioux perception of the world. Should this moral base become established and humans were to take a personal approach to the rest of the cosmos, new ways of living and acting would be made possible. In such a situation, the universe becomes a cooperative, complex community in which each species has a vital role to play and there are no anomalies.

Some interpretations of scientific methodology argue that we now must include the scientist as part of the experiment, and this recognition is a step forward in reducing the requirement of total objectivity. The question we must now ask is: "What kind of participant is the scientist in the experiment or the observation?" And we must answer, "He must be a whole person; he or she must include their emotional responses to the data and must bring to the gathering of knowledge the sense of self and self-discipline that characterizes a whole person."

Notes and References

1. A. McG. Beede, "Western Sioux Cosmology", unpublished paper in the North Dakota State Historical records, Bismarck, and the Newberry Library, Chicago, p. 3.

2. Ibid., p. 4.

3. Ibid., pp. 5-6.

4. Ibid., p. 6.

5. Ibid., pp. 6-7.

6. John G. Neihardt, *Black Elk Speaks,* University of Nebraska Press, 1972, p. 4

7. Thomas Kuhn, *The Structure of Scientific Revolutions,* University of Chicago Press, 1962, p. 37.

8. See, for example, Barbara Beddall, "Wallace, Darwin, and the Theory of Natural Selection" in *Journal of The History of Biology*, No. 1, 1968. Also, John L. Brooks, *Extinction and the Origin of Organic Diversity,* Connecticut Academy of Arts and Sciences, December 1972.

9. Werner Heisenberg, *Across the Frontiers,* Harper and Row, 1974, p. 22.

10. The suggestion of a middle ground has an eerie parallel in Heisenberg's description of the probability wave. In *Physics and Philosophy,* Harper Torchbooks, 1974, he writes:

> *The probability wave of Bohr, Kramers, Slater, however, meant more than that; it meant a tendency for something. It was a quantitative version of the old concept of 'potentia' in Aristotelian philosophy. It introduced something standing in the middle between the idea of an event and the actual event, a strange kind of physical reality just in the middle between possibility and reality. (p. 41)*

11. See, for example, *The Secret Life of Plants* by Peter Tompkins and Christopher Bird (Harper & Row, 1973) and their description of plant experiments by Backster, Vogel and Bose in which it was necessary for the experimenter to establish a warm personal relationship with the plants prior to any effort to measure their responses, emotional or mechanical, to the experiment.

12. Readers should consult especially: James Lovelock, *The Ages of Gaia,* W. W. Norton, 1988; *Gaia: A New Look at Life on Earth,* Oxford University Press, 1979.

13. Frances Densmore recounts an example of this ability in *Teton Sioux Music.* It is worth reproducing here:

> *Goose, a prominent medicine-man, also dreamed of the sacred stones. He said that he had two of these stones in his possession some time before he tested his power over them. One day a fur trader ridiculed the medicine-*

men in his hearing. This white man said that all the medicine-men did was by sleight of hand, and that he would have to see an instance of their power before he would believe it. Goose entered into conversation with the trader on the subject, who offered him ten articles, including cloth and blankets, if he would call a buffalo to the spot where they were standing. Goose sent both the sacred stones to summon a buffalo. The trader brought his field glasses and looked across the prairie, saying in derision, 'Where is the buffalo you were to summon?' Suddenly the trader saw a moving object, far away. It came nearer until they could see it without the aid of the glasses. It was a buffalo, and it came so near that they shot it from the spot where they stood. (Teton Sioux Music, Bureau of American Ethnology, Smithsonian Institution, Bulletin 61, 1918, p. 210)

14. The strong sense of personal identity among the Indians can be exemplified by the frequent changing of names to keep track of the change in the personality as the individual went through life. Most Indians had several names by which they were called, each giving specific information on their talents or accomplishments. Within the family, people would refer to each other by kinship terms in order not to interfere with personality growth and to remind themselves of family responsibilities. Some Indians who did not want to shame their most personal name used "secular" names to sign treaties which they believed the United States would not keep.

15. Densmore records the explanation of Eagle Shield of the Crow Owner Society of the Teton Sioux regarding the self-discipline of the Indians on this point:

The Crow is always the first to arrive at the gathering of the animals in the Black Hills. The reason why the Black Hills were so long unknown to the white man was that Wakantanka created them as a meeting place for the animals. The Indians had always known this and regarded the law of Wakantanka concerning it. **By this law they were forbidden to kill any of the animals during their great gatherings.** *(p. 319) (Emphasis added.)*

16. This classification is used primarily to determine economic and health similarities. There are other sets of relationships that deal with vocation, powers of interpretation, family and other aspects of human life. These classifications are mutually exclusive but are seen as illustrative of the breadth of the larger whole so not in conflict.

17. But see footnote 11 for recent scientific observations which show movement toward the Indian knowledge from observation.

18. An important research project might be to gather the stories of trees, tribes, and shelters since the cedar and the pinon pine also tell the people how to use them in building houses. Hence architecture in some of its aspects may be information that is given by trees to humans.

19. The Lummi Indians who live near the Canadian border in Washington state have a Rain Dance. It seems ludicrous for people who live in a virtual rain forest to have a rain dance. This dance is used on those rare occasions when it snows so hard that the houses are buried in snow and the people cannot get out of them. The rain melts the snow and rescues the people.

20. See Stanley G. Smith, "Multiple personality disorder with human and non-human subpersonality components", in *Dissociation,* Vol. 2, No 1, March 1989, pp. 52-56. Smith identified seven animal alters while engaged in therapy with a 70-year-old Indian man who had suffered abuse during his training by an even older medicine man. The therapy involved unusual difficulties in integrating the animal and human parts of the personality because of incessant demands on the patient to perform ceremonies, parts of which simply triggered dissident alters. Smith attempted to integrate this case with existing psychoanalytic theory and was partially successful. But he did not mention the possibility of tracing the animal components back through the man's family history. Although this instance is a tragic example of the human-animal relationship, it nevertheless does give evidence of connections far beyond what science would have predicted.

21. See note 15.

22. Joseph Nicollet led a government expedition to the Pipestone Quarries in 1838 and he reported:

The idea of the young Indians, who are very fond of the marvellous, is that it (the Quarry) has been opened up by the Great Spirit, and that whenever it is visited by them, they are saluted by lightning and thunder.

We may cite as a coincidence our own experience in confirmation of this tradition. Short of half a mile from the valley, we were met by a severe thunderstorm, during which the wind blew with so much force as to threaten the overturning of Mr. Renville's wagon, and we were obliged to stop for a few minutes during the descent into the valley. Sen Doc. 237, 26th C, 2d Sess, vol. V, Part 2, p. 15

23. John Neihardt, "When the tree flowered" in *Why the Island Hill Was Sacred,* University of Nebraska Press, 1970.

24. George Will and George Hyde, *Corn Among the Indians of the Upper Missouri,* University of Nebraska Press, 1917, pp. 171-191.

25. Indians placed considerable emphasis on the pre-birth stage of life, believing that it influenced everything else. Charles Eastman recounted the Indian attitude in his book, *The Soul of the Indian* (Houghton and Mifflin, 1911), explaining:

From the moment of her recognition of the fact of conception to the end of the second year of life, which was the ordinary duration of lactation, it was supposed by us that the mother's spiritual influence counted for most. Her attitude and secret meditations must be such as to instill into the receptive soul of the unborn child the love of the 'Great Mystery' and a sense of brotherhood with all creatures. Silence and isolation are the rule of life for the expectant mother. She wanders prayerful in the stillness of great woods, or on the bosom of the untrodden prairie, and to her poetic mind the immanent birth of her child prefigures the advent of a master-man—a hero, or the mother of heroes—a thought conceived in the virgin breast of primeval nature, and dreamed out in a hush that is only broken by the sighing of the pine tree or the thrilling orchestra of a distant waterfall. (pp. 28-29)

26. Roman Nose, the great Cheyenne Dos Soldier warrior, was told that he would be invincible unless he had touched metal before he went into battle, since the metal in his body would then attract bullets. In one fight with the cavalry he deliberately rode three times across the whole line of cavalry in order to encourage them to fire at him and heat their guns. He was not wounded. At Beecher's Island, asked to lead the third charge against the Colorado Volunteers, he knew he would be killed because he had eaten food given to him with a metal spoon. The basic outlines of his life were already given to him in the Vision Quest. But he had a choice when his death would occur if it was to be in battle—and he deliberately chose to end it on behalf of his warriors at Beecher's Island.

27. Beede says the Sioux could substitute a blanket for a buffalo robe because the blanket was made of wool and therefore was a natural part of an animal. See "Letting Go of the Ghost", Unpublished paper in the North Dakota State Historical records, and the Newberry Library, p. 52.

28. Lucien Levy-Bruhl, *How Natives Think,* Princeton University Press, 1985, p. 112.

29. Here the theories of Rupert Sheldrake, particularly the idea of "morphic resonance", need to be given serious attention. The Sioux have a complex and very sophisticated understanding of the particularity of both individuals and tribes which is connected with their star knowledge but we do not have space to delineate it here. For Sheldrake's ideas, see in particular *The Presence of the Past,* Times Books, 1988; *The Rebirth of Nature,* Bantam, 1991.

30. Since Jung was frequently accused of racism by people who protested his support of German psychotherapists during the Nazi era, it seems unlikely that he would concentrate on developing a specific interest in the racial collective unconscious. But some of his essays indicate that he was using a racial unconscious as a tool for articulating certain themes. Thus "Wotan" deals with the German unconscious, "Mind and Earth" with American Indians, and "Woman in Europe" with European women. (All essays are in *Civilization in Transition,* Vol. 10 of the Collected Works, Princeton University Press, Bollingen Series XX, 1970.)

31. A. McG. Bede, *Western Sioux Cosmology* (see note 1), p. 2.

32. Luther Standing Bear, *Land of the Spotted Eagle,* Houghton-Mifflin, 1933, p. 207.

33. Bede, p. 13.

34. See, for example, Peter Russell, *The Global Brain,* Tarcher Inc., 1983, who says:

> *What then might be our function in relation to Gaia? One possible response to this question suggests that humanity is like some vast nervous system, a global brain, in which each of us are the individual nerve cells. The second, more pessimistic response supposes that we are like some kind of planetary cancer. (p. 31)*

35. There are studies describing self-regulation of wolf populations with respect to deer on certain Great Lake islands. See for example Barry Lopez, *Of Wolves and Men,* Scribner and Sons, 1978, pp. 26, 55, 57.

New Wine in What Kind of Wineskins?
Metaphysics in the Twenty-First Century

by Arthur Zajonc

Metaphysics is a hazardous business these days. After all, it purports to reach beyond the evident report of the senses to the ultimate nature or meaning of existence. Yet, all attempts to shun metaphysics are undercut by its universal, if unconscious, presence as the basis for meaning in our lives. In the end, we presume the world and ourselves to be something, and that presumption is metaphysical. The presupposition we live by may view the world as interacting mass points, or a fallen angelic creation, but ultimately life rests now, as in the past, on a metaphysical foundation.

In the closing chapter of his classic study *The Metaphysical Foundations of Modern Science*, E. A. Burtt concluded with the observation that post-Newtonian metaphysics, as embraced by science through the nineteenth century, was characterized by

> the ascription of ultimate reality and causal efficacy to the world of mathematics, which world is identified with the realm of material bodies moving in space and time.[1]

Reality, in this view, was comprised of material bodies moving through an absolute space and time according to mathematical laws. Burtt traced the impact of this metaphysics on the prevailing conceptions: a) of reality, b) of causality and c) of the human mind. We may now inquire, how has the "ultimate reality" of post-Newtonian metaphysics fared over the last one hundred years, and especially in the last two decades? What has become of space, time, causality and the human mind?

We can approach the first two of Burtt's three categories by focusing on the specific examples of quantum physics, and, to lesser extent, on chaos dynamics. They can show us something of the character and significance of the metaphysical changes now taking place. We should remain modest in our early proclamations, as only the outline of tomorrow's metaphysics is clear today—much still remains to be filled in. Yet, for all our care and caution, we can fruitfully ask modern physics about the metaphysical foundations of the twenty-first century. What will be the figure and form of future "reality", the shape of its space and time?

Following a response to this question, we can turn to still larger issues. Will the new conceptions of time, space and matter urged on us by science be integrated into the dominant material imagination of our universe, or will they find a more congenial home in a thoroughly revised metaphysics? In what kind of wineskins will the new wine be held? If metaphysics is recast, what will it look like, and what will be its implications? In addressing these questions, we will be drawn to examine the thought of Goethe and Rudolf Steiner.

I. From Atomism to Entanglement

There is a limit to what a person can handle. A bricklayer lays one brick at a time, its size fitted nicely to the human hand. Even a crane operator places one girder at a time into the structure that will one day be a skyscraper. Things of this world seem to be built up piece by piece. Under such impressions atomism arises.

If the world is constructed brick by brick, understanding it would seem to require a congruent conceptual framework, one that predicates isolated units whose identity is never lost by juxtaposition. From bricks a house may arise, from hydrogen and oxygen may come water, but in both cases we still "see" bricks in the facade and atoms in the molecule. The mortar that binds does not dissolve.

Nevertheless, for all its usefulness and power, unrelenting atomism of the classical vintage is not only passé, but simply false. In the embryo it seems that one cell is added to another until a fetus is formed. But isn't it cell division, not addition, that reigns here? One cell becomes two, four and so on. Already in the first cell, the whole physical form is, in some sense, enfolded in a way sufficient to develop the physical form of an infant child. The living world seems to seethe with wholeness, but it is a "soft" kind of wholeness: one whose specific contours are elusive and therefore easy prey to the thrusts of "hard" science critics. Now, however, the hardest evidence against simplistic atomism is found within physics itself, in quantum mechanics, in the form of what are broadly called non-locality and entanglement.

At the turn of the century the brilliant successes of atomic physics seemed to affirm atomism, carrying it even into the atom itself, so that today the world is built up from quarks, gluons and leptons. Light, too, became atomic, at the hands of Planck and Einstein (1900-1905)[2] with the concept of the photon. Ever smaller and more elementary particles or "quanta" were being discovered. These were the building blocks of nature.

Yet since their inception, one by one, every elementary particle large or small, massive or massless, has shown effects that defy our naive notion of the atom. The Greek root of the word atom means "indivisible". With these indivisible, elementary objects we have, since Aristotle, always associated a place. One would naturally expect the simplest object to have the simplest place—a point location. Point by point, atom by atom, the world might then be constructed. The wonderful irony has been that in the struggle for absolute simplicity, physics has had to overturn the classical concept of location, and replace it with "non-locality".

The intellectual current of atomic thinking, of analysis, still runs fast and deep. Contrary notions appear vague and muddled. Yet if quantum theory is any guide, it is only our imagination that is limited. Nature, and even our mathematical descriptions of her, are unambiguous in their indications. Atomism and localism are only impoverished, limiting cases of a far richer and more subtle order to the universe. I would like to describe that order as exactly as possible based on the "simple" facts of quantum phenomena. Behind each statement is an experiment, some of which I will describe. I have done these experiments, as have hundreds of other physicists in laboratories around the globe. To these investigators the experimental results are routine—no surprises; but the demands they place on our imaginations are enormous. It is to this aspect that I appeal, to the need for a renewal of thinking, the birth of a richer imagination. Like demands are being made on us by biology, ecology, cognitive science, medicine, and a myriad other fields. We are at a threshold. In what follows I would like to sketch the outline of the new imagination, its logical features and their wider implications on the evidence of quantum physics. This is part of the "new wine". Once we have sampled it, we will pass on to an examination of the metaphysical wineskins that can contain it.

Non-locality

As stated above, in classical physics every object has a unique place. In order to connect one such object with another, something must travel from the first object to the second, from one location to the other. If I am here and you are there, it may be the sound of my voice (a wave-form impressed on air that travels at about 700 miles per hour), or light reflected from my face to your eyes (another "form" traveling at 186,000 miles per second). If we sever the links provided by sound, light, etc., then our world would be utterly soundless, black and without the slightest externally induced sensations. A state of deep sensory deprivation would result. Thus all objects communicate or relate to one another through the passage of signals, be they sound, warmth, light or whatever. That transmission takes time, and the limiting velocity, relativity theory tells us, is the speed of light. No communication can travel faster. Everyday experience as well as the phenomena of classical physics support these considerations, but the subtle phenomena of quantum physics do not.

At the quantum level (and this need not be identified only with the microscopic world of atoms and electrons) spatial relationships change fundamentally. A single, "indivisible" quantum such as an electron, neutron, or photon (or even a compound object such as a sodium atom) can be put into a non-classical quantum state which is "non-local". Let me explain the concept of non-locality by means of a specific example, by reference to an experiment that has been recently performed.[3]

Neutrons are one of the elementary constituents of atoms; they are uncharged and have a mass about 1800 times greater than that of the negatively charged electron. They are produced in large numbers in nuclear reactors, and from there can be directed to experimental areas adjacent to the reactor. Neutrons certainly seem to be substantial objects, particles in the traditional sense. If one directs neutrons onto a thin sheet of crystal silicon, a fraction of them are reflected (by Bragg scattering) and the remainder are transmitted. The silicon sheet acts as a beamsplitter (see Figure 1-A,B next page).

One can attempt to follow the trajectory of an individual neutron, at least in thought. Imagine an incoming neutron initially in state i. Upon reaching the beamsplitter it can be reflected up (trajectory a), or be transmitted (trajectory b). In quantum theory these two "modes" (that is, trajectories) are both possible for each individual neutron, and there is, therefore, a quantum mechanical probability amplitude for each mode. One must be clear at this point. It is not the case that the single neutron somehow splits into "sub-neutrons" with half going one way and half the other. Rather, we should attempt to think of a unitary quantum state where the two modes a and b are both simultaneously occupied. This is a new kind of concept, corresponding to a non-classical situation. The single neutron is in what physicists call a "superposition state". It is still a single neutron, but that single state can only be described as the sum of two quantum mechanical amplitudes, namely the amplitudes for modes a and b. Having encountered the beamsplitter, the neutron is put into a superposition state, which is inherently "non-local".

The non-local nature of the neutron state after it has passed through the beamsplitter can be made apparent very easily and in a number of ways. The simplest is to recombine the modes, thereby causing an interference pattern. The mere presence of interference already demonstrates that, in some sense, the neutron "traveled by both paths". We can make this much more dramatic by

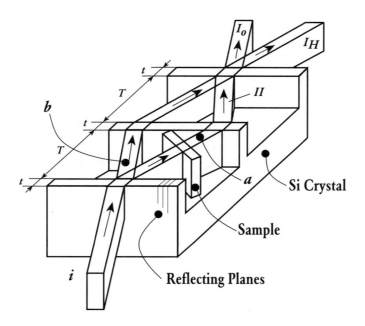

Figure 1-A:

Neutron interferometer.

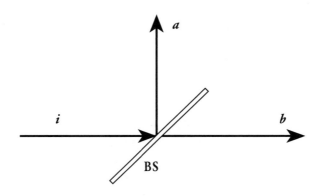

Figure 1-B:

Beamsplitter.

putting a piece of aluminum foil in one path, say mode a. This slightly delays the neutron in mode a, or equivalently affects the phase of the quantum amplitude for that neutron path and so changes the interference pattern. In other words, doing something in either path (and these can be separated by large distances) affects the single neutron interference pattern. One neutron interferes with itself in a spatially non-local way.

Another important feature of such single-quantum interference experiments is that the two quantum amplitudes for modes a and b add "coherently". Usually when one adds things together they are simply "mixed". Cement, water and sand make concrete. In the above situation modes a and b are not added to become a mixture (a so-called "mixed state" in quantum mechanics), but they are added "coherently" and form what is called a "pure state". The evolution of a coherent state is like the synchronous movements of a military drill team, many soldiers moving rigidly together. The oddity of single quantum interference is that one object can be moving all parts of the drill at once—like a one-man band who is a whole orchestra in himself! The ontological status of a single neutron, coherent superposition state (that is, a pure state) is every bit as solid as the state of the neutron before encountering the beamsplitter. Although spatially extended, it really is one thing.

Therefore, the neutron state after the beamsplitter is consummately strange when viewed from the standpoint of classical physics, but is a perfectly acceptable state in quantum theory, no less (or more) real than the initial neutron state i. Yes, it is non-local in the sense described above, and yes, we are unsure how to picture such a state; but is that anything more than a reflection of the limitations of our thinking, of our powers of imagination?

I have used only two modes in the above discussion in order to keep matters simple, but obviously there could be many more modes involved. A pure state of the neutron would then be a superposition of all these many, potentially very distant and differently directed, modes. Also, experiments exactly analogous to the neutron experiments have been performed using photons, electrons, and, most recently, with atoms.[4]

One final disconcerting matter. Quantum superposition states of the kind I have been describing can only exist in the absence of measurements. If we were to put detectors in paths a and b, we would always find the neutron either in path a or b, but never in both simultaneously. One only detects whole neutrons, and detects them locally. Here we see the illusive nature of non-locality. When, using physical detectors, one asks directly, where is the neutron? one receives a specific reply. If, however, one probes only by indirection, through interference, then the evidence is compelling for non-locality.

The challenge, therefore, is to conceive of an indivisible object which can show a highly structured and sensitive non-local nature over all conceivable distances. Yet when detected it always shows its entire self locally, as if instantly collapsing at detection.

Entanglement

In addition to non-locality, and intimately related to it, is the quantum concept of "entanglement". The idea of entanglement was first introduced by Erwin Schrödinger in 1935 as part of his formal discussion of the seminal "EPR" paper by Einstein, Podolsky and Rosen which appeared just months before.[5] The concept of entanglement was, for Schrödinger, the characteristic trait of quantum mechanics—"the one that enforces its [that is quantum mechanics'] entire departure from classical lines of thought".[6] While the single-quantum interferometer discussed above is also formally an instance of entanglement (in that case with the vacuum!), the canonical example of entanglement (and also non-locality) refers to two-particle systems of the type treated in the EPR and Schrödinger papers. We turn, therefore, to them.

Imagine that two quanta, be they neutrons, electrons or photons, are produced at distant and unrelated sources (see Figure 2 next page). Imagine them coming together until they interact with each other by some means. After the interaction the two separate, again to large distances from each other. How are we to think of this collision/interaction in quantum mechanical terms?

According to classical physics, one would treat the interaction as a microscopic game of billiards. One particle collides with another, then the two separate, each going its own way. But the analysis of Einstein, Podolsky and Rosen, which recent experiments have convincingly confirmed[7], tells us that the billiard-ball model of the collision is completely untenable for quantum systems. In fact, once the two particles interact, they form, according to Schrödinger, an "entangled state", very much like the superposition state of the neutron interferometer. In the entangled state there is no meaning (prior to measurement) to the notion of separate, autonomously moving objects, even long after the collision. The two have become one.

If a third quantum object were to interact with the already entangled two-quantum system, then a more complex entanglement would occur. Once again the individual identity of the quanta disappears and the three are now one. Clearly this process can go on indefinitely. Unlike the bricks that make up a building, Schrödinger's entanglement asks us to dissolve the concept "brick" as soon as the different elements are brought together. The entangled system is an emergent reality. Through the interaction, a novel ontic entity or relationship arises, one whose entire meaning is dependent on a loss of reality of the original quanta.

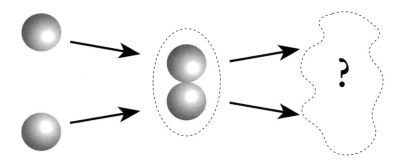

Figure 2:

Two-particle entanglement in EPR experiment.

Yet what has been entangled can be disentangled. Quanta are entangled by interactions; they are disentangled by measurement. With our normal sense apparatus, or with the physical instruments of the laboratory, we detect only classical disentangled objects. Niels Bohr made much of this fact, burying entangled states under epistemological considerations.[8] Others have attended more closely to the implications of entanglement. The puzzle of how entangled states become disentangled has been with quantum theory from the beginning, and is known as the "measurement problem". No acceptable solution has been found, although David Bohm's "quantum potential" theory goes some distance toward an answer.[9]

One's immediate reaction might be, but is all this really true? Or is this just another story told by academics (a la Thomas Kuhn, and the sociology of knowledge[10])? In reply, one can say that quantum theory, together with its features of non-locality and entanglement, really does work where all classical theories fail. The powerful theorem of John Bell, and the recent experiments that use it, have shown that no "local, realistic" theory of physics can account for the experimental facts.[11] However, at another level, I think the interesting question is not whether the new physics is more true than the old physics, but rather to first acknowledge that it is radically different; and second, to see the new physics as indicative of a new consciousness, which will gain dominance over the next two hundred years in much the same way that the Copernican and atomic views did. From this vantage point the absolute truth of these views is not the essential point. Rather, the move from old physics to new physics is indicative of a shift in Western consciousness toward a non-local and entangled imagination of our world.

Nor is the shift only taking place in physics. Within the life sciences, molecular biology and neo-Darwinian evolutionary theory are now repeating the grand accomplishments of classical physics in their own domains. But a few individuals such as Brian Goodwin (see his chapter in this volume) are able to argue with conviction that while these are powerful paradigms, they leave out much that is essential to the understanding of developing organisms. The mechanical imagination of molecular biology must reside within the more capacious imagination schooled on morphogenesis. Likewise, I see the work of John Todd on "living machines",[12] of Francisco Varela and Evan Thompson in cognitive science,[13] of Wes Jackson concerning perennial polycultures,[14] of Will Brinton on the soil,[15] and many others, as the vanguard of a new imagination or paradigm constructed on "post-modern" metaphysical foundations. Nor by any means is the new imagination ineffectual. It has already given rise to technologies in waste treatment, agriculture and medicine. In the face of ecological and social disasters, this burgeoning imagination will be critical to our well-being and the well-being of the planet.

Toward a Modern Conception of Time

The reconfiguration discussed above treats spatial order only. In most presentations of the new physics, the impact of recent developments on our conception of time is treated little or not at all. Yet here, too, profound structural changes have occurred. Relativity Theory, formulated in the early years of this century, deals with time in a way perfectly analogous to the way it deals with space; in fact the three dimensions of space join time to form an inextricable foursome. The ideas of relativity, therefore, affect time and space in equal measure. Moreover, recent explorations in quantum theory have upset the usual, well-ordered time sequence associated with causality complicating our sense of the relationship between time profoundly.[16]

Still, as Roger Penrose has recently written:

> Our present picture of physical reality, particularly in relation to the nature of time, is due for a grand shake-up, even greater, perhaps, than that which has already been provided by present-day relativity and quantum mechanics.[17]

Let us consider first of all our classical view of time. In his *Timaeus,* Plato put forward a geometrical atomism in which all five elements were conceived in terms of primordial triangles. In the hands of physically minded atomists, Plato's abstract geometrical atomism of pure forms became the substantial material atomism with which we are all familiar. In a less obvious but equally influential way, Plato can be seen as the father of modern temporal atomism.

The relevant discussion is treated by Simplicius in his *Commentary* concerning Plato's dictum to astronomers. Simplicius writes:

> Plato lays down the principle that the heavenly bodies' motion is circular, uniform, and constantly regular [that is, always in the same direction]. Thereupon he sets the mathematicians the following problem: what circular motions, uniform and perfectly regular, are to be admitted as hypotheses so that it might be possible to save the appearances presented by the planets?[18]

The complex observed motions of the planets were to be reduced to a set of uniform, circular motions, a task brilliantly performed by Ptolemy and generations of ancient astronomers.

Spacial atomism decomposes static objects into elementary particles. Astronomers, by contrast, treat objects in motion. Following Plato's demand, these motions were also decomposed. What we see as the irregular motion of planets is thought of as the sum of many different, but perfectly periodic, motions. The description of motion thus entails time as well as space, and the cycles demanded by Plato provided the absolutely regular basis for the mathematization of that temporal dimension. Planetary cycles are but the ticking of an astronomical clock.

In his analysis of this development, Pierre Duhem made clear that the reasons for choosing this particular solution were explicitly metaphysical.[19] That is to say, Plato's charge to astronomers was derived from considerations that were beyond physics (that is, "meta"-physical). Planetary motion should be thought of as fundamentally circular because, on theological grounds, planetary substance was known to be perfect (of the "quintessence") so planets must display the most perfect of all motions, namely circular motion. Implicit in this reasoning is a metaphysical basis for time.

Looking at the roots of time invariably led one to the rhythms of sun, moon, planets and stars. In the ancient world, time was given primarily through them, whether the division be into years, seasons, months, days, or parts of days. Yet the observed motions of the heavens are complex. Plato, and astronomers after him, regularized that motion according to the dictates of circular motion. What atomism has been to space, the relentless cycles of the heavens, and later the mechanical ticking of the clock, have been to time. Over the centuries we have divided and sub-divided time into smaller and smaller bits, ever more accurately regulated. We organize our lives according to this fragmented image of time.

Are there any indications that Penrose is right, that physics may provide as great a shake-up in time as with space? One youthful area of research that seems to point in that direction is chaos dynamics. By far the greater part of nature—in fact one could argue all nature—shows rhythms that are not reducible to the periodicity of the clock. They show their own peculiar kinds of "chaotic" rhythms. When seen from the standpoint of classical regularity, such motions appear chaotic and have been rejected by scientists for centuries. Yet once one enters into the mindset appropriate to such phenomena, a rich, patterned world opens up, whose time-order is not constrained to the relentless regularity of the mechanical timepiece.

Since antiquity, cosmos (the Greek word for "order") and chaos have been irreconcilable adversaries. Today, however, we are drawn into the marvelous region between these two absolutes. Within the rhythms of pure order the tendrils of chaos can be found, and the path from cosmos to chaos is peopled by magnificent forms displaying the most varied temporal and spatial arrangements, including those of life. Very recent investigations point to yet more intriguing connections between chaos and Plato's periodic motions in the area of "controlled chaos".[20]

If one adjusts the parameters of a driven pendulum, its behavior can be made to run the gamut from perfect regularity to a very un-clocklike chaotic motion. Surprisingly, chaotic motion can be "controlled" by very small periodic perturbations to the pendulum. In this recent series of research papers, physicists have reported on their investigations of the control of chaos from both a theoretical and experimental perspective. The significance of this research is likely to be great. In traditional physics it has always been thought that the strength of an effect is in direct proportion to the size of the driving force. The harder you push, the faster you go. The so-called "butterfly effect" from chaos dynamics undermines that idea, and, in these papers, specific means for controlling chaos by subtle forces, periodically applied, are investigated.

This research suggests ways in which subtle period influences can cause dramatic changes in the large scale behavior of systems. Possible applications to biological systems are obvious. Medicine, for instance, has been dominated by the ideas of traditional mechanics. According to this way of thinking, the effects of long-term exposure to toxins, electromagnetic fields, etc., should scale linearly. Thus, if short-term studies find no effect then, by extrapolation, there should be no long-term effects. But in non-linear regimes, which are the regimes in which we live, one cannot extrapolate; very small perturbations can, under certain circumstances, cause huge effects. Likewise, the approach to therapies has been one of frontal assault. Gentle therapies that work with microdoses, remedies or rhythms have had no theoretical basis on which to stand.

Quantum physics and chaos dynamics are often heralded as harbingers of a new science, and so of a new consciousness. Most such claims are little more than journalistic bravado. Still, one can legitimately see developments in quantum physics, along with many other developments in contemporary science, as symptomatic of important changes in the metaphysical foundations of modern life. From this vantage point quantum physics is not causing a transformation in consciousness; rather its own development reflects the more original changes now underway in thinking generally. Read as symptoms, quantum mechanics and chaos dynamics reveal certain important features of a dawning metaphysics. We can look, therefore, at science "symptomatically", reading from it an image of ourselves, and glimpse thereby the nascent forms of a future mentality.

II. The End of the Modern Era

The question still remains: how will the restructuring of space, time and causality be taken up? We probably assume that scientifically, well-informed philosophers will consult among themselves and converge on a single reasonable metaphysics. After all, post-Newtonian metaphysics as described by Burtt appeared to command the field essentially unchallenged. Yet, dissident voices have always existed, and in the first centuries of the modern era, when the scientific revolution dawned during the Renaissance, the battles were real and vociferous. At that time, a spiritual, hermetic metaphysics competed with, and lost to, the rising orthodoxy that became scientific materialism. Today, the burgeoning facts of modern science wonderfully complicate and subvert the complacency of the metaphysical establishment, but as discussions heat up once again, the outcome remains unclear. The reign of the modern era, begun in the Renaissance, seems to be ending without an heir apparent.

The most conservative reaction will likely be the denial of any metaphysical implications to modern science. Like the Aristotelians of the Academy who refused to look through Galileo's telescope, or having looked, refused to re-imagine their world, today's traditionalists will reject the promptings of science. Ironically, the role played by reactionary clergy in seventeenth century Padua is now likely to be played by scientists themselves, who could well become the vigilant guardians of an outmoded mentality.

Even among those who acknowledge the facts of a post-modern civilization, a range of responses is probable. At such moments of uncertainty, extreme positions possess a power disproportionate to their merits. We could envisage that at one end of the spectrum, scientific materialism will undergo a modest realignment by incorporating the data of modern science unreflectively into its corpus. Non-locality, entanglement, and the rest, will be co-opted into a slightly retooled materialism that becomes all the more compelling, while at the opposite end, spiritual visionaries will trumpet a New Age and the final overthrow of Matter. Crystal pendants and pyramid power will flourish in the vapid aura of an unthinking spirituality.

But like most dichotomies, this one is false. In order to avoid the excesses of one extreme, it is not necessary to plunge into those of its opposite. Surely there is a middle way that steers clear of the shoals of single vision, whether it be materialism or spiritualism. We can look with both eyes instead of one.

That middle way will not only need to accommodate the facts of new science, but it must also be competent to connect science to the cultural, ethical and spiritual dimensions of human life. In doing so, it will move decisively beyond the strictures of the contemporary metaphysics of science and technology with its hollow pieties about value-neutrality. Recognition of the real links between science and life will be more important than ever, because the enormous powers of the new science, like the old, will be equally open to corruption. Biotechnology and artificial intelligence will be no less vulnerable to greed and the lust for power than the discoveries of Einstein or Cortez. If our new imagination of nature is separated from the ethical and spiritual, then we will have persisted in reducing the most profound entanglement of all—that which entwines material and spiritual existence.

For entanglement can be thought of as vertical as well as horizontal. Technical problems are also moral and spiritual problems. They are wedded like two interacting quanta into a coherent state. Science has sought for centuries to disentangle body from soul, subject from object, scientific knowledge from spiritual values. The distinction has been useful, but the division of one from the other is a dangerous illusion. From the twelfth to the eighteenth centuries, science struggled for its intellectual freedom, to be unfettered from the shackles of religious ideology. But now that we are, by and large, free of them, we are also free to recognize the entwined nature of our world: body, soul and spirit.

I am advocating, therefore, a metaphysics that embraces not only a holism of space and time, but also a holism of the sensory and the moral. One of my influences in this is the poet-scientist, Johann Wolfgang von Goethe (1749-1832), who rightly saw the danger of separating these two. Best known for his *Faust*, Goethe valued his scientific accomplishments even more highly than his literary ones—a fact which few people realize. He worked in the areas of color science, botany, biology and geology to name a few of his many interests. In each of these fields he combined serious empirical research with the desire to see the unity within nature, a unity that reached into the artistic and ethical as well as the mathematical and abstract.

Goethe refused to leave the phenomenal for the abstract, and his scientific writings are therefore more a poetic re-enactment of the phenomenal than an abstraction of them. He always saw the sensory as inseparable from the "moral" or spiritual. As long as the sunset itself was in view, as long as the rainbow arched majestically overhead, the dangers of abstraction were mitigated, and the voice of the qualitative could be heard. When such phenomena, however, are reduced to schema or the equations of optics (even if quantum mechanical or non-linear), then quantitative reasoning dominates, and a gulf widens between the objective and subjective, between quantity and quality.

This gulf still characterizes even those areas of science which I have outlined as potentially revolutionary. Research in quantum physics rests firmly in the quantitative, a strength when speaking with those who will listen to nothing else, but it has no phenomenal or qualitative component. One cannot "see" the entanglement of neutrons, one can only deduce it from the response of detection electronics. Chaos dynamics is, by and large, a phenomenon of high-speed computing, showing itself best in the lovely fractal geometries of Mandelbrot sets. One stands, therefore, as the contemporary physicist always has, apart from nature, an onlooker.

I would maintain, therefore, that in addition to a metaphysics that allows values and holism, science also needs a methodology that includes qualities as well as quantities. Goethe and, after him, Rudolf Steiner (1861-1925) offer a promising framework for developing such a science, which is always aware of its vertical as well as its horizontal entanglements. As a poet-scientist, Goethe was ever mindful of the vast range of realities reflected in each phenomenon, and proceeded accordingly. Following his lead, Rudolf Steiner sought to perceive the occurrences of life in the spiritual context that would illumine them most fully. He viewed the spiritual as inherently intelligible, and therefore susceptible to objective inquiry. Both Goethe and Steiner, however, recognized that in order to include cultural, ethical, and spiritual aspects, the methods and scope of science requires change.

From Image to Archetype

Goethe viewed research as taking place in three steps which are depicted in Figure 3.[21] The first moment of scientific encounter is best characterized by wonder. Plato wrote that all true philosophy begins with wonder, and in the intervening 2000 years little has happened to change this opinion. We pass by countless phenomena without "wondering" about them. If we pause before them to marvel, we have taken the first tentative step toward scientific engagement. Phenomena studied at this level Goethe termed "empirical phenomena". No understanding of them is required, merely an openness, an ability to wonder. This naturally leads one to focus one's attention.

The act of attending is a powerful factor in human development. Without it, conscious learning is impossible. In attending to a phenomenon, a transformation occurs within the observer; a realignment or growth takes place. This fact was central to Goethe's understanding of research, for one is forever blind to that for which one has no eye. Through wonder, one is brought into a lively,

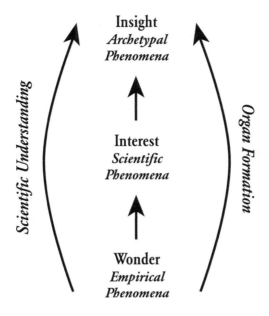

Figure 3:

Research and cognitive development, according to Goethe.

focused relationship to a phenomenon. That engagement is formative. As Goethe wrote:

Every object, well-contemplated, creates an organ for its perception.[22]

At the heart of Goethe's worldview, and certainly of his science, was the conviction that human beings undergo real development throughout their lives, spiritual as well as physical. Lively engagement with a phenomenon is essential for its understanding because, in Goethe's view, we are changed in the process; we develop faculties adequate to comprehending what is before us.

While the whole process begins in wonder, it is interest that animates the central period of organ formation. We take the naively given phenomena and begin to reproduce them for ourselves, changing the conditions to see which are required for its appearance, and which are minor factors. We distinguish the essential from the unessential. Goethe termed these "scientific phenomena". On them we train ourselves, and forge new faculties.

At this point it is important to note that Goethe remains with the phenomena throughout. He does not replace them with abstract concepts (point masses, postulated forces, unseen mechanisms . . .). Goethe's "scientific phenomena" retain their full range of associations, which meant for Goethe a moral-spiritual aspect intimately related to the purely sensory. The glow of oranges and reds in the evening sky is a moral-spiritual phenomenon as much as a physical one, and while the two might be distinguished, they cannot be divided.

The final step is the most difficult, but also the most important. It is the move from interest to insight, from scientific phenomena to what Goethe termed "pure or archetypal phenomena". Once again Goethe holds to the epithet: phenomena. Yet, at this point one moves beyond the concrete occasions of individual phenomena to exemplary or archetypal instances. In their purest form, such phenomena do not really exist outside the mind, but they can be seen within or through the most refined phenomena characteristic of an area of study. One never really sees, for example, the parabolic trajectory of a thrown stone, but under certain circumstances one comes close; and so one learns to see in the particular, the universal. Insight into the universal is a sublime moment, a "eureka" experience treasured by every discoverer. In order to apprehend the universal in this way, one must have labored long with "scientific phenomena", fashioning organs for insight.

The insight, once gained, needs to be communicated. But how? The only true way is to lead others to the same insight, which they must earn for themselves by traveling, like you, along the path of scientific experience, for they cannot see through your new-won faculties but must fashion their own. The alternative, almost unanimously adopted by the modern scientific method, is to reduce the experience to an equation, a mathematical relationship. Gone from it are the rich layers of meaning and association inseparable from real insight, but it retains the raw physical power of the original insight. Then, like a machine invented by some modern day Daedalus, the formula can be used without fully appreciating its moral import. Goethe foresaw the dangers of this approach, which are now, in the face of ecological disasters, the ethical implications of biotechnology, and our nuclear arsenal, becoming evident to us all. Like young Icarus, we fly on wings not of our manufacture, insufficiently aware of the hazards of flight and forgetting Blake's injunction: "No bird soars too high if he soars with his own wings".

Goethe sought inventors and discoverers, not technicians. He wanted an original, Daedalean relationship to scientific and technical knowledge, not an inherited relationship like that of Icarus, and he persisted in a unified view of knowing, including both the physical and the spiritual. An archetypal phenomenon, for all its purity, is woven of two worlds, one sensory and the other "moral". By attending to one face alone, we may forget, or lose sight of the other. The sentimental poet may lose the physical force of insight, while the scientist, embarrassed by the sublime, may rush to strip insight of her glory. Goethe steadfastly refused to sunder one world from the other; he insisted on vertical entanglement at every moment and in every instance.

One of Goethe's most careful students, Rudolf Steiner, sought to extend and apply Goethe's method of inquiry. Trained in the sciences and philosophy, but also an individual with singular spiritual gifts, Steiner saw Goethe's understanding of science as one capacious enough to hold an objective inquiry into the ethical and spiritual, as well as physical aspects of life. The archetypal phenomena were, as Hegel termed them, windows opening out onto a phenomenology of mind or spirit. Rudolf Steiner published his epistemology and spiritual philosophy in numerous books.[23]

Like Goethe, Steiner held that through disciplined inquiry faculties are developed, but he held that these could include faculties suited particularly for spiritual as well as conventional scientific research. The phenomena of nature and of life can be approached in a way that leads through archetypal phenomena to genuine spiritual experiences. The fruits of his own spiritual investigations led Steiner to a complex spiritual conception of the world in all its aspects. Of particular significance for our considerations is his understanding of human evolution. If we live in a period of metaphysical change, what light can Rudolf Steiner throw on its origins, character or relationship to a re-conceived space-time?

An Evolutionary Perspective

The revolutions of science, the rise of novel artistic achievements, or social and economic change are usually treated exclusively within the framework of external historical realities, perhaps including a modest psychological dimension. What I would like to suggest, and in this I follow Rudolf Steiner and Owen Barfield,[24] is that such developments are best understood as reflections not of external forces primarily, but of profound, if subtle, shifts in our consciousness, a shift that occurs very widely and so becomes of cultural as well as individual importance. Moreover, Steiner and Barfield suggest that the basis for such changes in consciousness is to be found in the changing soul-spiritual configuration of the human being. The driving forces that determine these changes in the human soul are as much inward as outward in nature. Although not a widely held position, I find their view of value, and would therefore like to apply this understanding to our previous considerations.

One can approach the evolution of consciousness in many ways, and it is a complex subject open to misconceptions and over-simplifications. Specifically I am not speaking about "progress", nor about a linear time-development in which the past is harvested for the future. A linear, mechanical conception of time can all too easily dominate our thinking in treatments of evolution, whereas there is perhaps no area where an organic or entangled notion of time is of greater importance than here. We need a conception in which the past is resurrected in the present and anticipates the future; where the future, as it were, works back into the present. With these cautions expressed, I would like, nonetheless, to venture an interpretation of the events we see being played out in quantum mechanics, chaos dynamics, ecology, etc.

If, as I have suggested, a form of thinking is emerging that is newly sensitive to holistic and ethical entanglements of our world, we may rightly ask: what has changed in us that brings these aspects newly to the fore? Why have we missed these features of our world for so long? How could we have been so blind? Rudolf Steiner maintained that such developments (or the lack thereof) are the reflection of inner, soul-spiritual changes. What are the specifics of such soul-spiritual changes and how do they occur? In order to answer this question I will need to briefly present Steiner's understanding of the "spiritual anatomy" of the human being.[25] Constraints of length will force me to be schematic.

Based on his spiritual experiences, Rudolf Steiner considered the human being to have a four-fold nature.[26] The aspect evident to us all is that which presents itself as the physical body, which includes that in us which is solid, liquid, aeriform and warm. The mineral, plant, and animal kingdoms obviously also possess a physical nature. To this Steiner adds, however, three other "bodies" or dimensions to the human being. The one most proximate to the physical he calls by the name "etheric" or "life" body. It is a body of formative forces, responsible for the form and life of the human being. Plants and animals, but not minerals, also possess such a body. The spatio-temporal order of the etheric is quite different from that of the physical, and will be of particular concern to us in understanding non-locality, entanglement and the rhythms of a new dynamics. To physical and etheric bodies are added two others, called by the names "astral body" and the "Ego". With the astral body there arises the inner world of simple, sentient consciousness which we share with the animal world. Finally, Steiner sees the human being as possessing an Ego responsible for self-consciousness. Details of the four-fold nature of the human being can be found in many of Steiner's books.[27]

Although in a certain sense all four of these aspects of the human being have been present for many thousands of years, the relationship of thinking to them has changed fundamentally over that time. In order to understand this, one needs to allow the activity of thinking to have a reality which is not brain-bound. That is to say, in its essence, thinking is not a product of physical or bio-chemical processes of the body. Thinking, rightly understood, is a spiritual activity. However, according to Steiner, that activity can be realized or imaged in one or another of the four bodies. Over the long course of time, thinking has been realized first by the Ego, then by the astral, the etheric and, since the fifteenth century, by the physical body. The kind of thinking evidenced in an epoch reflects the relationship of thinking to one or another member of the soul-spiritual nature of the human being. For example, Greece at its height lived in a form of consciousness which brought thought to consciousness in the etheric body. The vital, living quality of art and philosophy during that period is a reflection of the etheric basis for thinking in the Greek soul.

In the time between the ninth and fifteenth centuries a significant change took place, and thinking "fell", as it were, further down into the physical body. On the one hand, in Steiner's view, this form of consciousness led to the possibility for true freedom (an essential gain), but on the other it led to the modern, materialistic conception of nature. In a 1924 "Letter to the Members", he described his view as follows:

> The reason materialism arose is not that only material things and processes are to be seen in the outer world of Nature; it is because human beings, in the course of evolution, had to go through a stage which brought them to a form of consciousness that is at first only capable of seeing material revelations. The one-sided development of this requirement in human evolution has resulted in the modern view of the natural world.[28]

Materialism climaxed in the mid-nineteenth century. By the turn of the century, many forces—artistic, religious and political as well as scientific—were shaking the bastions of complacent materialism, and advocating other aspects as both real and significant in life. During the first two decades of the century, Germany was swept by a "Life philosophy"—*Lebensphilosophie,* as it was called.[29] The Blue Rider School and many prominent literary and scientific figures threw themselves into the movement. After the tragic intervention of two world wars, which capitalized on the neo-Romantic excesses which were sometime a part of the movement, we find ourselves in a situation once again where a philosophy of life as opposed to matter, of ecology as opposed to atomism, seems in the air. Why? In his letter of 1924, Steiner stated that the present time marked the beginning of another shift of consciousness, one that would move the basis for thinking back from the physical body to the life body, or etheric body, of the human being. As this occurs, the "thought-shadows" of physical thinking will once again acquire life. According to Steiner, thinking will gradually come to reflect, in form and function, the character of the etheric which is inherently holistic. Individuals will be drawn toward new "living" thoughts as they lift their thinking itself to the level of life.

Stated frankly, I think that this is what is occurring in our time. By honest, forthright efforts, and with a heartfelt concern for others and for the planet, our thinking is being lifted into a realm of life. The laws of that realm are inherently non-local and entangled, and its rhythms are those of living things. The new ventures in quantum physics, chaos dynamics, agriculture, medicine, cognitive science, and biology are at root a reflection of a dawning cultural shift toward "living thinking", that is at once moral and intellectual. Much hangs on our self-awareness of this fact, and on our efforts to promote it not only in ourselves but also in others.

We have to come to understand that every phenomenon is an opportunity for an engagement that is qualitative as well as quantitative—that considers wholes as well as parts, chaos as well as order. These are but different aspects of the same unitary reality, which we should be careful to cultivate as well as investigate. The metaphysical foundations of science for the next millennium should be broad and deep enough to see science as a spiritual endeavor, as an aspiration of the human soul and an inseparable companion to art and religion. If we succeed in this, even if only modestly, then the transformations of culture and society will reach far beyond the provinces of academic science. Technology itself will change, becoming the hopeful basis for a sustainable future.

Technological Implications

Both Alfred North Whitehead and Martin Heidegger[30] understood modern technology to be the touchstone or insignia of our contemporary world. Whitehead wrote: "What is peculiar and new to the [twentieth] century, differentiating it from all its predecessors, is its technology".[31] Its particular features, which differ from those of antiquity, both represent our culture and continue to define it. The transformations wrought by science and technology have brought unparalleled mastery of physical forces and substances, and, inseparable from that mastery, the potential for hitherto inconceivable destruction. What deep and essential changes within the practice of technology and science might lead us through this dangerous time of passage?

Rejection of technology and science is not only infeasible, but an illusion. As Heidegger writes,[32] those who reject modern science and technology are no less chained to it, even intellectually, than those who enthusiastically embrace it. Aversion is as compelling as lust. To establish a free relationship to science and technology is of utmost importance. Otherwise we are held hostage by them, whether as enthusiasts or neo-Luddites.

How does one establish a free relationship to science and technology? Bluntly put, only by standing fully within the field of danger, and finding a way to the essence of each. In his seminal essay on *The Question Concerning Technology*,[33] Martin Heidegger quotes the German poet Hölderlin:

But where danger is, grows

The saving power also

and comments: "precisely the essence of technology must harbor in itself the growth of the saving power". Thus, knowledge of the essence carries with it the possibility of establishing a truly free relationship to science and technology. But one needs to go on, freely developing the saving power from out of the essential itself, surrounded by danger.

The old masonic legend of Hiram, who was master builder to King Solomon, contains a powerful image of the saving power within the danger. As the crowning ornament to the Temple, Hiram undertook to forge a huge brazen sea. As the molten bronze was poured, the mold failed because of sabotage by three jealous apprentices. In the moment of disaster, Hiram called out to his long line of spiritual ancestors for guidance. The voice of Tubal-Cain (the first artificer of bronze) arose, urging him into the fiery molten sea itself. In response, Hiram threw himself directly into the flaming metal. By doing so, he was granted the magical means to save the casting. By dying into one's craft, one can bring it new life.

Is it possible to transfigure the crafts, be they physics, cognitive science, computer technologies, biology, medicine, agriculture or waste treatment, by staying with them, or to put it figuratively, by dying within them? I believe that the answer is "Yes". The thinking such technologies require will have the figure and form of entanglement and the rhythmical dynamics of life. We can find instances of them already about us. In agriculture, the organic and biodynamic movements are proving that caring for the Earth is not incommensurate with growing health-giving food. In medicine, the significance of mind, so long belittled in Western medicine, is now reasserting itself, as thousands of practicing physicians diagnose and treat their patients as soul-spiritual beings, as well as physical bodies. Even the wastes we produce in such prodigious quantities are being penetrated and transformed by a new kind of technology— the waste water work of John Todd, and the composting projects of Will Brinton, mentioned above, being but two examples with enormous potential.[34] All of these are predicated on an understanding of nature and human life as an integrated whole; they are based in a nexus of values that reach beyond profit and power to a recognition of the entwined order, moral and physical, in which we live.

In his February 4, 1992, speech to the World Economic Forum, Vaclav Havel recognized the fall of communism not as the victory of capitalism, but as the end of the modern era. According to Havel, the post-Newtonian metaphysics described by Burtt is crumbling. A truly fresh metaphysics, one amply exemplified by Goethe and Steiner, remains in the wings vying for attention. When Havel writes, it could be Goethe speaking:

> We must try harder to understand than to explain. The way forward is not
> in the mere construction of universal systematic solutions, to be applied to

reality from the outside; it is also seeking to get to the heart of reality through personal experience. In a word, human uniqueness, human action and the human spirit must be rehabilitated.[35]

That same revitalized spirit must come to shine through every human enterprise, and nowhere more brightly than in science and technology. Then will the new wine, vintage 2000, be borne in fitting wineskins.

References

1. E. A. Burtt, *The Metaphysical Foundations of Modern Science,* Doubleday Anchor, 1954, p. 302.

2. See Arthur G. Zajonc, *Catching the Light,* Bantam, 1993, Chapter 9.

3. Daniel M. Greenberger, "The Neutron Interferometer as a device for illustrating the strange behavior of quantum systems" in *Reviews of Modern Physics* 55, 1983, pp. 875-906.

4. A. Tomomura, J. Endo, T. Matsuda and T. Kawasaki, "Demonstration of single-electron buildup of an interference pattern" in *American Journal of Physics* 57, 1989, pp. 117-120. Also, see the report in *Science* 252, May 1991, pp. 921-922, "Making waves with interfering atoms" for an overview of atom interferometers. For photons, see P. Grangier, G. Roper and A. Aspect in *Europhysics Letters* 1, 1986, pp. 173-179.

5. A. Einstein, B. Podolsky and N. Rosen, "Can the quantum-mechanical description of physical reality be considered complete" in *Physical Review* 47, 1935, pp. 777-780.

6. Quoted in Max Jammer, *The Philosophy of Quantum Mechanics,* John Wiley and Sons, 1974, p. 212.

7. See, for example, the papers by Aspect et al. in *Physical Review Letters,* 47, 1981, pp. 460ff; 49, 1982, pp. 91ff; 49, 1982, pp. 1804ff.

8. Arthur G. Zajonc, *Catching the Light,* Bantam, 1993, pp. 315-316.

9. Bohm's theory is attractive in several respects. Massive particles retain their autonomous character throughout, and the mysteries of non-locality and entanglement are carried by a ghost-like quantum potential, unique to his theory. See D. Bohm, B. J. Hiley and P. N. Kaloyerou, "An ontological basis for the quantum theory", in *Physics Letters* A, 128, 1988.

10. See, for example, Larry Laudan, *Science and Values,* University of California Press, 1984, especially Chapter 1.

11. John F. Clauser and Abner Shimony, "Bell's theorem experimental test and implication", in *Reports on Progess in Physics* 41, 1978, pp. 1881-1927; and refs. by Aspect above.

12. See Donella H. Meadows, "The new alchemist" in *Harrowsmith* 38, 1988, pp. 38ff. on Wes Jackson.

13. Francisco J. Varela, Evan Thompson and Eleanor Rosch, *The Embodied Mind,* MIT Press, 1991.

14. See Evan Eisenberg, "Back to Eden" in *The Atlantic Monthly,* November 1988, pp. 57-89.

15. See *Wall Street Journal,* July 31, 1991, p. 1.

16. J. D. Franson, "Bell inequality for position and time" in *Physical Review Letter* 62, 1989, p. 2205; Z. Y. Ou, Z. Zou, L. J. Wang and L. Mandel, "Observation of non-local interference in separated photon channels" in *Physical Review Letters* 65, 1990, p. 321.

17. Roger Penrose, *The Emperor's New Mind,* Oxford University Press, 1989.

18. Quoted by Pierre Duhem in *To Save the Phenomena,* translated by Edmund Dolan and Chaninah Maschler, University of Chicago Press, 1969, p. 3.

19. Ibid.

20. See for example E. R. Hunt in *Physical Review Letters* 67, 1992, pp. 1953-55 and references therein.

21. Johann Wolfgang von Goethe, "Empirical observation and science" in *Scientific Studies,* edited and translated by Douglas Miller, Suhrkamp, 1988, pp. 24-25.

22. *Goethe's Werke, Hamburger Ausgabe,* edited by E. Trunz, 1961, 5th edition, Vol. 13, p. 38.

23. See for example Rudolf Steiner, *Philosophy and Freedom and Theosophy,* Anthroposophic Press, 1972.

24. Owen Barfield, *History, Guilt and Habit,* Wesleyan University Press, 1981. *Saving the Appearances,* Harcourt, Brace and World, 1988.

25. Rudolf Steiner, *Theosophy,* Anthroposophic Press, 1988, Chapter 1.

26. In other instances, he writes of a three- and nine-fold way of the understanding the human being.

27. See for example *Theosophy* (1981) and *Occult Sciences* (1982), Anthroposophic Press.

28. Rudolf Steiner, *The Michael Mystery,* Anthroposophical Publishing Co, 1956, p. 20.

29. See for example Paul Forma, "Weimar culture, causality and quantum theory (1918-27)" in *Historical Studies in the Physical Sciences,* edited by Russell McCormmach, University of Pennsylvania Press, 1971, Vol. 3, pp. 1-116.

30. Martin Heidegger, *The Question Concerning Technology,* translated by William Lovitt, Harper and Row, 1977.

31. Alfred North Whitehead, *Science and the Modern World,* The Macmillan Co., 1925, p. 22.

32. Heidegger, *The Question Concerning Technology* (see reference 30), p. 28.

33. Ibid.

34. See references 12 and 15.

35. Vaclav Havel, "The end of the modern era" in *The New York Times,* Sunday, March 8, 1992, Op-Ed page.

Radical Empiricism and the Conduct of Research

by Eugene Taylor

The only thing worse than someone with bad metaphysics is someone who thinks he has no metaphysics at all.

—C. S. Peirce

When we try to define precisely what is meant by scientific research, two opposing viewpoints immediately seem to emerge. One maintains that science is driven by consensually accepted theories about the physical world that organize a large body of accumulated facts. The purpose of research is thus to verify the theory. The other asserts that, because there are a number of possible theories that might be in conflict, all of which may be able to explain a body of facts, science must be defined by the more stable criteria of the methods used to produce it. Opponents of method often point out, however, that very few scientific disciplines adopt exactly the same experimental technique. Therefore, method alone cannot be an acceptable criterion.

While the struggle for supremacy between the theorists and the methodists in science has never abated, and, in fact, has probably driven an untold amount of new research in very creative ways, the battle is actually only very recent. For within the history of world knowledge, science has only developed into a superior force for change within the last four hundred years. For almost two thousand years prior to that, the historians tell us, only periodic attempts by isolated individuals marked the slow progress of objectively accumulated knowledge.

Several factors, we are told, must have been at work to account for such a long slow incubation period followed by rapid acceleration. Objective verification was a substantive advance on mere subjective impressions, partly because it subjected the results of each experiment to the crucial test of repeatability. The conceptual differentiation between induction and deduction was important, as it enabled the dogged empiricism of trial-and-error learning by individual investigators to be replaced by schematic generalizations, models, and rules about the working of particular phenomena known in common and verified by a larger community of colleagues. Knowledge accumulated and prior investigations as they became known did not need to be repeated. Also, the philosophy of positivism has certainly played a major role in guiding scientific thinking. Its main function has been to guide inquiry toward a deterministic view that the universe operates according to causal laws, that these laws can be objectively known, and that rational control over the forces of nature can best be achieved by precise measurement.

But objective verification, deductive thinking from theories to facts, and positivist epistemology, in addition to being benchmarks in the history of science, are also mental operations. They suggest in the present discussion that science is neither wholly driven by theories nor methods, but is perhaps better represented as an attitude or motive, that is, a particular state of consciousness based on certain consensually validated assumptions about the world, held by a community of individuals called scientists. There is a sense therefore in which we may refer to a psychology of science.

The problem with this definition, however, is that scientists, aspiring to be objective, universal, and neutral, maintain a rigid distinction between the subjective and supposedly spurious world of the perceiver and the more immutable and concrete world of objects. To relegate the enterprise of science to the status of an attitude is to call into question the absolute existence of an objective world independent of the mind. This world simply exists without question for the reductionistic scientist.

Philosophers, meanwhile, especially phenomenologists, have always been fond of pointing out that all cognitive thinking is based on presuppositions of some kind. Scientists get around this by agreeing that, while certain first principles must be assumed, these principles cannot actually be questioned because their discussion leads to the realm of metaphysics, the conclusions of which are essentially unprovable. That science actually works in representing and controlling the forces of the physical world is, for them, sufficient justification for its perpetuation. Metaphysics and science are therefore considered radically different domains of inquiry.

The Phenomenology of the Science-Making Process

Even though the underlying assumptions of science are not usually analyzed, but must be accepted as *a priori* givens in order for research to go on, some philosophers of science have occasionally made forays into that forbidden zone where metaphysics and science overlap. Indeed, the scientific community often must engage in the exercise of justifying its activities, and, because one of the great drawbacks of science is that it cannot tell why it is good to pursue itself, these self-proclaiming advertisements often contain revealing metaphysical statements about the normally hidden aspects underlying the way that science is conducted. At the same time, the history of science is strewn with numerous sophisticated attempts to address assumptions implicit in the scientific enterprise. It is in this domain of intellectual inquiry that science as a specific kind of attitude or special state of consciousness is more directly addressed.

I would like to examine four such self-conscious attempts to examine the presuppositions of science. The ones I have chosen come from psychology and psychiatry, since these disciplines have some special considerations of their own regarding the problem of consciousness as their subject matter which separate them from the natural and biological sciences. In particular, I would like to advocate one of them, the radical empiricism of William James, as a still viable tool which can be used not only to critique the on-going enterprise of science-making in psychology, but also to suggest, because of its focus on the phenomenology of the science-making process, some useful new directions germane to experimental research.

Koch on Cognitive Pathologistics

Sigmund Koch of Boston University, historian and philosopher of science and experimental psychologist, has spent the last fifty years analyzing the methods and theories of scientific psychology. He has concluded that, despite a large mass of idealized rhetoric to the contrary which has been spoon fed to successive generations of graduate students, government panels, and grant funding agencies, psychology today is in no sense a unified science.[1]

In the first place, he maintains that there is no consensually agreed upon body of accumulated knowledge that constitutes the core of the discipline. He gives numerous examples from history. The experimental laboratory methods of Wundt and Titchener from one hundred years ago dealing with the controlled introspective analysis of consciousness by trained observers were displaced by Watsonian stimulus-response theory after 1910. Meanwhile, the data of psychological tests and measurements, such as the intelligence scales and the interest inventories, began to accrue after World War I and represented a competing and unintegratable body of information when compared to stimulus-response learning theories. Today, cognitive theorists have largely abandoned the strict behaviorist paradigm as overly simplistic, suggesting that the efforts of the previous fifty years, constituting hundreds of thousands of man-hours of research, untold lives of experimental animals, and millions of dollars in grant funding, carried on for the purpose of unifying all of psychology under rat learning theory, amounted exactly to zero.

Second, Koch maintains that there is no commonly agreed upon method for conducting laboratory research. Even after the introduction of inferential statistics, one laboratory would use analysis of variance designs, another would adopt correlation methods, and yet another opt for simple probability quotients. Stanley Milgram's behavioral study of obedience, for instance, relied much more on situational factors and idiosyncratic responses of subjects than on the large-scale statistical evaluation of measurements on just one small, specific variable.[2] B. F. Skinner scandalized the experimental establishment by choosing only to perform an in-depth study on a subject sample of one.[3] His results were presented not as the statistical summary of a large sample of measurements, but rather as the simple graph of the altered behavior of each single organism.

Third, there is no central theory unifying all the subfields together. Indeed, ideologies abound in both psychology and psychiatry. One school promotes psychoanalysis, another biochemical interventions in mental illness. In psychology, the fractionated period of the individual schools in the 1920s gave way to the Age of Theory, which lasted almost thirty years, in which attempts were made to construct a single hypothetico-deductive model based on mathematical formulas for all research, deviation from which would be arbitrated by laboratory analysis. The failure of this endeavor led to the age of mini-theories in the 1950s, where the word "theory" in the grand sense was replaced by the generation of little models, whose empirical rightness, it was hoped, would later lead by their summation to the grand system. This result, of course, also did not come about.

Koch's detailed analysis of the failure of specific research programs in psychology has led him to look into the metaphysical foundations of experimental research in other branches of science as well. His conclusions he organized into an entirely new field, which he calls Cognitive Pathologistics, an analysis of the scientifically engendered disease of "ameaning" that is not only endemic to the sciences, but by now also thoroughly pervades the arts and the humanities in modern culture. By ameaning, Koch refers to the cognitive epistemopathy of scientific rhetoricians who limit the scope of the human experience in all its myriad and complex forms only to that which can be measured. Thus, since consciousness cannot be measured but behavior can, and since people were too complex but lower animals more easy to control, psychologists were forced for five decades to confine themselves to the measurement of how long it took for a white rat to run down to the end of a maze or to press a lever in a box. The success of rhetoricians at defining scientific psychology in this way was achieved only by rigidly applying a set of arbitrary rules lifted from the physical sciences and distorted to fit psychology.

The simple set of directions still taught to all graduate students for writing up an experiment provides an instructive example. One is told to first outline the problem (an exhaustive historical review was never considered necessary, or even desirable). One then quickly moves on to a statement of the hypothesis. The method is then presented, a statement usually made up of the selection of subjects, the instructions given of manipulations performed, and a description of the statistics used to analyze the data that have been collected. A results section gives the numerical conclusions, and a discussion section permits the generalization of the specific data of the experiment to whatever wider realm serves the experimenter's purpose. This may be either the destruction of another's cherished theory, or else the grandiose generalization of the findings from this one study to all of human and animal behavior in every circumstance conceivable (while replication of someone else's experiment was ideally considered most desirable, in reality it was almost never done; the emphasis was, rather, always on "original research"). Finally, in order to tone down the grandiosity and to set the stage for further grant proposals, the author is always instructed to end with the same phrase: "the results show that further research is needed".

For at least the last seventy years, psychological journals have been burdened with this model of writing. When we examine its total impact over the course of history, we find that the main effect has been to make psychology appear scientific, even though the total accumulated factual results suggest the contrary. Psychology, Koch concludes, has thus unwittingly contributed to the larger social problem of an information glut, most of it largely meaningless.

For Professor Koch, these trends toward ameaning, defined in terms of the scientist's penchant for indulging in "demystification", and excessive rule-bound behavior, are based on a set of metaphysical assumptions that have had profound influence on almost every aspect of culture. In fact, their effect is so pervasive as to demonstrate how the so-called objectively neutral stance of science has been elevated to the major orienting philosophy of life in the modern world. Indeed, one might claim that the implicit assumptions of the scientific worldview have become hypostatized into the form of a *sub rosa* religious institution. Science now represents the ultimate secularization of the religious impulse and defines the only acceptable form of contemporary spirituality able to be propounded by the arbiters of culture, modernity, and higher learning today.

MacMurray on a Science of Consciousness

Professor John MacMurray from the University College in London has also looked into the metaphysical assumptions of the scientific enterprise. His position was that we are rapidly approaching a time when, as the limits of science are more clearly understood, the scientific worldview will lose its place of supremacy and be seen as only one of several competing forms of knowledge within modern culture.[4] His thesis can be divided into two parts. First, he pointed out that the choice to pursue science as an objective discipline is essentially a subjective event on the part of each individual. Subjective forms of knowing, such as the Divine Right of Kings or the revelations of the priesthood, ruled collective definitions of reality in the pre-scientific age. This situation prevailed until the rational and empirical methods of the scientists were taken up by individuals such as Galileo, Newton, and Copernicus, each of whom chose as a personal commitment to pursue experimental methods against the prevailing worldview. Since then, things have not changed. While science remains an objective pursuit, the choice to pursue science is still a subjective event in the life and career of each budding scientist. Paradoxically, such an individual decision cannot be accounted for strictly by the methods and theories of science itself. Human, subjective factors are always operating in the urge to produce science.

Second, while historical circumstance and collective endeavor helped science and technology gain the ascendant, there is no doubt that most of the early gains occurred because they were within the realm of the inorganic physical sciences. As momentum, and hence power over affairs, increased, the scientific enterprise then progressed swiftly into the organic realm. The early history of science thus develops almost uniformly from physics, through chemistry, to biology. Only within the last one hundred years has the scientific attitude taken over the domain of psychology. It is perhaps no accident that objective experimental investigation focused first on physiology and behavior and has only now progressed to the cognitive processes of consciousness. Science has only recently discovered the domain of the mind. Yet here we may have also reached the limit of the scientific mindset. A science can objectively study any phenomenon by externalizing it from the processes of cognition and perception, but it cannot objectively study itself.

For these reasons, subjective factors continue to bedevil psychological and psychiatric research. When we try to scientifically study psychotherapy, we find that outcomes are not so different between the faith healer and the scientifically trained and legally certified psychiatrist.[5] Rather than objective scientific knowledge, the results seem to depend more on a complex set of variables that are in harmony between the therapist and the patient and these cannot be scientifically measured or objectively taught. When we survey, for instance, the progress of psychiatric medicine over the last thirty years, we find great advances in all areas of research and patient care, except that psychiatrists still seem able to best help only those who come from the same socio-economic bracket in society as themselves.[6] When in the laboratory we apply the scientific method to a very small area of chemical activity in the brain by abstracting a reaction out of its context, we discover an inverse ratio between precision and application to real-life events. The specific action of drugs in a test tube, for instance, must always be weighed against the ever-present problems of real-life side effects, which can only be discovered later in clinical practice once the drug is tried on actual human beings.

Thus, according to MacMurray, even though the scientific endeavor has become the greatest achievement of Western thought and will long endure beyond the culture that created it, we may be witness to an era in which the production phase of science has come to an end. As a culture we are now in transition toward a more permanent maintenance phase of science as a world industry. In the production phase, we could afford to ignore the noisome by-products, such as environmental, ethical, and quality-of-life issues. In the maintenance phase, however, all these questions now must be addressed. A science of the future will either have to alter its basic presuppositions in order to account for the problem of self-consciousness, or else reconcile itself to a more subordinate position as just one of many other forms of useful knowledge within culture.[7]

Peirce on Abduction

Another philosopher of science who has attempted to fathom the gray area between subjective and objective forms of knowing in science has been the logician and mathematical philosopher Charles Sanders Peirce.[8] Even though he was well aware of numerous extra-scientific factors impinging on the research situation, Peirce nevertheless sought to address the question of how science-making is possible.

To attack the problem, he created a new category in analyzing the methods of deduction and induction, which he called "abduction". While induction argues from facts to theories, and deduction from theories to facts, abduction deals with the process of creative hypothesis formulation. It does so by asking: "How does a scientist, without knowing the outcome of an empirical experiment beforehand, choose a testable hypothesis in the first place?"

Peirce explained abduction by telling the following story: he had been abroad in the early 1870s on an international scientific mission for the US Coastal Survey and was returning to the United States by steamer. When the boat docked in New York, he vacated his cabin in such a hurry that he left his raincoat and a valuable watch in a case which the Survey had given him to take precision measurements. He discovered his loss after he had landed and went immediately back to the boat, but found the cabin empty of the items.

He approached the captain, who was very sympathetic to his cause. A search was made of the ship and all employees were lined up for detailed questioning. There was evidently a sizable number of people who might have had access to his cabin and Peirce began to question each one of them individually. He realized he had no idea what to ask them, for surely if he confronted everyone openly, each would deny it. He decided, instead, that he would conduct each interview in private and simply spend a moment getting the person to talk about anything that came to mind.

As the last few employees approached, Peirce realized that he would soon have to come to some conclusion, but he did not have any earthly idea what that would be, or how he would come to it. When the last person had returned to the assembled ranks, Peirce, who at first stood with the captain in front of them, began walking up and down the line. Suddenly he abruptly halted before one man, why he did not know, and asked him point blank if he had taken the items. The man denied any knowledge of the affair. The employees were dismissed and Peirce immediately left the ship.

Still trying to decide what to do, Peirce went to the Pinkerton Detective Agency and told them what had happened and everything he had done. They laughed at his method, but said they would make an immediate investigation using their own professional techniques. Nothing turned up, however. One of the agents then made the suggestion to Peirce that he advertise a large reward among the pawnshop owners of the city for information leading to the return of the goods.

Within a few days, one such pawnbroker came forward with the missing watch and the claim ticket, on which was written the name and address of the man who had pawned it. The police went immediately to his house and found the watch case and the raincoat. They promptly arrested the man, who turned out to be the very gentleman Peirce had confronted at the end of his interviews on the ship.

The question now confronted Peirce: exactly how, without any preconceived theories and without the ability to collect specific facts that were obviously relevant to the case, was he able to pick the right man? Prior training as a scientist was obviously essential, but its relevance had to reside in the overall mass of his experience rather than in specifically identifiable elements. At any rate, the answer was that his training had brought about the honing and activation of faculties which also must operate in the experimental situation that are beyond sense perception and rational analysis alone.

Yet, what was the lesson of this particular exercise? The answer is quite important for the conduct of research. At one level, Peirce was dealing with the place of the "intuitive hunch" in normative experimentation, a topic consistently and self-consciously jettisoned by the hard-core positivist. At another, as a logician, Peirce was really engaging in the much larger and more novel epistemological agenda of appropriating intuition into the processes of reason for purposes of furthering scientific inquiry.

The lesson is that against the dictates of normative experimentation and the way science is traditionally taught, facts and theories must be held in abeyance for the intuitive faculties to come into play. A leap of faith must be taken if information from beyond the bounds of the known is to be forthcoming. Under these circumstances, Peirce's doctrine, which he called synechism, echoes the insight of Louis Pasteur, who said: "Chance favors the mind that is prepared".

James on Radical Empiricism

Yet a fourth thinker, one who has probably come closer than any other philosopher to redefining the proper purview of experimental psychology by extending it into the phenomenal, subjective realm of the perceiver, was William James.[9] The essential problem for James was that there cannot be a science of any kind without some consciousness to name and interpret it. Objective realities always exist not as independent entities, but as a function of something else. The name he gave to this view was radical empiricism, by which he meant not "sense perception alone", but "experience first".[10]

Radical empiricism is a way of defining the basic data of the sciences in terms of experience. Rationalism, as a scientific outlook, deals with universals and makes wholes prior to parts in order of logic as well as in that of being. Empiricism, on the other hand, stresses the part, the element, the individual, and treats the whole as a collection and the universal as an abstraction. Empiricism generates a mosaic philosophy since it allows the parts to speak for themselves and treats the wholes as being of a second, and therefore not quite so significant, order. It is inductive, since it starts with facts and reasons to theories, rather than deductive, which is driven by models in search of facts to corroborate them.

But empiricism as a way of knowing and constructing the world is not mere sensory stimulation. Rather, it deals with the entire phenomena of experience, whether generated from within the person or outside. Empiricism becomes radical when it refuses to admit into its constructions any element that is not directly experienced, nor exclude from them any element that is directly experienced. It deals both with reality and how we take it. Thus, within the entire range of human experience, all claims are a potential topic of scientific investigation, although not all may be ultimately verified.

Radical empiricism is also ultimately pluralistic. There can be many ways of taking reality. One person's phenomenological description may differ in large ways from another's. In fact, the appreciation of individuality is a hallmark of the radically empirical view. At the same time, two or more minds can know the same thing. Therefore, consensus occurs, but it is never complete. There are always exceptions at some point. Unanimity is never permanent. Experience is in a constant state of flux. What was fixed today will be moving tomorrow. Radical empiricism thus admits no single fact or theory as explaining the whole (although monism can always be one of a pluralist's options).

Radical empiricism is also pragmatic. There must be some sorting mechanism which differentiates and weighs the value of a variety of experiences, and that standard in the radical empirical view is always outcome. In other words, the reconciliation of all ultimate truth claims must be in the actual arena of living. It is not simply enough to have a thought, there must also be an act. The testing ground for all ideation is experience. Beliefs are proven or disproven by their effects. At the same time, effects infer belief. Acts are motivated by ideas, even if not consciously realized. Acts can never be the sole determinant, however. Rather, both ideas and their consequences must constitute our perception of the whole.

Radical Empiricism as a Research Strategy

James intended his metaphysics of radical empiricism to function as a critique of experimental scientific research. In his view, while positivist episte-mology had to exclude metaphysics in the initial phases that marked the launching of any science, this was not a permanent condition. As all sciences mature they need to be overhauled periodically, but, by the very untestable nature of their first principles, they do not contain the inherent ability to renovate themselves. This is, rather, the job of metaphysics, by which James meant the speculation of reasonable men and women about meaning, value, and relevance, with regard to the effort and outcome of any human enterprise, given the certainty of change and the possibility of error.

He put forth his ideas with the assurance that human factors eventually had to be figured into any scientific endeavor. The problem was that prior to the first articulation of his radical empiricism in the 1890s, he believed that no metaphysical system was sophisticated enough to confront the enormously successful results of the scientific mindset, which had even then forced a single conception of reality on modern culture. James died before he could articulate the full details of his metaphysical system, and his theory has had to be adapted to a variety of scientific endeavors by others in a somewhat entrepreneurial fashion. This is the task of the following section.

Three Case Studies

Radical empiricism suggests that the underlying assumptions of all scientific disciplines are at base philosophical, and that the radically empirical view can be brought to bear as a way to

1) critique the work of scientific reductionists in light of their own metaphysical criteria, as well as

2) explain phenomena amenable to scientific scrutiny not normally adjudicated by the metaphysics of physicalism.

The most basic question, however, is that if subjective factors play such a hidden role in experimental investigation, then how can research even go on? To address this issue, I would like to take up three contemporary examples of scientific analysis, examine their methodology, and critique them from the standpoint of radical empiricism. The first is a statement about scientific research in a well-known introductory psychology textbook. The second is a recent government study of the American human potential movement. The third is an attempt to redefine how we can do cross-cultural research in epidemiological psychiatry.

A Textbook in Psychology

One function of the metaphysic of radical empiricism is to provide a useful tool for the analysis of philosophical assumptions underlying scientific truth claims. A case in point is the rhetoric employed in an elementary textbook in psychology designed to give undergraduates their introduction to laboratory methods and to scientific ways of thinking. The work I have chosen is the widely adopted *Introduction to Psychology* by Munn, Fernald, and Fernald, which went through three editions between 1946 and 1976, and which would have influenced the present generation of practicing professionals in academic psychology.[11]

The opening statement of the book defines the nature of psychology as the science of human behavior. This was the required definition of all introductory textbooks for the period and was based on the pre-eminence of stimulus-response learning theory on laboratory studies of the white rat. The orthodox view was that scientific psychology dealt with only that which could be observed and measured. The authors then spend two pages backtracking by redefining scientific psychology with a plethora of contradictions. Having once appeased the establishment definition of psychology as the study only of what is overtly observable, they then admit that "some psychologists are interested in experience", a position which the authors identify as phenomenology, or how a person uniquely perceives the world. The authors hedge on making any claim as to the scientific status of phenomenology (and they omit altogether any mention of the extent to which laboratory measurement is phenomenological), except to infer that the communication of one's feelings and perceptions about the world is not as accurate as the laboratory measurement of observable behavior. They also admit that, even though psychology is the biological science of observable behavior, organisms exist in groups, so that psychology is also a social science. One gets the feeling here that the subject matter of psychology is defined not by the subject being studied, but by the methodological restraints and by lines politically drawn between different academic departments.

The authors then follow with a long section on the unscientific study of behavior, meaning pseudo-psychology, or that which is "unscientific" and therefore not "real psychology". They attack first the ability of every individual to develop their own intuitive norms about character. "Common sense" is debunked as inferior to scientific knowledge and "available evidence". Their idea of common sense is a list of stereotypic cliches, unrelated to any in-depth study of a single person's internally coherent worldview, or even to any of the numerous studies in the current psychological literature where personal philosophy of life has been reported as relevant to outcome.

Their most concerted attack, however, is reserved for what they call "fallacious claims concerning training in psychology". This is based on the idea that one cannot call oneself a psychologist "without appropriate training in the science of psychology". The authors then offer as evidence what can only be judged as the uncontrolled assessment of a single graduate student. This student, the authors tell us, had visited fourteen mental health providers, all of whom had advertised themselves in a phone directory as qualified to deliver psychological services. Visiting only "once or twice", in each case, the student had presented the same syndrome of fictitious symptoms. The student concluded that "more than half . . . were psychoquacks and that six had good intentions but were unqualified", but we are not informed of the criteria used to reach this judgment.[12]

The authors then conclude more generally that "the properly trained psychologist is a scientist or practitioner who uses scientific methods and the information resulting from scientific investigation". But this assertion cannot possibly be the case. The majority of psychologists in the American Psychological Association, for instance, are clinicians in private practice who do various kinds of psychotherapy in no way derived from experimental laboratory studies or other scientific experiments of any kind.

This claim is actually a literary device in order to turn to a discussion about the nature and assumptions of science, the scientific method, and scientific thinking. Here, the true metaphysics of physicalism is revealed.

The most philosophical and unscientific aspect of the authors' thinking comes at the beginning when discussing the aims of science. What they call the "ultimate aim of scientific inquiry" is to "achieve through increased understanding . . . the betterment of man".[13] One must note the injection of a true teleology into this endeavor, as "better" is a value judgment that must be defined by some unspecified, personal, and ultimately phenomenological criteria. Their gender specific language referring to the "betterment of man" is also of some consequence, since the authors also include the rhapsodic soliloquy of one writer who speaks of the aims of science as "man's 'love of Nature untainted with hidden plans for Her exploitation'". One can only imagine what this loving embrace of Man and Nature (who is supposedly a woman) through science may mean, given the present systematic destruction of the natural environment through these same scientific and technological achievements, not to mention current debates over the exploitation of women.

Nevertheless, the aims of science, the authors continue, are realized through description, prediction, and control. Information is to be collected "without imposing value judgments". Differences are subsumed under commonalities, which allow for the classification of observations and the development of a taxonomy. Prediction is essentially hypothesis formulation, "which may be stated verbally or mathematically".[14] Statistics are the psychologist's foremost means of prediction. Then they categorically assert, in a gross overstatement of the precision of their method, that "using probability tables and related measures, [the psychologist] can accurately predict such varied aspects of human behavior as activity cycles, school performance, and responses to advertisement".[15]

When they turn to a discussion of experimental control, the authors give examples not from psychology, but from manned space flight and the control of disease in medicine, before also including in the same sentence "the success of psychologists in dealing with problems of behavior disorders".[16] Besides being grammatically awkward, the authors are clearly engaging in a kind of rhetoric designed to associate psychology exclusively with the natural sciences. To buttress this assertion, they show the performance graph over an eight-week period of a single mental patient (of unknown diagnosis) who has been taught by operant conditioning to feed himself (a behavior that was desirable to train into the patient, the authors explained, because the nurse would always spill food all over the patient when she fed him).

When the authors turn to the assumptions of science, they discuss orderliness and causality. All their examples for orderliness come from physics, and they readily admit that "this assumption is most readily made with respect to the physical world".[17] Their only reference to psychology is a quote from another textbook which says that the older psychology as a science gets, the more order it discovers in behavior. Then they take up the discussion of "limited causality", which is the assumption that only a limited number of events are related to any other event. Basic to the worldview of the scientist is the idea that his own personal characteristics do not affect the tides or that the drinking behavior of New York truck drivers is in any way affected by the activities of African tribesmen. "For any particular circumstance, it is assumed that the number of related factors is limited".[18]

They admit that there is no one single scientific method, but "many approaches in different areas". Rather, the enduring task of science is "developing improved research methods". Most scientific inquiry is conducted by observation, hypothesis formulation and testing, and verification. More important, however, is that the inquiry should be characterized by objectivity, meaning explicitly defined operations so that others may replicate one's findings, and by reasonable interpretation.

In the discussion of objectivity, the authors at least note that "personal inclination determines which problem a scientist studies".[19] They quickly recover, however, by saying that "once the problem has been selected, [the psychologist] characteristically pursues a course which is independent of his feelings". His aim is to "let the results speak for themselves".

Interpretation, on the other hand, which is probably the most complex and value laden step in the entire process, the authors counsel is to be "developed in the context of all relevant factual data". The only clue given to the student about problems of interpretation is to caution that "the simplest or least complex explanation is to be preferred".[20]

One of the most interesting statements in this section comes from the authors' assertion that "The chief characteristic of science might be described as empiricism, which refers to the seeking of evidence through direct experience".[21] According to their own definition, psychology appears to have no relevance to this chief characteristic of science, if psychology itself, to be truly scientific in the orthodox sense, is strictly defined in terms of observable behavior. To admit experience, however, is to shift the focus of psychology away from an exclusive reliance on a metaphysics of physicalism toward a metaphysics that sounds like radical empiricism. Their point in making this claim, however, was more general, as they merely wished to conclude that evidence through observation is the hallmark of science, not dependence on authority and speculation.[22] Nevertheless, they seem to infer that experience is the final standard.

The last section that we will deal with concerns the authors' comments on scientific thinking. The general tone here is to convince the reader that scientific facts are not absolute and unequivocal, that the good scientist remains always skeptical, and that any conclusions drawn are always tentative and subject to revision with newer and more conclusive data. "The problem of interpreting scientific findings requires just such an attitude", they say paradoxically, "particularly when 'unobservable' phenomena are involved".[23]

The discussion then turns to the nature of constructs and theories. In general, the authors tell us, scientific thinking is made up of what is observed and what is inferred. In their example, if a student is seen running, this is an observed behavior, but why he is running must be inferred, as he could be afraid, eager, or just exercising. Psychology must infer certain topics, such as "thinking, remembering, feeling, perceiving, attending, and many others, that would otherwise have to be excluded".[24]

We must note that these divisions of internal mental functioning are themselves hypothetical, and a holdover from the categories of the mind bequeathed unquestioningly to modern psychology from the Scottish moral philosophers of the early nineteenth century. In any case, unobservables abound in the sciences, the authors assure us, giving an example of the inferred nucleus from a collision experiment in physics. Again, in the mind of the reader this classically conditions the rhetoric of psychology to the subject matter of the natural sciences.

Psychological theory, meanwhile, is full of inferred entities. The construct of memory, for instance, is purely theoretical, since we have never actually been able to see or isolate memory from any other brain function. The best scientists have done is to posit the existence of the engram, a non-existent physiological something which is thought to be the carrier of individual memories, but no such engram has ever actually been discovered.

Operational definitions, the authors tell us, are a means to be more precise about inferred constructs. To operationally define something, according to the authors, is to define something unobservable in terms of something that is observable which is thought to produce it. This division must be considered arbitrary, however, because they have already stated that agreement can only be certain when specific observables are measured. There are no rules for establishing any relation between the unobserved and the observed. What is defined as a relation and what is also simultaneously left out must always be a matter of dispute. For example, just because love is defined by a particular set of autonomic responses, such as increased heart rate, pupillary expansion, and rapid breathing, this does not automatically mean that this is all there is to love, or that this even measures that mysterious something called love at all. The authors' only justification for theories and constructs in psychology is that such model building is better than something "less precise—hence less scientific ..."[25]

Analysis of this section from an introductory psychology text is particularly instructive for several reasons. It tells us that the rhetoric of scientific psychology is full of philosophical contradictions in a discipline that claims to have jettisoned philosophy entirely from its makeup. It suggests that the methods and assumptions of the physical sciences have been indiscriminately borrowed from the inorganic and biological realm and naively superimposed onto the psychological domain uncritically and in violation of the careful skepticism which is put forth as the hallmark of scientific inquiry in the first place. It also suggests that psychology as a discipline has an identity crisis characterized by the need to appear truly objective, reductionistic, and free of subjective contamination, when in reality it is deeply influenced by personal phenomenology.

Human Potential

The second case I wish to analyze is a project assessing techniques believed to enhance human performance. This project was commissioned by the Army Research Institute in 1984 and carried out by a committee appointed by the National Research Council. The findings of the Committee were reported by the NRC in two publications, *Enhancing Human Performance: Issues, Theories, and Techniques* (1988) and *In the Mind's Eye: Enhancing Human Performance* (1991).[26] The committee, which consisted of "fourteen experts, selected for their expertise in relevant basic-science areas", was appointed by the Commission on Behavioral and Social Sciences and Education within the NRC.[27]

The project itself focused on the evaluation of "techniques, developed largely outside the academic research establishment", which "offered the potential to accelerate learning, improve motor skills, alter mental states, reduce stress, increase social influence, foster group cohesion, and—in the parapsychological domain—produce remote viewing and psychokinetic control of electronic devices".[28]

While the project was far ranging and included an evaluation of topics as varied as pain control, team performance, and subliminal self-help tapes, I would like to focus exclusively on only one assessment, that of meditation.[29] The chapter on meditation "considers what is known about effects of meditation and discusses the problem of application of meditation techniques in diverse situations . . ."[30]

In evaluating the chapter on meditation, one must realize from the outset that the authors are not reporting on any original investigations involving experimental and control groups, but rather they are only reviewing a narrow selection of scientific literature published in English, in some cases relying solely on summaries of summaries. Their pronouncements are therefore particularly open to philosophical analysis, because they make large assumptions and come to many general theoretical conclusions.

Overall, one can say that their comprehension of meditation is naive, their characterizations trite, and, in several instances, they indulge in linguistic inaccuracies and statements of central principles which show complete ignorance of the subject under discussion. This seems unfortunate at the level of the doctorate in psychology, when such information is readily available to them from anthropologists, sociologists, and scholars in comparative religions, as well as from indigenous practitioners.[31]

In their opening sentence, for instance, the authors attempt to define meditation: "Meditation is generally defined as a class of techniques designed to influence an individual's consciousness through the regulation of attention".[32] This is implausible for several reasons. First, there is no general, universally accepted definition of meditation as the manipulation of attention. Second, if they are analyzing a technique from some Asian system, it must be specified by its linguistic referent because the terms have different meanings in different systems. Third, because there is no commonly accepted definition of meditation, its usage must always be interpreted within the context of a particular school, anchored in a definite historical time period, and taken from a specific text. But they make no attempt to anchor their discussion anywhere other than the current scientific literature.

To justify their misstatement, the authors backtrack and try to suggest that there is some controversy over agreement on the conceptualization of meditation. We are never told among whom their generalizations are considered controversial, since they do not appear to have a grasp of the different schools. It is also hard to see where the controversy is located when most reductionistic scientists do not even consider the topic worthy of investigation anyway.

The authors then clearly express their lack of knowledge by stating what they say "seems" to them to be the "necessary procedural elements". But we are not told what criteria they used to choose these elements. Nevertheless, they list: lying or sitting quietly, attending to one's breath, the adoption of a passive attitude, being at ease, and sometimes chanting a word or phrase. To the knowledgable reader, these steps appear to be taken right out of Herbert Benson's *Relaxation Response* but without attribution.[33] Moreover, no practitioner considers these to be the only procedural elements, and Benson himself recognizes that these techniques are only conceptually generic. In particular, belief systems and conceptual sophistication of a cognitive language of consciousness mark the practice of advanced meditators, especially within the context of a particular tradition and within the sphere of a personal relationship between the student and a meditation teacher. None of these factors are recognized by the authors, however.

The authors further make a number of erroneous claims that are inaccurate from the standpoint of both scholarship and meditation practice. They claim that yogic practices originated exclusively on the Indian subcontinent, ignoring, for instance, the long tradition of Taoist meditation in China, which appears underived from Indian roots. They assert that there are "three streams in the history of meditation", and then give three categories in no way comparable: the "Buddhist" (we are not told what particular brand of Buddhism); that of Maharishi Mahesh Yogi (as if transcendental meditation were capable of representing all of Hindu meditation); and that of the "Western mystical tradition, both Christian and Jewish", speaking as if "Buddhist", "Maharishi Mahesh Yogi", and all of the "Western mystical tradition, both Christian and Jewish" are equally weighted. This is like an English sentence comparing the different races of mankind by referring to them as Chinese, John Smith, and a single group made up of Negroids and Australoids combined.

The authors then claim that the central principle of Buddhism is that "God is knowable", when Buddhism is not even a theistic religion. And they make the absolutely absurd statement that "Unlike Buddhist meditation, transcendental meditation did not require radical lifestyle changes or extended practice . . . " Technically, these are vague generalizations, certainly not based on sound empirical comparisons of two specific meditation systems. And, claiming to be speaking from the rational point of view, they explain away the tradition of *mantrayana*, or chanting, with reference to a quaint Anglo-American superstition: "Generations of insomniacs have been instructed to lie quietly and count sheep. It is doubtful that this homespun remedy for sleeplessness would persist over the years if it did not help some people some of the time."

The text then delves into the problem of experimental control. As the authors put it, there are seldom found in the many studies that demonstrate positive effects any controls for distraction or for just sitting or lying quietly and undisturbed.[34] They cite two separate studies to buttress their point which are not methodologically comparable, where no replication whatever has taken place, and they presume that "meditation" is defined the same way in each. Then they reach the egregious overgeneralization that "overall, our assessment of the scientific research on meditation (primarily transcendental meditation) leads to the conclusion that it seems to be no more effective in lowering metabolism than are established relaxation techniques; it is unwarranted to attribute any special effects to meditation alone".

Another methodological flaw is the frequently presented argument that, if they cannot find any data from the scientific literature for a particular effect, nothing can be said about it. This seems satisfactory by itself, but this statement is often presented in tandem with another, more nuanced generalization, such as "the laboratory findings that do exist fail to demonstrate that meditation itself fails to enhance a person's ability to reduce arousal from a stressor". Another way to read the same statement, however, is that no data means no one has investigated a particular problem, which is as much a reflection on choice of politically correct research problems as on the lack of data. Moreover, where researchers actually have done a few studies, methodological flaws alone could have led to the conclusion that meditation had no effect. In other words, the two statements presented together, that there are few studies in the literature and that what there is shows no effect, do not in themselves warrant any conclusion about meditation per se.

The authors then appear to contradict themselves when they examine the phenomenon of pit burial. When yogis in India have been buried underground or in a box for extended periods and measured under controlled conditions, the authors acknowledge that there is obviously some kind of inner control gained over body metabolism. Not only do they make light of this remarkable and potentially significant admission that consciousness can be trained to voluntarily alter metabolic rate, but they have already previously established in the reader's mind that experimental studies show that there is no significant change in metabolism.

Perhaps the greatest misunderstanding of these authors is that they presume the physiological effects mastered by advanced meditators are the cause of altering cognitive thinking. What they fail to realize is that a practitioner does not enter his chosen path just to voluntarily alter his heart rate or his metabolism. He enters because of religious motives and a desire to embark on the process of self-realization. Because of his attainments in terms of higher states of consciousness achieved, the physiological controls follow, not the other way around.

But there is more. Instead of reviewing the experimental basis of the meditation literature themselves, the authors rely on a single outdated six-year-old review of meditation that looked only at 300-odd scientific studies out of the more than 1,200 available. Then, in order to give the impression of fairness, the NRC commissioned a yoga adept to comment on this single review. The person they chose was Shannahoff-Khalsa, a Western-born Kundalini Yoga practitioner, who claimed that his own practice of yoga according to Yogi Bhajan was superior to all the other forms and, moreover, he maintained that it was the only style capable of being used by the military to develop so-called soldier-saints.[35] He gave a good analysis of the shortcomings of the single review, which the authors duly noted, but his own claims were then easily dismissed as overblown and unproven, therefore discounting his analysis.

The most important caveat given by the authors is recognition of their own limited frame of reference. This appears in a separate paragraph, titled "A cautionary note on Epistemology", which is worth quoting in full:

> It must be noted that it is very difficult for nonmeditation experts and thoroughly Western scientists like the members of the committee to evaluate many of the claims like those of Shannahoff-Khalsa. He is deeply

immersed in Kundalini Yoga and conducts both his personal and professional life in keeping with the philosophical and procedural requirements of that practice. He asserts, as do some psychoanalysts, that one cannot know a complex and powerful system unless one experiences it in a deep and thoroughgoing way. No one on our committee has done this with Kundalini Yoga or, for that matter, with the other meditation practices we have reviewed. This epistemological issue has important policy implications. Contemporary science is but one way of knowing. It is, however, the way of knowing that characterizes the work of this committee. At the same time, it seems appropriate to be mindful of the constraints that science, as well as culture, background, and personal life experience, places on how the committee views the field of meditation.[36]

This disclaimer is disturbing for several reasons. First, the authors have been led to think that they have to be meditators to discover what meditation really is. This is only true to a point. My claim is that they have not even thoroughly used the methodology they espouse. They limited themselves to a simple review of reviews without dealing significantly with the meditation literature that does exist. They did not confront the methodological problems inherent in mixing together studies that are not legitimately comparable, yet they mixed them anyway and presented their conclusions only by editorial fiat. They did not avail themselves of the opportunity to get several opinions instead of just one from a yoga practitioner. And they themselves never actually went out to have first-hand contact with different groups of meditators.

I am at a complete loss to see how one can come to any rational conclusion when based upon such faulty evidence, especially since the opinion of this board, enhanced by the name of the National Research Council, was intended to carry so much weight. From the standpoint of the radical empiricist, these researchers engaged in poor science by their own standards, and failed to realize that they had overstepped their bounds when, by their own admission, they came to conclusions based almost solely on the presuppositions of normative positivistic metaphysics. Their failure to examine the entire body of experimental literature and their inability to consult a rich scholarly literature outside of contemporary scientific periodicals for purposes of conceptual confirmation is a further indictment of the methodological short-sightedness currently plaguing psychology. Thus, the conclusions which they assert so definitely about meditation simply do not follow.

Cross-Cultural Psychiatry

The third application of radical empiricism in a scientific setting concerns the problem of how scientists trained in a Western laboratory tradition are able to carry on cross-cultural research when their own background biases them against the phenomena to be studied in the first place. A case in point is the Harvard Program in Refugee Trauma, carried on through the Indochinese Refugee Mental Health Clinic at the Brighton Marine Hospital in Boston, Massachusetts.

The Clinic opened eight years ago when an enterprising young psychiatrist, Richard Mollica, an epidemiologist from the Harvard School of Public Health, first recognized a need to serve the community of 18,000 Cambodians living in the Boston area. Mollica, a colleague of Fritz Redlich, had participated in the twenty-five year follow-up of the famous Hollingshead and Redlich study, which had shown that the lowest classes of American society were being denied access to psychiatric care in a consistent and enduring pattern of unconscious discrimination by a system that was itself suffering from a deep endemic illness.[37]

Mollica turned to assist the Cambodian community for several reasons. First, he had been radicalized by the failure of psychiatry to address the problem of the underserved. The twenty-five year follow up of the original Hollingshead and Redlich study showed that psychiatric services had improved vastly in scope and quality, while poor psychotic patients received even less of these services than before, chiefly because of deinstitutionalization.[38] Second, he noted that when the 18,000 Cambodians had been resettled in Boston from refugee camps in Southeast Asia, all of them had passed through the Brighton Marine Hospital, but not one had received a psychiatric exam, despite the fact that the entire community had been the victim of the Pol Pot genocide in their native country.

With the assistance of a small staff of American and Cambodian mental health workers, Mollica took over a wing of the Brighton Marine Hospital and set up his clinic. His team fanned out into the Cambodian community; they established ties with monks in the only Cambodian Buddhist temple in the Boston area, they contacted the Cambodian Mutual Assistance Societies, and his staff was able to start a women's therapy group, all of which drew patients to the clinic.

The first problem before Mollica was how to document the true mental health status of this refugee population. The patients were obviously depressed, but there was no word in Khmer for depression. If you asked the patients, usually through an interpreter, if he or she ever felt "blue", they were completely confused. Eventually, the major symptoms of depression according to the DSM-3R had to be reinterpreted in terms appropriate to the life world of the Cambodian. Only then could symptom checklists be developed and translated into Khmer for a variety of different diagnostic problems, and the staff be properly trained to take a psychiatric evaluation. The fact was, there was no precedent already established in the psychiatric literature for dealing with severely traumatized individuals from a non-Western population on their own terms.[39]

A second problem quickly arose. The staff at first had an extremely difficult time acknowledging that they were dealing with a severely damaged population. A several year transition period was needed for the professional staff to come to terms with the extent of trauma before them. In the end, they were able to document that almost every patient who came to the clinic had experienced an average of twenty-five trauma incidents during the course of resettlement. The women had been repeatedly raped in the camps by Thai soldiers. Many were torture victims or had seen their family members tortured and killed in front of them by the Khmer Rouge. All of their possessions had been stolen. Many had nearly starved. Many suffered from injuries to the head and body that had never been properly treated. Psychologically, these people were experiencing nightmares, depression, and numerous somatic aftereffects associated with mental and physical trauma.

Revealing the extent of damage done to this population often carried additional problems. For instance, the staff found that, while finally telling the trauma story was in many cases liberating for the patient, the effect on the therapists was sometimes devastating. In one case, a prominent Boston psychiatrist finally consented to visit the clinic and with much bravado took over the interview of a new patient. By the time half of the patient's story had gotten out, the psychiatrist called a halt to the interview and had to leave, admitting nausea and disgust. In yet other cases, some of the sickest patients would often become entranced with the telling and retelling of their trauma story. So too would some of the more inexperienced counselors.

Of particular importance was the difficulty that the staff had in assimilating how the torture victims understood what had happened to them. Because they were a Buddhist population with a deeply held belief in the doctrine of karma, the Cambodians felt that the reason they were tortured was due to some thought, word, or deed of their own that they had produced in a past life. The effect of this belief was in many cases to completely exonerate their torturers. This view was in many cases incomprehensible to Western mental health care workers.

One difficulty faced by the clinic director concerned the question of how to teach methods of cross-cultural research to the psychiatric fellows rotating through the service. A strategy was devised to expose the younger psychiatrists first to the basic principles of classical epidemiologic research, then to show them critiques of this methodology, such as the Popperian analysis of testing hypothesis by falsification. The problem of the metaphysical foundation of empirical research was then framed in the context of Husserlian phenomenology and James' radical empiricism. The result was a series of research projects which stressed methodology, but tried to account for extreme epistemological differences in the life worlds of the subjects and the experimenters.

A case in point is the recent survey undertaken by the clinic staff to ascertain the status of a group of elderly Cambodian women who had each been through extreme suffering before being resettled in Boston, but who were somehow able to sustain exceptional levels of health once in the United States. The results showed that the strength of individuals was derived from the mutual support network sustained by the group. But rather than this being just another instance of social cohesion, a look into the history of Cambodian religion suggests that the group had a continuity of identity with important forms of the old Khmer culture. Specifically, the cult of the Mother in Hinduism, which had profoundly influenced early Khmer society, had become organized into a matrilineal tradition of elderly women's groups which held an important position of power in the social hierarchy. The Cambodian groups in Boston were an attempt to reinstate this old tradition, which was thought to greatly empower the individual members by giving each one a sense of identity and purpose. Here one must first abandon the preconceived notions of experimental social psychology in order to inquire into the phenomenology of meaning structures within traditional Khmer culture to get at this alternative explanation.

The Site 2 Studies

These were but home practice sessions, however, for a massive epidemiologic survey that the Refugee Clinic Staff undertook in cooperation with the World Federation for Mental Health and the United Nations Border Relief Operation. Since the patients at the Brighton Clinic were almost all products of long term confinement in refugee camps outside their native country before coming to the United States, the Clinic Staff ascertained that it was of vital importance to examine the mental health conditions at these camps. The place chosen for the surveys was Site 2, a holding camp during the day and a *de facto* prison at night, which housed 186,000 people who had been living in temporary over-night quarters for ten years. Half the population were children who had been born in this camp.

The first survey, published in 1989, endeavored to document the deteriorating mental health conditions in the camp, the causes, and potential remedies, and the segments of the population most at risk for further injury and psychiatric illness.[40] General guidelines were suggested there for a restructured mental health system in the camp that would meet the needs of this population and at the same time act as a model for a much broader system that might be put in place once these inmates were repatriated to their own country, which now appears imminent. The framework for this new mental health care system de-emphasizes traditional Western psychiatric strategies based on pharmacology and one-to-one psychotherapy. Instead, it relies more on an indigenous chain of Cambodians trained as psychiatrists, physicians, nurses, and social workers, and on the reconstitution of the elderly women's groups, the community of monks as teachers and spiritual healers, and the Khrou Khmer, or traditional Cambodian herbalists.

The second major survey was published in 1991 and involved a more in-depth look, not just at the extent of illness in the camp, but also the extent of knowledge residents had about their traditional culture, the persistence of cultural folkways despite the attempt at total eradication during the Pol Pot genocide, the prevelance of religious practices, and the extent of knowledge about religious principles and moral values.[41]

The instruments designed for these surveys involved modification of the Hopkins Symptom Checklist, the Harvard Trauma Scale, and other survey instruments to more accurately reflect the linguistic and phenomenological realities of Khmer culture. These means of collecting information were augmented by training a group of educated camp members who were native Khmer. These trainers then conducted interviews with selected cohorts of the population. In the second survey, for instance, interviews were conducted with parents and their children on the same subjects to ascertain intragroup reliability on certain content areas and to assess the extent of differing perceptions of the degree of trauma and illness between the generations.

The single most important finding for the present discussion is that the children in the camp are perceived as being sick a large part of the time in the absence of actual physical illness. Two reasons are given by the experimenters for this: the first is that depression, malaise, and psychosocial maladjustment, that is, psychological factors, are the cause of the symptoms. The second explanation is that the children exhibit symptoms of traditional culture-bound illnesses which would normally be dealt with by native healers in the wider psychosocial context that is now missing from the artificial environment of the camps, in which case, one must reconstruct the cultural milieu to deal with the illness. But whichever the cause, the surveys are presented as the first of their kind to elaborate in such detail the psychiatric needs of a Cambodian refugee population. They are meant as much to contribute to a general scientific understanding of extreme trauma as they are to serve as working papers in the establishment of effective mental health policies for the Cambodians in the future. They also contribute to an important discussion on methodology and the underlying philosophy of research.

Conclusion

In the current context, I therefore conclude by baldly stating that the philosophy of radical empiricism may be helpful in the conduct of research for several reasons:

- It broaches the possibility that science is a consensually validated attitude in a state of constant transformation, not a fixed and immutable reality with power to give the ontological status of permanence to laws it articulates.

- It seems to raise some important but as yet unexamined epistemological problems about so-called value-free research in the objective sciences.

- It is person-centered, relegating the experimental method to the place of an auxiliary tool for clarifying and corroborating reality.

- It gives a few clues about what to look for in the initial chaos or gestalt of experience.

- It asks certain important questions about the interaction of two or more human beings who live in different realms of experience, especially where one presumes to exercise some form of objectivity over another's worldview.

- It forces a look at the part in the context of the whole.

- It returns the central focus of psychology and psychiatry to the problem of consciousness-as-immediately-experienced.

While one may readily reject this philosophical view as irrelevant to the practice of basic science, no basic scientist who has ventured out beyond the laboratory into the real world of patient care can deny the epistemological gap between knowledge and experience. Serious medical practitioners who at once must be good scientists and effective clinicians will readily recognize the dilemma. It serves no purpose for them to retreat into the safe dogma of scientific rhetoric when at some point they must face their own helplessness and uncertainty in alleviating the suffering of others.[42] Here one sees into the limits of science, is confronted with the fallibility of human inquiry, and yet is still called upon to find the true locus of healing. Its discovery, in addition to all our scientific manipulations, must certainly be bound up in the dynamics, as well as the mystery, of both human relationships and one's own level of self-knowledge.

Here we have two extra-scientific factors that may well become more important areas of exploration in the future. That is, we may find that laboratory measurement, especially where it involves human subjects, is always an experiment in social psychology. There is no such thing as a completely isolated independent variable.[43] At the same time, the sophisticated researcher of the future will most likely be far more sensitive to the inevitable effect which his or her own presence has in defining the parameters and the outcome of any experiment.

But the major epistemological problem that emerges in considering the phenomenology of the science-making process is one we have not yet even touched upon. In a word, I do not see how the various sciences and all the systems of mathematical laws that allegedly govern causality can have an existence independent of the human mind that has conceived those laws in the first place. The antinomy is that we profess to know and control everything about the world of matter, and we know absolutely nothing about the state of consciousness which observes it. In our quest for objectivity, we have even denied that consciousness exists.

My personal view is that at the core of his radical empiricism, James resolves the dualism of the mental and the physical by asserting that the one should not be subsumed under the other, but, rather, that no external world of objects can exist except as a function of some consciousness. This means that there can be no objective science without human consciousness to create it; no world of causal mathematical laws except in so far as they are a product of human thought. If this is true, then it becomes clear that contemporary definitions of objective science do not banish subjectivity, but rather they serve only to hold the discussion of consciousness in abeyance.

For when consciousness is so fixed by the will, all its products appear ordered, and through this filter, rational consciousness, projected outward, constructs the world of reasonable categories. But when consciousness turns back upon itself and attention turns inward, consciousness itself becomes fluid and undergoes a transformation in the direction of whatever conditions are present at that moment. The unconscious becomes visible; consciousness now has to deal with a flood of previously unconscious contents. One may witness a vision of one's self that lies within. Then, upon a return to a state of fixation by the will, now oriented not inwardly, but outwardly, a new order to external reality emerges.

The crux of the matter is that when one opens one's self to the uncertainty of pure experience, which is the radically empirical point of view, one runs the risk of being changed ultimately. Whether one discovers transcendence or is captured by psychopathology is then the question. I am reminded here of the saying inscribed on the back of Merlin's chair in Tennyson's *Idylls of the Kings*. In Old English, it said, "Siege Perilous", a warning to all those who would embark on the Grail Quest that the inward journey toward self-knowledge was a path fraught with danger. But, as many an erstwhile seeker in the visionary tradition knows, this inward risk must be taken if any real outward transformation is to take place.

Notes and References

1. Sigmund Koch, "Language communities, search cells, and psychological studies", in *Conceptual Foundations of Psychology; The Nebraska Symposium on Motivation*, 1975, University of Nebraska Press, 1976, pp. 477-559.

2. Stanley Milgram, *Obedience to Authority: An Experimental View*, Harper and Row, 1974.

3. B. F. Skinner, *The Behavior of Organisms: An Experimental Analysis*, Appleton-Century Crofts, 1938.

4. John MacMurray, *The Boundaries of Science: A Study in the Philosophy of Psychology*, Faber and Faber, 1939.

5. Jerome Frank, *Persuasion and Healing: A Comparative Study of Psychotherapy*, 3rd edition, Johns Hopkins University Press, 1991.

6. Richard Mollica, "Upside down psychiatry: A genealogy of mental health services" in *Pathologies of the Modern Self: The Social and Cultural Dimensions of Psychiatric Illness,* edited by David M. Levin, New York University Press, 1986.

7. One may view traditional political, economic and social forces as competing forms of knowledge with science. What good is the scientific information that burning forests causes ozone depletion, for instance, if the economic ability of Brazil to pay interest on its third-world debt depends on slash-and-burn techniques in the Amazon? Scientific information will undoubtedly sway some minds, may even prevail in the end, but it is clear that extra-scientific forms of knowledge continue to direct the environmental carnage.

Similarly, the psychologist Howard Gardner has proposed a theory of "multiple intelligences", in which rational and analytic modes of knowledge are considered only one of several competing sources of knowing within the structure of the normal personality. See H. Gardner, *Frames of Mind: The Theory of Multiple Intelligences*, Basic Books, 1983.

8. Hartshorne and Weiss, *The Selected Papers of Charles Sanders Peirce*, Harvard University Press, 1938.

9. Exceptions include Koch, Giorgi and Maslow.

10. F. B. Burkhardt, F. Bowers and I. K. Skrupskelis, editors, *The Works of William James: Essays in Radical Empiricism,* Harvard University Press, 1976.

11. N. L. Munn, L. D. Fernald and P. S. Fernald, *Introduction to Psychology,* 2nd edition, Houghton Mifflin, 1969.

12. p. 6.

13. p. 7.

14. p. 7.

15. pp. 7-9.

16. p. 9.

17. p. 9.

18. p. 9.

19. p. 10.

20. p. 10.

21. p. 10.

22. p. 11.

23. p. 11.

24. p. 11.

25. p. 11.

26. Daniel Druckman and John A. Swets, editors, *Enhancing Human Performance: Issues, Theories, and Techniques,* 1988, and Daniel Druckman and Robert A. Bjork, editors, *In the Mind's Eye: Enhancing Human Performance,* National Academy Press, 1991.

27. In turn, the project was approved by the Governing Board of the National Research Council, whose members are drawn from the councils of the National Academy of Sciences, the National Academy of Engineering, and the Institute of Medicine. The report begins by stating that "The members of the committee responsible for the report were chosen for their special competences and with regard for appropriate balance" (p. iv), as if stating that this was their intention actually achieved the desired result. Objectively, they appear to have failed to meet their own criteria. Obviously, a third and more disinterested party is needed. Scholars in the humanities might play such a role as more philosophically oriented psychologists might do in psychology.

28. *Mind's Eye,* 1991, p. vii.

29. This particular chapter was drafted by two of the Committee members. The first is Gerald C. Davison, a professor of psychology at the University of Southern California, and former director of clinical training. He received the AB from Harvard, and the PhD from Stanford. His research interests include cognitive assessment, stress, and hypertension. He has published on cognitive behavior therapy and experimental personality research. He has also co-authored three books, although we are not told which.

The other author of the chapter is Francis J. Pirozzolo, Chief of the Neuropsychology Service and Associate Professor in the Department of Neurology, Baylor College of Medicine. He received his BA from Wilmington College in psychology, MA from the University of Chicago, and PhD from the University of Rochester in neuropsychology and learning. His interests span age-related neurodegenerative disorders and human performance, especially the biochemical basis of the behavior of elite athletes.

30. Ibid., p. 9.

31. This, I believe, derives from an erroneous assumption that the relation between traditional academic scholarship and laboratory experimentation is well-defined and broadly known. A trained laboratory technician is not, perforce, an expert in academic scholarship. Most psychologists today do not have the slightest idea about how to utilize the research tools of a library, just as most philosophers and historians cannot perform an analysis of variance.

32. Ibid., p. 120.

33. Herbert Benson, *The Relaxation Response,* Morrow, 1975.

34. Ibid., p. 122.

35. We can only imagine the type of personality that would evolve as both a saint and a trained killer.

36. Ibid., p. 130.

37. Richard F. Mollica and Fritz Redlich, "Equity and changing patient characteristics, 1950-1975", *Archives of General Psychiatry* 37, November 1980, pp. 1257-1263.

38. Richard F. Mollica and Mladen Milic, "Social class and psychiatric practice: A revision of the Hollingshead and Redlich model", *American Journal of Psychiatry* 143:1, January 1986, pp. 12-17.

39. Richard F. Mollica, "The prevention of torture and the clinical care of survivors: A field in need of a new science" in M. Bosoglu, editor, *Torture and Its Consequences: Current Treatment Approaches,* Cambridge University Press, in press.

40. Richard F. Mollica and Russell R. Jalbert, *Community of Confinement: The Mental Health Crisis in Site Two (Displaced Persons Camps on the Thai-Kampuchean Border)*, World Federation for Mental Health, February 1989.

Richard F. Mollica, James Lavelle, Svang Tor and Christopher Ellis, *Turning Point in Khmer Mental Health: Immediate Steps to Resolve the Mental Health Crisis in the Khmer Border Camps,* prepared for the United Nations Border Relief Operation by the World Federation for Mental Health and the Harvard School of Public Health Task Force on the Mental Health Crisis in Site Two, December 1989.

41. Richard F. Mollica et al., *Repatriation and Disability: A Community Study of Health, Mental Health, and Social Functioning of the Khmer Residents of Site Two; Vol. 1, Khmer Adults; Vol. 2, Khmer Children (12-13 years of age)*, Working Document, Harvard Program on Refugee Trauma, Harvard School of Public Health and the World Federation for Mental Health, 1991.

42. An important statement on the impact of the health care worker's response to patient trauma is Richard F. Mollica, "The social world destroyed: The psychiatric care of the refugee trauma survivor" in J. Gruschow and K. Hannibal, editors, *Health Service for the Treatment of Torture and Trauma Survivors,* American Association for the Advancement of Science, 1990, pp. 15-34.

43. For a statement on the socio-political approach to psychiatry, see Richard F. Mollica, "Psychiatry in quest after orientation", *Analecta Husserliana* XX, 1986, pp. 101-124.

Toward a 'Science of Wholeness'

by Willis Harman

We posed a fundamental question in Chapter 1, namely: has the time arrived for a reassessment of the ontological and epistemological assumptions underlying modern science? In the chapters following, various responses to this question have been put forward. This final chapter is one more such response. It is not a summing up, bringing the discussion to some final closure—that would be premature. How this matter is ultimately resolved is, to a major extent, up to the scientific community. However, the implications of the issue are so pervasive and so profound that it is a matter of public concern as well. As stated in the beginning, our objective is to help bring this important issue into active dialogue, among scientists and among the informed public as well.

Modern industrial society, like every other in history, rests on some set of largely tacit, basic assumptions about who we are, what kind of universe we are in, and what is ultimately important to us. The answers assumed to these questions are strongly influenced, in modern society, by the findings and pronouncements of science. The scientific materialism which so confidently held forth its answers to these questions a couple of generations ago, is now—as a social force at least—a dying orthodoxy. Most scientists would agree that there has been a shift away from the extreme positivistic and reductionistic tendencies that characterized mid-century science, especially in the United States. Laughlin et al. (1990, p. 5) identify in this shift two principal themes:

1) A shift away from a fragmented, mechanical, non-purposive conception of the world toward a holistic, organic, and purposive conception; and

2) a shift away from a concern with objectivity toward a concern with subjectivity, including the role of perception and cognition in the process of scientific inquiry.

Simultaneously and not unrelated, a cultural change has been increasingly evident over the past third of a century which emphasizes

a) some sort of deep sense of wholeness, of oneness, of everything being a part of a *uni*-verse, and

b) a sense of the validity of deep intuition as one of the ways in which we contact the greater reality.

One might say that a respiritualization of society appears to be taking place, but one more experiential and non-institutionalized, less fundamentalist and sacerdotal, than most of the historically familiar forms of religion.

Thus at the same time that there has been growing public interest in rediscovering the spiritual aspect of human experience, scientists have begun to seek ways through which science might better accommodate the human spirit and the conscious awareness that comprise our most direct link with reality. If this accommodation turns out to involve a change in the fundamental underlying assumptions of science, and hence of society's prevailing worldview, that must inevitably be accompanied by a long-term shift in value emphases, priorities, and even socio-economic and political structures.

Toward a More Holistic Science

As observed earlier, scientists typically take their ontological and episte-mological assumptions to be inviolate, to be an inherent and ineluctable part of the definition of science. But it is precisely here that we seem likely to find the source—and possible resolution—of some of the most long-lasting and fundamental puzzles in science. In this chapter we will explore the possibility that this resolution might come through extending the accepted "separateness science" (based on the ontological assumption of separateness and the episte-mological assumption that all knowledge is based on physical sense data) to an extended "wholeness science" (based on an ontological assumption of oneness, unity, interconnectedness of everything) within which the present "separateness science" is a particular domain.

This proposed shift from an ontological assumption of separateness to one of wholeness may seem innocuously simple—perhaps even simplistic and naive. But in fact, there is at least as sound a basis in human experience for the latter assumption. As noted below, in the "perennial wisdom" of the world's spiritual traditions, and in the understandings of most indigenous peoples, it would seem the natural assumption. Furthermore, as Brian Goodwin has pointed out (Goodwin, 1987) the Renaissance nature philosophy of Francesco Giorgi et al., based precisely on the "oneness" assumption, initially competed with the "separateness" science of Descartes and Galileo, but in the end was rejected as being less suited to contributing to the developing passion for "controlling nature" through technology.

There is today increasingly widespread agreement that science must somehow develop the ability to look at things more holistically. However, some of the more radical implications of such an extended science are not immediately apparent. Let us imagine for a moment what science would look like if we start from the holistic assumption that everything—not only physical things but all things experienced, including sensations, emotions, feelings, motivations, thoughts—is really part of a single unity. If things are so interconnected that a change in any one could affect all, then it follows that any accounting for cause is within a specific context, for a specific purpose. In the broadest sense, there is no cause and effect; only a whole system evolving. What our present science does, in this view, is to study relatively isolatable systems where causal factors can be considered limited, and, in particular, where no volitional factors need be taken into account. (To recall how special this is, note that the judicial setting comprises another special case; here volition and motivation are considered to be central causal factors.)

In general, as Michael Scriven pointed out in Chapter 3, causes are limited explanations that depend upon context. If in the ordinary social context I inquire into the cause of steam coming out of a teakettle, I may be satisfied with the answer that someone plans to have a cup of tea and hence put the kettle on the fire. On the other hand, in the context of a science course, the expected answer may be in terms of thermodynamic concepts, completely ignoring the crucial act of placing the teakettle on the stove.

In a whole-system view, a change in any part affects the whole. Only when a part of the whole can be sufficiently isolated from the rest that reductionistic causes appear to describe adequately why things behave as they do, do the ordinary concepts of scientific causation apply.

Thus, a "wholeness science" would seek understanding, rather than singular, exclusive "causes". Its aim would be illumination more than the ability to predict and control. It would contain most of present science, but in an expanded context. It would not foster the temptation to assume that consciousness is nothing but brain function, or to insist that the course of evolution can be completely explained by mutations and natural selection, or to extrapolate physics from the laboratory back to a completely mechanistic "Big Bang" origin of the physical universe.

One of the main implications of such an extended science is the epistemological conclusion that we contact reality in not one, but two ways. One of these is through physical sense data—which form the basis of normal science. The other is through being ourselves part of the oneness—through a deep intuitive "inner knowing". In other words, the basic epistemological issue involved is precisely whether our encountering of reality is limited to being aware of, and giving meaning to, the messages from our physical senses (sometimes referred to as "objective"), or whether it includes also a subjective aspect in an intuitive, aesthetic, spiritual, noetic and mystical sense. (The fact should not escape our notice that an intuitive and aesthetic factor already enters into normal science in various ways, for example, the aesthetic principle of "elegance"; the "principle of parsimony" in choosing between alternative explanations.)

Relationship to the 'Primordial Tradition'

If this subjective aspect of knowing is to be taken seriously, it necessarily leads to a new openness regarding what might be learned—and how it might be learned—from knowledge systems that start from a different perception of reality, such as Chinese medicine, Tibetan Buddhist psychology, or the Native American relationship to nature.

The central finding of the study of comparative religion over the past half century or so has been that within any of the world's spiritual traditions there are typically various exoteric or public versions, and an "inner-circle", esoteric version. The latter tends to be more experiential and less sacerdotal, and usually involves some kind of meditative discipline or yoga. Although the exoteric versions may vary greatly from one another, and from one tradition to another, the esoteric versions are essentially the same. This "primordial tradition" or "perennial wisdom" (Huxley, 1945) is to be found in every religion and can be owned exclusively by none.

> The Primordial Tradition is not merely an ancient system of belief and practice. . . . It is, rather, a whole set of archetypical realities waiting to be discovered, at the highest reaches of the human consciousness, by all people. (Rossner, 1989)

The perennial wisdom tends to include such convictions as that Nature is directed from within by a higher intelligence or mind; that all minds in the universe are linked together by participation in one universal mind or source; that various mental or physical rituals can sometimes effect what they symbolize, or set the proper conditions in motion for the desired events or result to occur; that prayers, thoughts and mental projections might directly aid in the healing of sick and diseased persons through the release of powerful, life-giving energies; that all individuals have a powerful, if hidden, motivation to discover and identify with a higher Self which is, in turn, in immediate connection to the universal mind. Since this perennial wisdom has been distilled from inquiry persisting over a far greater span of time than the duration of modern science, it can hardly be simply set aside as inconsequential.

The distinction between modern Western science and an extended science based on the oneness assumption becomes sharply defined when we contrast Western science with classical Indian thought. India appears to have specialized on inner exploration for longer than any other society. The classical writings go back thousands of years, and modern summaries are available in the writings of Sri Aurobindo, Rabindranath Tagore, Swami Vivekananda, and others.

The most fundamental principle, at the core of this body of "inwardly empirical" knowledge, is that the subjective (mind, consciousness, spirit) is causal, and the objective is effect. Obvious superficial examples come to mind—the idea comes before the action; the vision before the creation. The Indian concept of karma, so misunderstood in the West, takes the principle a bit deeper. But most important, at the most fundamental level of continuous co-creation of the universe, the subjective—in the form of a Universal Mind, in which we all participate, albeit outside ordinary conscious awareness—is the cause of the objective world which we then experience with our physical senses. Western science—alone among the thought systems of all known societies—turned this on its head. The objective is causal, says modern science, and what physicists study—fundamental particles, quantum fields—are ultimate causes.

The Western concept of scientific causality is easily included in the Indian cosmology as a special case. The reverse is not true; Western science would have to be "extended" in the sense proposed here in order to accommodate the Indian view, or, for that matter, any other version of the primordial tradition.

Characteristics of 'Wholeness Science'

The above arguments suggest the potentiality of an extended science which would include present science as useful, but having limited application. Present science, tremendously effective in its chosen context, is based on

a) an ontological assumption of separateness and

b) an epistemological assumption of physical sense data as the sole empirical evidence on which the scientific picture of reality is to be based.

The prospect of a "wholeness science" would build upon

a) an ontological assumption of oneness, unity, interconnectedness of everything, and

b) an epistemological assumption that there are two available "windows" onto reality, namely, the objective, through the physical senses, and the subjective, through the intuitive and aesthetic faculties.

Thus at least four classes of data are to be considered:

1) Those data admissible in the strict logical empiricism model, namely measurements of physical parameters.

2) Data depending on the connoisseurship of expert judges, such as those on which systematic (taxonomic) biology is based.

3) Data which are essentially self-reports of subjective experience, obtained in an environment that promotes high levels of trust and candor, subjected to sophisticated skepticism because of our known capability for self-deception, and checked in other ways wherever possible.

4) The subjective self-reports of trained "inner explorers" of various cultures.

In none of these four categories are data to be accepted without some sort of careful consensual validation.

The data on which a science is based will not always fall neatly into one or another of these categories, of course. In the Native American knowledge system, described by Vine Deloria in Chapter 12, the way of observing is such that the four tend to merge.

Laughlin et al. (1990, pp. 338-341) speak of the introspective data of type (4) as the result of "mature contemplation" and note that exploration of this kind of knowledge in the scientific spirit involves:

a) Injunction: "If you want to know this, do this." For example, the meditative exercises of various esoteric traditions.

b) Apprehension: cognitive apprehension and illumination of the "object domain". For example, the subjective experiences of deep introspection including the noetic quality of mystical experience.

c) Communal confirmation: results are checked with others who have adequately completed the injunctive and illuminative operations.

The similarity will be noted between these steps and parallel ones in conventional science:

a) Technique, technology, and criteria for measurement;

b) Obtaining empirical results;

c) Consensual validation.

Combining Separateness and Wholeness

Once we recognize the non-necessity of the separateness assumption and its reductionistic corollary, there is no reason to assume that the biological and cognitive sciences can be reduced to the physical sciences (materialistic, reductionistic, deterministic), let alone to physics. The biological sciences involve more holistic concepts (for example organism, function of an organ) which have no counterparts at the physical sciences level. Similarly, there is no reason to assume that the characteristics of consciousness are reducible to biology. In other words, while theory reduction (as, for example, the laws of optics explained through electromagnetic theory) will be welcomed whenever it proves to be possible, it is not a dogma of wholeness science that it must be, in general, possible.

This matter of the hierarchical nature of science deserves elaboration. A homely analogy may help. Consider a book. To a beetle, a book is simply an obstacle in its path. To a dog, we may assume, it has other characteristics to be noted; the dog may recognize it, for example, as belonging to his master, perhaps to be mouth-carried to her. An ape might find the pages of interest, particularly if there were illustrations. A very narrowly focused quantitative scientist might find it of interest to note the relative frequencies with which various characters and combinations of characters appear. A more broadly literate person might find the book to be an important treatise in Eastern philosophy. The ape might find the scientist's quantitative preoccupations puzzling and meaningless, or the narrow scientist might contend that the philosophical concepts are not real and valuable knowledge. There is no apparent way to resolve these differences of perceived significance short of the ape learning the scientist's craft, or the scientist becoming experientially aware of the philosophical concepts.

Imagine a hierarchy of sciences (after Popper, 1977) something like that shown in Figure 1:

Figure 1

Spiritual Sciences (?)
Human Sciences
Biological Sciences
Physical Sciences

Let us leave as an open question whether anything belongs in the top cell. The point is that someone trained in botany or zoology may see things that a physical scientist would not tend to be sensitive to; hence there might be an argument between the two as to whether understanding of biological organisms can be reduced to physics and chemistry. A similar dispute on the issue of consciousness as agency might occur between biological and human scientists. Such disputes are resolvable only by recognizing the validity of all levels or grades of significance.

Another critical departure from "separateness science" relates to the act of observation. Starting from the holistic assumption, there is no separation of observer from observed—or rather, such separation is contrived, not real. Scientific methodology is then understood as naturally participatory; we simply recognize that, whereas we learn certain kinds of things by distancing ourselves from the subject studied, we get another kind of knowledge from intuitively "becoming one with" the subject. Thus in the social sciences, the "researchee" (the person or community being researched) becomes a full partner in the inquiry, not only helping to guide the research but sharing control of how the information obtained is put to use.

The kind of scientific knowledge derived from setting up situations where the observer is relatively separate from the observed would be expected to give only a restricted kind of information; more complete information would include that which one obtains through being intuitively in touch with, identified with, that which is being observed. For instance, it is not necessarily illusory anthropomorphism to "know" when your pet dog or cat feels something akin to jealousy, or expectation, or embarrassment. (Michael Polyani has dealt with this in his book *Personal Knowledge*, 1958.)

Dealing with the Anomalies

"Action at a distance" has been a problem for science from the very beginning. There was much resistance to Newton's law of gravitation, because it seemed to say that one body could affect another thousands or millions of miles away, without any intervening "mechanism"; the difficulty was overcome through inventing the fiction of the "gravitational field" which, psychologically, served to fill up the intervening space. But with the "oneness" assumption, action at a distance does not pose a particular problem; there is no necessity to hypothesize fields or particle exchanges to account for it.

This extended science will be concerned with "downward causation" (Campbell, 1974, Sperry, 1987) as well as the reductionistic "upward causation" which presently dominates the scientific world. Likewise, the presence of teleological factors in the biological realm presents no particular problem once there is releasing of the insistence that biology be reducible to physics and chemistry. We observe teleology in ourselves; why not, then, the larger system of which we are a part?

Neither do consciousness, conscious awareness, and the concept of the volitional self present any fundamental problem to the extended science. With the "oneness" or "wholeness" assumption, one does not find volition, other states of consciousness, teleological influences, "meaningful coincidences", etc. to be anomalous. If volition or purpose or meaning exist in myself, then *ipso facto* they exist in the universe; there is nothing of their existence to be explained, only explored.

Certain aspects of the unity that is the Whole will continue to be quite profitably studied by means of separateness science. That kind of science, however, would, as only part of a more extended science, no longer have the authority to insist that we are here, solely through random causes, in a meaningless universe; nor that our consciousness is "merely" the chemical and physical processes of the brain.

Openness to alternative theories and explanations, and healthy skepticism, are at least as important in wholeness science as they have been in the present separateness science. Consensus validation also remains of central importance, but it will be accomplished in a somewhat different way.

Many of the questions about such an extended science have been expressed by other current thinkers. Lincoln and Guba, for instance, have discussed what they call "naturalistic inquiry" (Lincoln and Guba, 1985), the purpose of which is understanding, not prediction and control. They emphasize tacit knowledge, qualitative inquiry, and the human as the instrument of knowledge.

Brian Goodwin's "science of qualities" (1987) also shares many of the aspects we have been considering. He urges that we

> ... return to the vision of the Renaissance magi, in which subject and object, known and unknown, can relate and participate in an appropriate unity, made possible by the fact that reality is a single coordinated domain.

The Concept of the Self

The self constitutes a particularly challenging aspect of reductionistic science. As previously observed, the conscious self is ineluctably involved in observation, yet the science constructed from those observations appears to contain no place for it.

Yet consider the implications of the following:

- Research on the well-documented placebo effect implicitly assumes that there is a "self" which believes in the efficacy of the placebo.

- Research on subliminal perception, hypnosis, psychotherapy, and other areas reveals that there is a "hidden mind" (unconscious processes) which basically does all the things the conscious mind does—and possibly much more.

- Research on hypnosis reveals that there is within the human mind a "hidden observer" which is not deceived by the suggestions of the hypnotist (or, presumably, by the "suggestions" from the person's cultural surround) (Hilgard, 1986).

- Research in the area of psychic phenomena, although results are admittedly erratic and findings are controversial, seems to suggest that at some deep level our minds are interconnected in some nonphysical way (see, for example, Mitchell, 1974, Inglis, 1992).

- Research on creativity and intuition reveals that the capabilities of the "hidden" creative/intuitive mind appear to be influenced by beliefs and by the extent to which one trusts in and depends on that part of the mind. Thus we do not know what are its ultimate limitations (if any).

- Research on out-of-body experiences and near-death experiences seems to suggest that consciousness is something other than just physico-chemical processes in the brain (Ring, 1982).

- In research on multiple personalities the shift from one self to another may be accompanied by measurable physiological changes, suggesting that "personality" is a holistic, non-reducible concept that can have real effects in the world.

- In such cases of multiple personality there appears to be, in every case, one alternate personality, called the "inner self-helper" which is different from the rest in that it claims to neither be born nor die, but to simply "be" (Damgaard, 1987).

- Research on children's recollections of past lives seems to show that these can sometimes be successfully checked for veridicality, lending strength to some sort of concept of reincarnation (Stevenson, 1987).

- There exists a great body of evidence, some meticulously gathered, that suggests survival of the personality after physical death, in a form that may subsequently communicate back to living persons in various ways. Although science by and large ignores this evidence and its implications, to most who have chosen to look deeply into the subject, the amount and quality of the evidence are quite impressive (Inglis, 1992).

- In studies of comparative religion it appears that, besides the many exoteric (public) forms, there is within any of the major traditions an esoteric or "inner circle" form, which is essentially the same for all traditions. This perennial wisdom seems to recommend an inner search involving some sort of meditative or yogic discipline, and discovery of and identification with a "higher" or "true" Self (Huxley, 1945, Rossner, 1989).

The typical scientist at some point disembarks from this train of argument; the latter items in the list are too "far out" to take seriously. But on what basis does he/she make this judgment? Really because the phenomena seem to violate the implicit assumptions of logical empiricism. From the point of view of the "oneness" assumption, the self, with or without capitalization, poses no particular problem.

Dialectical Evolution

In the Darwinian concept of evolution, organisms adapt to a changing external environment which poses problems that the organisms solve through evolution. The organism and its environment have separate existences, separate properties. The environment changes, through its own processes; the organism changes in response to the environment.

The outlook of wholeness science leads directly to the dialectical view of Levins and Lewontin (1985), in which the explanation of change is seen in terms of the opposing processes united within the evolving system of organism and environment:

> What characterizes the dialectical world, in all its aspects, is that it is constantly in motion. Constants become variable, causes become effects, and systems develop, destroying the conditions that gave rise to them. (p. 279)

In the dialectical view, organisms are both the subjects and objects of evolution: they both make and are made by the environment and are thus actors in their own evolutionary history. The most striking example is found in Lovelock's (1988) Gaia hypothesis, which proposes that the conversion of the reducing atmosphere that existed before the beginning of life to one that is rich in reactive oxygen was carried out by living organisms themselves.

Of course, the time scales of change of organism and environment may be very different. For instance, in studying population ecology, it is typically permissible to assume that the various species are not changing genetically while their populations adapt to a changing environment. On the other hand, in studying some aspects of evolutionary processes it may be quite appropriate to assume that the environment is relatively fixed while biological changes are going on. But these are always approximations of a process in which both organism and environment evolve together. We do not know, for example, that the apparent constancy of scientific "laws" is not a matter of evolution.

We argued in Chapter One that modern Western science is based on an ontological assumption of separateness. There is a second ontological assumption as well, that of "uniformitarianism", supported and advanced by Sir Charles Lyell in his book *Principles of Geology*. Uniformitarianism is the hypothesis that the laws of nature have always existed, have never changed, and never will change.

In the "oneness" view of the world, uniformitarianism is challenged, as well as separateness. What we have is one universe, evolving, with the individual human observer as part of the whole. Whatever perception of reality is arrived at by the scientist, it is a consequence of the interaction of perceiving organism and environment as they have evolved together.

It is the Darwinian thesis that human consciousness has biologically emerged from animal consciousness. But in the "oneness" view, as Owen Barfield puts it (1982), "Sooner or later a certain truth is brought home to you"– namely, that consciousness

> is the inner side of the whole, just as human consciousness is the inside of one human being. . . . Although it makes sense to inquire how and when consciousness developed into what we now experience as such, it makes no sense at all to inquire how and when mind emerged from matter. . . . Once you have realized that there is indeed only one world, though with both an inside and an outside to it, only one world experienced by our senses from without, and by our consciousness from within, it is no longer plausible to fantasize an immemorial single-track evolution of the outside world alone. It is no longer possible to separate evolution from evolution of consciousness.[1]

Further Characteristics of a 'Wholeness Science'

An inquiry that starts from the presupposition of wholeness implies that the basic method of observation is much more participatory–observation through identification with, rather than separation from. Strict interpretations of objectivity and of reliability through replication are inappropriate in participatory research, and so other criteria will have to be developed which are appropriate. Something like the Buddhist ideal of "nonattachment" might come to replace the concept of strict objectivity; and something like "trustworthiness" (perhaps based on multiple imperfect tests) may replace strict replicability of controlled experiments as the basis for judging reliability. Lincoln and Guba (1985) propose four criteria to establish trustworthiness in what they term naturalistic inquiry—credibility, transferability, dependability, and confirmability—and suggest tests for each.

Up till now, science has started with a limiting set of assumptions and has then found it necessary to deny the validity—and even the possibility—of a host of reported phenomena that do not fit within those limits. A tremendous amount of effort has been expended within science to defend the barricades against, or to explain away, these outcasts, which include not only such phenomena as "miraculous" healings and "psi phenomena", but also more ordinary experiences such as volition, selective attention, and the hunger for meaning.

Rather than having to defend itself against the anomalous, wholeness science permits the assumption that any class of inner experiences that has been reported, or of phenomena that have been observed, down through the ages and across cultures, exist in some sense and have a face validity that cannot be denied. We seek, in other words, a science that can accommodate all that exists.

We are aware that there are many subtleties to be encompassed in doing this. Whole societies can perceive things that observers from other societies do not, so it is necessary to be very cautious about claiming that some class of experiences is universal, even potentially. There is a tendency among some persons today to regard it as a mark of New Age distinction to be willing to believe almost anything. It is not total gullibility we seek, but rather new agreements about consensual validation.

In addition to what has already been said about the role of the observer in participatory research, one other important point should be noted—the fact that in such research the experience of observing brings about sensitization and other changes in the observer. A willingness to be transformed himself or herself is an essential characteristic of the participatory scientist. The anthropologist who would see clearly a culture other than her own must allow that experience to change her so that the new culture is seen through new eyes, not eyes conditioned by her own culture. The psychotherapist who would see clearly his client must have worked through his own neuroses that would otherwise warp perception. The social scientist who would use a participatory approach to understanding and guiding organizational arrangements and processes will almost certainly be changed through his/her involvement. The scientist who would study meditative processes and those "other states of consciousness" so treasured in the various spiritual traditions has to be willing to go through the deep changes that will make him or her a competent observer.

Further Implications

Some further implications for science are worth noting.

Non-Local Causality

It was only the physicalist and reductionist assumptions that made non-local causality into an anomaly. The universe is whatever it is found to be through open and impartial scientific inquiry; if it includes non-local causality, we had better learn to live with that fact. In human experience, the assumption of local causality appears to be valid when certain types of situations are set up, not with others.

Non-Reductionist Causation

As discussed above, the assumption that reductionist kinds of "causes" should account for everything has been, it turns out, a prejudice of science in its present form. With the "oneness" assumption, there is no unique causal explanation for any phenomenon; cause depends on context. In one context, reductionistic "causes" receive the primary focus; in another, volitional factors take center stage. Both kinds of explanation (as well as others) may be useful; no one is exhaustively and uniquely "true".

Speaking personally for the moment, I seem to experience (as did Aristotle) four levels of cause:

> **Level 1:** Physical cause (scientific cause in the usual sense)
>
> **Level 2:** Biological cause (will to live, reproductive drive, evolutionary drive, etc., in the human as well as other biological organisms)
>
> **Level 3:** Volitional cause (conscious and unconscious will and choice in humans and perhaps other organisms)
>
> **Level 4:** Intuitional cause, "inner knowing", spiritual yearnings.

I find all four of these operating in my life all the time, and experientially they are all qualitatively different. These would seem to lead to four different realms of science: physical, biological, cognitive, and spiritual (say). Each level has its own appropriate kind of cause; they operate simultaneously, and, alone or together, they do not provide a "complete" explanation; that is a goal to be sought only in the deep understanding of the Oneness.

'Mind Over Matter' and the 'Mind-Body Problem'

Again, these are paradoxes only because of the metaphysical assumptions of the modern view. If we start from the "oneness" assumption, then it is obvious that mind and matter are interacting all the time. The interesting question is how isolated situations can be set up (such as the usual technological applications) in which the effects of mind are locally negligible or ignorable. The still more interesting question, sociologically, is how we ever persuaded ourselves that those situations represent the norm, and the totally ordinary interaction between my mental volition and physiological response is an anomaly—a "mind-body problem".

'Meaningful Coincidences' (Synchronicity)

With the "oneness" assumption, meaningful coincidences are to be expected, but there remain interesting questions worth extensive exploration. For example: why do we not experience meaningful coincidences more often? What is it that creates the apparent separation between ourselves and others, or the world? Why do we seem to have a reluctance to manifest what we presently (and erroneously) term "paranormal" phenomena? Should this reluctance be overcome or respected?

Altered States of Consciousness

Reports of non-ordinary states of consciousness have, by and large, been considered by modern science to be aberrations or pathologies. However, in the "oneness" view these are potentially explorations of the whole, of the "Great Mysterious", to be employed judiciously, with the lessons thereby learned to be shared and added to the totality of scientific knowledge.

Many individuals have found in these experiences of altered states of consciousness the most convincing evidence regarding the nature of the death process. In many societies, especially those of the indigenous peoples around the globe, the individual is taught by the culture to perceive the universe as alive, and the self as intimately connected to nature, so that death is a natural process inspiring awe but not fear. In modern society, by contrast, we are taught that we are separate from nature, and our relationship is one of seeking to control nature. Death is thus a defeat, and a fearsome thing. The tyranny of positivist reductionist science undeservedly raised to the status of a worldview is particularly telling here. Not only is ours a society in which the fear of death is responsible for untold personal agony; its consequences in terms of the expensive medical compulsion to keep the physical body alive as long as possible have nearly brought modern health care systems to financial ruin.

Implications for Society

In all of this reassessment of underlying assumptions we are not trying to suggest that the presently prevailing metaphysical foundations of science have been a huge error. They were not necessarily a mistake at the time when they were formulated, and they have certainly brought about a spurt (lasting several centuries) of a certain kind of knowledge which has been extremely useful for its own purposes.

But to allow these assumptions to dominate our thinking as they have in the recent past—that would be a great mistake. The destructive effect of positivistic science on society's fabric of meanings and values is well documented and well known.

To re-emphasize the point, none of present science is invalidated in the limited domains where it was generated. However, some of the common extrapolations of scientific findings into the area of human affairs become questionable. For example, the fact that genetic characteristics are involved in behavior should not be extrapolated to conclude that the complete explanation for behavior is ultimately to be found at the molecular level. The fact that random mutation and natural selection are clearly factors in evolution should not be extrapolated to conclude that they are sufficient to account for the forms and diversity of organisms actually found. It is even in doubt whether we are justified in extrapolating the scientific laws we observe today back to the time of a hypothetical "Big Bang".

If science were to come to include a complementary body of knowledge based on the unitive or "wholeness" assumption, several important consequences can be postulated:

1) It would tend to foster different attitudes toward nature.

We can imagine very different attitudes toward such issues as taking care of the environment; preserving species and habitat; avoiding irresponsible climate change, desertification, salination, etc.; raising animals for slaughtering; using animals in research, etc. This is not just a theoretical point; we have examples to study. The worldview of the Native American Indian (and most other indigenous peoples as well) is just such a wholeness-based view, and the associated attitudes toward the Earth and our fellow creatures are there for anyone to observe. The Indian's relationship to his environment has proven to be sustainable over many centuries, which has not been true for most of the civilizations that have appeared throughout history.

2) It would result in science being more sympathetic to, and more amenable to, research relating to meaningful coincidences.

Survey research discloses that most people are aware of these coincidences in their lives; they definitely do not feel like random events. These include, for example, the coincidence of feeling that a distant loved one is in danger, and then receiving a confirming report. Other types are sometimes described as paranormal or religious phenomena, "hunches" or "miracles".

3) It would tend to stimulate research in the entire spectrum of states of consciousness.

These include religious experiences; experiences of mystical states of consciousness, of "other dimensions of reality". These experiences have been at the heart of all cultures, including our own. They have been among the main sources of the deepest value commitments. They cannot be ignored; yet modern science has denied their significance.

4) It would tend to foster a worldview supportive of the highest values of all societies.

Such a worldview would contribute toward societal consensus with regard to central values, meanings, and purposes.

Resolving this issue of need for a wholeness science deserves to be high-priority agenda for science. It should help achieve unity among the various sciences, and help resolve long-standing dichotomies and paradoxes of science (such as mind vs. matter; objective vs. subjective; free will vs. determinism). It could help science move toward paradigms that are rigorous and valid, and yet more in accord with the kind of wisdom we attain through life experience. It could clarify the relationship between science and values.

The past three decades or so have seen a worldwide reaction against the materialistic worldview. Part of this reaction has looked toward the past, toward a revival of traditional religion. But another—and probably more important part—has envisioned a new spirituality based on the "oneness" assumption. Drawn from diverse sources—spiritual renewal in Judaism and Christianity, shamanism and the Native North American traditions, feminine spirituality and goddess religion, "deep" ecology—this new spirituality acknowledges the sacredness of the body, sexuality, emotions, and the natural world. Rather than focusing on salvation in some disembodied realm, it sees the world of matter as divine and as worthy of love as the immaterial spiritual realm. Because "fallen" nature is redeemed and divinized, this new spirituality gives rise to an ecological vision that honors the planet and its multitude of species as a single living entity with whom we can learn to live with greater harmony and reverence. (See, for example, Miller, 1991.)

The Time is Ripe

Richard Tarnas (1991), in an epic story of the evolution of Western culture's consciousness, speaks to the timeliness of the project we have undertaken in this volume—perceiving the challenge of a truly holistic science as the culmination of a millennia-long evolution:

> An epochal shift is taking place in the contemporary psyche, a reconcilia-
> tion between the two great polarities, a union of opposites, a sacred
> marriage between the long-dominant but now alienated masculine and the

long-suppressed but now ascending feminine. And this dramatic development is not just a compensation, not just a return of the repressed, as I believe this has all along been the underlying goal of Western intellectual and spiritual evolution. *For the deepest passion of the Western mind has been to reunite with the ground of its being.* The driving impulse of the West's masculine consciousness has been its dialectical quest not only to realize itself, but also, finally, to recover its connection with the whole, to come to terms with the great feminine principle in life, to differentiate itself from but then rediscover and reunite with the feminine, with the mystery of life, of nature, of soul. And that reunion can now occur on a new and profoundly different level from that of the primordial unconscious unity, for the long evolution of human consciousness has prepared it to be capable at last of embracing the ground and matrix of its own being freely and consciously. (p. 442)

A great deal of cultural change has taken place since the early attempts to deal with some of these issues within the framework of science. The new emphasis on wholeness, and the legitimating of intuition and related aspects of inner knowing, have brought us a completely new climate. The time seems very ripe for insisting on a re-examination of the metaphysical foundations of modern science. Until this is done, the six "puzzle areas" described in Chapter 1 are likely to remain unresolved, and to stand as testimony to the fact that the modern scientific worldview is inherently flawed and misleading in ways vital to the well-being of individuals and societies, and inimical to the future viability of human civilization.

Note

1 If we accept Barfield's characterization, the lower levels of the hierarchy of sciences (above) comprise the kind of science we get from experiencing the world "by our senses without", whereas the upper levels tend to be science derived from experiencing "by our consciousness from within".

Assumptions, Corollaries, and Characteristics of Two Sciences: A Comparison

Separateness Science

1) Basic ontological assumption: the universe is made up, ultimately, of fundamental particles and quanta which are separate from one another except insofar as there are specifiable connections (such as fields).

2) A scientific explanation of a phenomenon (understanding of causes in a scientific sense) consists in relating the phenomenon to more general and fundamental relationships or "scientific laws". The ultimate scientific explanation is in terms of the motions and interactions of the fundamental particles and quanta involved. (This desideratum is approached, for example, in thermodynamics or physical optics.)

3) All scientific knowledge is ultimately based on data obtained through the physical senses. Such information is, then, ultimately quantifiable.

4) The truest information about the objective reality is obtained through the observer being as detached as possible. There is an ultimate limit to objectivity, in that there is inevitably some "observer effect" in any observation.

5) The universe is scientifically understood to be ultimately deterministic.

Wholeness Science

1) Basic ontological assumption: the universe is basically a single whole within which every part is connected to every other part. This wholeness includes every aspect accessible to human awareness—the physical world as discerned through our physical senses, and all the contents of consciousness.

2) Pragmatically useful scientific explanations enhance understandings of phenomena by relating them to other phenomena and relationships. Since things are so interconnected that a change in any one can affect all, then any accounting for cause is within a specific context, for a specific purpose. The search for ultimate reductionistic cause is futile; there are not cause and effect, but rather the evolution of a whole system. Order is observed in the physical world, but it is never free from the possibility of "downward causation" (from consciousness "down" to the physical).

3) Reality is contacted basically in two ways. One is through physical sense data. The other is inner, through being ourselves part of the oneness—through a deep intuitive "inner knowing". Our encountering of reality is not limited to the objective, being aware of, and giving meaning to, the messages from our physical senses. It includes also a subjective aspect in an intuitive, aesthetic, spiritual, noetic and mystical sense.

4) Understanding comes, not from being detached, objective, analytical, coldly clinical, but rather from identifying with the observed, becoming one with it. (This is not to deny the usefulness of objective knowledge, but only the recognition that it leads to a partial understanding.)

5) The concept of a completely deterministic universe (even in a statistical sense, as in quantum physics) stems from the "separateness" assumption; there is no reason to expect it to be borne out in experience.

6) The material universe evolved to its present state from the "Big Bang" by random physical process and, after the advent of life, mutation and natural selection. Consciousness (whatever it is) is a product of material evolution.

6) There is no *a priori* reason to assume that "scientific laws" are invariant; rather, it seems more plausible that they, too, are evolving. Hence extrapolation to the "Big Bang" may be suspect. Evidence seems to point to consciousness either evolving along with, or being prior to, the material world.

7) There is no evidence for mysterious drives or purposes in evolution. What appears as a "survival instinct" is merely the result of natural selection; any organisms that did not have such a drive were selected out. There is no scientific evidence for anything in the universe resembling purpose or design. The biological sciences use teleological language for convenience, but what it really means is that those structures and behaviors that contribute to survival survived.

7) Since we humans are part of the whole, and experience drives or urges such as survival, belongingness, achievement, and self-actualization, there is no *a priori* justification for assuming these are not characteristics of the whole. Similarly, since we experience purpose and values, there is no valid justification for assuming these are not also characteristics of the whole. In other words, the universe may be genuinely, not just apparently, telic.

8) The wide range of more-or-less commonly experienced phenomena known as meaningful coincidences (including the great preponderance of so-called anomalous phenomena)—where two or more events appear to be meaningfully connected, but there is no discernible physical connection—must ultimately be shown either to have a physical connection or to be, in fact, merely coincidence.

8) Meaningful coincidences are not to be explained, but rather apparent separateness. In other words, the question is not "How can we explain apparent telepathic communication?" but rather, "How can we explain why our minds are not cluttered by all that information in other minds?" Not "How can we explain apparent psychokinetic phenomena?" but rather, "How should we best understand why our minds have such a limited effect in the physical world?"

9) Non-normal states of consciousness, dissociation, etc. are phenomena to be studied largely in the context of the pathological, and in terms of their effects on behavior.

9) The entire spectrum of states of consciousness are of interest. These include religious experiences; experiences of mystical states of consciousness, of "other dimensions of reality". These experiences have been at the heart of all cultures, including our own. They have been among the main sources of the deepest value commitments; they may be an important investigative tool, a window to other dimensions of reality.

10) The explanations of ontogenesis, morphogenesis, regeneration, and related biological phenomena are to be sought in terms of coded "instructions" in the genes and similar mechanisms.

10) The ultimate explanations of ontogenesis, morphogenesis, regeneration, and related biological phenomena will probably turn out to have to include something in consciousness analogous to "image" or "idea".

References

Owen Barfield, "The evolution complex", *Towards 2,* no. 2, Spring 1982, pp. 6-16.

Donald T. Campbell, "'Downward causation' in hierarchically organized biological systems", in *Studies in the Philosophy of Biology,* edited by F. Ayala & T. Dobzhansky, University of California Press, 1974.

Jacqueline Damgaard, "Inner self helper" in *Noetic Sciences Review,* Winter 1987, p. 24.

Brian Goodwin, "A science of qualities" in *Quantum Implications: Festschrift for David Bohm,* edited by B. T. Hilary and F. D. Peat, Routledge and Kegan Paul, 1987.

E. R. Hilgard, *Divided Consciousness: Multiple Controls in Human Thought and Action,* John Wiley, 1986.

Aldous Huxley, *The Perennial Philosophy,* Harper and Row, 1945.

Brian Inglis, *Natural and Supernatural: A History of the Paranormal,* Prism Press, 1992.

C. G. Jung and W. Pauli, *The Interpretation and Nature of the Psyche,* translated by R.F.C. Hull and P. Silz, Pantheon, 1955.

Charles D. Laughlin, John McManus and Eugene d'Aquili, *Brain, Symbol, and Experience: Toward a Neurophenomenology of Human Consciousness,* New Science Library (Shambhala), 1990.

Richard Levins and Richard Lewontin, *The Dialectical Biologist,* Harvard University Press, 1985.

Yvonna S. Lincoln and Egon S. Guba, *Naturalistic Inquiry,* Sage Publications, 1985.

James Lovelock, *The Ages of Gaia: A Biography of Our Living Earth,* W. W. Norton, 1988.

Ron Miller, *As Above, So Below,* Jeremy Tarcher, 1991.

E. D. Mitchell, *Psychic Exploration,* G. P. Putnam's Sons, 1974.

Michael Polyani, *Personal Knowledge*: *Towards a Post-Critical Philosophy* (University of Chicago Press, 1974).

Karl R. Popper and John C. Eccles, *The Self and Its Brain,* Springer-Verlag, 1977.

Kenneth Ring, *Life and Death: A Scientific Investigation of the Near-Death Experience,* Morrow, 1982.

Fr. John Rossner, *In Search of the Primordial Tradition,* Llewellyn Publications, 1989.

Roger W. Sperry, "Structure and significance of the consciousness revolution", *The Journal of Mind and Behavior 8,* no. 1, Winter 1987.

Ian Stevenson, *Children Who Remember Previous Lives,* University Press of Virginia, 1987.

Richard Tarnas, *The Passion of the Western Mind,* Harmony Books, 1991.

Subject Index

abduction, 58, 351-352
absoluteness of truth, 92
acausal epiphenomenon, 112
acceptance, of consciousness and subjectivity
   in science, 98
action at a distance, 3, 8-9, 383
adaptation , 254
Age of Theory, 348
agere, 235
aim of scientific inquiry, 357
alchemy, 4
alienation, 6, 10, 181, 247, 253, 270
alternative mentalism, 110
ameaning, 348-349
analysis of mechanics, 137
androcentric organizing principle, 35-37
androcentrism
   as a factor in science, 34
   in methods, 18, 34, 38
   in ontologies, 18
   in theories, 18, 33-34, 38
animistic superstition, 6
anomalies, 7, 23, 111, 139, 158-162, 168-170,
   172, 174, 176, 262-263, 291, 312, 317, 383
   consciousness-related, 174
   human and machine, 160, 162, 170, 176
anomalous phenomena, 4, 9, 174, 177, 210,
   395
anomaly, 7, 228, 259, 279, 292, 388-389
anomie, 253
Anthropic Principle, 126-127, 156, 264, 282
anxiety, 283, 314
Apaches, 298
apprehension, 185, 239, 243, 251, 265-266,
   285, 316, 380
approximation, 58, 67-69, 78, 204
archetypal phenomena, 239, 336-337
Army Research Institute, 360
arrow of time, 195
artificial intelligence, 108, 114, 333
assumption(s)
   alternative, 11
   basic, 2, 7, 9, 21, 375, 394
   epistemological, 2, 7-9, 375-376, 379-380
   foundation, 1, 6, 21
   metaphysical, 8, 10, 12, 17, 21, 24, 27, 37,
     39, 43, 267, 269, 349-350, 389-390
   of separateness, 8-9, 393-394
   ontological, 2, 7-10, 27, 375-376, 386, 394
   positivistic, 9
   theoretical network of, 7
astral body, 338
astrology, 3, 68
atomic structure, 169
Atomism, 97, 322-323, 329-330, 339
atomistic determinism, 102
autopoietic, 234
awareness, conscious, 9, 100, 275, 376, 379,
   383
barrier penetration, 169-170
basic meaning, 59, 68
Bear Butte, 303

behaviorism, 8, 49, 55, 60, 65, 77, 100, 106,
   108-109, 114, 118-121, 241
behaviorist, 50, 56, 77, 100-101, 106, 108-109,
   348
   assumptions, 56
   paradigm, 348
belief(s), 29, 49, 67-68, 71, 78, 81, 89-90, 121,
   125, 257-259, 262-263, 269, 272-273, 278-
   279, 281-282, 288-289, 292, 295, 306, 354,
   362, 366-367, 378
   evaluation of, 68
Bell's theorem, 2, 10, 100, 113, 342
Bergson, intuition of pure duration, 191
bidirectional emergent interaction model, 102
Big Bang, 9, 126, 377, 390, 395
Big Crunch, 126
biological cause, 388
biological clock, 190
biological determinism, 42, 46
biology, 16, 26, 34, 36, 39-45, 105, 114, 119-
   121, 133, 143, 156, 182, 196, 211-212, 215-
   216, 220-221, 223, 225-226, 228, 230, 233,
   237-238, 240-241, 243-244, 247-250, 271,
   282-284, 317, 323, 329, 333, 340-341, 350,
   380-381, 383, 393
   evolutionary, 26, 36, 114, 220, 329
biophoton(s)
   emission in malignant and normal cells,
     205
   emission of, 201
birds, 1, 128, 167, 180, 204, 292, 294, 296,
   298-301, 303-304, 306, 310, 314-315
Black Hills, 303-304, 315, 318
Blackbody radiation, 167
Blue Rider School, 339
Bohr's principle of complementarity, 129-130
bootstrapping, 51
Brahman, 130
bridge laws, 73
Brighton Marine Hospital, 365
capitalism, 5, 10, 341
Cartesian body-mind problem, 107
Cartesian doubt, 82
Castalia, 179
causal determinism
   bidirectional model of, 114
   influence of mental states in brain func-
     tion, 104
   macromental model of, 103
   operator, 267, 281
   reciprocal form of, 102
   status of consciousness, 106
causality, non-local, 3, 388
causation, 3, 47, 58, 70-71, 79, 97, 102-104,
   107-108, 114, 116, 134-135, 141, 143-144,
   149, 151, 155, 207, 233-235, 251, 253, 255,
   263-271, 274, 277-278, 281-284, 377, 383,
   388, 393-394
   at a distance, 70, 278-279
   backward, 264, 282
   cognitive and emergent, 97
   cognitive, 97, 114, 282
   downward, 3, 103, 107-108, 383, 393-394
   emergent, 97, 102, 104, 114, 116, 141, 149

Names Index

About the Authors

Jane Clark is a free-lance editor and writer specializing in the relationship between science and the perennial wisdom. She studied engineering and physics at Birmingham and Warwick Universities, England, and has been a student of the Beshara School of Intensive Esoteric Education in Scotland for nearly fifteen years. She was the editor of *Beshara* magazine until 1991, and is currently helping to launch a new academic publication called *The Journal of Consciousness Studies.*

Vine Deloria is Professor of American Indian Studies and adjunct Professor of Law at the University of Colorado, USA. He is a member of the Standing Rock Sioux Tribe (Fort Yates, North Dakota) and has been an active member of the Indian community all his life, working with numerous organizations on poverty, land rights, education, and the preservation of Indian culture. He has degrees in science, theology and law, and has written widely on the history and culture of the Indian peoples of North America. His books include *Custer Died for Your Sins* (1969), *The Metaphysics of Modern Existence* (1979) and *American Indian Policy in the Twentieth Century* (1985).

Richard Dixey is Director of the Bioelectronic Research Unit at St. Bartholomew's Hospital, London, England. This has involved him in studies over the last ten years into the biological action of weak electronic fields and their possible medical uses. He also has interests in promoting the cause of healing in general. Alongside these activities, he is concerned with the social and philosophical impact of scientific knowledge and its comparison with Eastern worldviews. He recently edited a translation of a Tibetan text from the Bonpo tradition, *Heart Drops of Dharmakaya* by Sharzda Tashi Gyaltsen (Snow Lion, 1993). He has an MA in Physiological Sciences, a Doctorate in Biophysics, and an MSc in the History and Philosophy of Science.

Brenda Dunne is Laboratory Manager of the Princeton Engineering Anomalies Research Laboratory, New Jersey, USA, a position she has held since the program's inception in 1979. She holds degrees in psychology and the humanities from Mundelein College in Chicago and a Masters degree in Human Development from the University of Chicago. She has lectured internationally on consciousness-related anomalies phenomena, and is coauthor with Bob Jahn of the book *Margins of Reality* (1987), along with many technical publications in the field.

Brian Goodwin is Professor of Biology at the Open University, England. He has degrees in Biology (McGill) and Mathematics (Oxford) and studied under the great embryologist C. H. Waddington at Edinburgh, where he developed a lifelong interest in evolution and the nature of biological form. He is the author of numerous scientific papers and books, including the forthcoming *How the Leopard Changed Its Spots: The Evolution of Complexity* (1994), which have explored the principles of organizations and transformation in biology. Although now officially retired, he continues to be active in research programs both at the Open University and elsewhere in Europe.

Willis Harman is Professor Emeritus of Engineering-Economic Systems at Stanford University, USA, and President of the Institute of Noetic Sciences and Director of the Causality Project. He has degrees in Electrical Engineering (Washington and Stanford), and for many years was Senior Social Scientist at SRI International of Menlo Park, California, where he worked on long-term strategic planning and political analysis for corporations, government agencies and international organizations. He has written on electrical and systems engineering, futures research and social policy. His books include *An Incomplete Guide to the Future* (1979), *Global Mind Change* (1988), *Higher Creativity* (1984, with Howard Rheingold) and *Creative Work* (1990, with John Hormann).

Mae-Wan Ho is Director of the Bioelectrodynamics Laboratory at the Open University, England, where she researches on bioelectrodynamical coherence in living systems and teaches biochemistry and biophysics. She has degrees in Biology and Biochemistry (Hong Kong), and is author of numerous scientific papers covering biochemistry, genetics, evolution, development, and biophysics. Her latest book, *The Rainbow and the Worm: The Physics of Organisms* (1993), outlines a science of organic wholeness that synthesizes many areas of contemporary physics and biology. She is also painter and poet, and writes and lectures on the inter-connectedness of art and science.

Charles Laughlin is a professor of anthropology at Carleton University, Ottawa, Canada. He is the coauthor of *Biogenetic Structuralism* (1974), *The Spectrum of Ritual* (1979), *Extinction and Survival in Human Populations* (1979), *Science As Cognitive Process* (1984), and *Brain, Symbol and Experience* (1990). He has done ethnographic fieldwork among the So of Northeastern Uganda, Tibetan lamas in Nepal and India, and the Navajo in New Mexico.

Robert Jahn is Professor of Aerospace Studies in the Princeton Department of Mechanical and Aerospace Engineering, USA, and has had a long and distinguished career as a research engineer and lecturer. Since 1979, he has been the director of the Princeton Engineering Anomalies Research Laboratory, in which capacity he has written and lectured on consciousness-related anomalies. He is the coauthor, with Brenda Dunne, of *Margins of Reality* (1987).

Ilja Maso occupies the chair of Philosophy of Science, Methodology and Research at the University for Humanist Studies, Utrecht, Holland. He has published books and articles on ethnomethodology, qualitative research, and explanation. Articles have been published in *Husserliana*, *Quality and Quantity*, *Kennis en Methode (Knowledge and Method)* and in several readers.

Lynn Hankinson Nelson is an Associate Professor of Philosophy at Rowan College of New Jersey (formerly Glassboro State College), USA. She has a BA (Rutgers) and PhD (Temple) in Philosophy and has published articles on the philosophy of science and feminist theory. She is the author of *Who Knows: From Quine to a Feminist Empiricism* (1990), guest editor of a special issue of *Synthèse* devoted to Feminism and Science (1994), and coeditor (with Jack Nelson) of *Rethinking the Canon: Feminist Perspectives on Quine* (1994) and of *A Dialogue Concerning Feminism, Science, and the Philosophy of Science* (Kluwer, 1995).

Michael Scriven is currently Professor and Director of the Evaluation Institute at Pacific Graduate School of Psychology, Adjunct Professor of Philosophy at Western Michigan University, and Senior National Lecturer in Evaluation for Nova University, USA. He has degrees in Mathematics (Melbourne) and Philosophy (Oxford), and has written prolifically on philosophy, critical thinking, philosophy of science, turbine engine design, evaluation, word processing, computer studies and technology studies. His books include *Concepts, Theories and the Mind-Body Problem* (1958, with H. Feigl and G. Maxwell), *Primary Philosophy* (1966, reprinted six times up to 1988), *Reasoning* (1976), and *Evaluation Thesaurus* (1977, fourth edition, 1991).

Roger Sperry (1913 to 1994) was Board of Trustees Professor Emeritus and Hixon Professor of Psychobiology at California Institute of Technology, USA. He was best known for his split-brain research, for which he was awarded the 1981 Nobel Prize in Medicine and Physiology. His earlier work on neurospecificity in the growth of brain connections won the President's National Medal for showing how intricate neural networks for behavior are formed through an elaborate scheme of chemical coding of individual cells, findings that put nature-nurture issues in a new light. He had degrees in English (Oberlin), Psychology (Oberlin) and Zoology (Chicago). His many publications on mind-brain issues include *Science and Moral Priority* (1985) and *Nobel Prize Conversations* with Eccles, Prigogine et al. (1985).

Eugene Taylor earned the AB and MA in Psychology and Comparative Religions and the PhD in the History and Philosophy of Psychology. He currently holds the titles of Lecturer in Psychiatry at Harvard Medical School and Consultant in the History of Psychiatry at the Massachusetts General Hospital, USA. He is also author of *William James on Exceptional Mental States: Reconstruction of the 1896 Lowell Lectures* (1982).

George Wald is Higgins Professor of Biology Emeritus at Harvard University, USA. In 1967, he was awarded the Nobel Prize for Physiology or Medicine (with Harline and Granit) in honor of work he had started in the 1930s in Germany, when he was the first to identify vitamin A in the retina. He is the recipient of numerous prizes and awards, including the Paul Karrer Medal (1967) by the University of Zurich, which he shared with his wife, Ruth

Hubbard. Since retirement, he has devoted much of his time to what he calls "survival politics", traveling the world talking on such subjects as nuclear power and weapons, human rights and First World-Third World relations.

Arthur Zajonc is Professor of Physics at Amherst College, Massachusetts, USA. As a research physicist specializing in optics, he has been involved in "metaphysical experiments" which explore the fundamental tenets of quantum mechanics. As a historian and philosopher of science, he has developed courses and projects which connect the worldview of physics to other areas of human experience, working in particular with science museums. He has degrees in Physics and Engineering Physics (Michigan) and has written widely on the scientific work of Goethe and Rudolf Steiner. His book *Catching the Light: An Entwined History of Light and Mind* was published in 1993.

About the Institute of Noetic Sciences

An Overview

The Institute of Noetic Sciences (IONS) is a research foundation, an educational institution and a membership organization. It was founded in 1973 and currently has approximately 40,000 members worldwide.

The word *noetic* is derived from the Greek word *nous*, for mind, intelligence or ways of knowing. The "noetic sciences" bring the full range of knowing to the interdisciplinary study of consciousness, the mind, and human potential. Research topics at the Institute range from mind-body health and healing, meditation, and exceptional human abilities, to emerging paradigms in science, business, and society. The Institute conducts its research by providing seed grants to leading-edge scientific and scholarly researchers, organizing lectures, and sponsoring conferences. New ideas are disseminated through publication of selected books, a quarterly review, research reports, and a monograph series commissioned from leading scientists, philosophers and scholars. The Institute also publishes a quarterly newsletter, a periodic annotated catalog of books and tapes, and supports a variety of member research projects, networking opportunities, and local group activities.

The Central Role of Research at the Institute

Research informs the Institute's work. The Institute's seed grants build and sustain fruitful relationships with key researchers and organizations doing work in the field of consciousness studies, resulting in a stimulating cross-fertilization of ideas. While maintaining scientific rigor and scholarly integrity, these working partnerships are enlivened by the creativity, vision, and hope that inevitably accompany the exploration of new ideas.

The Institute's research strategy supports ideas and individuals judged to be both at the forefront of the exploration of consciousness, and particularly significant to its understanding. This strategy incorporates the following elements:

- Identifying key ideas and researchers
- Providing modest seed grants to support their work
- Linking them to other researchers
- Supporting recognition and legitimacy by publishing their work and providing opportunities to speak

- Creating a forum for open exploration of innovative ideas
- Assisting in making key ideas accessible to an informed public.

Scope of Research

The Institute has a threefold interest in the exploration of consciousness:

I. Emerging Worldviews: Many agree society is undergoing a profound transition. The Institute has been addressing this transformation for two decades, and today it continues to occupy a central place in research efforts. Unlike many other institutions in our society, the Institute is addressing social change at the level of worldview, beliefs and values. It is inquiring into the process of transformation for the individual, for organizations, and for key sectors of society (business, medicine, and science). The Institute's work is based on a belief that this transformation is fundamentally about an emerging worldview in which science and spirit are understood as integrated aspects within a unified whole, leading to such emerging concepts as "sustainable development" and "deep ecology".

II. The Nature of Consciousness: Work here focuses on detailed inquiries into ancient consciousness traditions, as well as recent Western scientific work arising from quantum physics, biology and the neurosciences. The Causality Project, a current major program, involves leading Western scientists in questioning the metaphysics of contemporary science based on challenges arising from within science itself. Research into consciousness over twenty years points out the inadequacies of our Western scientific paradigm and strongly confirms the need to identify a suitable answer to the question: How is knowledge validated in subjective areas? The Institute believes that the time is opportune to examine the fundamental assumptions on which Western science has been based for hundreds of years, and to forge an alternative set of assumptions—and a new epistemology which offers the tools currently lacking to strengthen inquiries into consciousness, mind, spirit and related areas.

III. Applied Research Areas: The third major focus is in selected applied research areas that are particularly relevant to emerging worldviews and an understanding of consciousness. Foremost among these has been work in health and healing. IONS has funded research in imagery, biofeedback, psychoneuroimmunology (the role of the mind, emotions, beliefs and personality in physical health), the role of the spirit in health and healing, the importance of "connection" (family, community, and support groups). Documenting and attempting to understand spontaneous remissions has been an area of special focus. Altruism has been a research interest both because it appears to be a natural outcome of personal transformation and because research in healing suggests that altruism positively affects health. The role of consciousness in human performance has included the study of peak performance in athletics and the work place, remote viewing, psychokinesis, and channeling. The Institute also has maintained a long-standing research program into different states of consciousness, as exemplified by meditation and the exploration of other altered states. Redefining health and healing also involves reconceptualizing death; the role of spirit in our lives and the question of survival after death of the physical body are long-standing and current research interests.

The Role of Research in Membership at the Institute

Institute members are at the forefront of positive social change—committed to their own development and to societal transformation. In partnership with members, the Institute explores both the inner dimensions of human experience and the implications of consciousness research for personal and social change. We feel it is important to link what we do to the growing segment of contemporary society committed to exploring these ideas and integrating them into the social structures of our time. This grounding effect delivers an essential element of practicality to our work. As a consequence, the Institute's efforts are tied to fundamental changes as they emerge both in research and in members' lives.

INSTITUTE OF
NOETIC
SCIENCES
475 Gate Five Road, Suite 300
Sausalito, California 94965
415-331-5650 Fax: 415-331-5673